THE ECONOMIC BORDERS OF THE STATE

The Economic Borders of the State

Edited by

DIETER HELM

OXFORD UNIVERSITY PRESS
1989

Oxford University Press, Walton Street, Oxford OX2 6DP
Oxford New York Toronto
Delhi Bombay Calcutta Madras Karachi
Petaling Jaya Singapore Hong Kong Tokyo
Nairobi Dar es Salaam Cape Town
Melbourne Auckland
and associated companies in
Berlin Ibadan

Oxford is a trade mark of Oxford University Press

Published in the United States
by Oxford University Press, New York

British Library Cataloguing in Publication Data
Helm, Dieter
The economic borders of the state.
1. Great Britain. Economic policies
I. Title
330.941'0858
ISBN 0–19–828607–4

Library of Congress Cataloging in Publication Data
The Economic borders of the state/edited by Dieter Helm.
Bibliograhy   Includes index.
1. Economic policy.   2. Government ownership.   3. Privatization.
I. Helm, Dieter.
HD75.E26   1988   338.9–dc19   88–32667
ISBN 0–19–828607–4

Typeset by Joshua Associates Ltd., Oxford
Printed in Great Britain
by Biddles Ltd.
Guildford & King's Lynn

Preface

This volume has developed from the first three years of the *Oxford Review of Economic Policy*. The editors and editorial board have provided, through formal and informal discussion, a forum for debate on economic policy from which many of the articles in this volume evolved.

The *Oxford Review*'s production editors—first Kate Ryan and then Hilary Hodgson—have helped to steer this volume to its conclusion. Their help has been invaluable. Typing by Hayley Bell and Monica Hyde has been patiently completed, and Judith Payne's excellent copy-editing has much improved this volume.

Contents

Introduction

DIETER HELM

This volume brings together economists and political scientists to present an assessment of a central theme of the new policies which have dominated the 1980s and which have come to be known as 'Thatcherism'. That central theme is the rolling back of the economic borders of the State, placing greater emphasis on the role of the individual choice and markets in allocating resources.

The papers presented here focus on the underlying political economy, and re-examine the role and purpose of the State in the economy. In keeping with the traditional political economy approach, the authors are drawn from a wide variety of viewpoints and backgrounds. As well as examining the philosophical basis of State intervention, the volume attempts to set the new ideas in a historical context and show how they have been translated into practice. To this end, a number of areas of policy—taxation, social security, nationalized industries, macro-economics, and local government—are focused on in the latter part of the book to draw out the practical consequences of this process. Versions of some of the papers previously appeared in an issue of the *Oxford Review of Economic Policy* (Summer 1986) devoted to this topic; most, however, have been specially commissioned for this volume.

The economic borders of the State are perhaps more controversial now than at any time since the 1945–51 Labour government set up the Welfare State, nationalized the basic infrastructure industries, and embarked on macro-economic demand management. This controversy, again as in the 1940s, is not confined to the UK. Indeed, the UK now exports 'Thatcherism' as it once exported the Welfare State. The retreat from the belief in the powers of government action to enhance economic performance is worldwide.

The parallels with the 1945–51 period are marked. Many of the questions bear a striking resemblance and, if the answers are markedly different, the focus on ownership, on the proper limits to individual choice, and on the ability of government to provide a stable macro-economic framework suggests much can be learnt from comparing the two episodes in economic policy.

The new much more pessimistic 'conventional wisdom' is that whatever the benign intention of State intervention, governments have failed to deliver the increases in efficiency and the relief of poverty promised. The nationalized industries did not yield allocative efficiency, nor did they engender good industrial relations. Demand management brought with it inflation, and the long-term balance of payments deficits persisted. The Welfare State soon lost its safety net aspects, and became an ever more expensive redistributive tool, without solving the basic problems for which it was designed.

These failures are, on this view, inevitable. Governments, run by politicians and bureaucrats, are riddled with inefficiencies. The officials pursue their own objectives. Furthermore, even if they did pursue the public interest (supposing it to be definable), the informational problems inherent in planning are bound to induce a less satisfactory result than that provided by the market. By contrast, the price mechanism has the great advantage of channelling individual efforts into the allocation of resources and economizing on information. In the market, price governs behaviour, rather than the complex guidance of the planners.

The new conventional wisdom stresses not only the impact of 'government failure', but also the negative effects on economic efficiency of taxation, and hence the limits to redistribution. Whilst adherents to the social market believe that transfers from the rich to the poor involve relatively straightforward progressive income taxation, the new conventional wisdom stresses the distortion induced by higher marginal rates on work incentives. Unemployment, far from being caused by deficient macro-economic demand, is, it is argued, the result of the very redistributional policies designed to help the poor. Social security prices workers out of jobs.

The new conventional wisdom extends beyond economics. Ultimately, the power of the new ideas comes from their philosophical underpinning. Instead of laying stress on the capabilities of co-operative social behaviour, and the social origins of many of the problems which beset the UK in the 1970s, the emphasis was shifted back to the individual. The merits of individual choice, individuals' property rights, and the liberty of the individual against interference by the State have been marshalled as central elements in the defence of markets. Indeed, it has been assumed that only in a free market economy could these fundamental freedoms be protected.

The ideas of philosophers and economists of the right—most notably Nozick, Hayek, Friedman, Buchanan, and Tullock—have played a major part in this rethinking. They have provided an intellectual basis to underpin the political reforms. Yet, the temptation to overstate their part must be resisted. Many of the ideas were not new: nineteenth-century liberalism provided the main political theories and, despite the advances in the formal theoretical framework of neo-classical economics, much of the focus of policy prescriptions could be (and indeed has been) traced back to Adam Smith. Thus, while the intellectual and philosophical framework must be addressed, and cannot be denied a major role in reshaping policy, its role must not be overstated. It is not so long ago that it was thought political suicide to 'let' unemployment cross the 1 million mark, inconceivable to privatize major State-owned utilities, and impossible to withstand a miners' strike. The ideas of the new right did not suddenly arrive in 1979: as Gillian Peele's paper shows, it took a major political shift in the practical conception of what was and what was not politically possible.

The politics of the 1980s have been dominated by this programme. There has been little effective opposition at the political level and, while economists have challenged the design of policies, it is hard to see a coherent alternative policy framework. The reasons for the political position are well known. The split of the Labour right, the formation and then splitting of the Social Democrats, and the defence issues of the Falklands and nuclear weapons have contributed to the Conservatives' ascendancy. But, at a more fundamental level, the left has thus far failed to come to grips fully with the new conventional wisdom. The new libertarianism and the new market philosophies have not been forcibly challenged. There has as yet been little rethinking of socialism. Rethinking amongst Liberals and Social Democrats has perhaps advanced further at the intellectual level, in part because of the need to provide the new party with a coherent set of ideas. But it is far from convincing the British electorate.

This volume attempts to provide an analytical framework to begin this reappraisal. The first part deals with the type of arguments which underpin the new economic policies, and the second looks at their applications. The volume begins with an overall assessment by Dieter Helm of the case for and against intervention, setting out a framework within which the subsequent contributions can be categorized.

Following this assessment, the next two papers, by Alan Ryan and Wilfred Beckerman, pose the question: to what extent is the degree of State intervention a matter of economic analysis, and to what extent is it a matter of value-judgement? Welfare economics has been largely focused upon the Paretian welfare principle, whereby any change in economic arrangements, and hence any intervention by the State, must be justified by demonstrating that at least one person will be better off, and nobody worse off. This apparently simple principle forms the basis of the justification of decentralized market systems by showing that a perfectly competitive economy will be Pareto-optimal.

Though the debate in the economic literature is then conducted in terms of the validity of this judgement, philosophers have been careful to distinguish different forms of value-judgement. Ryan points to the naïvety of conventional economics in lumping all its value claims within the one Paretian basket. One way of approaching the welfare basis of economic policy appraisal is to ask what information is considered relevant in the comparison of alternatives. In the traditional neo-classical approach (outlined in Beckerman's article), the economist restricts appraisal to utility information. This apparently general idea that economic arrangements are justified by appeal to their degree of preference satisfaction is, however, much disputed by philosophers, who point to the requirements of distribution, equity, and freedom. Efficiency in providing utility is not the only concern in deciding the optimal level of State intervention.

The moral basis of the market thus depends upon the information used in deciding upon the basis of intervention. Amartya Sen's article tackles this question and provides an insight into the 'new' welfare economics, which he has been central in creating. He argues that by expanding upon alternative sources of moral information—about rights and entitlements in particular—wider judgements can be made, which better capture distributional objectives and reinterpret the meaning of economic efficiency.

These considerations concerning rights, entitlements, and the capabilities of individuals point towards a rather different concept of freedom from that advocated by the new right. They provide a more robust case for intervention, and for the provision of basic social primary goods through the Welfare State. Partha Dasgupta's paper shows how modern informational theory can justify the provision of goods rather than services, and how these basic goods might be provided.

The new welfare economics, advanced here by Sen and Dasgupta, is thus largely based on the premiss that utility information is an insufficient basis on which to decide the degree of intervention. Furthermore, it is the requirement of freedom to certain positive rights which necessitates redistribution from rich to poor. This new approach provides the basis for a comprehensive case for State intervention in the provision of welfare services.

The concentration on freedom rather than utility is shared by writers of the new right. Their emphasis, however, is on a more individualistic concept of freedom, and tends to focus on the negative aspects of State intervention. These liberal thinkers have stressed the threat to liberty posed by the State, and pushed the case for stricter limits on its extent.

The new right is, however, heterogeneous. There are a number of distinct approaches which need to be carefully separated out. For example, the economic liberalism of Friedman is rather distinct from that of Hayek. Indeed, at least four schools of thought can be identified in this tradition.

First, there are libertarians, whose stress on individuals and their rights points towards the absence of all but the most limited functions of government. These theorists follow Nozick. Second, there are the constitutionalists, who argue for the imposition of rules to limit the State's activities. Hayek is the main representative of this group. Third, there are the economic liberals, who base their case on the economic efficiency of markets. Friedman is often associated with this group, though he tends to shift his ground. Fourth, there are public choice theorists who argue that government and bureaucracies are inevitably inferior to markets because the incentives and information available to them are necessarily weaker than those of private market agents. Buchanan and Tullock fall into this category.

To do justice to all these schools of thought is well beyond the scope of this volume. Rather than including articles on each, this volume pursues a different tack. Looking back to the earlier origins of the debate on the economic borders of the State which developed before the Second World War, two key antagonists were Hayek and Keynes. They differed on the causes of the Great Depression, and they differed over monetary theory and policy. Behind these policy differences lay a deeper dispute. To caricature their positions, Hayek believed that the capitalist system could achieve a superior allocation of resources because of the superiority of the price mechanism in conditions of uncertainty, provided that a monetary constitution was enforced. Keynes, on the other hand, thought that the economy might fail to co-ordinate itself at the aggregate level, and hence would need the guiding hand of the State to correct it.

In the article by John Gray, the complexity of Hayek's thought on the efficiency of markets and the constitution required to guarantee liberty is brought out. Gray shows that Hayek's position can be defended against the criticisms which can undermine Nozick, that he has a theory of positive freedom, and the crucial role of constitutional rules in his argument.

But if Hayek's case for the market is much more subtle than often presented, so too is that of Keynes. Robert Skidelsky's article carefully disentangles Keynes's conception of the State, and demonstrates it to be much broader than that of 'government'. Keynes's distrust of politicians on the one hand, and his naïve belief in the guidance of the educated (something Mill would also have accepted) on the other, led him to view the State's likelihood of benevolent action in an optimistic fashion. The universities, the Bank of England, and the Arts Council would pursue the public interest, because they were run by the right sort of people, whereas government by politicians would not.

The power of ideas is manifest not only amongst intellectuals, but also amongst politicians. The careful distinctions which our contributors make between the strands of thought on the left and the right rarely transpose themselves with much precision into the political arena. Gillian Peele's article looks at the influence of these ideas on the modern Conservative party and the adoption of a much sharper ideological stance. She shows how ideas were moulded to fit practical political requirements.

The second part of the volume is concerned with the economic borders of the State in different applications—in macro-economic policy, in the Welfare State, in taxation, in industry, and in local government activities.

One of the great extensions of State intervention in the twentieth century has been the assumption of macro-economic objectives. Christopher Allsopp's article tackles the rationale for a macro-economic role of the State. He shows that co-ordination failures are at the root of Keynesian concerns about the economic role of government, and discusses the assumption of a growing role for the State in preventing large-scale disequilibria in the monetary and real markets.

John Kay examines the rationale for taxation. By returning to the underlying purposes of a tax system, he shows how the conflict of objectives—especially between efficiency and distribution—has led successive governments to place far more demands on the tax system than can possibly be consistently achieved. Reform of taxation, and the role of taxation in the economy, require a prior understanding of the underlying objectives.

The inconsistency of objectives which characterizes the design of taxation is also a feature of social security. Andrew Dilnot shows how the modern system has developed and deviated from the original Beveridge system, and how its very complexity derives from the conflicting objectives of social insurance, redistribution, and the provision of basic social primary goods. Only by a resolution of the conflict in the basic principles can a satisfactory reform programme be constructed.

Colin Mayer's paper focuses on a central question of State intervention—why does ownership matter? He examines the capital market allocation of shares amongst portfolios, and considers the conflicts that may arise between the interests of government, shareholders, and consumers. The ranking of industries according to the degree to which public ownership is appropriate, on this analysis, is based on the costs and benefits of capital market allocation of funds for investment projects.

Finally, Dieter Helm and Stephen Smith look at the conflict between the decentralization of decision-making, which provides a rationale for local government and the national distributional priorities. In contrast to the conventional economic wisdom which holds that policies with a redistributive content should be assigned to central government, and that the role of local government should be confined to the provision of local public goods, Helm and Smith stress the contribution of local government to the implementation of a wide range of national policies. The informational and organizational advantages of decentralized operation of major re-distributive government programmes, such as education and social services, are an important factor in determining the borderline between areas of central and local responsibility.

The papers in this volume thus focus on three levels of analysis—philosophy, economics, and politics—and provide a timely insight into the debates and unresolved questions at each level, as well as indicating their interaction. At the philosophical level, there is little consensus on the appropriate borders of the State. Amongst the right, there is a deep conflict between those who provide a neo-liberal defence of individualism, based upon the sovereignty of consumer choice (following Friedman and neo-classical economists), and those, such as Hayek, who base their case on liberty and require strong constitutions or rules, within which freedom of choice is defined. On the left, the interventionist aspects of thought emphasize the failure of markets to perform efficiently, and lay greatest stress on the positive aspects of freedom. One variant stresses the role of the positive rights of individuals to basic social primary goods. At the policy level, the application of these philosophical ideas has been con-strained by the detailed circumstances which confronted the Conservative party in 1979. Nevertheless, although incremental changes have typically been pragmatic, the underlying issues in the reform of taxation, social security, and industrial policy have turned on conflicts over objectives and therefore values. The final, and frequently neglected, level of debate con-cerns the translation of ideas into practice—how politicians, to borrow from Keynes, became the slaves of not only defunct economists, but also of philosophers. This volume, I hope, helps to illuminate the debate at each of these levels.

The Economic Borders of the State

DIETER HELM[*]

1. Introduction

The 'economic borders of the State' have shifted markedly in the twentieth century. Governments, throughout the industrialized world, have extended their activities from the provision of minimal basic services—such as the maintenance of the value of the currency, defence, and law and order—to a much more comprehensive role in allocating resources, in providing education, health, and social security, and in macro-economic management. In addition, a new feature of twentieth century government has been the conscious attempt to alleviate poverty and redistribute income. This expansion has involved the development and use of a wide variety of policy instruments and a vast expansion in the scale of public expenditure and taxation.

This transformation did not take place as a smooth and steady progression. The role of the State expanded markedly during the two world wars. Governments, forced to attain maximum output from their limited resources, were not prepared to leave production to the private market and indeed, during the Second World War, planned the mobilization of resources in great detail with considerable success. After the Second World War, a new consensus emerged based on the 'mixed economy' with considerable government intervention at both the macro-economic and micro-economic levels. In the UK, the foundations for the post-war economic order were laid with the Beveridge Report (1942), the Education Act (1944), the Employment White Paper (HMSO (1944a)), and the subsequent setting-up of the Welfare State and the nationalization of major sections of industry. The latter included the utilities, energy, and transport sectors.

In broad terms, this consensus remained intact so long as economic growth continued to finance the demands of welfare services and the

* Fellow in Economics at Lady Margaret Hall, Oxford. I would especially like to thank Christopher Allsopp for his continual encouragement and considerable contribution to the writing of this paper. Thanks are also due for helpful comments from Partha Dasgupta, Colin Mayer, Derek Morris, and Gillian Peele.

public sector. While it lasted, there was a tendency for politicians to compete as managerial teams, committed, in the 1950s and 1960s, to the achievement of ever more ambitious goals for output, employment, and welfare provision. The principles on which this consensus was based were not seriously challenged at the intellectual level until the revival of monetarist theory and the political philosophy of the 'new right' in the 1970s. Since then, the question of the proper role of the State has been one of the most contentious issues on the political agenda.

In Britain, the change in government in 1979 produced the first radical and sustained political challenge to the foundations of the mixed economy. The Medium-Term Financial Strategy (introduced in 1980) redefined the role of macro-economic policy, assigning it largely to the reduction of inflation. The Conservative government also embarked upon a *laissez-faire* policy toward the private sector and, with the general ambition of 'making markets work better', sought to reduce government interference and intervention. Department of Trade and Industry programmes of regional and industrial aid were radically reduced (and the then Secretary of State wondered whether the department itself might 'wither away'). Labour market monopoly was attacked in an attempt to liberalize its working, so that wages might adjust 'naturally' to restore full employment. Incomes policies, the traditional response to wage inflation in the consensus years, were abandoned. In theory at least, the goals of full employment and growth were to be achieved by free markets and micro-economic flexibility, whilst control of the money supply would ensure low inflation. (In practice, however, the macro-economic and micro-economic aspects have increasingly become mixed up, as the privatization programme has in part been geared to reducing the public sector borrowing requirement at the expense of efficient resource allocation.)

Though the details of these policies are of immediate concern, this paper attempts to look behind the practical aspects at the fundamental principles which provide a rationale for State intervention. For the relationship between these policies and the economic theory of the market upon which they are based is nowhere straightforward. The economist, faced with the diversity of practical policy questions and the complexity of their effects, can contribute to this debate in a number of ways. Some of the questions which arise are instrumental ones—what options are there available to pursue a specified objective? Is present policy the best means available? These kinds of question relate to such matters as whether particular taxes are well fitted to raising revenue, or are progressive or regressive; whether privatized firms are likely to be more efficient than nationalized ones; whether £M3 or Mo is more closely correlated to inflation.

The answers that economists can provide to these questions are necessarily incomplete. In part, this is because the data economists have available are themselves typically incomplete and unreliable. But, in addition, theory requires simplifications which necessarily involve divergence from the actual world. Model failure is inevitable. Yet despite these difficulties, the kinds of disputes which arise with instrumental questions are ones which can be tackled in a rational manner and progress can be made. We now know, for example, much more about the role and methods by which competition operates; about the transmission from money to economic activity; and so on.

But although some of the evaluational questions about the economic role of the State are instrumental, others are more elusive. These are questions about ends, goals, and values. Indeed, Thatcherism cannot be understood without regard to the attempt to initiate fundamental change at this deeper level. It is less clear at this level what the economist can contribute. On the one hand, the economist cannot say that one value-judgement is superior to another. But, on the other, such judgements cannot be avoided. An ordering of objectives must be made. Faced with this dilemma, the economist can, where a number of objectives are being pursued, at least indicate where there is or is not consistency and can further examine what the consequences in terms of practical policy might be of pursuing them. Recent developments in welfare economics have gone a considerable way towards opening up this discussion beyond the narrow traditional Paretian welfare grounds.

This paper examines the economic arguments at both the instrumental and value-judgement levels. It attempts to identify the various rationales proposed for the market allocation of resources and for State intervention. It looks at the ways in which the fundamental economic theories of markets and planning have affected the growth of the economic borders of the State in the twentieth century and, in the light of this analysis, re-assesses the instrumental case for government intervention and the values upon which it is based. The arguments are focused on market and government failure at the instrumental level, and the welfare case for liberty and social justice. The role and design of macro-economic policy will be largely neglected here, except in so far as it relates to the underlying principles of economic organization.

The structure is as follows. Section 2 looks at the arguments 'behind' the current policy debate, bringing out the theoretical case which economists have put forward for and against the market. Section 3 then turns from this abstract discussion to see what impact these theoretical arguments have had on the economic expansion of the State in the twentieth century. Section 4 reassesses the instrumental and value questions and suggests an alternative way forward, while Section 5 presents the major conclusions.

2. The Rationale for State Intervention and the Market Philosophy

There has been a tendency in academic economics to focus on ever-narrower technical modelling and to shy away from grander questions such as the rationale for the market system. Increasingly this field has been left to political theorists and politicians. Yet economics has much to contribute to this debate and has, in fact, provided the core arguments for the expansion and now contraction of State activity. 'The ideas of economists and political philosophers, both when they are right and when they are wrong, are', as Keynes (1936, p. 383) noted, 'more powerful than is commonly understood . . . Practical men, who believe themselves to be quite exempt from any intellectual influences, are usually the slaves of some defunct economist'.

The central question, to which economists have given different answers since Adam Smith, is whether or not the competitive market system, left to its own devices, free of government interference, will produce superior results, in terms of efficiency and social justice, than alternative systems of economic organization. It is this claim which again dominates the political and economic policy agenda in the UK and many other countries.

It is a claim about both means and ends. The market system is argued to be the best *instrumental* method for attaining certain predetermined fundamental goals. Thus the argument for a policy of *laissez-faire* rests upon two necessary conditions—the merits of the ultimate goals and the instrumental efficiency of the market in attaining them. The debate about ends is one which market theorists have not avoided. Indeed it is here that the political philosophy of the 'new right' and economic theory have come together. The defenders of the market are typically neo-liberals, rejecting the paternalism of the State (from the right and the left) and stressing the importance of liberty for the individual. These writers favour the competitive market system because, compared with alternative economic systems, it is argued to generate greater individual liberty through voluntary consumer choice.

At the instrumental level, the proponents of the market divide between those who optimistically claim great virtue for the market and those with less exacting views. The former group see the market as generating the maximum wealth and the maximum freedom, while the latter rest their case on the weaker and less exacting argument that the market—while not perfect—is better than the available alternatives such as State intervention.

Any economic system ultimately relies for its justification upon the effects it has on welfare. The different theories of the market make different assumptions about human behaviour—about what motivates people and how they react to incentives. They can be divided into those which view competition as an incentive system bringing out the best in individuals, and those for which competition acts as a necessary discipline on the tendency to idleness and the exploitation of monopoly profit. Thus the market can be seen either as a positive system of incentives or 'carrots' to encourage the development of talents, skills, and abilities of individuals, or as a negative 'stick' to force people to be efficient.

Unfortunately for defenders of the market system, the models which they employ at the instrumental level and the goals or values advanced at the deeper level can also point in the opposite direction. The neo-classical model typically employed in defending markets relates to decentralization of production and exchange—a perfect market or a perfect planner will both produce optimal results. And, in terms of values, the appeal to liberalism can also point in the direction of intervention. But this is to anticipate the reassessment in Section 4 below. We first examine the traditional arguments.

Economists have, typically, focused on the efficiency gains from competition and we shall follow this tradition by first examining the instrumental efficiency of the market. This approach requires both a positive theory demonstrating the merits of the market and, in addition, a negative theory about the defects of State intervention. We then turn to the debate about values which lies behind the market defence.

(a) *Instrumental Arguments and the Economic Efficiency of Markets*

The somewhat counter-intuitive notion that the pursuit of self-interest unimpeded by government interference might be superior in efficiency terms to co-operative behaviour is a legacy of Adam Smith's 'invisible hand' doctrine. Yet, as Viner has pointed out (1960, p. 65), 'The classical exponents of *laissez-faire* always qualified their enthusiasm for the free market by the condition that it should be a competitive market'. The defence of the market rested then on the consequences of its competitive nature. Yet, in the literature, there are two quite distinct broad accounts of the operation of competitive forces and, hence, two defences of market solutions generally. These are, first, the static neo-classical economic model (in the tradition of Walras and Jevons) and, second, that of the Austrian tradition, which has focused on the dynamics of competition (in the tradition of Menger, Mises, Hayek, and Schumpeter). The former is the paradigm used most generally in mainstream economic theory and relies on the model of perfect competition. The latter relies on the superiority of the price mechanism as a means of co-ordination compared with government planning where uncertainty is pervasive. Both rely on value-judgements, but again these (as we shall see) differ strongly. We begin with the traditional neo-classical case.

Perfect Competition

The traditional argument for *laissez-faire* is constructed by examining how a decentralized market system, unimpeded by distortions, would function. That competitive form is then shown to be compatible with an apparently acceptable and uncontroversial welfare judgement and hence demonstrated to be ideal.

A perfectly decentralized economy operates in markets where there are a large number of consumers maximizing their utility and producers maximizing profits. Everything is owned and the property rights are clearly defined. In each and every market, the product is homogeneous, there are no barriers to entry, returns to scale are constant, and relevant information is generally available and free of charge. Each firm has no market power and hence is a price-taker rather than a price-maker. In such an economy, firms maximize profits where price is equal to marginal cost. Any deviation from this would lead to loss of market share as new entrants came into the market and consumers turned elsewhere for their goods and services. Thus firms earn just sufficient profit to make it worth their while staying in the industry. There are no supernormal or monopoly profits.

The next step in the market defence is to show that a perfectly competitive economy, where these conditions are met, is one which would be desirable. This is demonstrated by invoking the seemingly harmless welfare criterion of Pareto optimality. A state of the world is Pareto-optimal if there are no possible changes which could be made which would make at least one person better off without making at least one other person worse off. The First Fundamental Theorem of Welfare Economics demonstrates that a perfectly competitive economy is Pareto-optimal.[1]

Apart from the immediate difficulties with the correspondence of the model to the real economy (to which we will return below), this economy lacks anyone to set the prices (since all are assumed to be price-takers). Thus a further assumption is invoked—that there exists an 'auctioneer' or co-ordinator who sets and adjusts prices.[2] This auctioneer is assumed cost-

---

[1] The Pareto principle is discussed more comprehensively by Beckerman (this volume). See also Sen (1975) for a discussion of this theorem and its converse, and more generally Sen (this volume).

[2] The alternative approach is to assume that co-ordination takes place through bargaining, where property rights are perfectly defined and the legal system is costless in enforcing them. See, for example, Coase (1960).

less. But since the co-ordination is costless, it could equally well be carried out by a planner, and hence a perfect allocation of resources could be achieved either through the market, driven by the price mechanism, or by a planned economy with quantities chosen by planners. There is nothing in this result which suggests that prices are better than quantities in co-ordination, precisely because the information is costless.

Thus the neo-classical model of perfect competition as the paradigm of an efficient economy relies upon a series of claims—that the economy approximates the assumptions of perfect competition, that it is costlessly co-ordinated, and that the achievement of a Pareto-optimal state is worthy of merit. Using this same model, however, it is also possible to produce an analysis of the reasons for State intervention, by examining the extent to which the assumptions of perfect competition are not met.

The perfect competition model is a model of an ideal economy. It shows what an economy would have to look like if it were to generate the most efficient outcome. To the extent that markets in practice deviate from these assumptions, they can be deemed to 'fail'. The model of perfect competition can be used 'backwards' to identify cases of market failure.[3] These then serve as necessary conditions for State intervention in the economy. Such cases are not, however, sufficient. The reason for this is obvious. The economy which exists today is complex and it is highly unlikely that there are any unique, simple, and perfect solutions to its failures. In intervening in the market, governments also make mistakes and hence the extent of 'government failure' must be balanced against 'market failure'. It is by no means clear that the latter is less severe than the former. In practice, market optimists have tended to focus on the negative aspects of government failure, while market pessimists have stressed market failure.

Market failure arises in a number of ways and it will prove useful to consider the major sources at this stage. There are a number of approaches, including classification into demand, supply, and market structure. In practice, however, market failure is rarely pure and this should be borne in mind in roughly following this classification. We begin then on the demand side, with consumer preferences. The demand for goods and services in an economy ultimately rests on the preferences of individual consumers. In conventional neo-classical theory, these consumer preferences are assumed to be consistent and complete. Given a choice between any two alternatives, the consumer can rank these in order. Furthermore, given a set of alternatives, consumers will choose consistently. However, it is clear that in practice consumers often lack the relevant information to yield

---

[3] The classic article setting out this approach is by Bator (1958).

a complete ordering of all alternatives, and hence preference orderings are often partial and incomplete. In addition, there is considerable evidence to suggest the existence of at least local inconsistency and the influence of non-rational factors on choice.[4]

Where these weaknesses arise, the State may be able to provide better information about the opportunities available to individuals so that choices may be improved. Alternatively, the State may act instead of consumers in a paternalistic fashion—by trying to alter or replace preferences. The most important examples of this sort of State paternalism are in health care, education, and social security—in smoking, school milk, and compulsory education. This sort of preference failure can in addition lead to the imposition of compulsory insurance provision and the development of social insurance as the basis of welfare provision. The position is even more complex where one person chooses for another, without the State being directly involved. There is, for example, a tension between the 'rights' of the parents to choose freely the appropriate education for children, and the 'rights' of the child. Should the State intervene here? Many people would argue that the State here does have a duty to intervene, though this view would not be shared by the 'new right'.

In addition to direct preference failures and issues about adjudication between different people's preferences, the market system might fail because insufficient incentives exist for individuals to reveal their true preferences. Public goods constitute such a case. A public good exists where the marginal cost of consumption of another individual is zero and there is no possibility of exclusion from consumption. For example, it costs society almost nothing more to defend one additional person than it costs for the other fifty or so million, and it cannot defend the others without also defending the one. The demand failure that arises is in determining how much of a public good to produce. Since the additional cost to myself of the production of an extra unit of a public good is very close to zero, the incentive is to demand increasingly greater provision. There is, therefore, no straightforward market mechanism for revealing the 'true' demand for public goods. Further, since the costs cannot be easily recouped (because of non-excludability), there is little or no incentive for the market to provide these goods.

The provision of public goods can be met either by the State choosing an appropriate level (and hence replacing individual choice) and financing the expenditure by taxation, or by the formation of 'clubs' whose members consume the good, paying an entry or membership fee. In the former case, the problem for the State is to choose the optimal level of provision. In the

---

[4] The reader is referred to the selection of papers in Kahneman, Slovic, and Tversky (1983).

latter case, the club internalizes the public good, yet is unlikely to set the membership fee at the 'correct' marginal cost.[5]

Supply failures arise when the private costs of production do not coincide with those of society and where there are economies of scale. In both of these cases, the assumptions of the perfect competition model are violated and the market will not produce at the optimal price/output combination. Social costs arise either because the social value of production is under-valued by the market, in areas like employment and the arts, or because private firms evade paying for the consequences of their actions in the production of externalities. Pollution is the obvious example of the latter case. Where externalities arise (and they tend to be pervasive), there are a number of solutions available to deal with them. Each involves an attempt to incorporate the costs of the externality into the firm's decision-making. The first method is the classic Pigou/Meade tax/subsidy technique. The level of externality is estimated and a tax or subsidy is imposed on the firm to adjust costs to their true social level. Second, firms may internalize externalities by merging. Third, the sufferers from the effects of the externality may be able to take legal action against the firm, provided that the ownership of the right not to suffer from the external effect is well defined (see Coase (1960)). Where it is not, the State may intervene to rectify this weakness.

Supply failures may also arise in the presence of substantial scale economies, though the impact of these typically comes about through the resulting industrial concentration. In the traditional analysis, as market structure tends toward monopoly, price increasingly diverges from marginal cost and output falls. At the extreme is 'natural monopoly', where scale and scope economies are so great that there can be only one firm in the industry (see Sharkey (1982)). This analysis derives from the standard structure–conduct–performance paradigm in analysing indus-trial markets. It neglects the competitive practice which typifies many oligopolistic markets.[6] However, the fact that oligopolies can be competi-tive does not detract from the general problem of monopoly. Indeed, the static analysis tends to neglect the social costs of anti-competitive practices which firms employ to gain market power and hence a host of additional problems.

---

[5] Sandler and Tschirhart (1980) provide an accessible survey of the theory of clubs.

[6] For an overview and analysis of the modern industrial theory of oligopoly and monopoly, the reader is referred to the issue of Oxford Review of Economic Policy devoted to the topic (Autumn 1985) and especially to the articles by Mayer (1985b) and Vickers (1985).

Co-ordination and the Austrian Theory

The perfect competition paradigm is clearly a weak basis for defending the market system. Its conditions are rarely, if ever, met, and in practice the various types of market failure pervade the economy. Far from being a basis for defending the market, it is much better suited as a basis for State intervention. Hence, market pessimists have pursued this framework as a guide to intervention.

But because perfect competition may be an inappropriate model upon which to base the argument for *laissez-faire*, it does not follow that there are no other alternative defences. As noted above, the possibility of 'government failure' typically serves this purpose. It is within this context that the Austrian model of competition has been exploited by market optimists.

The Austrian model rests on imperfect competition and in particular on imperfect information. For Hayek, the principal modern exponent of the Austrian view,[7] 'the argument in favour of competition does not rest on the conditions that would exist if it were perfect' (1948, p. 104). Indeed, perfect competition is for Hayek a state in which competition has ceased, when the market has reached its ideal equilibrium. The competitive process takes place out of equilibrium, in a world of uncertainty and imperfection. Innovations arise and are tested in the market-place. The incentive to engage in research and development, to develop new products, is the possibility of profit. The larger existing profits, the greater the attraction of entry.

On this view, the attraction of the market system and of competition is not, however, limited to research, development, and market entry. The market system is co-ordinated by the price mechanism. Each individual in society need only know the relative prices for all the goods and services in the economy. Given that information and each individual's knowledge of his or her own preferences and resources, the pursuit of their own self-interest will lead people to place demands on the economy and to supply goods and labour. The price system allocates the resources to best satisfy conflicting demands. By rises and falls in the price of goods relative to each other, it signals to individuals changing degrees of scarcity and resource costs, which enables gluts and shortages to be eliminated.

This property of the price system has one great advantage. It is informationally undemanding. Each individual need only know his or her own

---

[7] The presentation here closely follows Hayek's arguments. This is largely for ease of exposition, and many of the important differences between Mises and Hayek in particular have been suppressed. See Mises (1920), Lange (1938b), and Dobb (1969) for more details, and Gray in this volume.

preferences and the relative prices of goods and services available to him or her. Each firm need only know its costs and, again, the relative prices. By contrast, the State planner, if he or she is to replace the markets, must know much more. While in the price system each individual need only understand his or her own predicament, the planner must try to comprehend that of all. This differential in information requirements and the impossibility of 'socialist calculation' was for Mises and Hayek a central argument for the market.

The above argument is permissive. With the relevant information provided by the price mechanism, individuals *can* make efficient choices. They *do* in fact do so because of the enforcement powers of the market. The market selects out winners by their profit achievement and eliminates the inefficient loss-makers. This process of competition is indeed often argued to be analogous to the way in which the environment acts in the theory of evolution and natural selection. Inefficiency is weeded out by the forces of competition rather like ill-adapted mutations are in biological models.[8] Competition enforces efficiency by negatively eliminating inefficiency. As Keynes put it (1926, p. 284):

The parallelism between economic *laissez-faire* and Darwinism . . . is very close indeed. Just as Darwin invoked sexual love, acting through sexual selection, as an adjutant to natural selection by competition, to direct evolution along lines which should be desirable as well as effective, so the individualist invokes love of money, acting through the pursuit of profit, as an adjutant to natural selection, to bring about the production on the greatest possible scale of what is most strongly desired as measured by exchange value.

Competition then acts to eliminate inefficiency. But where cost conditions vary, market power may arise. Yet here again competition is seen as a panacea. Where monopoly profits arise, rivals are attracted and their entry into the market drives down prices. Thus competition protects consumers. It is this argument which the modern advocates of privatization have appealed to. As Beesley and Littlechild (1983, p. 5) put it, 'Competition is the most important mechanism for maximising consumer benefits and for limiting monopoly power. Its essence is rivalry and freedom to enter a market. What counts is the existence of competitive threats, from potential as well as existing competitors'.

The mechanisms of enforcement depend on constraints arising in the capital market (such as take-overs and bankruptcies), in managerial competition, and in the product market. Competition is an external constraint. As long as it exists, at least potentially, the firm is forced to act

[8] See Helm (1984) for an analysis of this relationship between evolutionary theory and individual and firm selection.

in the interests of consumers.[9] Provided that entry is relatively cheap, monopoly need not lead to exploitation, since competitive selection will undermine excessive prices. Such a view of competition, therefore, combines the virtues of the price system in circumstances in which information is imperfect with the self-regulating constraint of potential entry. Though the outcome of the market would not be perfect, it would be superior to an attempt by government to replace it.

In analysing government failure, Hayek (1944), in *The Road to Serfdom*, and Popper (1945), in *The Open Society and its Enemies*, advanced an additional argument purporting to demonstrate that State planners would inevitably worsen the welfare of the society if they attempted to replace markets. Since the social world, and in particular the economy, is extremely complex, planners and social scientists can only have limited understanding of it. Because of this complexity, unintended consequences of planning decisions inevitably arise. These would themselves tend to create further difficulties, being (they assumed) largely negative in effect. Hence well-intentioned planners were likely to lower welfare accidentally. The road to hell—the road of planning—is thus paved with good intentions. The alternative to the 'open society' is the 'serfdom' of socialism.

This particular argument is problematic. For, as Sen (1983a) has pointed out, the observation that policies and actions may have unintended consequences is hardly startling. It is the assumption that these will tend to be perverse which drives Hayek's and Popper's theory and that assumption has no direct justification. Many unintended consequences will, of course, be irrelevant. Others will be beneficial. There is no justification for the assumption of perversity.

But even if some interventions by planners did have unfortunate consequences, the comparison with what the price system achieves is somewhat misleading. Recall that, because of market imperfections, transactions typically take place at the 'wrong' prices. Now, unfortunately for Hayek, just as the price system can be very helpful in conveying the right information, this transmission property applies to all information contained in prices, and not just that of 'correct' prices. Hence, should prices be distorted, as they inevitably are by monopoly, externalities, and other characteristics of market failure, Hayek's supposed advantages in information transmission become disadvantageous in an imperfect economy. The decisive property of informational economy is advantageous if the prices are right, but quite the opposite in a distorted economy.

Thus, the case for the market system, as opposed to planning based

---

[9] This reliance on potential competition has been much exploited in the recent literature on 'contestable markets'. See on this Baumol (1982) and Shepherd (1984).

upon government failure, cannot be carried as a general rule. Rather, like the market failure approach, a case-by-case procedure must be adopted. Economic theory does not lead to a general presumption either for or against the market system.

Market Co-ordination and Macro-economic Failures

We have seen that co-ordinating the economy in the neo-classical theory relies on a costless auctioneer and in the Austrian approach is carried out by the price mechanism. There remains, however, the further complication of co-ordinating the *macro-economic* activity in an economy.

Neither of the above approaches adequately copes with this difficulty because for them, strictly, there are no macro phenomena. The economy is characterized by individual tastes, by technology, and by firms. 'Macro' aggregates are simply the sum of their constituent parts. Statements about these must be translated into statements relating to individuals.

Unfortunately, this simplistic view does not stand up to close scrutiny. First, the macro outcomes of individual actions can often be quite contrary to the individuals' aims and intentions.[10] Second, voluntary co-operation without government intervention is frequently not enough; in many cases the co-operative solution to problems fails because of strategic considerations, which have been well represented in the so-called Prisoners' Dilemma and subsequent developments in game theory.[11] Co-operative solutions are, in this scenario, superior to the pursuit of narrow self-interest, but each party to the potential solution has an incentive to encourage the others to engage in co-operative acts, while themselves exploiting the situation. Oil producers may, for example, all agree to cut back output to increase profitability for all, but if everyone else cuts back and you do not, the rewards to yourself (but not the others) are much greater. Opportunities to 'free-ride' on others are considerable and it can be governments who are best placed to enforce co-operation. Third, the aggregate of individual preferences may not yield a consistent democratic social ordering of alternatives, unless undesirable and strong assumptions are placed upon the derivation of the social welfare function. The aims and objectives of society are not, contrary to Hayekian individualism, a simple function of those of individuals.[12]

---

[10] See Schelling (1978).

[11] An introduction to game theory is provided by Bacharach (1976). See Vickers (1985) for a non-technical discussion of applications to oligopoly theory.

[12] This result is presented in social choice literature as Arrow's General Possibility Theorem. It demonstrates that even if we assume weak Paretianism, unrestricted domain, and independence of irrelevant alternatives, a non-dictatorial social welfare function cannot be defined if there are at least three individuals and three social states. See Arrow

Finally, and here Keynes's contribution is of greatest import, the private sector does not always produce a stable level of output and employment. The economy is liable to booms and slumps and can get stuck in inferior equilibrium positions from which only the State, by guiding and manipulating its policy stance, can rescue it. Capitalism is an imperfect system which may need careful guidance and control to save it from itself. This last co-ordinating role gives a rationale for macro-economic policy, while leaving open the question of its design. The debates on macro-economic policy (for example, between the Keynesian and monetarist camps) will not be discussed here, except in so far as they bear upon the overall case for intervention or *laissez-faire*.

(b) *The Liberal Defence of Markets: Arguments about Values*

So far in this section, the instrumental case for the market and competition in generating economic efficiency has been set out and a number of objections have been raised. However, even if the market were a good mechanism for creating wealth and allocating resources, ultimately the defenders of the market rest their case on a further requirement—that economic freedom and hence the free-market economy are a necessary condition for political freedom.[13] We now explore this claimed relationship between economic efficiency and freedom, and show that it rests on a particular narrow concept of freedom. Further, having identified that concept, we note that the two are not necessarily consistent.

The arguments for the market in the Hayekian tradition ultimately derive from the central neo-liberal tenet of individualism (see Gray (this volume)). The liberty of the individual always dominates the efficiency of the economy. Happily for them, the defenders of *laissez-faire* thought they had discovered a system which guaranteed both efficiency *and* the maximum of liberty. However, should any conflict arise, the latter would always dominate the former in liberal thinking. It is the individual upon whom ultimate moral worth is placed and society is nothing more than the sum or aggregation of the individuals who comprise it. Society is the slave of its individual components. Governments whose role is not restricted by rules and constitutions will inevitably try to impose the preferences and interests of particular groups of individuals upon others.[14] To be free

(1951a) and Sen (1970b) for expositions, and Sen (1979b) for an accessible account of why this result arises.

[13] See, for example, Friedman (1962) and Friedman and Friedman (1980).

[14] This approach is rooted in the liberal tradition, from Locke and especially Mill (1859) onwards. Hayek's *The Constitution of Liberty* (1960) is the classic modern treatise on this brand of constitutionalism. Economists in the 'new right' tradition who have followed in this direction include most notably Buchanan and Tullock (1962) and Tullock (1976).

means to be free from interference, to have the maximum domain of choice within which an individual can do as he or she chooses. The role of government is to impose the rule of law to prevent unjustified interference of some individuals upon others, but at the same time to minimize its own interference. It is a restraining negative role, rather than an activist one.

Though the primacy of liberty is ultimately a value-judgement, its consistency with efficiency is one which modern social choice and welfare theorists have addressed analytically. One of the earliest and most famous attempts to reconcile them was by Adam Smith, who tried to demonstrate the natural harmony of liberty and the market. He claimed (1776; 1976 edition, p. 687) that:

All systems either of preference or restraint, therefore, being thus completely taken away, the obvious and simple system of natural liberty establishes itself of its own accord. Every man, as long as he does not violate the laws of justice, is left perfectly free to pursue his own interest in his own way, and to bring both his industry and capital into competition with those of any other man, or order of men. The sovereign is completely discharged from a duty, in attempting to perform which he must always be exposed to innumerable delusions, and for the proper performance of which no human wisdom or knowledge could ever be sufficient; the duty of superintending the industry of private people and of directing it towards the employments most suitable to the interest of the society.

Hence liberty meant the absence of constraints, and since governments constrained the market when they interfered and the market was voluntary to its participants, economic freedom from government interference could not but enhance political freedom. Indeed, Smith is quite precise on the exact duties of government. He goes on to state these as follows:

According to the system of natural liberty, the Sovereign has only three duties to attend to . . . first, the duty of protecting the society from the violence and invasion of other independent societies; secondly, the duty of protecting, as far as possible, every member of the society from the injustice or oppression of every other member of it, or the duty of establishing an exact administration of justice; and, thirdly, the duty of erecting and maintaining certain publick works and certain publick institutions, which it can never be for the interest of any individual, or small number of individuals, to erect and maintain.

Such an automatic harmony of interests and such a weak domain for government cannot, however, be taken for granted. One of the central difficulties in neo-liberal thought which has not been fully explored is that the market is itself a social institution. It cannot be accounted for by individual elements; rather it is, as we saw above, the co-ordinator of individuals. Hence the need for rules by which social institutions, like markets, are to function. The price mechanism may bring individuals into balance in trading between goods and preferences, but this is only possible if some individuals do not exert undue influence and power over others. *Laissez-faire* cannot be anarchic; it must be strictly confined by rules. The market thus must maintain neutrality between individuals and must be free from governmental interference. Hence social institutions must have rules, or constitutions, and the society as a whole must have an agreed code of conduct which meets the liberal criterion of fairness. These rules then define the role of government and the limits of competition.

The problem then is how to frame these rules. What is to be a 'fair' code of conduct? What is a 'fair' competition? It is on this question that the *laissez-faire* advocates of the market turn to the liberal theorists of the State. For much of liberal political theory—in the tradition of Hume, Locke, and Mill—has been concerned with justifying the rules of a constitution, by reference to the choices of individuals. The modern liberal theory, as developed most notably by Nozick (1974) on the right and Rawls (1971) on the left, seeks to justify the principles of a social arrangement, by asking what individuals would choose if they were abstracted from society. In particular, for Rawls, the choice is based on what they would choose if they were ignorant of the place in society they might come to occupy once it had been set in motion. The liberal rules for the framing of the role of government, the limits to *laissez-faire*, and 'natural' competitive forces are those that idealized individuals would choose. Thus the central tenet of individualism is preserved and made the guiding arbiter of the structure of the State and its legal arrangements.

Though ultimately this is the foundation of the neo-liberal case, it is not at all clear that the market solution is the best preserver of individual liberty, nor that individuals would select such a constitution. For the market system to maximize the degree of freedom, there must be no conflict with Pareto-optimal efficiency. Unfortunately, it has been demonstrated by Sen (1970a) that to hold both Paretianism and liberalism simultaneously can be inconsistent. This result arises because the Paretian concept is applicable to the degree of preference satisfaction with unrestricted domain. However, the requirements of liberty restrict the domain of preferences that individuals may exercise to prevent interference in one person's choice by others. Hence one person could be made better off without harming others in the utility sense, but at the same time, exercise choices which the liberal would find objectionable. Satisfying preferences may conflict with the restriction of the domain of choice. As Sen concludes, 'while the Pareto criterion has been thought to be an expression of individual liberty, it appears that in choices involving more than two alternatives it can have consequences that are, in fact, deeply illiberal'.

But even if liberty and efficiency were consistent, there is no guarantee that the resulting income distribution would meet the requirements of social justice. Since much of the expansion of the economic role of the State has been in redistribution and that redistribution has reduced the 'natural' efficiency of the market system, the critique of State intervention also relies on an argument about the importance of distributional considerations in social welfare. A more positive concept of freedom, which included a degree of equality, would undermine the case against government intervention. This will be discussed in greater detail in Section 4 below.

3. Theory and Policy in the Growth of the State

We have seen in the previous section that the arguments for and against market solutions to economic organization are complex and typically combine both instrumental and welfare arguments. Politicians who use economic arguments when considering State intervention tend to draw on them to support their prior value-judgements. But because this use is inevitably selective and because these arguments do not necessarily mesh well together, the outcome can be other than might be expected.[15] This section looks at the growth of the State in practice, comparing the arguments used with those discussed at a theoretical level in the previous section.

The role of the State prior to the First World War was largely that of the 'night-watchman'. The State guaranteed property rights, provided for defence, kept law and order on the streets, and maintained the value of the currency. Redistribution of income was largely left to charity, and revenue-raising was restricted, in the main, to customs and excise, monopoly, and commodity taxation. The State was thus largely restricted to the three roles allocated to it by Adam Smith.

The First World War required economic mobilization to a degree not previously experienced by western countries, and led to an expansion of the economic role of the State in production, labour mobilization, and taxation. Though the State tried to withdraw after the First World War and return to the pre-war world of the gold standard, the inter-war period witnessed the development of social assistance in response to unemployment, involvement in labour relations, and a tendency towards greater emphasis on corporatist solutions.[16]

---

[15] This theme is developed in Allsopp and Helm (1985).
[16] See Middlemas (1979), especially Chapters 5–8.

(a) *The 1930s Debate*

The intellectual debate of the 1930s, with the growth of Keynesian economics and socialist planning theory, was in part a response to the growing economic 'crisis of capitalism' and the political growth of fascism and communism. While textbook classical theory suggested that markets were either in equilibrium or tending towards it, the reality of collapse in Europe and the United States of capital and labour markets pointed elsewhere. The theoretical responses were diverse. At one extreme, both classical and Austrian theorists redefined their theories of the market and pointed to 'distortions' (such as unions, the concentration of capital, and government intervention) as the source of depression. At the other, theorists of the left explored alternative economic arrangements where markets were replaced by planners. Ironically, both sets of theorists could and did appeal to the perfect competition paradigm as their starting-point. The free market theorists looked to the removal of market distortions; the left identified the market failures associated with monopoly, cartels, and the absence of proper accounting for social costs, and attempted through planned solutions to increase the accountability of industry to public needs.

A third, and largely new, strand argued that macro-economic failure could occur—that there were co-ordination problems at the macro level regardless of what happened at the micro level. Thus aggregate demand could be deficient, even if labour and capital were competitively supplied and paid their marginal products. This Keynesian approach recognized that the economic system was not necessarily self-correcting. But it could be saved from collapse by a little guidance and support from the State. The government should inject demand into the economy when there were signs of slack and recession, but restrain demand when inflation threatened. This did not involve interfering directly in markets, but rather providing the right macro-economic framework.

For somewhat distinct reasons, pressure for a more concerted effort by the State to redistribute the rewards generated by the market intensified after the First and then again after the Second World War. Though it had been on both liberal and socialist agendas in the nineteenth century, the wars had a socially levelling effect and led to much greater expectations of social justice in their aftermaths. The liberals and the socialists did, however, have distinct approaches to the question of social justice and these were well established by the time that Beveridge laid down the principles for the post-war Welfare State.[17]

---

[17] See Clarke (1978) and Freeden (1978) for analyses of the origins and development of the splits between the new liberals and social democrats in the late nineteenth and early twentieth centuries.

Neither the neo-classical nor the Austrian paradigms gave satisfactory justifications in terms of social justice as to why the distribution of income generated by the market should be socially and politically acceptable. The debate about the proper redistributional policy to adopt was partly one about means and partly one about ends. On the one hand, social insurance was advocated as a method of overcoming the accidents which might befall individuals—such as sickness, unemployment, maternity, and so on. On the other, direct redistribution was advocated by those who identified the 'causes' of poverty as beyond individual control. In other words, the social insurers saw poverty as the consequence of market failure (the insurance market and preference failure), whereas the redistributionalists saw it as a separate issue, regardless of the perfection of the market. Perfect markets do not, on this latter view, produce just distributions of income. It was, as we shall see, the liberal approach—that of the social insurance principle—which dominated the design of the Welfare State, whereas the redistributional approach dominated taxation design.

(b) The Three Pillars of the Post-war Consensus

The Welfare State

The design of the Welfare State was loosely based on a number of theories which had been developed in the inter-war years. At a fundamental level, the concept of a 'Welfare State' represented a political and moral concept, invented to stand as a central war aim to be contrasted against Hitler's 'warfare state'.[18] From the wartime experience of co-operation between parties in planning almost every aspect of social and economic life, emerged the consensus around a new social partnership between capital, labour, the State, and the market.

But the moral and political commitment lacked an instrumental basis— the practical aspects of implementing this vision were less clearly spelt out. In reality, many of the important caveats of the economic theory were ignored and a series of *ad hoc* measures employed. Thus market failure arising from monopoly and collusion was 'solved' by nationalization, without due attention to 'government failure' and hence little careful attention to the form of controls. Similarly, the insurance and redistributive aspects of welfare were conveniently merged.

The Beveridge system relied upon social insurance and universal benefits. Though its origins go back to the early social insurance legislation of Lloyd George's 'People's Budget' in 1909, the first major steps during the Second World War were taken by the coalition administration. The

---

[18] Marwick (1982).

Butler Education Act laid down the principle of equal access to education for all, and the Beveridge-inspired 1944 Social Insurance White Paper (HMSO (1944b, 1944c)) extended the macro-economic commitments of government and set the scene for the extension of the provision of social insurance. That in turn was based upon the new assumption that the State was both capable of and had a positive duty to generate full employment. The Beveridge system had a number of key features which were taken over by the Attlee Government and, since they remain to a greater or lesser extent the dominant characteristics today, it is worth reminding ourselves of them.[19] First, Beveridge considered that poverty was an absolute concept—being poor related to absolute levels of food, clothing, health care, and so on. As the economy grew and expanded, it would therefore tend to disappear. Second, poverty was caused by 'accidents' and could, therefore, be insured against. But since people tended, for a variety of reasons, to under-provide for these contingencies, an element of compulsion was required to ensure that nobody fell below a certain minimum standard of living. This provided the rationale for State intervention to correct for what was referred to in Section 2 above as a preference failure. Benefits were then paid to those upon whom such 'social accidents' as unemployment or sickness fell. The Beveridge system did not purport to deal with inequality and thus the 'means-tested' entitlement to benefits was inappropriate.

Beveridge's approach also rejected a general income basis for benefits. These were to be in kind. Poverty related directly to the absolute levels of certain defined goods for which a minimum of consumption was required to enjoy a basic standard of living. Hence, under Beveridge, 'experts' (in practice, Civil Servants and politicians) would select and provide these basic goods on behalf of individuals, rather than give them cash to exercise their choices in the market. State paternalism was justified by preference failures. Now, in practice, it was best to provide some basic goods—like health care and education—free of charge and on demand, rather than incur complex insurance administration. Others, such as unemployment benefits, were more directly related to premiums paid.

The Beveridge scheme did not, however, work out as its inventor had imagined (as Dilnot (this volume) demonstrates). The reasons were partly practical—the reality of the post-war UK economy—and partly theoretical. First, Britain had emerged from the Second World War as a virtually bankrupt economy. The war had been essentially debt-financed, and this accumulation could be repaid in one of the following ways—by higher taxation, by export-led growth, by debtors 'aiding' their clients, or by cuts in expenditure. Britain, unlike its defeated European and Japanese rivals,

[19] See Dilnot, Kay, and Morris (1984, ch. 1) and Creedy and Disney (1985).

continued to aspire to world power status and hence could not rapidly run down its military and diplomatic services. Its capital stock was much depleted by the war effort, and Marshall Aid was insufficient to offset this and less generous than that received by other European countries. World markets outside the US were not expected to expand with the rapidity which was actually experienced. The consequence was a continuation of wartime austerity, with rationing and controls holding back domestic demand to enhance the current account of the balance of payments. Many of the more expensive aspects of the new Welfare State had thus to be trimmed, starting with the introduction of prescription charges in 1948.[20]

The second reason was the growing realization that poverty could be the result not only of social accident, but also of more fundamental social and economic factors. The consensus of the post-war period took a much more relativistic view of poverty, and the development of supplementary benefit as both means-tested and income-based was a significant departure from the Beveridge ideal.

Private and Public Ownership

If the design and introduction of the Welfare State derived from a confusing mixture of principles and practical reality, the nationalization of industry and the emergence of national planning were even more complex. Like privatization much later, the rationale for nationalization owed much to political principle and political expediency. The politics were then bolstered by appeal to economic arguments.

The economic rationale of nationalization was complex. At one level, the socialist concept of a planned economy required that the 'commanding heights' be under State control. This was both a macro- and a micro-economic argument. It was macro-economic to the extent that national-ized industries were seen, under the auspices of national planning, as instruments for economic management, and it was micro-economic in so far as planning was considered superior to the market allocation of resources. But, in addition to these general arguments, there were more industry-specific reasons, associated with monopoly, social costs, and cross-subsidization. Finally, the desire for workers to control and par-ticipate in their work-places also played a part, especially when these arguments coincided with powerful union interests as, for example, in the mines. This mix of arguments led to a neglect of the price mechanism in economic planning under the Labour administration. As Cairncross (1986, p. 308) summarizes the position:

---

[20] See Morgan (1985) for an account of the politics of the period, and Cairncross (1986) for the economics.

It corresponded to a fundamental cleavage between two approaches to economic planning: a socialist, egalitarian, approach which saw planning as a purely organisational activity akin to the planning that goes on within a productive enterprise, an army or, for that matter, a political party; and a liberal, Keynesian, approach which saw planning as a corrective to the operation of market forces and dwelt particularly on the need for a level of effective demand adequate to maintain full employment.

Thus little consideration was given to pricing, and the catch-all 'break-even' financial objective left 'social' non-profit-maximizing activities (such as employment and rural railways) to be set at levels dictated by boards and met by cross-subsidization.[21] Yet, despite the rather ill-defined form of control, the State sector of industry set up in the 1940s remained largely intact until the 1980s (with the exception of steel which has been pushed back and forth between government ownership and the private sector). Successive governments (especially those of Wilson (1964–70) and Heath (1970–4)) added further companies as they fell into bankruptcy. 'Lame ducks' like British Leyland and Rolls-Royce fell into this category.

Co-ordination and the Macro-economic Role of the State

In addition to the Welfare State attending to the relief of poverty, and nationalization as an aid to planning and the solution of monopoly problems, the third major pillar of the post-war period was the new macro-economic role of government in co-ordinating the economy to maintain a high level of employment, whilst restraining inflationary pressure. The 1944 Employment White Paper (HMSO (1944a)) is significant in that it took on the commitment to tackle what had been the major problems of the inter-war years. To fulfil this objective, there were essentially two possible types of policy—on the one hand, demand management and, on the other, planning to ensure that the outcome of micro behaviour would aggregate to produce an acceptable macro level of employment.

Demand management was the Keynesian solution; planning was that of the socialist theorists. Though the conventional wisdom had it that the former was the chosen instrument, that was true much more of the period after 1951 than of the Attlee Government. The Attlee Government saw employment less in terms of overall fiscal stance, and more in terms of the extent of planned intervention. Though not averse to deficit-financing, full employment was to be achieved by positive (micro) public works, not general spending. Furthermore, the immediate post-war chronic balance of payments position, and the desire to maintain sterling's artificially high level against the dollar, were hardly conducive to Keynesian expansion.

[21] For a detailed account of the intentions and consequences of the organizational structures, see Chester (1975).

Planning for the Labour government was to be a mix between short- and long-term plans, as well as special cases. Though there were different views and emphases, the Crippsian approach was perhaps the most cohesive. As he saw it,[22] the 'basic' industries were to have long-term plans, 'economic budgets' were required for macro aggregates such as the national income and expenditure aggregates, and manpower and 'special measures' would deal with problems such as the external position, capital investment, and fuels.

With the increased provision of welfare benefits and a State production sector, these three pillars of post-war economic organization remained intact—as indeed they did throughout western Europe—during the 1950s and 1960s. The challenge that was finally presented came as the perceived costs began to rise to unacceptable levels. At the micro-economic level, the continued financial burden imposed by the nationalized industries and the provision of social benefits required increased rates and levels of taxation. More generally, the onset of inflation, continued external payments problems, and the impact of oil price shocks led to a questioning of the underlying validity of the mixed economy. These developments in turn led to the reopening of the intellectual questions raised in Section 2 of this paper—had the expanded economic borders of the State brought benefit, or had they caused inflation and 'crowding-out' of more efficient private sector activity? The intellectual challenge of monetarism and of the philosophy of the 'new right' translated into a radical political redirection of policy after the 1979 Conservative election victory.

(c) *The Challenge of Thatcherism*

The Thatcher Government since 1979 has pursued fundamentally differ-ent policies in each of the major areas of economic policy from its post-war predecessors. Rather than expand the economic borders of the State to meet greater social and economic pressures, it has explicitly attempted to curtail the role of the State in the economy, with the intention of enhancing the freedom of the individual and encouraging the growth of 'the enter-prise culture'. The basis of this redirection has been an explicit appeal to a mix of Austrian and neo-classical market theories, and to libertarian values. In this section, the major policy changes will be briefly reviewed, and related to the underlying philosophy.

The corner-stone of the first Conservative administration's macro-economic policy was the Medium-Term Financial Strategy (MTFS) intro-duced in 1980. The essence of the MTFS was a set of targets for the public sector borrowing requirement (PSBR) and £M3 which the government

[22] Economic Survey for 1947; see Cairncross (1986, pp. 305–7).

pre-committed itself to achieve. Its intention was to bind the government to its targets and to signal commitment, and hence gain credibility in financial markets. The philosophy which lay behind it was monetarist. Though monetarism has many interpretations, the Thatcher variant had a number of easily identified broad features. These can be summarized by two simple propositions—that the market system functions so as to generate full employment 'naturally' if left to its own devices; and that money is the main (or sole) determinant of the price level.[23] Monetary growth was in the MTFS directly linked to the PSBR, and, since increases in taxes were deemed to have undesirable effects, reduced public expenditure was the chosen route to implement the policy.

The emphasis on reducing public expenditure to meet the government's macro-economic objectives tied in well with a more general dislike of the growth of the absolute size of government in the post-war period. Aside from the more overtly political motives, government activity was deemed to be less efficient than that undertaken by the private sector. The State sector failed to reward risk-taking and enterprise, and lacked the discipline of the market-place to punish inefficiency. Furthermore, government borrowing 'crowded out' private sector activity, and the necessary taxation to finance it reduced the returns to innovation and enterprise, as well as the incentive to work.

The economic rationale for this pessimistic view of government economic activity was variously supported by three conflicting arguments—that private markets were 'competitive' and hence produced socially optimal results; that 'market failure' was less significant than 'government failure'; and finally, in an Austrian vein, that monopoly profits were transitory, and longer-run competition would eliminate them. Thus each of the approaches to defending the market identified in Section 2 above were, when convenient, appealed to. Those who believed in pragmatism could agree with those ideologically committed to the market in privatization cases such as Jaguar Cars, Amersham International, and Cable and Wireless, but would have greater reservations where market failure was more apparent in such cases as British Gas, the electricity supply industry, and the water authorities.

The privatization programme, which constituted a major part of the micro-economic attempt 'to make markets work better', came a little later. It was a much broader policy than asset sales,[24] involving a host of

[23] The best 'official' exposition of the intellectual basis of the MTFS is given in Lawson's Mais Lecture (1984). For a critical assessment of the MTFS, see Allsopp (1985). A wider survey and critique of the first stages of the Thatcher Government's economic policy is to be found in Buiter and Miller (1983). Matthews and Minford (1987) provide a more sympathetic interpretation.

[24] See Kay and Thompson (1986) and Yarrow (1986).

measures including the withdrawal of industrial aid, deregulation, and franchising. The policy followed a number of phases, as did the emphasis on its intellectual justification. At first, the State withdrew aid and subsidies, radically pruning industrial policy as traditionally conceived. If the market 'naturally' achieved an efficient equilibrium, the State could not better it, and indeed might make matters worse by preventing the discipline of the market from being imposed. The next step was to increase competition in the State sector. Deregulation of buses, the Oil and Gas (Enterprise) Act 1982, and the Energy Act in 1983 were the major legislative achievements of this phase, encouraging entry by the private sector and relaxing State monopolies.

The next phase concentrated more directly on ownership and the transfer of public assets to the private sector. Whilst this transfer of assets was initially viewed as a method to enhance efficiency by increasing the intensity of competition, to be judged 'by the extent to which it maximises competition' (Moore (1983)), it was soon apparent that asset sales, considered as 'negative public expenditure', provided a method of financing tax cuts, whilst remaining within the boundaries of the MTFS. In addition, there were a number of other variants of the new competition policy. These included the contracting-out of services traditionally performed by State organizations (such as dustbin collection and health service laundry) as well as more ambitious franchising arrangements. Thus, what had started out as a relatively well-defined policy came to be directed towards the achievement of other objectives which sometimes conflicted with competition.

The new market philosophy was also apparent in the labour market, and the attack on 'monopoly' as a source of market failure was nowhere more apparent than in this area. The cause of unemployment lay not in the stance of macro-economic policy, nor in the absence of the traditional method of restraining wages via incomes policy, but rather in the labour market's uncompetitive characteristics. Indeed, both of the traditional policies were now deemed to be self-defeating. The labour market displayed rigidities, and 'a more flexible labour market is the key to increased competitiveness and thus to lower unemployment'.[25]

In the competitive model of the labour market, equilibrium is attained where the wage is equal to the marginal revenue product of labour. Unemployment arises because of deviations of the world from that model. These deviations are caused by market failure, and in the labour market the most notable was identified as that of monopoly power from the supply side, and hence legislation was introduced 'to reduce the monopoly power of trade unions, and to make union executives more responsive to the

[25] *Economic Progress Report* (1986, p. 1).

wishes of their members. The aim has been to create a climate in which realistic pay bargaining and acceptance of flexible working practices become the norm.'[26]

A number of interesting points arise from this model. First, the traditional micro-economic model of the labour market does not rule out the manipulation of labour demand to enhance employment. Thus if supply-side policies are solely used, the reason must lie in the undesirable macro-economic consequences of demand stimulation for rejecting this method of coping with employment. Second, the rhetoric of union reform has not always lent itself to the reduction of either monopoly power or wages. Making unions accountable to their members does not reduce bargaining power necessarily; indeed, it might enhance it.[27]

With the third electoral victory, the market philosophy has been extended beyond macro-economic and industrial concerns towards the Welfare State and government institutions. Radical reforms based on individual choice have been extended most notably to education and housing. Further changes to the health service and to social services can be expected. In each case, the role of the State in directing provision is to be limited by a greater emphasis on market services and on the rights and responsibilities of individuals to make provision for their needs. Personal pensions, personal equity plans, parental choice over local authority provision of education, and residents' choice over housing estate management are the practical policy instruments, and as each government activity is addressed, the concepts of market allocation and individual freedom dictate the policy response.

Somewhat paradoxically to this broad market approach, when it comes to governmental institutions, a much more centralizing stance has been adopted. The reforms of local government (contracting-out, poll taxes, opting out for schools) considered individually fit into the market philosophy; jointly they represent a marked centralization of power. The political rights of individuals to choose more interventionist local authorities have been curtailed to meet economic objectives (see Helm and Smith (this volume)).

Thus the policies pursued by the Thatcher administration rely on both value-judgements and instrumental theories: it would be a mistake to perceive the policies merely in an economic framework, concerned with efficiency. Rather, the economic policy derives from an ideology which has a reasonably well-defined set of fundamental principles. It is from these

---

[26] *Economic Progress Report*, op. cit.

[27] See *Oxford Review of Economic Policy*, Summer 1985 issue, which was devoted to unemployment, (especially the article by Mayhew) for a more detailed appraisal of recent government policy in the labour market.

principles that the new emphasis on private market solutions arises. The philosophy of Thatcherism is remarkably close to that of the Hayekian brand of liberalism, outlined in Section 2 above. The starting-point is individualism. People realize their potential as individuals, and not primarily as social beings. That implies that individuals are the best judges of their own welfare, and that they have given (exogenous) preferences. The impact of the State is to constrain these choices, and hence the less government interference, the better. Unfortunately, a society without government tends towards anarchy because property rights and personal liberty cannot be guaranteed. Ownership requires protection from attempts to encroach upon it. A framework of law and order is required to prevent some individuals from interfering with others' property. Taxation does interfere with property, and hence it is justified only to the extent that it prevents greater loss of property from others. Defence is the external variant of the protection of property rights. Liberty and economic freedom are thus equated with the ability to enjoy property and to exercise consumer choice with the minimum of government interference. Law and order and defence spending enhance liberty; taxation (except where it aids law and order and defence) reduces it.

The prevention of encroachment upon property rights should not, however, be interpreted narrowly. Individuals may unjustifiably exploit others in a variety of physical and non-physical ways. One such way is by monopoly. Monopoly power and exploitation can in theory arise in both the capital and labour markets, but it is the latter case which has, as we have seen, received most attention. The former is 'solved' by arguing that monopoly capital exploitation is only transitory, and indeed may be a spur to competition. This is a variant of the Austrian approach to economics, which is quite different from the conventional market failure neo-classical approach used in the labour market case.

Consider now how the major features of the Thatcher administration's view of the State conform to these principles. Control of the currency and protection of its value defend the value of people's savings. Privatization reintroduces specified property rights and spreads share ownership. Tackling labour monopoly through trade union reform reduces exploitation. The sale of council houses gives people property rights. The encouragement of the private provision of health insurance and education increases individual choice and responsibility rather than reliance on the State. The reduction of taxation reduces the State's infringement of individuals' right to enjoy their income. Pay increases for the army and police, as well as greater expenditure on resources for them, enhance the power to curtail physical interference with individuals' liberty.

But, as with the setting up of the pillars of the post-war period, theory and practice do not always meet, especially in the political sphere. For despite the apparent consistency and coherence of the theory behind the general policy approach, the programme has frequently resorted to *ad hoc* pragmatism. Furthermore, as with the 1945 Labour government, economic theory has not been sacrosanct. Rather, it has often been plagiarized to meet political necessity. The result is frequently a mishmash of ideas, influences, and values. But what Thatcherism has done is to reopen the debate about these fundamental principles of the organization of production, the distribution of income, and individual liberty. In returning to the principles of *laissez-faire*, the debate has once more been couched in terms of the market versus planning, and market versus government failure. In the next section, we look for other alternatives.

4. Weighing up the Arguments

The economic borders of the State are not matters that economists can decide upon without reference to value-judgements. To that extent, as Beckerman persuasively argues in this volume, there will never be unanimity on where the boundaries lie.

However, the economist can analyse the relative merits of alternative policies for the achievement of pre-set goals, and can further analyse the foundations of economic policies by pointing out to which goals these ultimately relate. Thus in weighing up the relative merits of the arguments about the economic borders of the State, we must conduct the analysis at a variety of levels. These include the goals of economic policy, and the instrumental policies designed to achieve them.

(a) *The Argument So Far*

Section 2 considered the arguments for and against market solutions to economic organization. It was there shown that the two major defences of the market—the neo-classical and the Austrian—are quite distinct. The traditional neo-classical case rested on perfect competition and Pareto optimality conditions. However, markets quite generally fail to meet the requirements of perfect competition. Furthermore, the fundamental Pareto welfare judgement rests on efficiency alone, without due attention to distribution and liberty. It is individualistically based upon utility, and hence rules out a number of other morally relevant sources of information in adjudicating between alternative economic options. The Austrian case for the market, as best represented by Hayek, ultimately rests on a libertarian value-judgement, combined with an instrumental analysis of competition based on information costs and uncertainty. Thus Section 2 demonstrated first, that the case for the market depends on an instrumental theory of how the market works, and second, a deeper set of fundamental principles based on value-judgements. It showed why the two instrumental theories typically employed are open to objection, and a number of reasons why the value-judgements of both approaches are questionable.

Section 3 related this theoretical debate to the practical policies which have defined and redefined the role of the State in the UK economy. The Attlee Government's expansion of the economic borders of the State was based on a view of market failure, on the co-ordination role of the State through planning, and on the redistributive functions and powers of the State. The Thatcher period has seen an emphasis on the merits of competition, on the informational problems associated with State planning, and on a macro-economic conception of currency maintenance. The reasons behind this new conservatism about the capabilities of the State rest on a different view of how competition works, and a different emphasis on the relative merits of the fundamental goals when the inevitable conflicts between them arise. The neo-liberal emphasis on the rights of the individual against State interference, the merits of private property as opposed to State ownership, and the emphasis on markets rather than planning, all derive ultimately from this framework.

The consequence of this is that it is futile to question the present economic policy framework solely at the instrumental level, without analysing the merits of the underlying value-judgements and hence of neo-liberalism. In this section of the paper, the objectives and instruments of economic organization will be reassessed. It is argued that an alternative vision of liberalism provides an integration of liberty with equality, and can form an alternative way of defining the economic borders of the State. For while many policies raise difficulties at the level of the objectives, there remains a series of instrumental questions concerning the design and assignment of policy about which much can be said and considerable progress made. Let us start then by reconsidering the instrumental efficiency of the market system.

(b) Reassessing the Efficiency of Markets

That markets fail to meet the stringent optimality conditions of perfect competition is both obvious and crucial. For it follows that there will always be a prima-facie case for government intervention for efficiency reasons. Such a condition is not, however, sufficient, and the case for intervention at the micro-economic level must always be balanced against its costs. Just as markets are rarely, if ever, perfect resource allocators, so too governments are rarely, if ever, perfect planners. The argument must inevitably be a pragmatic one—is 'market failure' more serious than 'government failure' in the provision of particular goods and services? Despite the Hayekian attempt to show that government failure must always exceed market failure, there can be no general rule concerning the preference for or against market or government solutions so long as the neo-classical theory is the instrumental basis of the argument.

Market failure arises in a number of different ways—in public goods, externalities, and monopolies most noticeably. Where such cases do arise, there are a number of alternative policies available. Broadly, these can be classified into those which seek to *replace* the market by State provision and planning, and those which aim to make markets work better. In the former case, the government takes direct responsibility; in the latter, it changes the rules of the game, by regulation and taxation most noticeably, and perhaps acts as referee. Thus governments have a variety of policies available, ranging from nationalization to the use of quasi-government bodies, such as the Monopolies Commission, the Office of Fair Trading, the Office of Telecommunication (OFTEL), and the Office of Gas Supply (OFGAS).

Government failure also has many facets. At its most direct it involves corruption, bribery, and deliberate misallocation of resources. Though some on the 'new right' claim that this is likely to be endemic, it is not usually central to the critique of government. Rather, the critics point to the organizational behaviour of bureaucracies, to the lack of market discipline and accountability, and to problems of information management. The public service is open to persuasion and manipulation by interest groups which may 'capture' the administrators. These problems of control influence the extent to which intervention is justified at all, and the structure and form that intervention takes.

What a number of case-studies have shown is that the question of the extent to which competition can be enhanced (the degree to which markets can be made to work better) or government intervention increased (by replacing markets) to provide for greater efficiency is a complex one, and varies considerably between sectors of the economy.[28] The adoption of a general competition/privatization policy to deal with market and government failure relies ultimately on the assumption that this complexity of different cases is irrelevant, and hence denies this central result. To that extent, such blanket policies are straightforwardly wrong. Ultimately the methods by which competition and the market work are not simple; often they can be surprising and perverse. Thus simplistic advocacy of 'competi-

[28] A number of such case-studies are presented in Kay, Mayer, and Thompson (1986).

tion' will not itself solve market failure. Careful attention to entry conditions, the market power of dominant firms, the availability of information, and so on can critically alter the impact of competitive forces.

But although competition cannot necessarily solve market failure, its presence is nevertheless often generally advantageous. Indeed *competition*, rather than *ownership*, is more likely to enhance efficiency. The privatization programme (like nationalization) makes the fundamental error of confusing these two. Ownership transfers without competition have left the market failure in telecommunications probably as serious as prior to privatization, and arguably worse. The case of gas is also likely to follow this dismal path (see Hammond, Helm, and Thompson (1985)).

In both the nationalization and the privatization of major firms and industries in the UK, the political argument has tended to gloss over the importance of complexity. Economic arguments were employed either for or against the market without due regard to the caveats, assumptions, and restrictions which necessarily surround economic models. This process is nowhere better observed than in the economics of Thatcherism. In the early period (1979–83) the emphasis was on liberalization and competition. Thus simple market models (based on both neo-classical and Austrian economics) were marshalled to justify, for example, the abolition of statutory monopoly (the Oil and Gas (Enterprise) Act 1982, and the Energy Act 1983) and the appraisal of State monopoly by the Monopolies and Mergers Commission (the Competition Act 1980). As macroeconomic constraints began to bind, political factors influenced the shift towards ownership transfers, and economic arguments were marshalled to show how the capital markets enforce efficiency, as well as the virtues of wider share ownership. Most political positions can be bolstered by appeal to economic theory, but the disregard of the assumptions behind the models and the selection of theory according to the support for a prior political position are lamentable.

Not all the problems of applying economic theory to policy design arise from disregard of assumptions and caveats, however. Another source of difficulty arises because the objectives selected by politicians have over-determined policy. Especially since the Second World War, governments have assumed ever greater commitments—to generate full employment, alleviate poverty, increase growth, reduce inflation, and so on. If the government assumes a multiplicity of objectives which lead to conflicts and inconsistencies, a coherent interventionist policy cannot be devised, unless the trade-offs between the objectives are predetermined.

One of the major political failures of the post-war period has been the attempt by governments to achieve too much—to engage in a competition of promises for ever greater economic and social achievements. While the desires to attain efficiency in production and a fair distribution of income *and* to minimize interference by the State in individuals' lives are laudable, the conflicts between them and the failure on the part of governments to deliver are sadly inevitable.

Two examples will illustrate this. The first is the design of the tax system. As Kay (this volume) argues, taxation is required to raise revenue, to redistribute income, and to meet the requirements of social justice. Many of these functions it shares with the social security system with which it overlaps. But a tax system cannot be both simple and fair, if these objectives conflict. The laudable desire of virtually every post-war government to reform the tax (and indeed the social security) system has foundered on the problem of their political inability to relinquish cherished objectives. The second example is privatization policy. It has become (as we saw above in Section 3) embroiled in the conflict of economic objectives—competition, ownership, PSBR requirements, tax cuts, and wider share ownership. Multiple objectives thus cause inconsistency where they conflict. Inasmuch as recent policy has attempted to reduce the commitments made by the State, and to reduce people's expectations of what the State can provide, this problem has been somewhat alleviated. But while the reduction of commitment may reduce problems of consistency, it very much matters which objectives are dropped. And that brings us back to the question of values.

(c) *Reassessing the Value-judgements*

The market philosophers rest their case on its efficiency and ability to generate the maximum freedom. That freedom is ultimately the ability of individuals to exercise their choices freely without undue interference. But the type of society that individuals typically might choose to live in may not be one in which distributive issues are neglected. Indeed, the growth of the role of the State has been in part a response to a greater demand for social justice and hence the alleviation of poverty and the reduction of inequalities.

The value-judgements which provide the rationale for the State include a positive as well as a negative concept of freedom (using Isaiah Berlin's (1958) classic distinction) which has far greater interventionist implications. Rather than focus on individuals as abstracted out of society, to be protected from encroachment and limitation on their actions, positive freedom looks towards enhancing the capacity to enjoy a reasonable standard of living (see Dasgupta in this volume and Sen (1984)).

If the focus moves towards positive freedom then the question arises as to which goods and services best contribute to giving individuals the capacity to enjoy that minimum standard. Certain basic social goods—such as health care, education, nourishment, and employment—would typically attain widespread inclusion. Thus, to attain a certain level of positive freedom, the State would need to provide these goods universally.

Perhaps not surprisingly, this provision turns out to be quite close to what the Welfare State set out to provide. However, as we saw above, in three crucial respects this deviated from the Beveridge system. These goods were not provided as 'social insurance' against accidents; they were provided in monetary compensation as well as in kind; and they were not absolutely defined. The definition of basic social goods and the levels required to maintain a minimum standard of living may vary considerably between societies and within societies over time. It is a matter of relativities, and hence includes redistribution as well as the relief of poverty.

This argument is not, however, necessarily paternalistic, though it could be consistent with such a position. The choice of the basic primary social goods can be made through the political process, rather than via State selection. Nevertheless, in reality paternalism is regularly employed, given the practical difficulties of using the political system to ascertain detailed information about preferences and the theoretical problems referred to above in constructing a social welfare function.

The consensus years of the post-war period were largely founded upon a basic agreement about the fundamental value-judgements. Once the Welfare State was established and key industries nationalized, the major political parties concentrated on competition at the instrumental level. Each party sought to present itself to the electorate as better managers of the economy. True, there were differences of emphasis, between equality and liberty for example. But these were largely cosmetic in the battle for the centre ground of politics.

This broad agreement about the goals of policy lasted as long as economic growth continued. But with creeping inflation in the 1960s, devaluation in 1967, the drift up in unemployment, and the oil shocks of the 1970s, it broke apart. Thatcherism in the 1980s has been based upon a return to fundamentals. The goals of policy were questioned, and the State retreated from intervention and paternalism. The debate about the ends of economic organization was reopened. All this was to the good. The consensus over goals was in fact one which could only survive while there was enough growth to meet expectations—to provide for increased prosperity and redistribution, to finance the losses of the nationalized industries, and to pay for the Welfare State. But what occurred was not symmetrical amongst either political parties or academics. The right re-defined its ideology and its political machinery, and shifted away from the instrumental to the domain of values. The left, on the other hand, continued to emphasize its managerial skills at running the economy. While freedom of choice and the retraction of the State from interference in the lives of individuals became the justification of policy for parties of the right, the left continued to 'cost' its economic proposals carefully and to debate exactly how fast unemployment could be reduced.

That may now be coming to an end, at least at the intellectual level. We have seen that the concept of liberty which underlies the philosophy of the 'new right' is a negative one, which stands in opposition to that of equality. The new liberalism which underlies the positive approach to freedom—the capabilities and capacities of individuals required to be able to enjoy a reasonable standard of living—can be set against the negative approach. That in itself is not new, though neither are the central arguments of the 'new right'. Modern welfare economists have, however, added much in redefining the scope and limits of this position.

The more difficult step, which would be innovative, is to translate the concept of positive freedom into a practical and coherent set of policies. That attempt involves not so much a further round of debate on the merits of interventionism, but rather the attempt to answer the question of what the State should provide as the minimum conditions for guaranteeing individuals the capacity to enjoy a reasonable standard of living. The answer to that question, on this approach, lies in an identification of the basic goods and services which individuals need. In that sense it requires a return to Beveridge. But it is not necessarily consistent with the principle of social insurance. In a sense, the current debates on health and education reflect these arguments. The motives for State provision of these basic goods relate less to market failure and efficiency, and more to social justice. Though the argument does at times get bogged down in discussions of whether this provision should be by the private or public sector, by and large it is about the level of provision and the access to it.

5. Conclusion

Economic theory does not furnish an answer to the question as to where the economic borders of the State ought to lie. In part, this is because economic theory is an imperfect corpus of knowledge. But the major reason is that there is no 'right' answer to the question. It all depends on value-judgements.

Nevertheless, there are a number of aspects of the question on which economics can inform, which refer to the instrumental efficiency of markets and the consistency between market-based solutions and underlying fundamental principles. It is worth restating them here. First, economic theory does not provide any evidence to support a general preference *either* for markets *or* for planning. Markets always fail in some degree and so do governments. The relevant question to ask is not whether they fail, but where, when, and by how much they fail. Similarly, given a particular potential intervention by government, the questions should be how much information do administrators and Civil Servants have, how likely are they to be 'captured' by vested interests, and how good are the instruments of intervention available? Pointing out the complexity of market and government failure does not lend itself easily to simple political platforms, but it does underline the desirability of a pragmatic approach to defining the economic borders of the State.

These efficiency reasons for intervention arise not only in micro-economic examples, but also at the macro-economic level. Economies do not seem to adjust 'naturally' to equilibrium, and the persistence of unemployment throughout the industrialized world well illustrates this. A major economic role of government is, therefore, in co-ordinating the actions of individuals to achieve greater efficiency. Governments can bring parties together and encourage desirable outcomes in ways in which individuals cannot.

Pragmatism in State intervention in industry and a macro-economic role for the State in co-ordinating individual behaviour were two central pillars of the post-war consensus. The third was the commitment by government to guarantee a minimum standard of living for the poor via the Welfare State. The system created in the 1940s set the task of government as the provision of basic social primary goods—such as health care and education—to provide for that minimum. It deviated from Beveridge's concept of social insurance in so far as it rapidly took on a more relativistic view of poverty and hence involved (with the tax system) a redistributional aspect. Economic theory suggests that poverty has very few of the relevant characteristics of an insurance problem and hence social insurance is not the appropriate way to achieve social justice.

Before turning to social justice, however, it is worth restating the conclusions reached on the relationship between the theory of the market and certain value-judgements to which its defenders have appealed. Economic theory clearly suggests that the requirements of economic efficiency, as represented by Pareto optimality, and those of liberty can be inconsistent. It is, therefore, not true, contrary to conventional belief, that the market necessarily always maximizes liberty. The light that economic theory does, if properly employed, throw on the question of the economic borders of the State is thus often negatively directed. It shows what cannot be claimed. It shows that general rules favouring the market or State intervention are inferior to pragmatic approaches, and it shows that liberal values and market-based economic organization may be inconsistent.

Political arguments about economic policy tend to start with ideology and progress to a search for an economic rationale. Economic theory does, however, have a greater role to play than as fodder for political argument. Ideologies do not simply emerge. Indeed, economic theory has provided many of the arguments that have influenced both the form ideologies have taken and their political acceptability. One of its most abiding influences has been to enhance the appeal of neo-liberalism by (mistakenly) emphasizing the compatibility of freedom and the market, thus neatly side-stepping the problem of distribution. The rewards which individuals get arise, in traditional neo-classical theory, not from any 'rights' or entitlements that they might have, but as returns to their ownership of factors of production—their own labour and any capital that they might have. On all the really interesting distributional questions, however, neo-classical theory is silent. This state of affairs has meant that one of the major pillars of the post-war consensus—the Welfare State—has been without an economic rationale. Indeed, worse than that, it often seemed to be inconsistent with received theory. Providing goods rather than money, it is argued, undermines freedom of choice, and income-based supplements reduce work incentives. Thus the Welfare State weakens the very market forces which will maximize economic efficiency.

This critique of the Welfare State results from a confusion about means and ends. For the above arguments reduce the question of the design of the Welfare State to one of means, conveniently forgetting that the principles upon which it is based (distributive justice and positive freedom) conflict directly with those underlying the appeal to markets as conducive to the freedom of the individual. Neo-liberalism and distributive social justice are conflicting moral sets of principles. To reduce the question of the rationale of the Welfare State to the instrumental level begs the fundamental value-judgements. The appropriate policy must depend upon the value-judgements. The 'new' welfare economics, referred to above and which Dasgupta's article in this volume addresses, is based on alternative value-judgements. These are what the debate on the distributive role of the State is about, and to discuss policy solely in terms of economic efficiency and market failure is incorrect.

Recent government policy has reopened these debates by challenging the pillars of the post-war consensus. The policies which have been introduced—the MTFS, privatization, and labour market reform—represent an attempt to return to a *laissez-faire* economy, with the State retreating towards a night-watchman's role. The residual role of the State to which such a position leads is the protection of property, law and order, defence, and maintenance of the value of the currency. To the extent that this approach derives from old-fashioned defences of the market, the

Thatcherites provide a good example of Keynes's dictum. They are 'the slaves of some defunct economist'. The new welfare economics, on the other hand, points towards a positive set of criteria to provide a rationale for the Welfare State and intervention as mechanisms for the achievement, not of neo-liberal values, but rather of social justice.

2

Value-Judgements and Welfare

ALAN RYAN[*]

1. Welfare, Psychology, and Evaluation

Although economists and political theorists have much to say to each other, they do not always find it easy to communicate. The economist is likely to find the political theorist oddly unconcerned with questions of formalization and measurement; the political theorist is likely to find the economist lumping together considerations he is professionally committed to separating out. So here, economists will find my remarks about the concept of welfare quite unlike those they would find in a welfare economics text. My aim is to remind them how disparate the elements are that enter into ordinary non-technical assessments of 'welfare', before I embark on the main task of arguing for the primacy of non-welfare values in drawing the economic borders of the State. These include both negative and positive freedom, as understood in the liberal tradition from Mill down to Rawls and Nozick, as well as the non-liberal conception of freedom defended by Marx. I also argue for the importance of various distributive and justice-based values, egalitarianism, 'maximin' justice, and 'baseline' justice among them. This paper is barely a preface to a theory of the relative roles of market and State, but I hope I shall persuade my readers that the diversity of arguments for and against both State and market provision is interesting as well as daunting.

(a) A Simple Analogy

If economists have been tempted to distinguish between technical analysis—their professional concern—and 'value-judgements'—every-one's concern—this may be because of the intuitive appeal of a simple picture of the way moral evaluation relates to economic analysis, one which trades on the following analogy.[1] At a given state of technology, it is possible to build a motor-car engine (or any similar device) with a range

---

[*] Professor of Politics, Princeton University.
[1] Cf. the contrast Mill (1965, II, i, 1) draws between the laws of production and the laws of distribution, the former non-optional laws of nature, the latter wholly a matter of choice.

of different properties which we want engines to have. These properties are in competition with one another. Power competes with fuel consumption; fuel consumption competes with longevity; and so on. What combinations of these desiderata may be had is a fact about the world fixed by the laws of nature and the existing technology. The imperative to employ the best available technology is the desire to minimize the sacrifice of any one desideratum in securing an increase in any other.

We could complicate the question by making the analogy more concrete and asking whether efficiency implies the use of the best technology, or the use of the most cost-effective technology, but this is irrelevant to our purposes. What we need from the analogy are three items: first, the existence of various feasible combinations of engine desiderata; second, a conception of 'efficiency' which is tightly tied to the thought that the technology embodied in an engine is 'efficient' when there are no costless improvements to its performance to be had; and third, the thought that the customer for the engine simply picks an engine with one or other of the available combinations of characteristics. The consumer's choice simply expresses the consumer's evaluation of the preferred engine; it cannot be 'deduced' from any number of facts about the engine. It is a value *given to* the preferred outcome by the consumer.

Economists will have seen what is coming. The economy is much like an engine; it is 'efficient' in the familiar Paretian sense when nobody's welfare can be increased without someone else's being diminished. But there are innumerable Pareto-efficient situations which strike observers as intolerable, and others which attract different observers for a host of reasons unconnected with their efficiency. The 'value-judgement' supervenes when we decide for or against any particular economic outcome.[2] The textbook illustration does well enough. An economy in which all resources belong to one person and everyone else is starving to death is Pareto-efficient, since there is no way in which anyone's welfare can increase without someone else's diminishing. It is also repulsive. We may appeal to Bentham against Pareto, and hold that a transfer from the holder of all the resources to the others would increase *total* welfare and so be justified on utilitarian grounds.[3] Adam Smith's (1976) 'impartial spectator' might ignore 'total welfare' but find his sympathy with the worse-off so intense that he could not help thinking the situation unjust. Almost any modern theory of distributive justice would condemn such an unequal distribution.[4] The

[2] Beckerman's essay (this volume) is engaging in itself, and engages one's sympathies on Pareto's behalf, too; none the less, it treats the 'value-judgement' in much the way I describe here.

[3] See Harrison (1983, pp. 246-9) on Bentham's belief in diminishing marginal utility.

[4] Whether Nozick's 'entitlement' theory is an exception is hard to decide; it seems in intention not to be a theory of distributive justice at all. See Nozick (1974, ch. 7).

point of the textbook illustration is always the same: whatever the basis of the objection, it cannot be derived *from* the economic facts but must be imported *to* them.

I want to proceed cautiously by first of all distinguishing a concept of 'moral efficiency' from Pareto efficiency, in order to show that there is at any rate one way in which my simple analogy is illuminating and the orthodox account persuasive enough. I shall then suggest that both my notion of moral efficiency and the orthodox conception of Pareto efficiency are partially subverted by problems in the logic of explanation which recur throughout the social sciences. In arguing this, I say a little about the efficiency and rationality as such, but only to glance at some outrageously difficult issues. Thereafter, I move on to showing that the concept of welfare is porous, but not so completely porous that it will absorb all the moral aspirations we may bring to bear. That is to say, we should distinguish between welfare-orientated and rights-, freedom-, and justice-orientated arguments, not collapsing the latter into the former. If the fact that it will enhance his welfare is a good argument for giving some-thing to a person, it is a different argument from claiming that it will enlarge his liberty, that he has a right to it, or that it would be unjust to withhold it.

My simple analogy yields a conception of the 'morally efficient economy' like this. An economy may be assessed in terms of its perfor-mance along several morally interesting dimensions. Does everyone receive resources sufficient to keep up a 'baseline' standard of living? Are workers free to change employers when they wish? Are raw materials and human capital squandered? It may be that freedom to change employers conflicts with non-squandering, or with the maintenance of baseline welfare. An economy will be 'morally efficient' if there are no 'cost-free' improvements in performance along one or another value line to be had. If there are several alternative outcomes which are in that sense efficient, the preference for *this* balance rather than *that* is an ultimate expression of value (Barry (1965, pp. 3–8)). This does not imply that all evaluation is merely a matter of announcing personal allegiances: 'I approve of freedom' or 'I approve of efficiency'. It is only to say that there may well be some point at which we must say, 'given the cost of efficiency in terms of freedom and so on, I would rather that this world existed than that its competitors did'. If there are such ultimate expressions of moral preference, they fit my simple model very well.

(b) *Problems with the Simple Analogy*

Having said that, I must subvert it. Neither moral efficiency nor Pareto efficiency are the determinate properties that I have thus far assumed. The concept of efficiency I have been employing has an undoubted heuristic value, but 'the economy' is not a real-world object with determinate properties governed by natural laws, and we cannot transfer the concept of efficiency applicable to a car engine, with its basis in our knowledge of chemistry and physics, to a context where we are talking of a system whose boundaries are fluid, and whose workings are only weakly explained by the 'laws' governing human behaviour. To claim that an economy is 'efficient', whether in my sense or the more familiar sense, relies on counter-factual claims about what choices economic actors would make in other circumstances than those that actually obtain. Our knowledge of physics and chemistry allows us to infer what *would* happen to engines constructed otherwise than they actually are; our knowledge of what choices economic actors would make is not so grounded (Davidson (1980, pp. 229–39)). Take any set of economic agents you like; without impugning their honesty or psychological make-up, or our own capacity to understand them, we may doubt whether *they* know how they would choose in anything but very similar conditions, and therefore doubt whether *we* can tell either. We are often mistaken about how we shall behave under new conditions; if we cannot predict our own reactions, how can we be sure of the reactions of others?

I do not mean that we can never be sure. Psychological research suggests that individuals manifest preferences that represent well-formed indifference curves only after they are told rather a lot about consistency and completeness, that is, when they are *trying* to behave like economically rational actors. We can *make* ourselves more like the actors assumed by orthodox economic theory; some situations reward such behaviour and penalize the reverse, and it is not surprising that orthodox economic theory explains them.[5] But this is a far cry from the universality enjoyed by the laws of physics. Our 'preferences' are less like solid facts about the world than many economists have hoped, and models of rational choice are very like theorems in deontic logic whose applicability to behaviour remains debatable (Hahn and Hollis (1978, pp. 10–17)).

If preferences are less solid than one might think, because beliefs and desires are less solid than one might think, it is tempting to fall back on the thought that some, but not all, behaviour is 'economic', and some

[5] Marx therefore insisted that Adam Smith was wrong to suppose that a natural inclination to truck and barter lay at the heart of economic behaviour; persons in an appropriate environment are *forced* to truck and barter. Cf. Hobsbawm (1964).

interactions therefore constitutive of an economy. We accept that there is much idealization in the analysis of interacting actors, whose goals and resources are assumed rather than discovered, but remain confident that the mechanisms of production and distribution (of an economy operating as a 'simple system of natural liberty', at any rate) will be well mapped by such an idealization. We then reach the traditional view that interactions of this sort will be good at achieving 'economic' efficiency, but, depending on the tastes of those involved, or on the distribution of endowments, or on the provision or not of public goods, may well be morally unattractive. We have the terms of a peace treaty between economists and moralists. Like all peace treaties, this one tempts both moralists and economists to violate it. Lionel Robbins's (1933) famous attempt to explain the nature of economics in terms of rules for economizing—which this peace treaty recapitulates—raises awkward questions. How does economic behaviour relate to other forms of behaviour—when 'ought' we to behave non-economically, and on what basis do we decide? What can we say about the rationality of 'non-economic' activity? Enthusiasts for rational choice will want to extend the realm of the economic; but if it is not impossible to turn the proposition that all behaviour is optimizing into a necessary truth, it does not much advance our understanding, since it merely turns the question 'what are they doing?' into the question 'what are they optimizing?'.[6]

But a division of labour which hands overtly maximizing (or satisficing) behaviour over to economics and leaves the rest to the other social sciences is unsatisfactory; economics cannot throw out all activities in which people engage without consciously optimizing. If some forms of employment offer the chance of enjoyable social relationships, this makes a difference to the optimal mix of work and leisure, even if part of the point of the pleasurable social relationships is that they are not treated in the optimizing mode (Elster (1983)). Nor is the concept even of means–end rationality very well understood. Parfit (1984, pp. 12–13) and others (for example, Hodgson (1966)) have pointed out occasions when it is rational to be irrational: faced by a kidnapper, you would be better off if the kidnapper thought your behaviour only randomly connected to his threats, and if the nuclear deterrent is a rational way to keep the peace, its deterrent effect relies on our enemies supposing that once they have used their weapons, we shall *not* ask what good it will do to use ours.

---

[6] But see Becker (1976) for the opposite view.

(c) *The Complexity of 'Welfare'*

Thus far, I have been conducting a spoiling argument against the view that 'economic' judgements about efficiency and welfare maximization can be firmly established, and lined up to be added to or trumped by 'value-judgements'. Before arguing that the economic boundaries of the State must be determined by conceptions of freedom, individuality, and social vitality, which are only dubiously analysable in welfare or utilitarian terms, I must conclude this spoiling campaign by adding that the economist's conception of 'welfare' is not the plain man's or the politician's.[7] To begin with a banality, our judgements about other people's welfare generally 'second-guess' the wants and wishes of those people themselves. My daughter may very much want to fill herself up with candy-floss, Coke, and potato chips before she embarks on the most terrifying rides the fun-fair possesses. I am likely to insist that doing so would be bad for her. As her father, I have her welfare in mind even more than her wants, and although I might succumb to pleading or to tears and let her have what she wants, giving her what she wants does not advance her welfare. Welfare is a matter of 'good for' rather than 'wanted'.

Welfare connects with wants, but does not collapse into them; at best, 'good for' latches on to long-term wants as opposed to short-term ones, but a man may be heedless of his own well-being throughout his—no doubt short—existence. Looking after one's own welfare contrasts with pursuing one's ideals, but not absolutely. St Francis was heedless of his welfare in embracing lepers, yet we do not always contrast ideals and welfare; I do not mean that the cynic maintains that saints expect a reward in heaven, rather that we might believe that pursuing ideals is good for us *per se*. We are 'better off' because we are 'better people'. 'Merit goods' such as education straddle ideals and welfare. Education is good because it enables its beneficiaries to satisfy their long-run wants, which is an argument from welfare. Or it is 'good to have' regardless, which is an argument from ideals. But if 'being better' is also doing better, an appeal to ideals is an appeal to welfare.

Judgements of welfare are thus judgements of how well someone is doing. However, it is not surprising that in political and economic argument, 'welfare' is largely identified with physical and psychological health—an employer heedless of his employees' welfare is heedless of the risks to their health or sanity they run by working for him, rather than simply mean about what he pays them, for reasons we shall see below. One

---

[7] What follows is heavily indebted to Beckerman and to Dasgupta (both this volume); my discussion goes in such a different direction that I do not quote them directly; but I write with them constantly at the back of my mind.

way in which judgements about welfare are very like factual judgements and are far from ultimate moral judgements is that we can agree that someone is heedless of his own welfare or that of others without having to conclude that he is behaving badly. It may not be his job to look after their welfare: the currency dealer is rightly uninterested in the welfare of his competitors, and if he is not, he had better get out of the game. Conversely, one only has to be concerned with particular aspects of their well-being to get credit for looking after the welfare of those under one's charge. The officer who leads his company into battle does what is intrinsically inimical to the health of his troops; none the less, if he ensures his men are well fed, well rested, treated courteously by the NCOs, and so not driven mad by the war, he has their welfare at heart. He may get them all killed, but they will be healthy when they meet their fate. By the same token, employers are not expected to pay their workers over the odds, but they are expected not to injure them while they are at work.

Barry (1965, pp. 187 ff.) long ago pointed out the natural affinity embedded in the US Department of Health, Education and Welfare. The idiom which refers to those in receipt of income maintenance allowances, unemployment benefit, or whatever as 'on welfare' picks up the thought that considerations of what people *need* as opposed to what they happen to want are decisive in considering their welfare. This is why it was plausible to run ideals and welfare together; if pursuing ideals is an essential part of the good life, people need culture, and being cultured adds to your well-being.

These observations bring us to the policy crux. The gap between market outcomes and the observer's estimate of how well people are doing is likely to be filled by paternalistic intervention. I mean by paternalism any instance of doing good to people by compulsion, whether to make them better people or to make them better-off. Take unemployment pay: we may *explain* the low incomes of the unemployed workers by their previous failure to estimate the chances of unemployment and to insure against it, or by insurance companies failing to offer adequate insurance, or whatever; but the political judgement is likely to be that the State should interfere with the workings of the insurance market to compel workers and employers to pay into a fund to finance welfare benefits for the unemployed. Again, we may think that it is miscalculation which accounts for the difference between what industrialists contribute to education and the additional output, and therefore welfare, that more education would provide. The obvious way to fill the gap is by compulsory taxation and supplying education directly. Paternalism, however, has a bad reputation in a liberal society; 'curing market failure' sounds less offensive, which is doubtless why policies justifiable on either ground are usually justified on the latter.

For those who are unabashed by occasional paternalism—like those who follow Beckerman (this volume) in being willing to see taxes used to buy Covent Garden performances on the grounds that society just ought to have such things—there is no problem. They do not flinch from justifying their approval of subsidies to the arts on pure 'ideal-regarding' grounds.[8] Whether they regard these activities as part of the activities of the *Welfare* State depends on how far they accept the view that people may 'do better' by 'being better'. They need not accept it. It is not *prima-facie* absurd to claim that governments ought to maintain a certain kind of culture more or less regardless of what wants it satisfies, and that the existence of Mozart operas is a good worth preserving for its own sake.[9] The way of life of the Falkland Islanders is an expensively preserved good of just this sort; so are elements of any distinctive natural culture.

(d) *Beyond Welfare*

Those who are abashed by paternalism have many options. Some eliminate the Welfare State entirely; some redraw its boundaries; some have interesting consequences for our usual view of what makes a policy more or less 'left-wing'. Few yield simple answers to questions about where to draw the economic borders of the State. I treat five in no particular order, and hope I display no particular bias in my treatment of them, at least until I come to draw some conclusions. The first three options have names associated with them—Rawls, Nozick, and Mill; the last two have traditions of policy implementation behind them, but I am not sure that any thinker has made them so much his or her own that one can simply gesture at the ideas in the way one can with the first three. In order of discussion, they are: (1) the view that individuals have a right to a certain quantity of 'primary goods', so that the State may legitimately intervene in the market to whatever extent is necessary to ensure that the worst-endowed member of society is endowed with the largest possible bundle of primary goods; (2) the view that the government may *only* enforce individual property rights, these rights themselves not being at the discretion of government; one brand of Marxist hostility to capitalism is based on the denial that there are any such rights; (3) the view that property rights are the creature of government and claims on resources are to be decided by an enlarged utilitarianism of a heavily libertarian kind; Mill's defence of market relations on this basis finds its counterpart in

[8] For the distinction between 'want-regarding' and 'ideal-regarding' principles, see Barry (1965, pp. 38–43).

[9] I think that it is, in the last resort, an unsustainable position; but see Moore (1903) for a famous argument in the opposite sense.

Marx's claim that freedom demands the abolition of the market; (4) the view that 'common goods' are particularly morally valuable and will generally have to be supplied by governments rather than the market; (5) the view that considerations of 'justice' are basic, cannot be exhausted by property rights, and are best met by securing a welfare 'baseline'.[10]

2. Justice, Rights, and Liberty

(a) *Arguments from Primary Goods*

Rawls's *Theory of Justice* has introduced innumerable readers to the concept of 'primary goods'. These, which are sometimes abridged by Rawls to 'wealth and power', are those goods which one needs, no matter what goals one chooses to pursue. They are sometimes described as the pre-conditions of self-respect, the thought being that nobody can have much self-respect in the absence of resources to pursue whatever goals he or she may turn out to have. The 'maximin' theory of justice with which Rawls's name is associated is the doctrine that justice demands that the least advantaged person's 'bundle' of primary goods should be as large as possible, that is, that we must *maxi*mize the *mini*mum holding of primary goods. There is no suggestion that the least favoured person's *welfare* should be maximized. The reason is partly that it is much easier to compare different-sized bundles of primary goods than to compare different degrees of welfare. There are also problems of so-called 'utility monsters', individuals who can consume any quantity of goods while becoming no happier and would therefore sabotage any policy couched in terms of making the least happy as happy as possible. These are merely technical issues, though; the more important reason buried in Rawls's account, and overlooked by critics obsessed with his attempt to resurrect the tradition of the social contract, is that it cannot be the task of the State to make us happy, but at best to give us a fair chance at the pursuit of happiness.[11]

What we have a right to is what traditional theories of natural right rather misleadingly said we had a right to—life, liberty, and the pursuit of happiness. The State has no business second-guessing our view of our own happiness or welfare; nor do we have any right to rely on others to ensure that our lives go as well as possible. If we have the resources to which we

[10] Rawls (1971), Nozick (1974), Mill (1965, 1967), Titmuss (1970, 1976), Barry (1965).
[11] Rawls (1971, pp. 60–95). Cf. Kant's claim that making other people happy in accordance with our conception of their happiness is the worst of all tyrannies: Reiss (1970).

are entitled, the rest is our business. This pulls the State's role in economic life out of a Paretian framework. The existence of unmade bargains which render a situation sub-optimal gives government no general licence to interfere to induce people to make the bargains economic theory says they should, nor to act to replicate them. It is not 'up to' government to do so.

Rawls's argument is intended to defuse egalitarianism and its opposites simultaneously. Rawls assumes equality of civil rights and moral worth, but thinks that rational individuals not unduly susceptible to envy will wish to maximize their own bundle of resources without reference to the size of other people's bundles. The device of the 'veil of ignorance', in effect the device of asking what sort of economic principles we would assent to, if we did not know how we in particular would do under them, is a way of enforcing the conclusion that we would agree to 'maximin'. This is very much not a utilitarian argument for equality—the only plausible version of which must appeal to diminishing marginal utility—both because it is hostile to talking in terms of utility, as we have seen, and because Rawls wishes to avoid awkward interpersonal comparisons. The thought is that a rational person will desire greater equality if and only if it pays him; only the envious would want equality even if it cost them. What Rawlsian justice aims to achieve is a situation in which the worst-off people can truthfully be told that further attempts to transfer resources to them will result in the worst-off being worse off than they are now.

(b) Entitlements

How Rawls's 'maximin' standard of rights to primary goods is to be cashed in practice is somewhat mysterious, but I return to it shortly. Before doing so, I move to the other options. Nozick's *entitlement* theory of justice is avowedly an extension of, and criticism of, Rawls's. It is anti-paternalist, handles utility at arm's length, and is even more squarely in the natural rights tradition. Where Rawls argues that we have no natural 'ownership' rights in ourselves, our abilities, or such external things as we can lay hold of, and derives such rights from the theory of justice, Nozick falls back on a view he ascribes to Locke, but which is even more reminiscent of Grotius (Tuck (1979)). Each of us is born the owner of himself or herself, ownership being understood as an unimpeded freehold. Nobody has claims on us which we do not give them; we and they may not invade one another, and that is all. Governments may not tell us how to live—Nozick (1974, pp. 155–7) explicitly defends sexual liberty and the right to take any kind of drugs we like; conversely, the fact of our need gives us no rights. I may die without the drug you have just invented; all the same, it is your drug, not mine, and I may have it only on terms set by you.

There is no quantity of primary goods to which I have a right; the only right I have is to use my holdings as I like, so long as I do not limit other people's freedom to use their holdings. If I have drawn a bad card in the natural lottery—nobody needs my abilities, nobody likes my looks—I shall do badly; but this is no injustice and grounds no claims. I am not entitled, as I am in Rawls's theory, to have the results of the natural lottery corrected.

It is plain this view leaves no great scope for government compulsion, let alone redistribution. It is less clear what else follows, since there is some awkwardness in getting from ownership of *ourselves* to ownership of such external things as houses, fields, patent rights, and General Motors. However, even if there is scope for getting a more expansive State out of Nozick's theory than he himself supposes, it is plain that it has to be done by an appeal either to preserving the freedom of the hard-done-by or by rectifying some former injustice. It cannot be done by asserting any general duty on the part of the State to maximize welfare generally, or to promote the welfare of those whose welfare nature has failed to secure.

The difference between Rawls and Nozick lies in the fact that Nozick is much more whole-hearted in appealing to the existence of natural rights prior to society or government. Rawls conceives of us entering the world rightsless and asks what rights a social contract drawn up behind the veil of ignorance would give us; Nozick (1974, pp. 160–2) maintains that this is sure to favour a teleological or instrumental conception of rights, and that what any of us was entitled to would depend on how far our having it promoted the goal which legitimated rights in general. That, however, is no right at all; the essence of a right is just its invulnerability to considerations of how far the right promotes some other goal. My bicycle would not be 'mine' if it were mine only when my having it maximized the mobility of the least mobile person.

The attractiveness of this vision can be estimated by the vigour with which Marx (1976, vol. 1, ch. 26) attacked it. Marx saw that the thought that we may do what we like with our own appeals to most of us. The question of how 'our own' comes to be 'our own' is decisive; on the face of it we acquire a title from a previous owner, whose title must either be natural or stem from some yet previous owner. It therefore matters greatly how the process started. Marx's insistence that capitalism began in the forcible expropriation of small farmers is well judged because it impugns the pedigree of present titles. Nozick certainly agrees that the economic borders of the State may be redrawn to rectify past injustices. Marx (1976, p. 895), of course, differs from Nozick in holding that capitalism could not have existed *without* the injustices.

(c) *Positive Liberty, Liberal and Marxist*

The interest of Mill's thoughts on this topic lies in the fact that he was by training sceptical of any theory of 'natural', or, as he called them, 'abstract', rights, but tried to reconcile his utilitarian upbringing with his passion for justice, and his conviction that the greatest of human goods was liberty. As a senior official of the East India Company and the most distinguished economist of his day, he had a strong sense of the positive economic potential of government, a detailed understanding of the merits and drawbacks of bureaucratic management, and a passion for economic self-government. He was closer to Rawls and Nozick than to successors who only took up his reflections on market failure and public goods, but was infinitely far from Nozick in seeing a positive role for government in reshaping ownership for the sake of freedom, and bolder than Rawls in demanding more than Welfare-State-modified capitalism to realize liberty (Mill (1965, IV, vii)).

Mill stated his position in *Liberty*, *Principles of Political Economy*, *Chapters on Socialism*, *Representative Government*, and dozens of long essays from the quarterlies of the day. He insisted that the notion of utility inherited from his father and Bentham was too narrow; the only happiness worth pursuing was that of 'a man as a progressive being'. He appealed to a principle of growth borrowed from German romantic writers such as Schiller and von Humboldt to fill out Bentham's prosaic picture of human nature. Where did economic theory fit in? Mill thought rules of efficient production were uniformly applicable and had the invariant quality of physical law. How mankind should organize itself in order to produce efficiently was locally modifiable; how the results were to be distributed was wholly a matter of choice (Mill (1965, II, i, 1)). The principles he appealed to—besides a concern not to be excessively inefficient—were vitality, individuality, progressiveness, and liberty. In India, the East India Company had a near-monopoly of entrepreneurial energy and uncorrupt administrative capacity—(thought Mill); it was therefore proper that much of the economy should be in its hands or at any rate under its control, so long as the goal in principle and in fact was the speediest possible emancipation of the Indian population from this state of tutelage. In Britain, a like monopoly would be absurd (Ryan (1973)).

Where do individual rights appear in this scheme? Mill's argument was both negative and positive; political, intellectual, and religious liberty were sacrosanct. Self-defence alone can abridge them, and self-defence is to be construed narrowly. Positively, these freedoms would encourage individuality, self-reliance, and a capacity for innovation. Property rights, on the other hand, were a social privilege not a natural right. The State offered to assist its members in realizing their wishes; in so doing, it allowed owners of property to realize their wishes in ways which their less fortunate fellows could not. From this fact follows a view of social justice. The existence of property imposes duties of self-restraint on the less favoured, and governments have a continuous obligation to ensure that the existing system is a good bargain to them. Hume had remarked that the rich enjoy their property only because the poor do not rise up and dispossess them of it; we may tell them any story we like about the grounds of property rights, but unless they get a reasonable bargain from the institution's existence, they can hardly be expected to tolerate its continued existence. Mill, who thought that working people would become increasingly exacting in the questions they asked, thought they would be right to ask whether their recognition of the rights of the rich gave them as good a bargain as possible. The same view is implicit in *A Theory of Justice*.[12]

Mill did not advocate sudden and drastic remodelling of the entire system. Expectations having been aroused by existing property rights, governments must go carefully, not perpetrating injustices in the process of doing justice; none the less, the justification of property rights is libertarian—Millian libertarian rather than negative libertarian—and governments should not think that liberty cannot be further extended by remodelling the property rights currently recognized. Individual property and the market have increased our potential for choice and innovation; but it is not to be assumed that the system is perfect and cannot further increase that freedom. Mill's discussion of the scope and limits of property in Book II and of government action in Book V of his *Principles* appeals to these considerations; though it was written a decade before *Liberty*, it rests squarely on the same concern for 'man as a progressive being'.[13]

It is worth noticing that Marx's conception of freedom, though owing much to the same German tradition as Mill's, is entirely hostile to the thought that the market has any libertarian claims on us. For Marx, the role of private ownership and the market in decision-making was wholly negative. Mankind had placed itself under the sway of an 'alien, inhuman power' by allowing the market to decide what was produced and how. The market system enabled capital to tyrannize over the individuals who notionally ran the economy. *It* controlled us, rather than vice versa. This does not mean that the economic borders of the State should extend so far that they swallow up the market; the unified decision-making system

---

[12] Nozick (1974, pp. 195–6) remarks that the 'best-endowed' have the right not to be exploited by the 'worst-endowed', so that Rawls's appeal to the terms which the latter will accept for co-operation is misjudged; that misses the point made by Hume, Smith, Bentham, and Mill, which is that the worst-off will not accept a theory like Nozick's in the first place unless they are tolerably well off.

[13] Mill (1982), 'Introductory', p. 70.

introduced by 'free association' replaces both the market and the State (Marx (1973)).

(d) *The Common Good*

It is sometimes said, and was said by Mill's Idealist successors such as T. H. Green (1894), that neither welfare as usually understood nor liberty as understood by the defenders of *laissez-faire* or by Mill himself was the key to assessing the optimal balance of market- and government-supplied goods and services. What is needed is a conception of 'the common good'. The conception in question is not very closely allied to the economist's conception of *public* goods, but arguments from 'the common good' do rest on the thought that markets fail to deliver it.

The thought is that goods enjoyed in common are superior to those enjoyed only privately; but there is no suggestion that they can only be enjoyed in common. The Idealists, and successors such as Richard Titmuss, appeal to classical ideals of friendship and communality of interests against what they see as the divisiveness of the modern economy. Aristotle described friends as those who enjoyed goods in common, and approved of an economy in which private property was employed in production but where as much as possible was used in common. He, of course, had in mind the common tables of the Spartans; but it is easy to think of modern examples—the maintenance of public parks rather than private gardens, education in schools rather than by private tutors, the promotion of concerts rather than simply pumping music into each home over the radio or down a cable.

Another appeal is to the thought that what we *all* need and enjoy is superior to what we value differently; we all need at least a minimum of health, education, and a decent environment. The provision of this takes moral priority over the provision of anything else. The market can be left to give beer to the beer drinkers and champagne to the champagne drinkers, but not to give blood to those who need transfusions. Both sorts of appeal rely on the belief that there are morally valuable side-effects from communality of consumption; the Spartans thought they got extra loyalty and comradeship, Green (1894) and Titmuss (1970) thought they got extra altruism on the one side, and gratitude and a sense of belonging on the other.

(e) *Baseline Justice*

Anyone tempted by any of these arguments is likely at the same time to be conscious that they cannot be pressed to extremes. It is only a certain

amount of one's needs for, say, health, education, and a decent environment which really form part of one's common humanity. Beyond that,
there seems nothing to object to in private provision; the liberal value of
individual choice seems to take over very soon. Conversely, an all out
defence of individual choice in the manner of Nozick's *Anarchy, State and
Utopia* seems much too cavalier in its dismissal of such values. Hence, we
may be led to think in terms, not of maximizing some value or even some
set of values, but of providing a baseline above which individuals must
advance by their own efforts, but below which they ought not to fall. To
my mind, the thought that justice demands the provision of a welfare
'baseline' is in fact the most popular and in ethics the most plausible
foundation for the Welfare State.

One attraction of 'baseline' thinking is that it is susceptible to any
number of different justifications: utilitarian, if we think that sub-baseline
utility outweighs supra-baseline utility; contractual, if we think that any
social contract would have insured us against falling below such a baseline
but would not have gone as far as 'maximin'; quasi-aesthetic if we think
that a society is simply disgusting if derelicts are begging on Merrill
Lynch's doorstep; based on justice if we think that everyone comes into the
world with a claim on the means of survival. It is politically attractive
because it does not threaten to gobble up resources indefinitely, and
because it is easier to get a consensus on where the line should be drawn,
below which it is intolerable that anyone should fall, than about anything
more positive (Barry (1965, pp. 152 ff.)). I suggest below that a rational
view might be two-sided, ready to rest on a baseline conception of the
minimum duties of the Welfare State and to appeal to something richer
and more contentious for its ideals.

(f) *Conclusion*

With these five simple pieces of apparatus in hand, we can finally ask, how
far do they help us to decide on the economic borders of the State? I shall
argue for a combination of Millian liberty as social ideal and the 'baseline'
view as a conception of social justice capable of securing consensus. The
attractions of Rawls's views to many readers rest on their resemblance to
this combination.

Rawls's account of economic justice in terms of 'maximin' suffers,
however, from excessive vagueness. In particular, his desire to protect civil
liberties against sacrifice for the sake of economic growth conflicts with his
egalitarianism, and is in any event not well handled by the 'hypothetical
contract' device. If we are to end with the two distinct values of civil liberty
and social justice, we might as well begin with them (Hart (1975)). Anti-

interventionist readers are apt to forget Rawls's insistence that civil liberties and personal freedoms take priority over economic justice-as-maximin. Nozick's teasing suggestion that on Rawlsian grounds the worst looking man ought to get the best looking girl is a good joke at the expense of any thought that we should distribute *everything* according to maximin, but harmless against the theory as stated, which has entrenched personal freedoms against any such idea (Nozick (1974, pp. 236–8); Rawls (1971, pp. 60–2)).

But this defence renders Rawls vulnerable to the suspicion that the sanctity of existing liberties will forbid almost all redistributive policies and place Rawls in the ranks of the conservatives. Rawls is aware of this, but the result is that the initially clear distinction between freedom and economic values, or between freedom and the value of freedom, is so eroded by Rawls himself that it is hard to tell when we may and when we may not tinker with political and civil freedoms for the sake of increasing their value to the least favoured. The way forward is not to scour the text looking for a solution, but to go back to the motivation of the theory in liberal values.

This lies in two views; the first that nobody is to be used as a mere means to the ends of others, the second that the sanctity of the individual is detachable from the sanctity of property—property is sacred only in securing the free choice of life-style. If private property in consumption goods is thus inescapable, these considerations seem to Rawls to provide no foundation for private property in producer goods. He thinks a different consideration tells in favour of a regime which leaves much to the workings of the market. This is the empirical observation that market economies, assisted by pragmatic government intervention, have out-performed their rivals in productivity; to realize maximin justice, our best option is a pragmatically mixed economy in which the market secures efficiency, and the tax regime is designed to secure maximin justice. This leaves it wide open *how* maximin justice is established; as between job creation, income transfers, or the provision of non-marketable benefits in kind the theory is silent. It does not, and ought not to, follow Dasgupta (this volume) in associating a concern for positive liberty with provision in kind. There may be many occasions when money will provide the 'ability' to make choices which positive liberty looks to. It does follow Dasgupta and Sen (both this volume) in looking to 'enabling' conditions rather than direct operations upon utility.

Going outside Rawls's framework, but remaining firmly inside liberal theory, it is entirely plausible to defend private property in producer goods on libertarian grounds both positive and negative. There is a positive argument from entrepreneurship—the encouragement of imagination and innovation and variety—up to a point an argument from productivity, but more importantly an argument from liberty; negatively, the argument is that although planned economies *need* not be coercive or a threat to political and civil liberty, they are more likely to be so than their rivals. Variety-maximizing and coercion-minimizing considerations together provide a non-entitlement-based libertarian case for the widest possible use of the market. Anyone tempted by this argument is tempted by what I have called Millian liberty. The economic borders of the State are to be drawn instrumentally and pragmatically, but with an eye to the liberal verities.[14]

To talk of defending freedom pragmatically is to reject Nozick's theory of rights. Nozick claims that the economic space occupied by the State is a vanishing point. Since each person owns whatever he or she has come into the world with, or has acquired by lawful exchange, or has picked up without violating the rights of others, the State has no right to transfer any of his or her holdings against his or her will. Presumably public goods will be provided if and only if everyone votes to have them provided and to be taxed for their cost. Nozick's only gesture to the usual argument about the predictable sub-optimality of their supply is to suggest that in the world he envisages, there will be so much more scope for benevolence that we shall not miss the services governments now provide (Nozick (1974, pp. 297ff.)). Because Nozick's theory of rights represents all rights as property-like rights which constrain government or other intervention absolutely, the only way to show that we need not accept this self-abnegating view is to show that property rights are not what Nozick thinks. This is a long business.[15]

It is perhaps permissible to continue instead with the argument on which we have already embarked; if it carries conviction it will also carry us past this issue. Mill's account of the proper balance of individual rights and government activity in terms of progress towards liberty relies heavily on empirical arguments from history and sociology as well as economics. Where Rawls appeals to moral intuition to legitimate his approach to theorizing justice, Mill's starting-point was the nineteenth-century enthusiasm for self-government, an enthusiasm both admirable and dangerous. The danger was that self-government might turn into majority tyranny. The danger would be increased if people acquired the habit of expecting to be looked after by their rulers. But the danger was worth running for the possibility that genuine self-government would be achieved. This required industrial democracy as well as political democracy; it also required enormous self-restraint, for democracy would only work if the citizenry

---

[14] Mill's account comes in Mill (1965, Book V).
[15] I do a very little towards this in Ryan (1985). See Paul (1980) for much more.

had a clear view of when it was *not* entitled to interfere with the freedom of action of individuals (Mill (1982, ch. V)).

This vision yields a complex story about the economic borders of the State. Property rights may be defended, not as sacrosanct and natural, but as artificial and freedom-enhancing. A reason for thinking hard about property is the liberticide quality of bureaucratic government. Unlike Spencer, Mill did not think that bureaucracies are inevitably less efficient than privately owned undertakings. In some conditions they are, but not always. Even where they are more efficient, however, there is a cost to relying on government activity; it centralizes talent and enthusiasm where we ought to spread it as widely as possible. So, if education is a 'libertarian merit good' (as it must be), groups of parents or local communities should set up schools and not entrust it to central government. Always the argument is that institutions have one task above all others, which is to secure the greatest degree of individual initiative and imagination.

Mill, however, was enough of a traditional utilitarian to accept the familiar argument for government provision of public goods such as light-houses and the like; equally, he was ready to accept government-sponsored research, did not demur at the thought that natural monopolies might be run by government where it was impossible to force competition and if not run then certainly supervised. All this was and remained the stock-in-trade of subsequent welfare economics and was about as sophisticated an account as could be generated without more technical apparatus than Mill possessed.

This reminder of the utilitarian side of utilitarianism makes his account more persuasive than that offered by enthusiasts for common consumption. Their doctrine is most attractive when contrasted with something like Edward Bellamy's vision of a socialist but autistic Utopia. *Looking Backward* boasts that in Boston in the year 2000, exquisite music can be had in every house without the need to go to a concert.[16] But it is an appalling thought that cricket or football matches might be played without spectators, save those watching television, that all shopping might be done by telephone, and so on. All the same, the positive argument for common-ness of consumption is frequently pretty feeble. Titmuss's arguments for a non-market system for securing and supplying blood are most compelling when most instrumental; if we get cleaner blood, more blood, and cheaper blood by appealing to volunteers, the voluntary system is to be preferred. The side-effects of gratitude on the one side and happy altruism on the other are unpredictable and much less important (Barry (1965, pp. 202–5)).

[16] Bellamy (1888) was hugely popular on publication, but its most important effect was to provoke William Morris into writing *News from Nowhere* (1891).

The more general point about common goods, however, is that everything hangs on the sort of community you wish to preserve. The Spartans wanted to preserve martial spirit, so dined in messes. What do we wish to preserve? There is something to the thought that we want each citizen to feel society is devoted to a collective battle against ignorance, poverty, and illness, and that this is a distinctive argument for State provision of education, unemployment benefits, and medical care. The difficulty with doing very much with it is that we hardly know what causes what in this area. People profess devotion to the National Health Service, but would they feel less to a privately supplied system where the State picked up the bill and charged individuals only what they could afford? Do they feel devotion only so long as they remember what it was like in the days when they were not sure whether they could afford to look after themselves and their children? The communitarian who simply thinks that people ought to make more collective provision for their needs and less private provision comes as close as anyone to making a 'pure' value-judgement, but where collective provision is neither more efficient nor gratifies some existing moral value, its defence is exceedingly difficult. Certainly in the work of Titmuss it sometimes seems that the argument simply leaps from the premiss that we all face the same fate, to the conclusion that we ought collectively to provide for that fate. We ought to remember, however, that we are not writing about the Sparta of the sixth century where private property was undeveloped and most people thought of themselves as members of families first and individuals second. Too much emphasis on altruism may produce less of it rather than more.

This finally brings us to the doctrine which sets out to avoid just that fate. It can, of course, be argued that even 'baseline' provision may run amok. Where should we set the baseline? If we set it at some highish percentage of average income, we are likely to stretch the willingness of the better-off to contribute; if we set it too low, it will not be even a baseline. The standard inflationary horror of our time is the thought that we first set a baseline, then find everyone trying to use their market muscle to preserve their differentials, then find the worst-off trying to push up the baseline to catch up . . . This is where an eclectic drawing on the insights of Rawls and Mill may help. If we think of the baseline in terms of primary goods and think of them in libertarian terms, we may get a consensus on the thought that the baseline should be construed as access to the resources which best enable their possessors to lead an independent life. Here, Dasgupta's defence of provision in kind rather than by marketable vouchers makes perfect sense; for it is likely to be the physical or psychological properties of the goods—teaching people how to fill in forms, say—which are vital, not the financial resources they embody. Sometimes money may liberate, sometimes training, sometimes information; the only constant is the deter-mination to promote independence. Paradoxically, to think along these lines suggests ways in which the economic borders of the State might need to be widened in order that they may contract again.

3

How Large a Public Sector?

WILFRED BECKERMAN[*]

1. Introduction

There are two good reasons why the desirable size of the public sector is a subject of constant, acute controversy. First, public expenditures—which by no means capture the full impact of the State on the economy—are a large proportion of national product, and the corresponding tax burden affects almost everybody in the community. This applies to every advanced country. As Table 3.1 shows, the average share of public expenditures in gross domestic product (GDP) in the (then) ten member countries of the European Community, in 1984, was almost exactly 50 per cent. The British share, at 44.3 per cent, was lower than that of any of the other countries except Greece.[1]

The second reason for the intensity of the controversy concerning the size of the public sector is that although most people feel some degree of altruism, on the whole those who expect to gain from a large public sector—for example, from State benefits, or public provision of particular services that they want—tend to be in favour of it, and those who expect that, on balance, they will lose from it—for example, on account of their tax liability—will be against it. Naturally, both sides usually dress up their particular predilections in some pseudo-economic rationalizations or bogus philosophy. For example, those who expect to gain from a more equal income distribution will usually parade the moral indignation aroused in them by the existence of distributive injustice, and those who expect to lose by more equality will preach the virtues of self-reliance and the importance of incentives for the development of personal character and public progress.

[*] Fellow and Tutor in Economics, Balliol College, Oxford.
[1] There are innumerable limitations on this sort of international comparison. One is that relative prices differ between countries and there is evidence that the relative prices of goods and services bought by government in Britain are lower than in other countries, so that in volume terms the British public obtain more for their (public) money. (See, for example, Statistical Office of the European Community (1983, Table 14, rows relating to 'volume in PPS'). The same point is made by Levitt (1984, pp. 39–40).)

Table 3.1. Shares of public expenditure in national products of member countries of the European Community, 1984[a] (percentages of GDP)

Country	Goods and services	Transfer payments[b]	Total
Belgium	17.4	36.1	53.5
Denmark	26.1	31.9	58.0
France	16.4	32.2	48.6
Germany	20.1	24.3	44.4
Greece	19.0	18.5	37.5
Ireland	19.0	32.4	51.4[c]
Italy	19.4	32.1	51.5
Luxemburg	15.7	30.0	45.7
Netherlands	16.8	41.2	58.0
United Kingdom	21.9	22.4	44.3
Average, all 10 countries	19.2	30.1	49.3

[a] The figures relate to general government current expenditure. The figures in the last (total) column are for 1984 and those in the first column are for 1983, the second column of figures being obtained as the difference between the two. The slight error that this involves will not affect the conclusions or the comparisons.

[b] Including interest payments on the national debt.

[c] 1982.

Source: OECD (1986), Basic Statistics: International Comparisons (following p. 71).

This is not to say that there are not serious and disinterested reasons for differences of opinion concerning the desirable size of the public sector. At the most general level, the size of the public sector raises the issue of the conflict that may exist between economic efficiency and the liberalist desire to minimize restrictions on individual freedom, to which Helm refers on pp. 22ff. As is clearly pointed out by Peacock and Rowley (1979), the importance that liberals attach to individual freedom and the threat to that freedom which they see arising from concentrations of economic power explains why the liberalist philosophy has not been destroyed by the increasing demonstration, in the theoretical literature, of the many ways that free markets fail to ensure productive efficiency.

Of course, many commentators on the sociological and political aspects of the size of the public sector would challenge the liberalist conception of 'freedom' on the grounds that it is excessively legalistic. To some extent the freedom of the individual to express his personality and maximize his

standard of living may sometimes be enhanced by increased State intervention in the economy. This is not just a matter of productive efficiency
and the increase in freedom associated with a rise in economic welfare. For
writers like Myrdal (1960, especially ch. 6), for example, it is more a
matter of a sense of participation in society and its direction when certain
activities are regulated through democratic processes rather than by those
private individuals who happen to control certain resources in the
economy.

But even without taking account of these wider political and sociological aspects of the problem, it still remains true that there is no objective
scientific method of determining precisely the optimal size of the public
sector. Much of the public debate is between conflicting interest groups
disguising their motivations in rhetoric of one kind or another. And
economic analysis cannot always indicate which side in the debate is
talking most nonsense. Nevertheless, it can make a major contribution to
clearer thinking about the role of the public sector both in general and in
particular instances. More precisely, the function of the economist in the
debate is to:

(1) set out the logical structure of the argument;
(2) identify at what points the answer depends on specific facts;
(3) provide some guidance as to what the facts are, or, in some cases, why
     they may be well-nigh impossible to ascertain; and
(4) identify where the argument depends on value-judgements and, if
     possible, give some guidance as to the importance of the value-
     judgements in determining the answer to particular questions.

It is this last feature of the argument which makes it impossible to arrive
at totally objective, scientific answers to many of the questions raised in the
area of public economics. For the value-judgements that are involved—
which are chiefly those concerned with equality or with components of
human welfare that cannot always be accurately captured in market transactions—affect every corner of the argument. Yet, by definition, they are
not amenable to scientific verification and reasonable people may easily
differ about them. But this does not mean that no answers can be found.
Individuals make value-judgements all the time and societies are able to
reach decisions based on them. One of the contributions of economic
analysis is to bring them out into the open. But it is also to show that value-
judgements are not enough and that the case for or against the incorpora-
tion of any activity within the public sector also depends on hard economic
analysis and on certain facts that the economic analysis reveals as being
crucial.

In this article, therefore, an attempt will be made to set out the analytical issues and to identify the relative roles of factual information and value-judgements in relation to major classes of the public sector's activity. Of course, there are innumerable ways in which the public sector's activities can be classified, depending on the purpose in mind. For example, the classification adopted in a recent important international comparison of the role of the public sector (OECD (1985)) includes government regulation as one distinct type of public sector activity, and there is no doubt that failure to allow for this and for many other ways in which the government influences private economic activity could result in an underestimation of the total impact of the State on the economy.

Alternatively, limiting the scope of our interest to those public sector activities that are reflected in public expenditures, the classification could be one that corresponded as far as possible to the main classic functions that public expenditures are expected to fulfil. This is the classification used in the OECD study and the main figures are summarized—for those countries for which the OECD Secretariat has been able to obtain comparable data—in Table 3.2.

Of course, this classification is very rough. As will be explained below, items such as education or health, which are included under the heading

Table 3.2. The structure of general government expenditures in selected OECD countries, 1981 (percentages of GDP)

Country	Total	Public goods[a]	Merit goods[b]	Income maintenance[c]	Other[d]
Australia	33.9	6.8	11.7	7.4	8.0
Denmark	59.5	8.0	17.4	16.4	17.7
France	49.2	7.5	16.0	17.2	8.5
Germany	49.3	6.8	14.3	16.7	11.5
Italy	51.2	7.0	14.0	15.8	14.4
Japan	34.5	4.2	12.5	6.9	10.9
Netherlands	61.1	n/a	n/a	17.7	n/a
United Kingdom (1979)	43.2	7.7	13.6	9.1	12.8
United States (1978)	32.8	8.4	10.2	7.8	6.4

[a] Defence and general public services.

[b] Defined in the source as comprising education, health, housing, and community and social services—many of which, of course, have a strong income maintenance component.

[c] Pensions, sickness benefits, family allowance, and unemployment compensation. See Table 3.3 for breakdown.

[d] This item, obtained here as a residual, includes public debt interest as well as various economic services not included elsewhere.

Source: OECD (1985), Table 9, p. 52.

'merit goods' in this table, are really provided by the public sector in most countries for a variety of motives, some of which may be purely resource allocation motives and have none of the paternalistic air of merit goods. Nevertheless, the table does demonstrate in a rough-and-ready way the order of magnitude of the major classes of public expenditure. (It also shows, incidentally, that compared with the other countries, public expenditures in Britain, as a share in GDP, are not particularly high.)

The classification of public expenditures shown in Table 3.2 can be related closely to the main economic functions of the public sector in the following way. These main functions are conventionally regarded as comprising stabilization, allocation, and distribution.[2] Of these three functions, the stabilization function relates to the role of the government in reducing fluctuations in economic activity or, more particularly, attempting to run the economy at a high level of employment.[3] But this function does not really concern us here, since—leaving aside monetary policy—this is largely a matter of the difference between government revenues and expenditures, not their absolute size.[4]

This leaves us with two main functions of public expenditures, allocation and distribution. The allocative function—i.e. the attempt to improve the allocation of resources between different uses—can be divided, in turn, into two main kinds of expenditure, namely expenditure on what are known as public goods (defence and the like) and expenditure on merit goods—of which education and health are partial examples, although, as indicated above, they both have resource allocation functions. The distributive function of public expenditures is served largely by means of social security benefits. But again, this classification is very crude and the provision of many goods and services—notably in the health and education field—is also designed to promote distributional objectives. Nevertheless, whilst the expenditures cannot be neatly divided up to correspond to different functions quite as easily as the OECD study might suggest, the functions themselves can be classified—in theory—in a more exhaustive and mutually exclusive manner.

[2] As set out, for example, in the standard treatise by Musgrave and Musgrave (1976, ch. 1).

[3] I shall ignore here the question of aiming, instead, at the optimum trade-off between high employment and other objectives with which it may be thought to conflict.

[4] This does not mean that the budgetary balance, or the particular method by which any given balance has been achieved, has no impact on resource allocation or income distribution; it usually will have. Nor does it mean that the question of how far the State should attempt to pursue a macro-stabilization policy at all is not an important question. But although over the course of the last century the stabilization function of the government's budget has become as important as its more traditional functions, it does not directly relate to the issue of the size of the public sector.

2. The Allocative Function

(a) *The Basic Framework*

Most of the concrete situations that give rise to a prima-facie case for some public sector intervention in the interests of improved resource allocation can be treated as situations in which the free market would fail to ensure that resources were 'optimally' allocated in the economy. The conditions that generally have to be satisfied in the interests of optimal allocation of resources are usually referred to as the Pareto optimality conditions. No economist has been so misrepresented in the economics textbooks as Vilfredo Pareto. Keynesians complain that Keynes was badly misrepresented in the standard textbooks on macro-economics of the post-war years. But the positions attributed to Pareto would imply that the man was a complete idiot! For example, the usual textbook analysis of Paretian optimality is based on individuals' preference functions—i.e. functions expressing the 'utility' that individuals derive from the consumption of alternative combinations of goods and services. It is then often disparagingly remarked that, in building an analytical edifice on this basis, Pareto had failed to take account of the fact that the amount of utility an individual obtains from a given bundle of goods might not be independent of other people's consumption levels and patterns. Furthermore, it is usually alleged that his analysis was severely limited by his failure to allow for distributional considerations.

Of course, nothing could be further from the truth. In fact, Pareto attached so much importance to both the mutual interdependence of people's satisfactions and the influence on them of distributional considerations that he distinguished sharply between two quite distinct concepts. One, which is referred to in the textbooks as 'utility', is actually what Pareto referred to as *ophelimité*, and which, indeed, in his treatment, was a narrow and strictly economic concept and which related to the satisfactions that consumers obtained from their own consumption of goods and services.

Pareto's—as distinct from the textbooks'—concept of utility was totally different.[5] It was not restricted to the satisfaction that a consumer would obtain from his own consumption and it included all the sources of satisfactions that an individual could obtain, including those aroused by the consumption and relative income levels of others. This meant that an

[5] It is true, however, that the contrast between utility and *ophelimité* appears to be greater in Pareto's *Traité de Sociologie Générale*, which was published in 1917, than in his *Cours d'Economie Politique*, which will be more familiar to economists and which was published twenty years earlier.

individual's utility (in Pareto's terminology) covered also the satisfaction that an individual obtained from different forms of social organization, income distribution, or provision for certain public goods or services even if they did not directly contribute to the purely self-concerning *ophelimité* of the individual.[6] In turn this meant that an individual's preferences over the wider domain covered by Pareto's concept of utility were not necessarily expressed only through market transactions of a conventional kind and could also be expressed in voting procedures or other forms of social decision-making.

One particular consequence of Pareto's view of the way that individuals' utility-preference patterns were formed was that—unlike *ophelimité*—they could not be taken as *given*; they could be influenced by the social context in which individuals found themselves. Of course, it may well be that the formation of people's preferences can be analysed in economic terms, as well as in psychological or genetic terms. But although most economic analysis necessarily takes such preferences and their background determinants as given, the fact that they are influenced by the social and economic environment limits how far one can analyse resource allocation problems purely in terms of the classic Robbins (1933) framework of the allocation of scarce means amongst competing ends, since the independence of the means and the ends is no longer clear-cut.

Nevertheless, following the conventional representation of Pareto, certain conditions relating to the optimal allocation of resources can be identified. In particular, it is possible to show that if certain conditions are satisfied (notably that prices equal marginal social costs of production), the economy will operate in such a way that it would be impossible to make any one person better off without making somebody worse off. Furthermore, it can also be shown that if one of these conditions is violated, it must be possible, by changing resource allocation in such a way as to eliminate the violation in question, to make somebody better off without making anybody worse off.

One then merely has to make what might appear, on the face of it, an irresistible value-judgement to the effect that any move that makes somebody better off without making anybody else worse off—commonly known as a 'Pareto-improving' move—*must* be desirable, to arrive at the conclusion that all possibilities for making such moves should be exploited. A Pareto-optimal situation is commonly defined as one in which there are no further possibilities left for making Pareto-improving moves. In such a situation, any move that makes one person better off will make somebody else worse off and, given the impossibility—in some scientific sense—of making interpersonal comparisons of utility, it is not possible to

[6] Pareto (1917, p. 1334).

reach objective scientific conclusions as to whether such moves add to total utility or not.

The various assumptions underlying this construction and the technical conditions that need to be satisfied to ensure that an economy operates at a Pareto-optimal situation are numerous and highly unlikely to be satisfied in practice.[7] But for present purposes what matters is how a free market economy would automatically lead to a Pareto-optimal allocation of resources. More particularly, how far can one identify certain classes of economic activity in which there is a strong case for believing that a free market could not provide optimal levels of prices and output, and that public sector supply is more likely to do so? In other words, the optimal size of the public sector is not something that can be decided in the aggregate. At best it would have to emerge as the result of an assessment case by case, industry by industry, activity by activity. In each individual case, it is necessary to replace the rhetoric of 'commanding heights' or 'market discipline' by a precise statement of how the particular features of the case in question do, or do not, imply that a free market would be unable to satisfy the conditions required for Pareto optimality and that public sector operation is the best alternative mode of operation.

Economic analysis has provided us with a classification of types of economic activity that constitute—in the light of this approach—prima-facie cases for being carried out by the public sector.[8] In what follows, therefore, specific types of situation that appear to call for public sector activity will be discussed in relation to the particular assumptions and conditions most important for the type in question and, unless otherwise specified, it will be assumed that other assumptions and conditions are being satisfied or are not important to the point being made.

However, one general assumption of overriding importance needs to be mentioned at the outset. This concerns the artificial separation of resource allocation criteria from income distribution considerations. It is well known that, at best, the Pareto rules only indicate what is an optimal allocation of resources *for a given income distribution* and that any other income distribution would generally imply a different optimal allocation.

[7] Pioneering comprehensive and critical analyses of the innumerable severe limitations on much traditional welfare economics were Little (1950) and Graaff (1957).

[8] Pareto had little confidence in the notion that progress could be made in identifying 'optimal' situations by means of simplifying assumptions that increasingly separated economic theory from the other social sciences. He wrote, 'Until the science [of economics] has made a lot more progress, it is less important to spend one's time on economic theory than on integrating the results of economics with those of the other social sciences. But this is something that does not appeal to many people because it requires a long and tiring study, involving a knowledge of a lot of facts, whereas, by contrast, anybody who has a scrap of imagination, some paper and a pen, can write a dissertation on economic theory' (Pareto (1917, pp. 1287–8, present writer's translation)).

For different income distributions will imply different weights, in the aggregate, for the varying preference patterns of the individuals in society. In other words, there are an infinite number of Pareto-optimal positions. Strictly speaking, therefore, it is illegitimate to assert that any one pattern of resource allocation is optimal without being prepared either to allow explicitly for distributional considerations or to reject explicitly their relevance.[9]

But one can be too perfectionist in this area (as in many others), and in practice numerous instances can be found where the micro-economic analysis of a resource allocation problem is unlikely to be affected significantly by almost any conceivable variation in assumptions of a distributional character. One might be able to imagine an income distribution and a set of value-judgements according to which the optimal way of disposing of garbage in Oxford would be not to dump it into disused quarries, or wherever, but to dump it instead in the front quadrangle of All Souls College, but the assumptions in question would no doubt be very unrealistic. And the range of plausible resource allocation solutions is usually much narrower once one is prepared to cut out the most extreme value-judgements and distributional assumptions.

(b) *Public Goods*

One of the classic types of product for which there is a strong presumption that a free market could not approximate to a Pareto-optimal level of output is the type known as 'public goods'. It will be already apparent that this term does not mean goods supplied by the public sector (which include also merit goods, those supplied by nationalized industries, and so on). It refers to goods (or services) that have certain technical characteristics—which are explained below—such that it is virtually impossible for the free market to approximate to an optimal level of output. The reason for this is as follows.

One of the analytical results emerging from the basic Paretian analysis is that goods should be priced at marginal cost. Ignoring the underlying construction leading to this pricing principle, the basic intuitive rationale is fairly simple. Few would dissent from the basic value-judgement that we want to maximize economic welfare.[10] Leaving aside distributional considerations, then, it is fairly obvious that if production of every good is

---

[9] For a most stimulating survey of this and related issues, see Dobb (1969).

[10] Of course, there is room for much difference of opinion as to (1) what constitutes economic welfare and (2) how far there is a conflict between economic welfare, on the one hand, and non-economic welfare—such as international peace and harmony, racial tolerance, love of one's family or neighbour, and so on—on the other.

pushed to the point where its contribution to economic welfare just covers its marginal cost (which, if correctly defined, equals how much social welfare it could create in an alternative use), then social welfare is maximized.[11] And the price that consumers are willing to pay does measure their evaluation of the satisfactions that they obtain, at the margin, from consuming a unit of the good in question, and it is these satisfactions that are taken as indications of economic welfare.

Public goods, however, are goods for which, over a relevant range, the marginal cost of supplying an extra unit to any particular consumer—once the basic facility to supply any consumer exists—may be zero. The reason for this lies in a particular technical feature of their supply, namely that of *non-rivalry* in consumption. This means that if the good is consumed by one consumer, it is still available for consumption by another. If one person eats an apple, it is no longer available for anybody else to eat, but if one person looks at a lighthouse, this does not prevent anybody else looking at it. The apple is hence a private good and the lighthouse is a public good. Other examples that have been commonly referred to in the literature as far back as Adam Smith are national defence and, to some extent, law and order.[12] Radio and television broadcasts are also in this category, as are, over a narrower range, various facilities such as museums, gardens, street lighting, and so on. Looking at the light from a lighthouse, or flowers in a garden, or paintings in an uncongested museum, or pretty girls in the street, are all examples of the consumption of a public good. Non-rivalry means that the enjoyment of the facility by one consumer does not detract at all from the amount of it left available for other consumers. Hence, the marginal cost of supplying one unit to any consumer—in the relevant economic sense of marginal opportunity cost—is zero.

Of course, there may be a marginal cost of producing an additional unit of *output*—for example, the fuel used in producing the light from the lighthouse, or the Oxford dons and other personnel required to make good television programmes. And beyond a point, the facility in question may become congested, so that additional users do impose costs on society (namely the disutility imposed on other users). In such cases, even when the basic facility (the lighthouse or museum or road) is installed, Pareto optimality requires the imposition of some charge. There are also capital costs associated with the facility in question, so that long-run marginal

[11] We also abstract here from various other conditions, notably second-order conditions.

[12] See Smith (1776, Book V, Chapter 1, parts 2 and 3) for assertions concerning the duty of the sovereign to protect '. . . as far as possible, every member of that society from the injustice or oppression of every other member of it . . .' and to erect and maintain those public institutions and public works that are socially desirable even though they may not be profitable for private bodies to provide.

costs of supply are crucial to determining optimum total output, and there is a large body of theory (closely linked to cost–benefit analysis) that is concerned with specifying what is the optimal level of production of such goods, given their capital and current costs of production and the total satisfactions that consumers would obtain from the optimum supply of the product in question, and the precise nature of the divergence between what would be supplied in a free market and what would be the socially optimal supply.

Another technical characteristic of many, but not all, public goods is that it would be impossible to charge for their use anyway. This is the *non-excludability* characteristic. Once the lighthouse is shining for one ship's benefit, it cannot stop other ships' crews from looking at the light. Hence, even if it was decided that lighthouses should charge for their services, there may be no way they could do so. Similarly, once the United States is being defended against the danger of invasion by Nicaragua, it is not possible to exclude any particular US residents from sharing in this defensive shield, whatever his preferences in the matter. This non-excludability characteristic of many public goods is often analysed in terms of the inability of the supplier of the service in question to protect his property rights.

Given these two technical characteristics of public goods, it is easy to show that, in general, they will not be optimally supplied through the free market. To take the simplest example, consider the case where the facility is installed (for example, the lighthouse, museum, etc.) and there is no congestion problem. In this case, as shown above, the marginal cost of providing the good to any individual user is zero. Hence, in the interests of Pareto optimality, the price ought to be zero. But clearly no private company will provide output at a zero price. And for public goods that are non-excludable it would be impossible to charge a price anyway, even if it were thought desirable. Even where the service is excludable—as, for example, with public gardens—so that private enterprise could provide the goods and make a profit, this would involve their supplying the good at a positive price. In this particular example, this would clearly be Pareto-sub-optimal (in the non-congestion case). For if, instead, the good were to be provided free, somebody who would otherwise have been deterred from consuming it would be more likely to do so, thereby being better off without having made anybody else worse off by preventing their consumption of the good in question. Similarly, it is easy to show that a free market will not lead to an optimal installation of the facilities in question—even in the excludable case.[13]

[13] There is an extensive literature on this topic, an admirable survey of which is Musgrave and Musgrave (1976, chs. 3 and 32).

But although there are clear grounds, in these instances, for concluding that the private sector would be unable to provide an optimal level of output, the conclusion that public provision is the best alternative is not always justified. In the first place, in some cases special steps can be taken to restrict access to the facility in question. This applies even to lighthouses. If there are not many ships around so that usually only one ship at a time is likely to be near the lighthouse, it would be possible to switch it on or off according to how far the ship in question had been deemed to have satisfied certain conditions, such as having paid dues at its last port of call. This facility was used, in fact, to operate private lighthouses in England in the past.[14] More commonly today, it is illegal to have a radio or television receiver without having paid for the licence and, no doubt, similar measures can be adopted to restrict access to other facilities, depending on their technical characteristics. Pay television in one form or another has been common for some time.

In other words, even with pure public goods, which are generally regarded as constituting the type of activity where the prima-facie case for public provision is strongest, there may be instances where other forms of market provision, backed up by legislation, franchising arrangements, or other supplementary policy measures, can approximate optimal output. For example, if private firms are given the right to sell advertising along with a free supply of radio or television programmes, then the service in question can be supplied without the intervention of the State.

Of course, the nature of the product being provided will inevitably be affected, since a new objective has entered the scene, namely the desire to maximize the audience for the advertising part of the activity. How far this product change is socially desirable depends on other considerations which are touched on below under the heading of 'merit goods' and which turn essentially on value-judgements. Most people who have seen the effect of nearly exclusively commercial television and radio in the USA would be terrified that a similar fate would overtake such services in any country opting for their full-scale commercialization. But aesthetic judgements are not the same as scientific proof. Other possible arrangements for such goods include, in fact, the regime of more or less benevolent competition that exists in Britain between publicly provided and privately provided television. The element of competition prevents the public output from disregarding consumers' interests entirely, whilst the element of regulation prevents the private output from degenerating entirely to the levels familiar to most people who have seen standard American television programmes.

And it is possible that there is much more scope for such forms of mixed provision. In the first place, there is scope for a wide range of goods and

[14] See Coase (1974).

services that have mixed public and private good characteristics, or that could be provided in either public or private good modes. For example, if policemen on the beat deter villains from attacking some people in the street, they are probably deterring them from attacking others as well. Hence, the marginal social cost of supplying this element of protection to any one individual is zero. It would be sub-optimal, and usually impracticable, to charge for it. But some forms of such protection are excludable and, depending on how the circumstances are defined, there are obviously marginal costs of sending extra policemen to any particular location. In fact, a public police force is only a relatively recent innovation. In the old days, guards were employed only by rich people and they probably regarded assaults on other individuals as being none of their business. (Nowadays, in most countries, they are employed in the public police force and often carry out the assaults themselves.) Even today, private protection in the form of personal bodyguards, security organizations, and so on is quite common. Some forms of cheaper private protection—such as better anti-burglar devices, fierce dogs, and so on—are available to most individuals.

In short, the dividing line between public and private goods is not always sharp and can only be made so by a fine breakdown of all the activities in question, many of which cannot be separately supplied. Many activities having mixed private and public good characteristics can be provided in approximately optimal amounts either by the public sector or—possibly accompanied by certain restrictions or obligations—by the private sector. In such cases, the choice between the two modes may turn largely on the overall effect on average costs (allowing also for efficiency incentives) of supplying the whole related range of activities by one mode rather than the other. And, as with the security example, there is often scope for mixed private and public supply or other special administrative arrangements to mitigate some of the market failure that pure public goods would normally exhibit.

Furthermore, there are many local or quasi-public goods servicing a relatively small number of people that may be provided as a result of negotiation between the people in question. Where the goods are excludable and congestion costs (psychic or otherwise) soon become significant—for example, swimming-pools—they are likely to be optimally provided by the private sector (in the absence of merit good considerations looked at below). When they are excludable but congestion costs are negligible, or when they are not excludable but numbers are small (for example, local associations to preserve amenities), the chances of arriving at a socially optimal level of supply collectively, without State intervention, may also be substantial. Of course, it is necessary for the potential beneficiaries of such an activity to be able to organize themselves in the appropriate manner, and numerous clubs of various kinds that fulfil this sort of function do exist. But, on the whole, it appears that the conditions necessary for private collective action to lead to an optimal supply of public goods are far too stringent to be universally feasible. They include breath-takingly implausible assumptions regarding the homogeneity of tastes, the scope for infinitely large numbers of possible clubs to choose from, the absence of significant costs of negotiating and providing information, the possibility of ensuring that parties to any negotiation reveal their true preferences, and so on.[15]

A second obstacle to the practical application of Paretian analysis to the provision of public goods, in addition to the fuzzy area of goods and services having mixed public–private good characteristics, is that even where there is agreement in principle that certain types of goods and services ought to be provided by the public sector, it is difficult to identify accurately the Pareto-optimal level of supply. Although major contributions have been made to the theoretical solution of the problem, notably by Lindahl (1919)[16] and Samuelson (1954, 1955), there are serious obstacles to their practical application. The Samuelson rule is that public goods should be provided up to the point where the marginal costs equal the *sum* of marginal benefits to individual consumers (corresponding to the intuitive point that the marginal benefit by one consumer does not detract from the availability of the good or service to other consumers, so that marginal benefits are not mutually exclusive, or rival, as in the case of private goods). But this approach, like the Lindahl approach, leaves aside the problem of how one could know the size of the benefits, i.e. what are consumers' real demand curves for the goods in question?

It is well known that simple questionnaires designed to find out how much people would value certain goods or services are not liable to elicit reliable responses. If people do not expect to have to contribute to the construction of the public good in question (for example, the lighthouse, or the bridge, or the local tree-preservation group or vigilante squad) in accordance with their expressed intensity of desire for it, they have an interest in exaggerating how much they value it. If, on the other hand, they suspect that they would have to contribute to its installation in proportion to how much they professed to value its subsequent facilities, they would tend to disclaim any interest whatsoever in the facility in question and expect to use it, nevertheless, as free-riders.[17]

[15] The seminal works in this area are those by Tiebout (1956) and Buchanan (1965).

[16] Published in German in 1919. The article is reprinted in Musgrave and Peacock (1958) in English, pp. 168–76. An extensive discussion and critique of the Lindahl solution is contained in Johansen (1965, pp. 129–40).

[17] This, of course, is also one of the obstacles to the efficient supply of public goods through voluntary associations and clubs.

However, whilst various complicated schemes have been suggested in the literature for inducing people to reveal their true preferences, these are not generally practicable. Various voting arrangements, particularly if these link preferences to payment, have been suggested to help solve this problem, but few people believe that they can suffice. But it would be out of place here to enter into the very complex field of social choice theory, although this is closely bound up with many of the issues discussed in this article.[18]

A third limitation on the scope for scientific answers to the question of how large should be the supply of public goods, is the assumption that all the other prices and costs entering into the calculation genuinely reflect the true economic costs and benefits to society. But for this condition to be satisfied, a host of totally implausible assumptions have to be made, such as the absence of imperfect competition, of externalities, of taxes, subsidies, tariffs, and so on, the existence of markets in all relevant activities, and so on. The fact that these assumptions will not, in general, be satisfied weakens the claim to be able to estimate accurately the ratio of costs to benefits for purposes of providing the optimal supply of public goods. But, again, one should not be too perfectionist or defeatist. Ingenuity and effort can often enable adequate allowance to be made for these distortions (and also for distributional considerations), and the literature of applied cost–benefit analysis is full of examples of such calculations having been made successfully.[19] Furthermore, all the reservations about the precise determination of the optimal provision of public goods enumerated above equally weaken the presumption that the free market will produce the optimal supply.

The three obstacles to the accurate identification of the scope for public goods, which have been identified so far, relate only to the limitations on our knowledge of relatively technical matters that are, in principle, objective. There is, however, a fourth category of obstacle that arises out of the inescapable role played by value-judgements.

First, any resource allocation problem has distributional implications. For example, if optimality required that some public good be provided free of charge, there is still a question of who should pay for it. This is not a matter of mere accountancy. The construction of the lighthouse, for example, will have used up scarce resources at one time or another (assuming full employment). Hence, somebody had to be deprived of the use of an equivalent command over resources. Given that it would generally be sub-optimal and/or impracticable to make the users pay the

---

[18] An admirable recent survey is by Mueller (1979).

[19] One pioneering analysis of the appropriate methodology, which has been applied— sometimes with variations—in many countries, is set out in Little and Mirrlees (1968, 1974).

full cost of the facility, charges have to be raised in some other way. This raises obvious income distribution and equity considerations. Why, for example, should the general public pay, via general taxation, for the provision of a service that benefits only shipowners? If the shipowners cannot be made to pay each time they look at a lighthouse signal, why not make them pay, say, a tax on ships or on the services provided to them in ports—as was the case in Britain in the past?

This sort of consideration was prominent, for example, in connection with the construction of a third London airport—the benefits of which might be thought to accrue largely to business men for whom a small saving of time was important. But in this case, the non-excludability condition does not apply (the airport authorities can charge for the use of the airport) and London airports are usually congested anyway, so that the marginal social costs imposed by individual users are not zero. But even if an airport is not obviously a public good in the technical sense, some features of its operation are certainly public *bads*—notably the noise created by the planes and possibly the increased approach traffic. It may well be that the measured benefits to the airport users exceed the estimated monetary counterpart of the loss of amenity to local residents. But this sort of comparison—as in any cost–benefit analysis—depends also on the relative income levels of the groups concerned. The validity of the answer depends on its not being sensitive to alternative distributional assumptions.

This illustrates the point made earlier to the effect that income distribution enters into the simplest resource allocation problem. And not only will different income distributions generate different optimal resource allocations, but measures to change resource allocation in the interests of optimality will influence the income distribution. However, provided these distributional effects are made as explicit as possible, it should then be up to policymakers to take steps to rectify or not the distributional effects according to their particular distributional preferences.

But there is also a second type of value-judgement entering into any calculation of the pros and cons of any public project, that is not of a simple income distribution character. For example, a cost–benefit analysis of a project, the benefits of which will accrue over time, involves the use of some discount rate. Quite apart from the well-known reasons why the market rate of interest may deviate from the true Pareto-optimal market rate, it may also differ from the social rate of discount on account of the possibility that society has some moral obligation to the interests of future generations that is inadequately represented in the balance of forces determining market rates of interest.[20] Or, again, in evaluating the relative costs

[20] I have never been very impressed by the moral claims of future generations, but I believe I am in a minority on this question. See Beckerman (1983).

and benefits of some public utility project in a rural area, how far should one take account not merely of income differences but also of indirect intangible effects, such as the value of preserving rural communities?

At this point, it becomes clear that in order to proceed further, one has to abandon the assumption of consumer egocentricity and to make allowance, as Pareto would have done, for the fact that consumers also see themselves as members of a society which provides a wide range of benefits for minority groups, which may sometimes include themselves but sometimes not, and which may sometimes accrue to groups that are better off than themselves. One does not begrudge the residents of Mayfair their publicly provided police protection, or subsidies to opera at Covent Garden, in a society which is also prepared to give a helping hand to its least fortunate members. This is what membership of a civilized society entails. Of course, once such considerations—which are discussed in more detail in the next section—are introduced, it is obviously even more difficult to adopt dogmatic positions concerning the optimality of any particular level of expenditure on most public goods. The value of the Pareto optimality rules, therefore, is not so much that they provide a precise scientific guide to the desirable level of provision of public goods, but that they provide a starting-point for asking the right questions about particular candidates for inclusion in the public sector on public good grounds and for providing some sort of constraint on unbridled log-rolling or totally irresponsible expenditures of other people's money.

(c) *Merit Goods*

Another type of economic activity which often appears to constitute a prima-facie case for public provision is the supply of merit goods. These are goods that, on basically ethical grounds, society believes should be supplied to—and, where appropriate, actually consumed by—everybody, perhaps only to certain minimum levels, whether they like it or not and whether they can pay for it or not. To go back to the initial construction of the Pareto optimality rules, it is important to recognize the enormous value-judgement embodied in the argument that a position in which no consumer can obtain higher utility without some other consumer sacrificing utility implies that no further exchange between them can make one of them better off without making the other worse off. No concept could be more value-loaded than the term 'better off'. At best, utilities merely represent individuals' preference orderings. To assume that they also correspond to welfare orderings—i.e. that being on a higher utility indifference curve is the same as having higher welfare—represents a gigantic value-judgement. It requires assuming, amongst other things, that consumers are the best judges of their welfare and that preference orderings and welfare orderings are identical. In other words, it assumes consumer sovereignty.

In fact, few societies are prepared to make this assumption—witness the numerous ways in which we interfere with consumers' freedom, positively, or negatively, because we do not accept that consumers are always the best judge of their interests. A prime example of a form of consumption that is made compulsory partly on merit good grounds is education. It is true that education also has some beneficial externality characteristics—i.e. that education of individuals not merely benefits them but also benefits everybody else, as a result of the contribution of an educated population to the desirable functioning of society. But this could have been handled by subsidies. Education also has distributional consequences, both short-run and long-run, but these could be handled, in principle, by distributional measures, such as means-tested fees or appropriate grants and allowances. It is because education is also believed to be something that people *ought* to consume, whether they like it or not, that it is made compulsory, and hence, has to be freely available to those who do not wish to pay for it or who cannot pay for it.

Similarly, there are 'demerit goods', or 'bads', like drugs. A recent addition to the list of merit goods is the automobile seat-belt. If it were thought that the only objection to the use of drugs or the non-use of seat-belts was the cost to the community of medical care or the disposal of corpses, the Pareto-optimal method of dealing with the negative externality aspects of these activities would be to tax the drugs and subsidize the seat-belts. Yet most societies impose laws about these forms of consumption on merit good grounds—i.e. the view that some people need to be protected, in their own interests, from maximizing their perceived utilities.

Now it is true that some people—such as Milton Friedman—would argue that the consumer sovereignty assumption is legitimate for everybody except children and criminal lunatics. But it is obvious, from a casual glance at the way the world operates, that the vast majority of the world's population *are* either children or criminal lunatics, so Milton Friedman's reservation would not, in fact, greatly reduce the proportion of the population for whom it might be dangerous to make the assumption that they are the best judges of their welfare interests. Once merit goods are admitted into the proper sphere of public policy, it is obviously easy to show that most of them will not be consumed to socially optimal levels unless they are provided or financed or subsidized by the public authorities in one way or another, or made the subject of mandatory legislation.

The type of merit good discussed above has the characteristic that people are not believed to have the information necessary to allocate their expenditures optimally from the point of view of their longer-run welfare.

In other words, in the same way that lack of information about the true demand curves for pure public goods restricts the accuracy with which the policymaker can determine the optimal supply, the lack of information available to consumers restricts the accuracy with which the demand curves for private goods indicate the contribution of these goods to consumers' welfare and can hence help ensure that a free market solution will be optimal.

But quite apart from information gaps and even without taking a strong paternalistic position—with all the threats and dangers to democratic organization that this can involve—there is another class of merit good. For there is no doubt that people do not confine their set of wants and needs and preferences to those provided by private goods. Most people have preferences relating to social goods that, as Pareto clearly recognized, contribute as much to their welfare as the provision of those goods entering into their egocentric *ophelimité* functions. Civic pride or national pride—both good old Victorian virtues—often takes the form of provision of public goods that would not be supplied privately (although these are not excluded).

Mention has been made of the merit good component of education, and a similar consideration may apply to health. If it is believed that, in a free market, many people may not receive as much health care as society regards as desirable in their own interests, then some form of public encouragement may be necessary, although how far this must take the form of public provision raises complex questions, such as the adequacy of insurance arrangements, the limitations on information, or the costs of alternative systems. But certain public sector activities, such as education and health, are not simply matters of dealing with externalities or with the weaknesses of consumer sovereignty. Even in the absence of such conditions, it is well known that rational behaviour by individuals not acting in concert may not lead to an optimal outcome from the collective point of view—as, for example, in the famous Prisoners' Dilemma. Nor should social welfare functions necessarily comprise only individual welfares irrespective of how these are obtained. 'Welfarism'—as it has been dubbed by one of its foremost critics, Amartya Sen—would lead to various conclusions that most people would find repugnant in a civilized society. Furthermore, as Sen has argued, the apparently attractive democratic features of Paretian rules in fact can lead to restraints on individual freedom in certain areas of behaviour that would be abhorrent to most liberals.[21]

For all these reasons, it may well be that society wants to provide certain public goods simply because public provision of them is the best means of

[21] See Sen (1982c), especially chs. 13–15. See also Johansen (1965, p. 128).

ensuring that they are distributed and consumed in a manner that people think is necessary in a civilized community. In the same way that it may be thought that a hallmark of any civilized community is that the citizens have a right to be protected against danger to life and limb irrespective of how far they can pay for it or how far their preference functions and income constraints induce them to pay for it, society may also believe that a hallmark of a civilized community is that its citizens have the same unqualified right to free education and health, and that these are best provided by the public sector.

In other words, there is a class of goods that a community may find is best supplied through the public sector on account of quasi-distributional grounds. Similar attitudes no doubt also apply to the community's policy towards housing. 'Specific egalitarianism', as this approach is often called, also often extends to the provision of basic goods or services, such as free milk for children, or subsidized television for old-age pensioners, and so on. Clearly, a society that is prepared to make such value-judgements—and most societies are—may also be prepared to make the further value-judgement that everybody should enjoy equal access to certain facilities, in the sense that private purchase of more than the minimum is to be ruled out. For example, this would no doubt be part of the case for banning private provision of education or health services. At this point, the scope for conflict between all the value-judgements referred to above and the objective of freedom of the individual emerges very clearly.

(d) Nationalized Industries

The case for public supply of certain goods or services that do not share the features of public or merit goods as described above is dealt with further by Helm (this volume). It must suffice here to point out that most of the difficulties mentioned above in connection with the precise identification of the legitimate scope for public goods—both as regards the estimates of the costs and benefits and as regards distributional and merit good considerations—will, of course, apply to any resource allocation problem, including those attached to the optimal conduct of nationalized industries.

For example, the industries usually regarded as prime candidates for nationalization on account of a specific form of market failure—namely that associated with natural monopolies—often exhibit the scope for alternative arrangements or for mixed public and private provision mentioned above in connection with other types of candidates for public provision. It may well be true that some goods are produced under conditions of decreasing costs per unit, at least up to the point of optimal total supply, so that the most efficient supply mode is a monopoly. But a private monopoly would not produce an optimal amount and would exploit its market position. In such cases, public supply is one alternative method of operation. But it is not the only one. Regulated monopoly is another. And in some cases the claims for economies of scale under monopolistic supply (private or public) are exaggerated. For example, it could well be that two postal services in Britain—one using, say, red stamps and red letter-boxes and the other using blue ones (no prizes for guessing which would be private and which public)—might lead to a more responsive and efficient postal service than that which we now have. People would soon find out which one delivered their mail more quickly. Of course, it may be necessary to impose certain obligations on the private service to deliver mail to outlying areas, but this raises other issues of a distributional character.

Another way in which nationalized industries illustrate the more general point made above concerning the ubiquity of distributional value-judgements in resource allocation problems is the question of the degree to which pricing in the public sector ought to emphasize distributional considerations. For example, one distinguished welfare economist, Graaff, has suggested that output of nationalized industries should be priced as much in the interests of society's distributional objectives as in the interests of optimal resource allocation.[22] In other words, if it is desired to reduce inequalities of real income, it would be better—as Adam Smith had suggested about two centuries earlier—to charge low prices to the poor and high to the rich, in the interests of distributive objectives.[23]

3. The Distributive Function

As indicated above, public expenditures—which, it will be recalled, are not coterminous with the public sector (largely on account of the nationalized industries)—can be divided into public expenditures on goods and services, and transfer payments. The latter comprise social security benefits and are determined almost entirely by the State's distributive objectives—i.e. the degree of income equality which is thought to be desirable. The same distributive considerations also influence, of course, the way that the

[22] 'The survival of the marginal cost pricing principle is probably no more than an indication of the extent to which the majority of professional economists are ignorant of the assumptions required for its validity . . . I suggest that the only price a public enterprise or nationalised industry can be expected to set is what we may as well call a *just* price . . .' (Graaff (1957, pp. 154–5)).

[23] Smith (1776, Book V, Chapter 1, Part III, Article 1) advocated tolls upon carriages of luxury relative to those on carts and wagons, so that '. . . the indolence and vanity of the rich is made to contribute in a very easy manner to the relief of the poor . . .'.

total tax burden is distributed, though here allocative considerations may also play an important role. (See Kay (this volume).)

There is no need for detailed explanation of why a nation's distributive objectives are basically value-judgements and hence not amenable to scientific determination. The notion of what is a 'right' degree of equality and of society's trade-off of equality against other possible conflicting objectives, such as liberty or efficiency, is clearly not something that can ever be established on the basis of scientific experiment or evidence. Consequently, there is no way of demonstrating scientifically that any particular level or pattern of social security benefits is optimal. For the notion of optimality has no meaning except in relation to some given objectives. The efficient resource allocation objective in connection with the allocative functions of the State has a superficially compelling appeal on account of its deceptive appearance of being derived from a totally uncontentious value-judgement, to the effect that we are simply trying to maximize welfare and that welfare orderings are identical with preference orderings. But nobody would expect to find what appear—however mistakenly—to be correspondingly compelling value-judgements from which to derive the rules that should govern the State's distributive function.

This does not mean that the desirable level of the State's transfer payments is entirely arbitrary, and that no facts are relevant, and that there is no scope for systematic analysis of, say, social security expenditures. First of all, at the theoretical or conceptual level, much useful groundwork has been done to clarify the various alternative concepts of equality that may be relevant—for example, equality of outcome or of opportunity; equality of income, or wealth, or something else; equality after allowing for family size, needs, time period over which income is measured, and so on. These conceptual issues are an indispensable preliminary to informed discussion of the impact of alternative policies on equality, as well as to a clearer formulation of what exactly one's distributive objectives really amount to.

At the practical, factual level, there is also clearly scope for systematic analysis of various kinds, such as of the extent to which alternative distributive programmes succeed in reaching their objectives and at what cost.[24] It is also important to analyse the comparative resource allocation effects of alternative distribution policies. And, at the aggregate level, although it will be impossible to make precise allowance for international differences in distributive objectives, international comparisons of expenditures on social security provide some guidance as to whether the level of such expenditures in Britain is flagrantly profligate or shamefully niggardly. If, for example, they appeared to be exceptionally high, then either we were

[24] See, for example, Beckerman (1979a) and Beckerman and Clark (1982).

aiming at much more ambitious objectives in the field of equality or we were being much less efficient in the pursuit of similar objectives.

But, as Table 3.3 shows, there is no prima-facie case for either conclusion. By comparison with the other countries included in some recent detailed OECD comparisons, for example, British expenditures on social security are relatively low.[25]

Table 3.3. Shares of social security expenditures in GDP in selected OECD countries, 1981 (percentages of GDP)

Country	Total	Pensions	Family allowances	Unemployment benefits
Australia	7.4	5.6	0.7	0.8
Denmark	16.4	8.1	1.2	5.1
France	17.2	11.9	2.2	1.9
Germany	16.7	12.6	1.2	1.4
Italy	15.8	13.1	1.2	0.6
Japan	6.9	4.7	1.6	0.4
Netherlands	17.7	12.9	2.0	1.0
United Kingdom (1979)	9.1	6.5	1.4	0.7
United States (1978)	7.8	6.7	0.5	0.4

Source: OECD Economic Studies, Spring 1985, Table 9, p. 52. The OECD term for what is described above as 'social security' is 'income maintenance'. The lack of more extensive country coverage could be accounted for by limitations on the comparability of the data easily available to the OECD.

Of course, international comparisons are always fraught with pitfalls in interpretation. For example, the relatively low level of State pensions in Japan may owe much to the widespread adoption of company pension schemes—i.e. indicating less need for State pensions. Similarly, the scale of pension payments will depend partly on the age structure of the population. It also depends on the objectives of the schemes. For example, the high figures shown for public pensions in France and Germany do not necessarily imply greater egalitarianism, and probably imply less, since they reflect partly the large component of earnings-related pensions in these countries. This may help equalize incomes between different income

[25] Comparisons covering a much larger selection of OECD countries and with an even greater degree of detail, but only for 1972 (or nearest year) are shown in OECD (1976), Tables 1 and 2, pages 18 and 20. These comparisons do not modify the conclusion given in the text. And, using a broader concept of 'social protection expenditures', the statistical services of the European Community show that Britain's share of such expenditures in GDP was lower than that of any other of the (1981) member countries.

groups at any period of time, but it perpetuates inequalities in lifetime incomes. For the greater are people's earnings during their working lives, the greater will be their State retirement pensions under such arrangements.[26]

Another source of international incomparability is the degree of efficiency in social security arrangements, in the sense of the proportion of the benefits that go to the people to whom they are primarily aimed. A country can spend less, relatively, than another, without sacrificing its redistributive objectives, by virtue of greater target efficiency.[27] However, such information as is available of a comparable nature concerning income distribution in various countries suggests that this is not more equal in Britain than in many other OECD countries.[28]

Another type of information that helps reduce the area of arbitrariness is the extent to which the State's redistributive activities have changed income distribution over the course of the years. Of course, one can never know whether it was optimal or not in any particular base period. Nevertheless, it might be thought (and is certainly often alleged in public discourse) that, in so far as the Welfare State had already brought about a considerable increase in the equality of income distribution, there would be less case for further moves in that direction—or that we may already have gone too far, with harmful effects on initiative, enterprise, and the spirit of self-reliance that, it is alleged, made this nation great. But such serious comparisons that have been made of income distribution in Britain, before and after allowing for the redistributive impact of the government budget, show that, in the end, the distribution of final income (i.e. allowing for all taxes and benefits, in cash and in kind) is no more equal in recent years than in the years immediately before the war.[29] And some very recent estimates of the way in which post-transfer equality has changed in Britain over the more recent past show that, according to a very wide variety of methods of measuring equality of net incomes, inequality has become greater between 1968 and 1983—according to some measures, by a considerable amount.[30]

[26] It is irrelevant how far such arrangements are part of a centralized State scheme or how far they are administered by separate funds for each category of employee, as, for example, is the case to a large extent in France.

[27] For a detailed discussion of alternative concepts of efficiency, in the context of an international comparison, see Beckerman (1979b).

[28] See Royal Commission on the Distribution of Income and Wealth (1980) and Sawyer (1976).

[29] See, in particular, Nicholson (1974). Of course, the redistributive impact of the whole of government activity is not confined to taxes and benefits and will include many other government activities, such as degrees of protection for individual sectors or groups of producers, subsidies, education, manpower training, and so on.

[30] Morris and Preston (1985, Tables 3.3–3.5).

In so far as the desirable degree of income distribution is a highly contentious concept, another relevant indicator of the adequacy of present spending on social security would be the more generally accepted concept of poverty and the extent to which society has succeeded in ensuring that nobody falls below the quasi-official concept of the poverty line (i.e. the supplementary benefit scale rate). Again, on the basis of this indicator, Britain is a long way from achieving its objectives. A country where (in 1983) over 3 million individuals were just at, or below, the poverty line can hardly be accused of an extravagant level of expenditure on benefits designed to mitigate poverty.[31]

Of course, the desirable degree of redistributive activity is not simply a function of the desired income distribution. It depends also on society's trade-off of equality against efficiency. Much opposition to a high level of social security is based on the dislike of the associated taxation, and this is usually supported by arguments to the effect that high taxes have high disincentive effects. However, no studies of this relationship have yet produced any reliable statistical evidence of there being any serious adverse impact of high taxes on working incentives.

4. Conclusion

It has been argued above that it is not within the scope of economic science to provide precise scientific estimates of the socially optimal size of the public sector. This is partly for technical reasons—such as that the quantitative estimates that the theory shows would be relevant are subject to large margins of error. But it is also partly because the very nature of the questions raised is such that value-judgements enter into all stages of the assessment. These are not restricted to value-judgements about obvious ethical issues, such as the desirable degree of income inequality in society. They include also value-judgements about the type of society in which one wants to live and the importance that one attaches to social and collective needs—whether tangible or desirable as a means of preserving social cohesion and of expressing society's vision of itself and its views on what constitutes a civilized community. No scientific tests can adjudicate between, on the one hand, a vision of society that is concerned with the distribution of welfare and the equality of consumption (even where the necessary public provision may benefit minority groups of all kinds) and, on the other hand, a vision of society as a free-for-all in which paradise is attainable only when everybody can buy shares at the local grocery shop.

[31] Morris and Preston (op. cit., Table 5.3).

At the same time, the limitations on the economic analysis of public expenditures must not be exaggerated. The technical economic arguments concerning the scope for public expenditures have greatly enriched our understanding of the criteria by which such expenditures need to be justified. Even though they can never provide scientific proof, they can often provide powerful evidence for the view that certain public expenditures are quite unjustified or that others are woefully inadequate. They replace vague waffle or rhetoric with a clear statement of what positive information is required and what value-judgements may be important. They provide an indispensable means of vetting nonsensical arguments one way or the other, as well as a valuable positive tool of analysis in situations where the social judgements have been made and are fairly clear-cut. Although 'the lore of nicely calculated less or more' can no more enable us to dispense with value-judgements concerning what constitutes the 'good' life in a humane society than it can determine whether building Kings College chapel was worth while, it is important to recognize when and where the value-judgements are relevant and what the answers ought to be for any given set of value-judgements. In many important instances, economic analysis will indicate answers that will be fairly robust in the face of alternative value-judgements or estimates of the relevant facts. And even where the analysis suggests that we do not know the answer and that there is no adequate prima-facie case for following one course of action rather than another, it is important, in a rational and civilized society, to have good reasons for not doing things.

4

The Moral Standing of the Market

AMARTYA SEN[*]

1. Introduction

How valuable is the market mechanism for practical morality? What is its moral standing? We can scarcely doubt that as individuals we do value tremendously the opportunity of using markets. Indeed, without access to markets most of us would perish, since we do not typically produce the things that we need to survive. If we could somehow survive without using markets at all, our quality of life would be rather abysmal. It is natural to feel that an institution that is so crucial to our well-being *must be* valuable. And since moral evaluation can hardly be indifferent to our interests and their fulfilment, it might appear that there is nothing much to discuss here. The market's moral standing 'has to be' high.

However, the value to an individual of a particular institution when society has been organized around that institution must be distinguished from how the society—and even that person—might have fared had the society been organized differently. We, as individuals, are thoroughly dependent on the market (as things stand), but that does not tell us much about the value of the market *as an institution*. We have to consider alternative ways of doing the things that the market does. The assessment of an institution cannot be based on examining the predicament of an individual who is suddenly denied access to it, without having the opportunity of being in another social arrangement with other types of institutions.

A second difficulty in treating the question as straightforward arises from problems in formulating the nature of the choice that is being considered. When somebody questions the value of the market, he or she is typically not considering the alternative of having no market transactions

[*] Lamont University Professor, Harvard University. This is a slightly altered version of an article first published in *Social Philosophy and Policy*, vol. 2, no. 2, Spring 1985. I am most grateful to Allan Gibbard for his discussion of the paper following my presentation at Bowling Green State University, Ohio, on 21 September 1984. I have also benefited from the general discussion, including comments by Jules Coleman, Donald Regan, Alexander Rosenberg, and Hal Varian, and from later correspondence with Varian.

at all. In fact, that is hard even to visualize. Markets, in the widest sense, enter into an enormous range of activities. Some social activities are formal market transactions; others are quite informal; and some have only a few market-type features. Those who rail against the market mechanism are not about to recommend the cessation of all such transactions. To see it as an 'all or nothing' question is to miss the point of the criticism altogether. It is a question of 'how much', 'how unrestrained', 'how supplemented'. Even the most ferocious critic of the market mechanism is unlikely to be looking for a world in which every person must produce every bit of the goods and services that he or she can consume. The question must be posed differently.

A third problem comes from a different direction. In so far as the market mechanism is valued as an instrument, its moral value must ultimately derive from somewhere else. We cannot begin to assess the moral standing of the market mechanism without first asking, 'To what intrinsically valuable things is the market mechanism instrumental?'. We have to place the role of markets in a fuller moral context.

I shall take up the question of instrumentality in the next section, and then go on to the problem of integration.

2. The Consequent Good or the Antecedent Freedom?

Most defences of the market are instrumental in terms of the goodness of the *results* achieved. It works 'efficiently'; it serves our 'interests'; it is 'mutually beneficial'; it delivers 'the goods'; it contributes to 'utility'; it serves as the 'invisible hand' by which man is led to promote an end which was no part of his intention.[1] On this view, the market is good because its results are. For example, Friedman and Friedman (1980, p. 222) argue: 'on the whole, market competition, when it is permitted to work, protects

[1] The last phrase comes from Smith (1776). Aside from indicating wherein the virtue of the market mechanism lies, it points to the fact that no individual participant in the process aims at *all* the results the market achieves. Friedrich von Hayek has seen in this a great new insight—indeed a great theory of 'the result of human action but not of human design'—initiated allegedly by Adam Smith, 'revived' by Carl Menger, and now enshrined by Hayek; see Hayek (1967, pp. 96–105). One has to be careful about what is being asserted here. It would be wrong to say that no one aims at *any* of the results achieved. In this model, each person is assumed to pursue, as far as is feasible, his own interest, and this pursuit is *fulfilled* by the market transaction. 'The butcher, the brewer, or the baker' did not aim at 'our dinner', but *we* presumably *did*. The fact that not *all* the results, nor the *pattern* of the results, were anyone's 'design' seems to be an unremarkable fact. Surely, Adam Smith's main contribution, in this area of analysis, was to show how the results of different people's 'designs' are *co-ordinated and achieved* by the market. I have discussed this question, among other issues, in Sen (1983a).

the consumer better than do alternative government mechanisms that have been increasingly superimposed on the market.' We need, of course, a criterion for judging the interests of the consumers and the relevance of these interests to the overall moral assessment of the market. We also need some methodology for interpreting the exact content of the Friedmans' claim before it can be properly assessed. But there can be little doubt that this approach to the value of the market mechanism—whatever its exact content and force—rests on assessing *results*.

Perhaps less obviously (but obviously enough), so is the claim that the market makes people 'free to choose', a freedom that might be seen to be valuable in itself (whether or not it also helps in other ways, such as the protection of the interests of the consumers). The goal of 'freedom to choose' provides an alternative (though not unrelated) basis for the assessment of the market mechanism by its results. 'That is the basic difference between the market and a political agency. You are free to choose. There is no policeman to take the money out of your pocket to pay for something you do not want or to make you do something you do not want to do.' (Friedman and Friedman (1980) p. 223.) Whether the freedom to choose is *itself* a fundamental value—not only instrumentally so at some 'higher level' of analysis—is a difficult question that need not be addressed in the present context.[2] The importance of the market, on this 'free to choose' view, derives from the more basic value of that freedom (no matter how the value of that freedom is itself obtained).

But there is also a different possibility that must be considered. It could be the case that what is at issue is not the value of the freedom to choose. People may be seen as having fundamental 'rights', and the exercise of those rights may be seen as not requiring any justification at all. If the market is seen as being part and parcel of the exercise of such rights, then markets may be defended on the basis of antecedent rights, rather than in terms of the results, including freedom of choice, that they may achieve. To assert that 'individuals have rights, and there are things no person or group may do to them (without violating their rights)'[3] would *entail* recognition of the freedom to make market transactions (given the way the rights referred to are characterized). The question of the consequences, in this procedure, arises later, *after* the right to transact (and thus to engage in market relations, in the broad sense) has already been given a stable moral status.

In this formulation, rights specify rules—of ownership, transfer, etc.— that have to be followed for a person's actual 'holdings' to be legitimate.

---

[2] See Hare (1981) on 'levels' of moral thinking and on the distinction between the 'intuitive' and the 'critical'. See also Gray (1983).

[3] Nozick (1974) p. 1.

The results of these rules are accepted precisely because they have resulted from following the right rules, not because the results judged as *outcomes* are in themselves good. The results (including serving the interests of consumers, or even enjoying the 'freedom to choose') may or may not, in fact, be judged to be good *as results*. But whatever the conclusion of that outcome analysis might be, the justification of the market, in this approach, is not based on the merits of the results. Indeed, it is apparent that there are consistency problems in an attempt to combine this approach with another that justifies actions (including, of course, trans-actions) in terms of preferring one pattern of outcomes over another, since that would over-determine the system.[4]

If this rights-based procedural view is accepted, then the traditional assessment of the merits and demerits of the market, in terms of the good-ness of outcomes, would be quite misplaced. The moral necessity of having markets would follow from the status of rights and not from the efficiency or optimality of market outcomes. This approach, incidentally, involves the rejection of the way economists—the professional group most immediately concerned with the assessment of the role of markets—have typically examined the case for and against the market. In the standard economic view of 'social welfare', rights are seen as purely institutional (typically legal) artefacts, without any importance of their own: rights are judged—in the typical welfare-economic framework—in terms of how they fulfil or thwart people's interests.

The failure to consider the procedural approach at all is certainly an omission that deserves some comment. Robert Nozick's analysis repre-sents one example of nonconsequentialist moral reasoning, and this type of reasoning must be seriously considered by welfare economists. Even if such reasoning might be ultimately rejected, there is no question that that approach deserves the most serious consideration.

It is also worth noting in this context that the force of a rights-based procedural justification of market operations is independent of our under-standing of empirical regularities in the real world, in a way that any consequentialist justification for market operations cannot be. For example, one could have a lively debate as to whether Friedman and Fried-man are right about what they say on the relative merits of the market mechanism in safeguarding the interest of consumers, or whether, in fact, it is the case that 'the freedom to choose' in any substantive sense is better guaranteed by the market mechanism than by some feasible alternative. If

---

[4] Robert Nozick does point to (what he calls) 'invisible-hand explanations' of the emergence of social institutions (such as markets), quoting Adam Smith (Nozick (1974) p. 18). But, consistently with his own approach, he does not proceed to assess such institu-tions in terms of the goodness of interest-fulfilling outcomes.

it is shown that the empirical relationships on which the consequentialist justifications depend are erroneous, then the case for the market mechanism, derived from such reasoning, would collapse.

The same applies to a moral assessment of the market based on the 'freedom' resulting from it. If that freedom is shown to be 'illusory',[5] then the case for the market mechanism, in this approach, would be disestablished. That assessment would have to be thoroughly dependent on the truth of the causal hypotheses linking markets and the resulting freedom. Questions can be raised on the empirical acceptability of the presumed causal connection.

In contrast, one interesting feature of the a priori rights-based justification of market operations is that it is not contingent on the empirical regularities that hold in the real world. The results of market transactions may be good, but even if they are bad or unassessable, they are still legitimate because they are sanctioned by antecedent rights. This can be seen as giving the nonconsequentialist approach a robustness that the consequentialist approach lacks, especially since empirical regularities are hard to establish, and predictive theories in this field can be extremely flimsy.

On the other hand, this robustness and the immunity from empirical critiques are also plausible sources of scepticism about that ethical structure. Why should our assessment of institutions be insensitive to results? Why must we accept the priority of these rights?[6] Do the rights of ownership and exchange have 'foundational' status? Must we really accept the notion that some arrangements required by the recognition of these rights are morally acceptable *irrespective* of their consequences—however bad they might be? What if the consequences are totally disastrous?

The last is not only a matter of purely theoretical speculation. As I have tried to argue elsewhere,[7] many large famines—in which millions of people have perished from hunger and hunger-related diseases—have taken place (even in the recent past) without any overall decline in food availability at all, with no 'natural cause' making the famines inescapable. People have been deprived of food precisely because of sudden and violent shifts in 'entitlements', resulting from the exercise of rights that people 'legitimately' have within the given legal system. Loss of employment and wage

---

[5] See, for example, the different analyses of this issue by Husami (1978), Steiner (1974), Cohen (1979 and 1981), O'Neill (1979), and others. See also Dworkin *et al.* (1977), Dasgupta (this volume), and Helm (this volume).

[6] Gibbard (1976). Gibbard examines the possible claim of 'property rights' to be 'grounded in principles of natural liberty', with or without Locke's (1764) qualification regarding the libertarian position, and shows why the claim is hard to justify.

[7] Sen (1981a).

income have often led to starvation. Changes of relative prices have sometimes driven the losers to the wall. The legal systems in question differ, of
course, from an *idealized* legal structure of the kind required by a theory of
rights of the type we are examining, but, nevertheless, in many respects
they have a good deal of similarity. In fact, it is easy to show that, with a
system of rights justified independently of consequences, it is possible to
have disasters of this kind occurring without anyone violating anyone
else's rights at all. The contingency of ownership, as well as influences that
determine transfers and terms of trade, can easily lead a particular
occupation group into absolute deprivation, destitution, and decimation,
without anything illegitimate and perverse having happened from the
perspective of rights.

It is not irrelevant to ask the question, 'If such starvation and famine
were to occur, must the results of the market operation be taken as
"acceptable", simply because they have followed from people legitimately
exercising the rights they have?'. It is not easy to understand why rules of
ownership, transfer, etc. should have such absolute priority over the life
and death of millions of people.

In response to this it can, of course, be claimed that only in these
extreme cases will it be right to override the requirements imposed by
rights and their legitimate exercise. There could be a caveat that nullifies
rights in these cases, but not in others.[8] Nozick himself keeps the question
open as to whether 'catastrophic moral horrors' should provide a ground
for violating rights. There *is* a dilemma here. If disastrous consequences
can be used as a ground for nullifying deep-seated rights, surely that
completely undermines the consequence-independent way of looking at
rights. If disastrous consequences would be adequate to nullify any rights
(even the most important ones), perhaps bad-but-not-so-disastrous consequences would be adequate to nullify other, less central, rights? Some of
the rights related to the ownership and use of wealth may well be seen to be
less 'deep-seated' than some other rights, for example the personal-liberty
rights with which civil libertarians have been, understandably, most
concerned. Once rejection, based on consequential evaluation, is admitted
into the picture of moral reckoning, it is difficult to find an obvious
stopping-place for a theory of rights that is based on a purely procedural
approach.

[8] Contrast the model of 'alienable rights' in Gibbard (1974), in which rights have
extreme sensitivity to the nature of the outcome. It is arguable that such a system of
outcome sensitivity may not do full justice to the procedural nature of rights, but on the
other hand it is very hard to see why rights should continue to be not alienable at all even
when the results of the exercise of rights are plainly terrible. Some connections between
outcomes and rights are discussed in Sen (1982a). See also Regan (1983) and Sen (1983c).

It is hard to argue that the value of the market can be divorced from the value of its results and achievements. This is not to say that the assessment of market operations, or the evaluation of the market mechanism, must be based exclusively on utility consequences only (defined in terms of satisfaction, desire-fulfilment, etc.). For example, it is quite possible to take into account what the market mechanism in general, and specific market operations in particular, would do to such things as the freedom of the individuals in society. If being 'free to choose' is regarded as an important part of a person's well-being (*or* regarded as morally important despite its not being a part of personal well-being), it would be perfectly sensible to include this in the assessment of the consequences of market operations. This would obviously be inadequate for producing a procedural moral system of the kind that Nozick and others have tried to develop. But by taking freedom into account in our calculation of consequences, the force of their criticism of narrow consequential systems can be partly accommodated.

I have, in fact, tried to argue elsewhere that taking note of the fulfilment or violation of rights, and of the realization or non-realization of freedom, in the assessment of social arrangements, does more justice to the importance of rights and freedom than a purely constraint-based (for example, Nozickian) system of rights and freedom can do.[9] This is not, as is often assumed, only a matter of the contrast between 'negative' and 'positive' freedom. Even if one ignores altogether 'positive' freedom, and confines one's attention to assessing 'negative' freedom, there is still a strong case for including the badness of violation of negative freedom in evaluating consequent states. Given imperfect compliance, the violation of negative freedom of A by B can sensibly figure in C's calculation regarding what to do, and a consequence-sensitive system can deal with such links. It is inadequate to try to deal with negative freedom through constraints only, since they have no relevance to C's calculations if it is B who violates A's negative freedom, even if C could have helped to stop this violation.

It could be argued that the consequential way of taking note of rights may not be able to pay adequate attention to the 'deontological' aspects of agent-relative action assessment. These aspects have been illuminatingly analysed by Williams (1973), Nagel (1980), Parfit (1984), Scanlon (1987), and others. Doing harm to someone directly may be seen to be morally worse than not preventing others from doing the same harm to the same person. This might be thought to be particularly so for the special role of 'negative' freedom. To this point some responses may be made, which I shall note here without elaboration or development.[10] First, this is really a

---

[9] Sen (1982a).
[10] I have discussed this question and other related ones in Sen (1987).

separate matter requiring *additional* structures,[11] and the correct starting-point for 'deontological' issues in personal morality may not be rights at all, but the assessment of agency linked with the position-relativity (in particular, 'doer-relativity') of moral evaluation.[12] Second, such additional structure for *personal* morals may be quite consistent with a result-orientated assessment of *institutions* such as markets and property. The different characters of the choice of institutions ('what institutions should we have?') and the choice of personal action ('how should I behave?') require different moral analyses, since these are distinct (though not independent) problems. The deontological issues are especially important for the latter.

No matter how that additional deontological question is dealt with, the *valuation* of freedom—even of 'negative' freedom—would demand a more consequence-sensitive approach, not reliant only on imposing constraints. Those who have argued that the traditional consequentialist approaches—most notably the utilitarian systems—take inadequate note of the importance of freedom have not been, in my view, mistaken in this claim. But the failure arises not so much from the concentration on consequences, but from the way consequences are assessed. If utilitarianism is split into three distinct parts,[13] namely 'welfarism' (judging states of affairs only by utility information), 'sum-ranking' (dealing with utility information by simply adding them), and 'consequentialism' (judging actions, rules, etc. ultimately by the goodness of the states of affairs resulting from them), then the primary failing, it can be argued, arises from 'welfarism'.

This is, of course, a more general question, and one which we need not really take up in this paper. If it is accepted that the moral importance of the market mechanism and market operations has to be seen primarily in terms of the market's results, then the need to go more deeply into consequential systems has to be recognized. The value of the market instrument is, then, consequential, derivative, and contingent. To assess that value, we have to understand the more fundamental social values of well-being, freedom, and justice.[14] We have to examine also the causal links

---

[11] See Sen (1983c and 1985a).

[12] One way of seeing the problem of personal morality in this type of context is in terms of a system of action evaluation that is consequence-sensitive, but not fully 'consequentialist'. Another way of dealing with it is to make the evaluation of states of affairs *position-relative* to the person doing the evaluation (including his or her own agency). There is, in fact, a case for such position-relativity on grounds of ethical cogency; or at least so I have tried to argue in Sen (1982a). See also the exchange between Regan (1983) and Sen (1983c).

[13] Discussed in Sen (1979a).

[14] On questions as to how these moral values may be interpreted, assessed, and integrated, there are—not surprisingly—enormous differences; see, for example, Arrow

between the institutional arrangements and the realization of the more fundamental values.

3. Optimality and Inequality

The assessment of the market mechanism in welfare economics has tended to rely—at least in recent decades—on the so-called 'basic theorem of welfare economics'.[15] Indeed, in the theory of welfare economics, the main rationale of the market mechanism has been typically viewed in the light of the dual relationship captured by this theorem.[16]

The first part of this 'basic theorem', asserting that every competitive equilibrium is a Pareto optimum, has been called the 'direct theorem'. The other part, claiming that every Pareto optimum is a competitive equilibrium, may be called the 'converse theorem'. Both theorems are established by making a set of restrictive assumptions. The assumptions are not exactly the same in the two cases, but they have several requirements in common (for example, the absence of externalities[17]).

The ethical force of the direct theorem in establishing the case for the market mechanism may be seen to be quite limited. A Pareto optimum does, of course, have the valuable property that not all the parties can be made better-off (in terms of utility) in any alternative feasible state. But it is easily seen that a situation can be Pareto-optimal but nevertheless quite terrible. If the utility of the deprived cannot be raised without cutting into the affluence of the rich, the situation can be both Pareto-optimal *and* truly awful.

There are two standard responses to this criticism of the relevance of the direct theorem. One is to argue that the criticism is based on making

(1951a), Harsanyi (1955 and 1976), Little (1957), Buchanan and Tullock (1962), Rawls (1971 and 1980), and Dworkin (1977 and 1981). On related matters, see also Varian (1975), Dworkin *et al.* (1977), Calabresi and Bobbitt (1978), Usher (1981), Roemer (1982 and 1984), Frey (1983), McLeod (1983), and Pattanaik and Salles (1983). I have tried to discuss some of these issues in Sen (1970b, 1980, 1982a, and 1985a).

[15] Arrow (1951b), Debreu (1959), and Arrow and Hahn (1971).

[16] As Dorfman, Samuelson, and Solow (1958, pp. 409–10) put it, 'More recently it has become common to sum up all these in one brief and easily understood theorem which comprises everything of significance and provides the backbone of welfare economics. This fundamental theorem states "every competitive equilibrium is a Pareto optimum; and every Pareto optimum is a competitive equilibrium."'

[17] This assumption is not in fact fully needed for each of the results; see Winter (1969) and Archibald and Donaldson (1976). These further results indicate the presence of an asymmetry, in the required assumptions regarding 'externalities', between the direct theorem and the converse theorem. Some other properties (for example, convexity) have very disparate relevance indeed to the two theorems (the direct theorem does not require any convexity assumption, whereas the converse theorem certainly requires it in some form or other).

explicit or implicit use of 'egalitarian' values, and many people would dispute whether such values have force. I have tried to address that issue elsewhere,[18] and this is perhaps not the occasion to go again into that old question. I shall have a little more to say on this in the next section, but for the moment I simply assert that indifference to the inequality of well-being requires some justification. The fact that equality is widely valued does not, of course, establish its validity. But it does demand a response, and a presumption of this kind calls for some serious argument as to why, in this case, inequality is acceptable. If the direct theorem is to be treated as one of great ethical significance, we must be told more about the *general* moral irrelevance of inequality of well-being, *or* of the moral case for the *particular* inequalities that would contingently occur in each case.

The other counter-argument suggests that we should shift our attention from the direct theorem to the converse theorem. Given welfarism, i.e. assuming that 'social welfare' is a function of utility information only (and this seems to be the common assumption in welfare economics), it is plausible to argue that the best of the feasible social states must be *at least* Pareto-optimal. Since, according to the converse theorem, *every* Pareto-optimal feasible state is a perfectly competitive equilibrium, with respect to some set of prices (and some initial distribution of resources), it follows that it is invariably 'possible' to achieve the very best through *some* market mechanism (provided the market is perfectly competitive). The fact that some particular Pareto-optimal states may be morally revolting does not affect this argument one iota, since we could have chosen another— better—Pareto optimum by having a different initial distribution of resources, and then by relying on the perfectly competitive mechanism to take us to the appropriate social optimum. Not surprisingly, Debreu (1959) describes the converse theorem as a 'deeper' result, and Koopmans (1957, p. 27) notes that it is the converse theorem, rather than the direct theorem, which is 'the central proposition of the "new welfare economics".'

The converse theorem is undoubtedly a major theorem in the literature of resources allocation. But to use it as a justification for the market mechanism requires further argumentation. The converse theorem points to the possibility that, if we get the initial distribution of resources right, we can reach the very best state of affairs through the competitive market mechanism *without requiring any political interference with the market mechanism*. That can certainly be seen as a conditional rejection of the necessity of a political mechanism.

On the other hand, how do we get the appropriate initial distribution of resources? The need for the redistribution of ownership is, of course, one

[18] Sen (1973a).

of the central political issues that divide the 'right' from the 'left'. Classical socialist arguments have been concerned primarily with the ownership of 'means of production', and only secondarily with such questions as 'externalities' and other problems with which the market mechanism allegedly cannot cope. If the real case for the market mechanism—through the high road of the converse theorem—is dependent on a major revolution in the distribution of resource ownership, then the case for *laissez-faire* and for using the allegedly 'non-political' route of the market mechanism is thoroughly undermined. The converse theorem belongs to the 'revolutionist's handbook'.

There is, in fact, a further difficulty, and this concerns the issue of incentives. Once the initial distribution is appropriate to the optimal outcome, the perfectly competitive outcome (if unique and globally stable)[19] will take us in the direction of the very best state of affairs. However, in order to determine the *appropriate* initial distribution of resources (for optimality in terms of the values usually invoked in traditional welfare economics, including 'equity'), one would need a great deal of information about each person's productivity, tastes, etc. It will not be in the interest of those who are likely to lose out in the process of redistribution to reveal these facts. The incentive to reveal information is absent in such a system, under the standard assumption of self-interested behaviour.[20]

It would thus appear that while the converse theorem is intellectually much more attractive, it is not easy to translate it into a practical case for the market mechanism.[21] If the *information* regarding individuals is inadequate for determining what the initial distribution of resources should be, *or* if there is an absence of—or reluctance to use—a political

[19] Uniqueness and global stability, incidentally, are additional assumptions and no mean demands either. See Arrow and Hahn (1971).

[20] This problem of the incentive to reveal information has to be distinguished from the problem of informational economy, to which the procedures for 'decentralized resource allocation' are addressed (see, for example, Malinvaud (1967), Heal (1973), Weitzman (1974), and Dasgupta (1982b). In such 'decentralized' procedures, each agent acts as a member of a 'team', and it is typically assumed that they have *shared objectives*, though disparate access to information. The problem of decentralized resource allocation, when the agents have their own respective goals, which may conflict, has not been much studied in the literature, and will certainly not lead to simple and comforting results.

[21] There are various 'incentive-compatible' mechanisms (see, for example, Groves and Ledyard (1977), Green and Laffont (1977), and Dasgupta, Hammond, and Maskin (1979)), which deal effectively with the problem of the 'free-rider' in terms of the incentive to *do* the right thing, *given* the initial distribution of resources, despite the presence of such problems as 'public goods'. These 'solutions' are not, however, addressed to the problem of how to deal with the incentive to reveal information of a kind that would permit the policymakers to make judgements about the right initial distribution of resources (in line with the distributional objectives of policymaking). Nor do they address the problem of revelation of

mechanism that would *actually* redistribute resource ownership and endowments appropriately, then the practical relevance of the converse theorem is severely limited. On the other hand, the direct theorem continues to apply without these qualifications (provided the other assumptions, such as the absence of externalities of particular kinds, can be legitimately made).[22] Indeed, for the 'non-omniscient', or the 'non-revolutionary', government, it is the direct theorem rather than the converse theorem that is of immediate interest in judging the market mechanism.

This, of course, does bring us back to the earlier question as to how good an outcome we might regard a Pareto optimum to be. If one is concerned about income distribution, or about inequalities of utility or well-being, it is very hard to settle just for 'any Pareto-optimal state', without looking further.

This particular difficulty brings out an extraordinary aspect of the market mechanism that is often overlooked. It is that the specification of the market mechanism is an essentially *incomplete* specification of a social arrangement. Even with the purest, perfectly competitive market mechanism, we are not in a position to understand precisely what will happen until we know something more about the rest of the social arrangement, in particular the distribution of endowments and resource ownership. It is an extraordinarily ambitious programme to judge one part of the social arrangement (the market mechanism) without assuming something specific about the other parts. It is not surprising, therefore, that our view of the market mechanism may well be thoroughly dependent on how the incomplete description of the social arrangement given by the market mechanism is completed by other substantive descriptions. For any moral approach that responds positively to equality of one kind or another (of well-being, or of resources),[23] the assessment of the market mechanism must be integrally related to the rest of the picture.[24]

I ought to mention, in this context, that there are a number of other

individual *judgements* to be combined in an 'aggregate' judgement (for example, to decide on equity). On the last, see Gibbard (1973), Satterthwaite (1975), Pattanaik (1978), Laffont (1979), Moulin (1983), and Peleg (1984).

[22] In fact, in so far as we value the market achievement not in terms of Pareto optimality (i.e. reaching an 'undominated' vector of utilities), but in terms of the corresponding notion of being 'free to choose' (i.e. having an 'undominated' n-tuple of individual freedoms to pursue *whatever* they decide to seek), the assumption of self-interested behaviour can be also significantly relaxed.

[23] See Dworkin (1981). See also Roemer (1984) and Varian (1984).

[24] There can, however, be useful *partial* criteria of judging achievements, for example, whether the mechanism satisfies specific requirements of 'horizontal equity' or 'symmetry preservation'. The market mechanism can be partially defended from these particular perspectives. See, for example, Schmeidler and Vind (1972) and Varian (1974).

'results' that are often cited in the literature dealing with the moral case for the market mechanism based on achievement assessment. For example, in dealing with the *effects* of property rights, reference is often made to Coase's (1960) theorem—that the optimality of the outcome is independent of the initial distribution of property rights, provided certain assumptions (such as absence of transactions costs) are made. However, the result depends upon a very weak definition of 'optimality', and the difficult issues discussed in the last few paragraphs are essentially not addressed.[25]

The only way of dealing with the problem of inequality in the outcome of market mechanism is to face that issue directly, rather than avoiding it, either by silence or by some peculiar definition of 'optimality'. It might be the case that inequality of well-being or of resources is of no moral concern, but if so, that position has to be made and defended. It becomes, of course, particularly hard to defend that proposition when inequalities are so great that some people live in extreme misery, or indeed die of starvation or hunger. But even otherwise, the question is far too important to be neglected.

4. The Producers' Rights to the Product

One other line of moral defence of the market mechanism (traced to different 'foundational' values) raises the question of who is 'producing' what, and argues for the right of the producer to enjoy the fruits. On this view, inequalities in the outcome are of no concern, unless they are out of line with the productive contributions made by the different individuals. This approach does directly address the issue of inequality, suggesting a method of dealing with it which is based on *the right of the producer* rather than on *the right of the needy*. I examine that approach next, by scrutinizing a powerful exposition of it by Bauer (1981).

Bauer's attack on 'the unholy grail of economic equality' has several features, but it includes *inter alia* what I have elsewhere called 'the personal production view'.[26] This issue is quite central to the moral assessment of the market mechanism. Bauer argues that 'economic differences are largely the result of people's varied capacities and motivations' (p. 19). Given this interpretation of economic differences, he sees little that is wrong with such inequality: '. . . it is by no means obvious why it should be unjust that those who produce more should enjoy higher income' (p. 17).

---

[25] For different interpretations of what Coase's line of reasoning achieves, see Buchanan (1977 and 1983), Calabresi and Bobbitt (1978), Cooter (1982), and Green (1982).

[26] See Sen (1982b). See also Bauer's rejoinder in the same journal (*New York Review of Books*), 10 June 1982; see also Bauer (1984).

Bauer argues that the high incomes of 'the relatively prosperous or the owners of property' are 'normally . . . *produced* by their recipients and the resources they own' (p. 12, emphasis added). Given this 'personal production view' of inequality, the moral assertion of the appropriateness of such an inequality can be seen as a variant of an 'entitlement' argument. However, the entitlement reasoning here does not take the procedural form it takes in the system of Nozick and others, since the rights that people have, on Bauer's view, are not those of ownership, transfer, etc., but of actually getting what one has 'produced'. Bauer is concerned with results and not just with procedural rules of contract.

In this respect, the entitlement reasoning of Bauer relates to a labour-entitlement system of the kind that one interpretation of the Marxian theory of 'exploitation' leads to. According to that view, labour 'produces' all the value of the output (or nature and labour do, with no residual left), and the entitlement of labour to get the output is related to that fact. Any shortfall reflects 'exploitation'.[27] In Bauer's system the output is produced not only (nor, in any Lockean sense, 'ultimately') by labour, but by the different factors of production (including capital). And the marginal productivity theory is given an interpretation of real contribution, as opposed to having only allocational usefulness in terms of counterfactual calculations.

It is not at all implausible to think that 'the personal production view', if correct, can lead to some case for inequality, even though it would still have to compete with claims arising from other considerations, such as that of needs. If, for example, a person has himself produced—unaided by others—some food, and another person wants to snatch that food away from the first, then the case for the first person rather than the second having that food might well be seen to be strong. While this judgement may be countered with competing arguments for a different distribution (e.g. the stronger need of the second person, if that is the case), there is undoubtedly some plausibility in arguing that the fact that the first person has produced the good in question *is* a matter of moral relevance. Also, if there are no strong contrary arguments, i.e. if the second person's needs are not noticeably different from those of the first, the case for the first having the food on grounds of having 'produced' it would seem to be quite strong, at least in terms of common-sense morality.

'The personal production view' is, however, rather difficult to sustain. If

[27] There are, of course, a great many difficulties in this way of seeing the Marxian system, as many contributions by Marxian economists have brought out. There is, in fact, a strong case for seeing the relevance of Marxian exploitation theory from a perspective different from that of production entitlement. On these issues, see Morishima (1973), Steedman (1977), Cohen (1978), Elster (1980), and Roemer (1982).

production is an interdependent process, involving the joint use of different resources, it is not generally possible to separate out which resource has produced how much of the total output. There is no obvious way of determining that 'this part' of the output is due to resource 1, 'that part' due to resource 2, etc. The method of attribution according to 'the marginal product' concentrates on the extra output that one incremental unit of the resource would produce, *given* the amounts of the other resources. This method of accounting can lead to problems of internal consistency, except under some special assumptions (in particular, constant returns to scale). But even if these assumptions are made, the relevance of the accounting to 'the personal production view' is deeply problematic.

In fact, the marginalist calculus is not concerned with finding out who 'actually' produced what. Marginal accounting, when consistent, has an important function in decision-making regarding the use of resources, suggesting when it would be appropriate to apply an additional unit of resource and when it would not. To read in that counter-factual marginal story one of 'actual production'—who in fact produced what part of the total output—is to take the marginal calculus well beyond its logical limits.

For example, if it turns out that using the marginalist calculus to evaluate factor contributions yields the result that 40 per cent of the output is 'due to' labour, 40 per cent 'due to' machinery, and 20 per cent 'due to' management, that just tells us something about the respective relative values of the marginal contributions multiplied by the total amounts of the respective resources. It would not, of course, follow that any of these three factors of production could produce their respective shares unaided by the others. Indeed, the apportioning is not even one that is done by adding together the marginal contributions of all the respective units one after another, but rather goes by weighting the *entire* amount of the resource input by the marginal valuation of the counter-factual additional contribution of that resource *at the point of equilibrium*. Under the competitive distributive process, that is what will determine the relative shares of income, and in this sense, it has predictive value as well as allocational use. But 'the personal production view' adds to this real use a spurious interpretation as to who has 'produced' what. This comes, as it were, from nowhere, and it is essentially a fiction. It might, of course, be seen as a 'convenient fiction', but that fiction is a whole lot more convenient for some than for others.

The problem becomes even more complicated when the comparison extends to incomes generated from the production of *different* goods, since the relative incomes would then depend on the relative prices of these products, introducing an additional element of arbitrariness into 'the personal production view'. The significance of the relative prices in terms of 'productive contributions' would require a further fiction in translating the marginal rates of transformation—again, a set of counter-factual magnitudes—into a set of actual production weights.

There is the further problem that 'the personal production view' applies only to resources, and to move from there to the contribution of the person *owning* the resources is a considerable jump. The right of the owners of productive resources to receive high income requires some justification of the moral relevance of ownership. It is not justified on the simple ground, to which Bauer refers, of the income-rights of 'those *who* are more productive and contribute more to output' (p. 11, emphasis added). Once again, the traditional socialist literature has not been so concerned with disputing the productive contribution of different resources as it has been with disputing the right of the *owners* of productive resources to grab what the resources produce.

If this reasoning is correct, the problem of inequality raised in the context of the other defences of the market mechanism is not disposed of by moving to 'the personal production view'. This is not because there is no intuitive appeal whatever to the idea that one ought to have a right to something one has produced 'oneself'. But (1) in a world of interdependent production, that condition is difficult to apply to resources; and (2) in a world of non-personal resources, it is difficult to translate it from resources to persons.

There are, of course, circumstances in which 'the personal production view' might be very powerful. If, for example, we are asked to arbitrate between two children fighting over a wooden toy, which has been made unaided and with free wood by one of them, and if we know nothing more about the two children, then it would be not unreasonable to be swayed by the fact of 'personal production'.[28] Utilitarians (and many others) will claim that this appeal is entirely explainable by some instrumental reasoning. Whether this is so is unclear. What is clear, and cannot be doubted, is that there is a strong moral intuition in that direction. But no matter what this appeal arises from, the possibility of applying it to judging actual market outcomes is so restricted by the fact of interdependence and the contrast between owning and producing, that this approach may be of little use in practical reasoning.

5. Concluding Remarks

The moral standing of the market mechanism has to be related to results, and it is, thus, derivative and contingent. While it is important to examine

[28] I have discussed this question in Sen (1981b).

the possibility that market operations might be justified on grounds of the exercise of people's 'prior' rights (irrespective of consequences), the implausibility and the arbitrariness of that approach are difficult to avoid. I have argued for the alternative of assessing market operations in terms of achievements, but also for treating achievements much more widely than 'welfarism' permits (including such factors as the importance of 'freedom to choose'). This has the advantage of taking note of the moral force of some of the arguments presented by the 'procedural' view, while making that force compete with other moral claims in the overall decision.

The second approach examined finds the moral standing of the market mechanism in the values of the outcomes. This is the standard approach in welfare economics, which then proceeds to take the more specialist form of judging the outcomes exclusively by the utilities generated. In terms of that general approach of 'optimality', while a case could be made for saying some nice things about the market mechanism, it is hard to go beyond some highly tentative statements. The crucial issue turns out to be our assessment of inequality. The 'direct theorem' ignores it. The 'converse theorem' deals with it in a way that is self-defeating, in so far as the non-interventionist 'moral' of the market mechanism is concerned.[29] Of course, we might refuse to judge the outcome in terms of utility information only. I have tried to argue elsewhere[30] against the 'welfarist' method of evaluation of states of affairs. But the issue of inequality does have to be addressed, whether inequality is seen in terms of utilities, well-being, incomes, resources, or freedoms (including the real 'freedom to choose').[31] The practice of avoiding this question through evasion or silence, on the one hand, or through peculiar definitions of 'optimality', on the other, seems hard to defend.

The third approach that was examined is one based on 'the personal production view'. Despite the possible relevance and force of that moral consideration, it appears that this gives us very little help in morally assessing market mechanisms in a world with (1) interdependent production, and (2) owned impersonal resources.

The argument that is much harder to dismiss is one that claims little for the market mechanism except superiority over other *practical* alternatives. Brittan (1983a, p. 37) has argued that 'too often the defects of the real world market are compared with the hypothetical action of a benevolent and omniscient dictator (as frequently—in the more technical writing—for reasons of mathematical convenience as from any deeply held convic-

---

[29] It is not surprising, in view of this, that the early contributions to the efficiency of the market mechanism came from socialist writers like Lange (1938a) and Lerner (1944).

[30] Sen (1970b, 1979a, and 1982a).

[31] On the last, see Sen (1980 and 1985a).

tion).'[32] Indeed, it is not unfair to ask a critic of the market mechanism what precise system he would put forward *instead*, how well does it work, and how does it compare?

Once the issue is seen in this way, it is clear that the question of the moral standing of the market mechanism cannot be given the kind of simple answer that some of the approaches examined have tried to give. It might well be the case that many alternatives suggested as substitutes for the market mechanism would do worse than the market mechanism, even in terms of the criteria used by the advocates of the change. It is also possible that, in terms of the criteria put forward by defenders of the market mechanism, replacement of the market in many spheres by other procedures would do much better.

The Chinese produced chaos by trying to do away with some features of the market mechanism. At the same time, they did expand the positive freedoms of many. For example, despite a per caput gross national product (GNP) only a fraction (about a seventh) of Brazil's and Mexico's, China has succeeded, through an interventionist regime, in raising life expectancy well beyond that of Brazil and Mexico. It is also no lower than that of South Korea, a country with a much higher level of income and a much faster rate of growth (based on a market economy with an active government policy). If we look at actual achievements across the world, the picture is a divided one, and there are many conditional conclusions to be drawn based on such empirical comparisons.[33] The difficulties in making the comparisons arise partly from the problem of isolating empirical regularities, but also from the formidable complications in getting an adequate moral criterion in terms of which the instrumentality of the market mechanism and its rivals can be judged.

When all the qualifications have been put in, the market mechanism certainly has some instrumental moral relevance, related to its handling of information and incentives. The result-oriented and contingent nature of that relevance does not make the lessons unimportant. The defenders of the market mechanism have often seen in hesitant acknowledgements like this one a tendency to damn the market with 'faint praise'. But while faint praise is no doubt one method of damning, unjustified and ferocious praise is certainly another. The vigour of the defence of the market mechanism examined earlier in the paper is not matched by its ability to meet criticisms. It also distracts us from the contingent importance of the use of the market mechanism in many real circumstances, and tends to make us overlook the relevance of these lessons for practical reasoning. There *is* a case for *faint* praise—not any less, nor much more.

[32] See also Little (1982).
[33] The question is discussed in Sen (1973b and 1981c).

5

Positive Freedom, Markets, and the Welfare State

PARTHA DASGUPTA*

1. Introduction

The comparative merits of market and certain distinguished non-market resource allocation mechanisms have continually been at the centre of debate in economics and political philosophy. Doubtless they will remain there. For here one faces the grandest of human concerns, embracing as it does issues bearing on liberty and welfare, the aspirations of people, their potential and realized capabilities, and the fulfilment of their needs. It enables us to see individuals in a social context, to ask about the possible features of a civil society, the obligations that people may have to themselves, to one another, and to agencies. Then again, we are able to enquire into the obligations that agencies have to people and to one another, the extent to which responsibility needs to be delegated among offices and persons, the role that dispersed information may play in answers to these, and so on. The debate is central to any discussion of the kind of society we ought to aspire to be members of.

The mix of market and non-market activities in the production and distribution of such commodities as medical care, education, insurance, social security, shelter, legal aid, and so forth, is a matter of immense practical urgency. However, in open societies, political positions and attitudes are always in need of justification; at the very least, in need of an argument. For this reason, the link between analytical discourse and debates on matters of direct practical concern has always been strong in this field. Political philosophers and theoretical welfare economists refer to actual problems for their motivation, and politicians and journalists scrutinize abstract theories. Periodically there is, as there ought to be, a reassessment of what one stands for and what is being accomplished. Today, perhaps more than ever before, there is a serious debate about the mix of market and non-market activities in the production and distribution

* Professor of Economics at the University of Cambridge and Fellow of St John's College, Cambridge. I am most grateful to Dr Dieter Helm for illuminating discussions on the subject matter of this essay and for his suggestion that I write the essay.

of those commodities whose public provision is the hallmark of what is, slightly misleadingly, called the Welfare State. It is, therefore, entirely appropriate to try to marshal our current theoretical understanding of matters that are pertinent to these problems. This is being done by many others and one hopes it will continue to be done. This essay attempts to provide such an assessment.

I emphasize at the outset that I will limit myself only to presenting and assessing various *theoretical* arguments which have been much discussed over the past many years and have shaped people's thinking. I will make no attempt to discuss those urgent problems, such as, for example, the appropriate size and composition of the 'welfare' budget in the UK today, which require for their analysis not only theoretical arguments, but also careful quantitative evidence. Furthermore, to have an exposition which is reasonably streamlined and which enables me to go directly to what seem to me to be the central difference among various influential doctrines, I will ignore pervasive scale economies in the production of certain commodities and, excepting for security and the legal system, ignore also collective consumption possibilities. These provide too familiar and exhausted a terrain. But more importantly, for the purposes of this essay, nothing will be lost in my ignoring them and much will be gained.

The link between individual liberty and the ability to engage in market transactions has been much discussed in the literature. Traditionally, justification of an exclusive reliance on market allocations has been based on an appeal to one type of liberty, of the *negative* kind (Berlin (1969)) and it has been argued that market transactions are an expression of negative freedom. But there have also been justifications resting on *instrumental* grounds, most especially discussed by economists. In Section 2, I will summarize these positions. In Section 3, I will suggest that there is another type of liberty, of the *positive* form (Berlin (1969)) whose promotion requires each person to have access to and command over certain commodities and resources, the most important of which are precisely those the Welfare State has traditionally been urged to make available.

In Sections 4 and 5, I will discuss *welfarism* (of which Utilitarianism is a special case), the dominant moral framework in the economics literature. I will distinguish welfarism from positive and negative freedom, and I will summarize how welfarism can justify a reliance on a mix of market transactions and State intervention by way of the imposition of taxes and subsidies. In Section 6, I will argue that in the face of uncertainty, even welfarism calls for certain patterns of non-market allocation mechanisms well beyond those discussed in Section 5. In Section 7, I will present a summary of the arguments presented thus far and suggest that, on the face of it, welfarism and moral theories founded upon positive freedom would appear to have identical *practical* policy implications. In Section 8, I will argue that this is not in fact so and that under a wide variety of circumstances, welfarism would advocate State allocation of what I will call positive-rights goods by means of transferable coupons, whereas doctrines appealing to positive freedom would advocate their allocation in kind. It would seem ironical then that certain practices of the Welfare State envisaged by the founding fathers can be justified, *not* by an appeal to welfarism, but by an appeal to freedom of a certain important kind.

2. Freedom and the Market

Defence, and in many instances outright advocacy, of the market mechanism have ranged from grounds that are near-mystical to ones that are unabashedly prosaic. At one extreme is the advocacy by Hayek, who claims not at all to understand the market mechanism and warns us all not to try to do so but asserts nevertheless that the mechanism is—most especially in theory—the best guarantee for his conception of *progress*.[1] At another extreme is a defence of a particular form of the market mechanism—the *competitive* form—on grounds that under certain conditions it sustains an efficient allocation of resources and that it does so with little by way of a need for central information pools and State interference.[2] At yet another extreme is an advocacy based on the primacy of such individual rights as those which are shown ultimately to justify a night-watchman State, a State whose activities are limited to the provision of a few public services, such as the enforcement of contracts and the protection of persons or groups against force, theft, and fraud. This is not the place to evaluate the ingenious notion that the *historical* entitlements which people have to commodities and resources have priority over all else, an idea which lies behind the celebrated recent advocacy of the night-watchman—or minimal—State (Nozick (1974)).[3] But we should note here

[1] Elsewhere, I have attempted to piece together exactly what Professor Hayek has been advocating in this area of discourse and have given reasons why his arguments—in so far as they amount to an argument—are unconvincing. See Dasgupta (1980, 1982a). Brittan (1983b) independently presents a reading of Professor Hayek's writings on these matters which is similar to my own. But for the most part, it is a reading, and a reverential reading, with little by way of an analysis of why we should find them compelling. A good representation of Hayek's views on the market mechanism can be found in Hayek (1948, 1960, 1976).

[2] The literature on this is vast and the efficiency statement itself is called the First Fundamental Theorem of Welfare Economics. Arrow (1971) presents a characteristically penetrating account of this line of argument.

[3] For an economist's evaluation, see Arrow (1978).

that this advocacy is not based on traditional instrumental grounds. Rather, it sees the unfettered and unassisted market mechanism—described in rich detail by Nozick—as the only justifiable mechanism for resource allocation because it alone is consonant with the protection of what Berlin (1969, Essay III) would classify as *negative freedom*; that is, an absence of coercion, an absence of '. . . the deliberate interference of other human beings (or human agencies) within the area in which [one] could otherwise act' (Berlin (1969) p. 112). For it is negative freedom which 'historical entitlement' in Nozick's sense ultimately protects and promotes.

It is worth noting that Nozick's 'libertarianism' is quite different from Hayek's and that in fact they are distinct doctrines. Hayek's advocacy of an unbridled market mechanism is on instrumental grounds. *Progress* is the goal which is sought. It is thus a basic virtue of a society to generate it. Negative freedom is only a means to this, it would not seem in Hayek's writings to be a primary moral good. ('. . . if the result of individual liberty did not demonstrate that some manners of living are more *successful* than others, much of the case for it would vanish' (Hayek (1960) p. 85, emphasis mine).) Contrary to what is often done, it does not do to bracket Hayek's and Nozick's conceptions together.

At yet another extreme is the advocacy of the market mechanism by Bauer in a series of penetrating and influential books and articles (see especially Bauer (1971, 1984)). Bauer's advocacy is based in parts on the promotion of negative freedom in the economic domain and in parts on the belief that it offers the best chance for the growth of material well-being for those who truly seek it. Partly too there is an underlying suggestion that State assistance diminishes and corrodes self-reliance and ultimately an individual's sense of responsibility and thus self-respect. (I shall argue in Section 3 that this suggestion *can* be very misleading.) There is, however, no suggestion that political democracy, in particular negative political freedom, is implied by well-functioning economic markets, nor that it implies them.[4]

These then are four positions from which the market mechanism has been justified. There are others, hybrid ones, such as Milton Friedman's, but these four span the most widely cited ones on offer. Of these, the second stands apart, not only because it *is* prosaic but also because it is a shade non-committal on the justifiable role of the government. Economic efficiency, or technically speaking Pareto efficiency, is a criterion which yields only a partial ordering over economic states or resource allocations: there would typically be a number of feasible economic states which

---

[4] For a lucid exposition of the logical independence of markets and political democracy, see Lindblom (1977).

cannot be ranked by the criterion of efficiency. The Second Fundamental Theorem of Welfare Economics asserts that, under certain conditions bearing on values, preferences, and technology, any efficient allocation of resources can be sustained as a competitive market equilibrium, provided the government in advance imposes a suitable lump-sum wealth redistribution.[5] Thus, a commitment to economic efficiency is consonant with far-reaching government intervention in the form of massive redistribution of purchasing power.

In contrast, the remaining three positions I have tried to outline are uncompromising in their advocacy of the limits of government interference. Details apart, they see the State supplying only those public goods, like security, an effective legal system, and certain types of information channels, which are essential for the market mechanism to be able to function. This is only to be expected. Based as these advocacies are in their different ways on individual rights to negative freedom, they insist that the State must guarantee those commodities which are necessary for the realization of these rights. But there are other rights, of seemingly no less urgency, which too have to do with freedom and they also require for their furtherance command over certain classes of commodities and, as I shall argue below, *individual* command over commodities. I turn to this.

3. Commodity Use and Positive Freedom

In his classic essay on liberty, Berlin disentangled two concepts of liberty which, although they had become fused in the literature and in one's thinking, had historically '... developed in divergent directions not always by logically reputable steps, until, in the end, they came into direct conflict with each other' (Berlin (1969) p. 132). In contrast with freedom from coercion—including, of course, freedom from State interference—Berlin spoke of *positive freedom*, the *ability* '... to be somebody, not nobody; a doer—deciding, not being decided for, self-directed ... conceiving goals and policies of [one's] own and realizing them', and of the ability '... to be conscious of [oneself] as a thinking, willing, active being, bearing responsibility for [one's] choices and able to explain them by reference to [one's] own ideas and purposes' (Berlin (1969) p. 131).

At one level the two concepts amount to the same thing. Both are concerned with the extent of one's feasible set of choices. At another they are, as Berlin elaborated, quite different, for they differ by way of the *sources*, or *agencies*, which constrain choice, which etch the contours of the

---

[5] For an exposition, see Arrow (1971) and Meade (1976).

feasible set.[6] For example, a person may be assetless and, more importantly, chronically malnourished, lacking thereby motivation and physical
capabilities necessary to be employable in a freely functioning labour
market, his sole means of escape from the bonds of deprivation. He does
not enjoy positive freedom. He is unable to be a 'thinking, willing, active
being'. Such a man does not have life plans, or projects, or 'own ideas and
purposes'. But if he is not prevented by others from seeking and obtaining
employment in a freely functioning labour market, he is negatively free. In
this example, what keeps him in wretchedness, what deprives him
systematically of his right to positive freedom, is not the dictates of a
person, or an agency, but the 'workings of the free-play of market
forces'.[7]

Positive freedom is concerned, among other things, with the *ability* of a
person to *function*. And a person's ability to function depends on his
personal characteristics, his command over commodities and resources,
the commodity and resource use made by others in his community, and so
on. What are often called 'basic needs' (see, for example, Streeten
(1981)), commodities such as basic food and shelter, medical care, and
sanitation facilities, are goods that are required in order that a person is
capable of functioning. Whatever else he requires or wants to have, he
needs these. Within bounds, a person can function better, more effectively, with greater availability and use of such goods. There is thus a
continuum of possible levels of use: it is not all or nothing. There is
evidence, in the case of nutrition, of threshold effects, where prolonged
restrictions in nutrition intake can produce severe stress in a person's
metabolism (see Dasgupta and Ray (1986b)). There are thus minimum
needs in this case.

Primary education is also thought of as a basic need, but it is of a *slightly*
different variety. It is not much use being literate if all others are illiterate
and if there are no books in sight. Primary education is near to this end of a
range, at the other extreme of which are commodities that are required for
one to be able to function only because others make use of them. These
commodities, of which telephones are a good example, offer 'network
externalities', in that if a sufficient number of poeple use them, one's own
need for them increases dramatically, as other channels available for being

---

[6] Positive and negative freedom are but two senses in which the word 'freedom' has been
used. Berlin (1969, p. 121) asserts that there are more than two hundred senses in which
the word has been used by historians of ideas! The mind boggles at the mere thought.

[7] For an analysis of how this may come about, of how it is that the assetless are the most
vulnerable, of how they may become utterly disenfranchised from the economic order
under the free-play of *fully-functioning* market forces, see Dasgupta and Ray (1986a,
1987).

able to function (for example, being able to keep in touch with others) are effectively foreclosed.[8]

In this essay, I shall concentrate on this side of the range, commodities like basic food and shelter, medical care, primary education, and sanitation facilities, which are thought of by many as 'natural-rights goods', goods that are necessary for one to be able to function.[9] In what follows, I shall refer to them as *positive-rights goods*, as they are necessary for positive freedom. There are, of course, other 'natural-rights goods', such as security and an effective legal system. But, as we noted earlier, such commodities are necessary for the attainment and protection of negative freedom, they are *negative-rights goods*, and the need for their centralized provision has already been much advocated in rights-based theories.

Rights can readily clash with one another, just as they can with other goals. There may need to be a dilution of some forms of negative freedom for the advancement of certain aspects of positive freedom, and vice versa. Since the protection and promotion of such forms of liberty require a command over resources, we are inevitably faced with a resource allocation problem and thus with the necessity for trade-offs. But it is not the need for trade-offs I wish to emphasize here. Rather I find intriguing the fact that security and a legal system, two of the primary commodities needed for the protection of negative freedom, are, technically speaking, public goods, in the usual sense that there *need* be no rivalry in their use.[10] Now, public goods are a notorious cause of market failure. This *may* go some way towards explaining why there has been so painless a confluence of what are, after all, two separate positions: the insistence on negative freedom and the demand for economic efficiency via the unfettered competitive market mechanism.

In contrast, the commodities that are necessary for the promotion of

[8] The term 'network externalities' has been borrowed from the telecommunications industry, where standardization of products (that is, compatibility of software to computers) is of paramount importance. There is now an interesting literature showing how the market mechanism can lead an economy astray from dynamic efficiency in the presence of network externalities among units of a durable commodity. This is because of the resulting scale economies in the *demand* side for the product. See, for example, Katz and Shapiro (1985) and Farrell and Saloner (1985).

[9] To be sure, 'basic food' is an aggregate concept and so there is much scope for debate over what specific food items, more pertinently, nutrient combinations, are necessary for 'food adequacy' among different categories of persons. And there *is* a great deal of debate. I have tried to discuss some of these issues in my E. S. Woodward Lectures delivered at the University of British Columbia. See Dasgupta (1986a). See also Dasgupta and Ray (1986b).

[10] This claim may read hollow given the extent to which the courts in many countries are overstretched. But if one thinks of the number of cases that come before the courts and the number of transactions that are undertaken because of the mere presence of the courts, the point is inescapable.

positive freedom range from those which are only partially public—such as medical services that contain or prevent the spread of communicable diseases—to totally private ones, such as shelter and food. The unassisted and unbridled competitive market mechanism can, under certain circumstances, produce an efficient allocation of resources involving the use and production of private goods. But it can *never* be guaranteed to distribute them in a way which ensures the protection of positive freedom for all members of society. An efficient allocation is consonant with a fraction of the population disenfranchised from economic activities and left cold and hungry and diseased. And the competitive market mechanism—even when fully functioning—can, under a large class of circumstances, be guaranteed to bring about precisely that.

4. Economic Welfare and Positive Freedom

Applied welfare economic theory has, for the greater part, been concerned with the production and distribution of individual *welfare*, where individual welfare is seen as being founded on the availability and use of goods and services. Thus, social and economic states—for example, commodity allocations—are judged solely on the basis of the individual welfare characteristics of these states. If two distinct commodity allocations produce the same individual welfare values, they are judged to be of equal merit: it is thought to be a matter of social indifference which of the two prevails. This is seen most clearly under Utilitarianism, which ranks social states on the basis of the sum of individual utilities, or welfares. If two distinct commodity allocations produce the same utility values and *thus* the same sum, Utilitarianism is indifferent between them.[11] This exclusive concern with the welfare characteristics of social states, often called 'welfarism' (see Sen (1979a)), has been much scrutinized in the literature on social choice (see Guha (1972) and d'Aspremont and Gevers (1977)). The point is, of course, that we may have good reasons *not* to be neutral between commodity allocations yielding identical welfare assignments to people if the assignment of rights-based goods in them is vastly different; for example, if in one of the allocations the assignment is much more unequal. Welfare is welfare and freedom is freedom. Hunger is not the same as undernourishment and it can be greatly misleading to confound them. The chain linking the availability of commodities, through commodity use and the ability to function, with individual welfare is a

[11] Of course, Utilitarianism is indifferent among a great deal more: it is indifferent between any two utility distributions which add up to the same amount. But it is not this feature of Utilitarianism which is my concern here.

most complex one. When judging social states, moral pluralism requires of us to scrutinize the entire chain, not merely some given part of it.[12] It is in this sense that both rights-based theories and welfarism are morally limiting.

5. Market Mechanism and Economic Welfare

As noted earlier, one justification of the market mechanism for the purposes of resource allocation has been based on an allegiance to welfarism. Both the sharpest and the bluntest form this justification takes is the First Fundamental Theorem of Welfare Economics which, as we noted earlier (see footnote 2), asserts that a competitive market equilibrium allocation, when there is a competitive market for each and every commodity, is Pareto-efficient. It is the sharpest because it makes precise an analytical feature of competitive market allocations: there is nothing mystical in the justification nor any appeal to historical evidence. And it is the bluntest because Pareto efficiency yields a mere partial ordering. But the point I want to note here is that competitive market allocations are, as this theorem in effect implies, fully consonant with welfarism: given initial endowments and technological possibilities, equilibrium allocations are determined solely by individual welfares (or utilities).[13] It follows that the only reason—and this is a big reason, let us admit—why a welfarist may not find competitive market allocations appetizing is that they do not necessarily get the *distribution of welfares* right. This, as the Second Fundamental Theorem of Welfare Economics makes clear, can be corrected for if the State engages in a redistribution of initial endowments before allowing competitive markets to operate.[14] In fact, the informational parsimony suggested by the Second Fundamental Theorem is totally illusory. The information the State is assumed to know is awesome in amount. It needs to know individual utility (or welfare) functions, technological possibilities, and initial endowments, if it is to get the final dis-

---

[12] These considerations have been carefully and lucidly presented in Sen (1985b).

[13] This, of course, assumes that individual market *choice* is based exclusively on individual welfare, not a negligible assumption, but I shall suppose it for brevity. Formally, the claim in the text is that competitive market allocations satisfy the neutrality (equivalently, welfarist) assumption in social choice theory. This may seem to contradict the assertion in Sen (1970b, p. 78) that they do not, but in fact it does not. Sen allowed for the possibility of missing markets, but in this case, we know that competitive market allocations are not even Pareto-efficient. By 'fully functioning markets', I mean that all markets are open.

[14] Such a move, of course, grates against negative freedom, but we are now looking at market allocations from the point of view of welfarism. Meade (1976) is arguably the most comprehensive account and defence of the twin roles of State intervention and the market mechanism based on the Second Fundamental Theorem of Welfare Economics.

tribution of welfares right. But if it knows all this, why bother with markets at all? Why not operate a totally command economy? Why not, that is, command the production and distribution of goods and services through quantitative planning?

The answer is, of course, no reason why not. The Second Fundamental Theorem of Welfare Economics—which is so often seen by economists as providing a reason why the State ought to rely on markets—holds true only in circumstances where there is no need to rely on markets at all. I have no explanation for this paradox.[15]

Now, of course, it can be argued that the Second Fundamental Theorem is not to be taken literally. No one is expecting the State to get things exactly right, even if it knew what *was* right. To be sure, the welfarist State does not know everything it would like to know. But it would have rough information, perhaps even statistical information. So it would try to get things approximately right, statistically right, by a combination of taxes and subsidies and a reliance on markets. But this needs further argument and is true only under certain circumstances. In others, the welfarist State would do better by a judicious mixture of markets and commands.[16]

In fact, even the efficiency property of competitive market allocations requires further clarification when the environment is shot through with uncertainty. In the next section, I discuss the complications that uncertainty introduces to the notion of Pareto efficiency and to the workings of the market.

6. Uncertainty, Information, and the Market Mechanism

In the face of uncertainty, Pareto efficiency can mean one of two things: welfare efficiency *before* the uncertainty in question is resolved, or welfare efficiency *after* it has been resolved. Economists refer to them often as *ex ante* and *ex post* efficiency. The efficiency of competitive market allocations which the First Fundamental Theorem refers to is *ex ante* Pareto efficiency. It can be shown (see Starr (1973)) that it is only when both individuals' subjective probability beliefs about the likelihood of the possible uncertain events are identical and each individual's *ex ante* welfare is the expected (or mean) value of *ex post* welfares, that *ex ante* Pareto efficiency results in *ex post* efficiency as well. Each is a very strong assumption, a great deal stronger than economists usually care to reckon.[17]

[15] Elsewhere I have discussed in more detail the role of information in the Second Fundamental Theorem (see Dasgupta (1980)).

[16] See Weitzman (1974) and Dasgupta, Hammond, and Maskin (1980).

[17] Hammond (1982) presents a lucid account of the problems facing a Utilitarian planner under uncertainty.

The point is not merely that beliefs can differ, but that they can differ because some beliefs may be wrong, more wrong than others. The fact that a person has wrong beliefs does not mean that the person in question does not take them seriously nor that his welfare is not influenced by them. But this only means that one should give *some* weight to such beliefs when judging the merits of alternative resource allocations under uncertainty. It does not mean that the fact that the beliefs are wrong should be ignored entirely. The weakness of *ex ante* welfarism is that it ignores it completely.

As it happens, the *ex ante* Pareto efficiency of competitive market allocations holds true if (and in general *only* if) a crucial additional assumption obtains, one which I have assumed implicitly so far. It is that *all* individuals possess the *same* information![18] If they don't—and in the world that we know, they don't—an entire cart-load of additional problems concerning the functioning of competitive contingent markets arise even for the die-hard welfarist. If people differ by way of what they know, information assumes the role of an exchangeable commodity. But the market for information is most likely to be shot through with inefficiencies—in the *ex ante* sense—and in extreme cases, they simply will not exist.[19] (For an excellent summary of what we know of the analytical features of markets with asymmetrical information, see Stiglitz (1985).)

To take an example, the purchase of a medical diagnosis is the purchase of an opinion, a belief, a probability distribution over possibilities, one may not even have thought about prior to the purchase. (Think of the many ailments one has not even heard of.) But how is the purchaser to know what he is purchasing prior to making the purchase? And how is one to expect the doctor to declare his diagnosis prior to a financial agreement, given that he will be unable to withdraw the diagnosis if payment is not subsequently made? Trust in the person assumes a central role in such circumstances, for it is a way of circumventing the anonymous trust that markets allow to be fostered. The acquisition of reputation through credentials and long-term behaviour are key elements in the resolution of such market dilemmas.[20] One must not allow fly-by-night medical practitioners to operate, because this would introduce vast additional uncertainties about the quality of the product the citizen is ultimately paying for. In his classic essay on medical care, Arrow (1963) argued how

[18] When this is so, the identity of beliefs is perhaps not as outrageous an assumption as would appear at first blush.

[19] We say 'A penny for your thought'; never, 'A penny if you are thinking of this and nothing if you are thinking of anything else'. For we know in advance what thoughts the thinker will claim he was having. This is the reason why it is injudicious to take bets on people's states of mind.

[20] I have tried to go into the question of trust formation and reputation acquisition in Dasgupta (1988).

the phenomena of moral hazard and adverse selection—both of which are an outcome of asymmetric information among people—can be a cause of massive failure in the market for risk, the failure being judged in the sense of *ex ante* Pareto efficiency.[21] The welfarist's advocacy of compulsory health insurance and entry restrictions into the field of medical practice is ultimately based on this failure.

7. Summary So Far

I have argued that unbridled and unassisted markets as a mechanism for the production and allocation of 'private' commodities have been advocated both on welfarist grounds (the Pareto efficiency of competitive market allocations) and on grounds of the primacy of rights to negative freedom (Sections 2 and 5). We have also seen that welfarists who are concerned with the *distribution* of individual welfare have often appealed to the Second Fundamental Theorem for a justification of a mechanism consisting of market transactions preceded by appropriate State-organized asset redistribution. Such State interference is, to be sure, otiose to those rights-based theories which concentrate exclusively on negative freedom— theories such as Nozick's. What both such philosophical positions would have in common, though, is an advocacy of private markets for mediating production and exchange.[22] But we also noted that the conditions under which the Second Fundamental Theorem holds are ones in which a welfarist may as well recommend the use of central quantitative planning. As *instruments* for attaining desired allocations of welfare, there is not much to choose between the two modes—provided one is a welfarist of course. Once the conditions postulated by the Second Fundamental Theorem are relaxed, however, rationales—more accurately, justifica- tions—for certain patterns of non-market resource allocation mechanisms begin to rear their head for the welfarist. We have seen, in the previous section, how uncertainty about future possibilities introduces a serious

---

[21] A problem of *moral hazard* is said to arise for a potential transaction between two parties when one of the parties cannot monitor the other's *actions* pertinent to the trans- action in question (for example, fire-prevention care taken by the insured). A problem of *adverse selection* is said to arise for a potential transaction between two parties when one of the parties does not know the *characteristics* of the other party which are pertinent to the transaction in question (for example, whether the second-hand car dealer is honest). Each of these problems has been greatly studied in recent years in the economics literature. In Section 8, I will analyse a problem of adverse selection which Welfare States inevitably face.

[22] In order to make the point in a sharp form, I am ignoring the production of public goods and the existence of large-scale economies in production. Welfarism and rights- based theories concentrating on negative freedom would display different attitudes to allocation problems in the presence of these.

ambiguity in the meaning of welfarism and that the Second Fundamental Theorem bears on the *ex ante* version. But of far greater importance is the contingent fact that people not only face uncertainty, they *know* different things and thus are uncertain *about* different things. This makes information a tradable commodity. We noted that there are intrinsic grounds for serious failure in markets for risk, and by implication markets for information, and that this on its own provides welfarism with a justification for recommending certain non-market channels for the allocation of such commodities as insurance, health care, and basic food and shelter, where the consequences under certain events, possibly low probability events, are shattering in terms of personal welfare.

It is *possible* for rights-based theories to be supremely unconcerned with such arguments. But, as we noted in Section 2, it is possible to be unconcerned only if primacy is awarded to the right to negative freedom, for State interference on matters of resource allocation are a form of coercion for at least some members of the population.

Negative freedom, however, is but one kind of freedom. Of seemingly no less urgency is another kind, positive freedom, the protection and promotion of which requires each individual in society to have access to and command over appropriate amounts of certain commodities, on occasion called 'natural rights goods', such as basic food, shelter, and medical care. Active State interference designed to guarantee individual access to such goods is, it would thus seem, perfectly consonant with rights-based theories, provided positive freedom is given due weight.

On the face of it, then, moral theories based on welfarism and positive freedom would have a great deal in common. Economists often seem to appeal to them interchangeably, not necessarily because they are moral pluralists—although they may also be that—but because on the face of it, the two doctrines appear not to have different *practical policy* implications. For example, a streamlined Welfare State is justifiable by an appeal to either doctrine.

8. Positive-Rights Goods in Coupons and Kind

In fact, there are important differences in their practical implications. I want to argue that among other things, a concern with positive freedom would have us, in a wide range of circumstances, advocate State guarantees of positive-rights goods *in kind*, whereas welfarism would typically advocate guarantees *in coupons*, with the resulting option of exchanging away the rights to these goods.

Earlier we noted that, among other things, positive freedom is concerned with the *ability* of a person to *function* and that it values a person's access to and command over certain specific commodities solely because they are a *means* to this ability. Rights to such commodities, therefore, turn out on inspection to be *derived rights*. But people differ, and in particular their *needs*—in the sense of enabling them to function—for these commodities vary: over time (as a person ages), across regions (because, say, of climatic differences), and by virtue of differences in their physiological characteristics. It follows that their (derived) rights to these commodities vary.[23] A positive-rights doctrine—that is, a doctrine which emphasizes the right to positive freedom—would, therefore, regard the just distribution of these 'positive rights' goods as being determined by needs. People's *preferences* for these goods relative to other goods would count for less.[24]

If all persons had equal income and identical welfare functions, the just distribution of such positive-rights commodities would have people in greater need receiving more of them. This would follow from both equity-conscious welfarism and positive-rights doctrine. In such circumstances, there is nothing to distinguish the two.

But income is not distributed equally. Moreover, as a matter of incontrovertible fact, the State always has incomplete information both about individual needs and about individual incomes. Suppose, for simplicity, that there is a given amount of a positive-rights commodity. What mechanism should we recommend for its allocation?

To make the point in a sharp way, suppose we appeal to the right to positive freedom; that is, that distribution ought to be according to needs, persons needing more having access to a greater amount. Suppose then that the State does not know who has what needs nor indeed who has what income, but has statistical information about both, and for simplicity of exposition I assume, not entirely unrealistically, that needs and incomes are uncorrelated. There are two allocation mechanisms which form the twin pillars of the debate under review: the price system and rations. I discuss them below.

To have a precise, but simple, problem I want to suppose that the State has control over the commodity in question. Under the rationing mechanism, the State distributes the commodity *in kind* and prohibits resale within the population. Under the price system, the State issues individuals with exchangeable coupons so as to enable people to purchase

[23] I should emphasize that the variability in needs that I am talking of here is a variability in functional needs, not a variability in individual *welfare* functions.

[24] To be sure, needs will typically be reflected in individual demand functions and I will, of course, assume this. But I will interpret demand functions broadly here by assuming that they are generated both by needs and by the person's sense of his own ability or welfare.

the commodity. Being wedded to positive freedom, the State desires to minimize the mean-square deviation of the realized distribution of this commodity from its *just* distribution.

Notice that in this example, the State faces a problem in adverse selection (footnote 21). Each person is assumed to know his own income and his needs, the State only has statistical information about these. If the State knew each person's needs, it could implement the just distribution of the positive-rights good, by simply giving each person his rightful amount and forbidding any further exchange. Alternatively it could, by relying on the Second Fundamental Theorem, implement the just distribution by lump-sum transfers followed by reliance on markets. So it might seem that the State could simply ask people to give it the needed information. But there are strong incentives for non-truthful disclosure. Since the State has announced its intention of distributing the commodity according to needs, everyone will have a strong urge to claim great needs! For this reason, the State has to resort to 'sub-optimal' allocation mechanisms and we consider below two of them: distribution in coupons and kind.

Since the State by assumption is uncertain of each person's needs and income, the best rationed allocation under this ignorance is *equal* allocation.[25] It is also simple to check that under such incomplete information, the best market mechanism would be one where the State issued an equal number of convertible coupons to each citizen.

It is clear that the distributions which would result from these two allocation mechanisms differ. (They would be the same only if persons are identical in their needs and have the same income.) This much is obvious. What is not obvious is which mechanism comes closer to the just distribution of this positive-rights commodity. In an important and interesting note, Weitzman (1977) showed, in the context of a simple example, that rationing is the better mechanism if the dispersion in income is large in comparison with the dispersion in needs across the population, and that the price mechanism is superior if the reverse is the case. The point is that if income variability is small, the price mechanism is better because people with greater needs will end up consuming more of it because their incomes are about the same as those with lesser needs, and this is precisely what positive-rights demands. But if income variability is large, this is no longer so, for people with high needs and low income will end up consuming less than people with low needs and high income. It is this possibility which the rationing mechanism prevents.

It is not *always* that aggregate welfare (say, total welfare, if one is a

[25] The implicit assumption I am making here, that all persons, both in terms of their needs and their income, are being sampled from the same underlying population, is, of course, not at all realistic, but nothing hinges on this.

Utilitarian) is greater when the government resorts to coupons in distributing a commodity, even though under the price system each person, having
been awarded an equal number of transferable coupons, has the *option* of
consuming as much of the commodity in question as he consumes under
rationing. This is because the relative prices of various goods, when the
positive-rights commodity is exchangeable, are different from what they
are when the commodity is not exchangeable. Indeed, some people may
well be worse off in terms of welfare under the coupon system. However,
the important special case I am considering here is one where it is a reasonable approximation that the relative prices of all other commodities and
services are the same under the *coupon* and *kind* allocation mechanisms
for the positive-rights good. In this case, welfarism recommends allocations via exchangeable coupons over the allocation in kind, for everyone is
better off under the coupon system. Furthermore, given that it is *fait
accompli* that the State has assumed control over the positive-rights good
in question, so do moral theories based on negative freedom. What the
example I have been discussing in this section illustrates is that if income
variability is large, positive-rights recommends measures that are at
variance with both such moral doctrines and stands apart in insisting on
the non-exchangeability of the rights to the good.

Paradoxically then, the conceptual problem for positive-rights doctrines
arises not when income variability within the population is large, but when
it is small. We have seen that when it is large, rationing is the favoured
mechanism. People are in this case forbidden to trade these rations, to buy
and sell their rights. Here, positive-rights doctrines are at one with
negative-rights doctrines in other spheres. We are all equal before the law
and, in political democracies, we each have one vote. And we are
forbidden to exchange these rights for other goods. So too with rationing
of positive-rights goods. Thus far the matter is clear enough. The paradox
that arises is when income variability is small relative to the variability in
needs. Here it is the dictates of positive-rights which require that people be
allowed to exchange their rights to the commodity. Of course, the reasoning here is straightforward. Since needs vary, the ideal distribution is *not*
an equal distribution. Incomplete information on the part of the government provides the State with the reason for allowing the market to perform
the allocation according to needs. It can do that effectively only when
income distribution is fairly equal.[26]

---

[26] Allocation in kind can, of course, be strongly justified as a means of protecting the
rights of children (free school meals as a means of ensuring that children have at least one
good meal). The fact that child allowances in the UK are paid to mothers and not to fathers
is a reflection of this justification. I am grateful to Carol Dasgupta for drawing my attention
to this fact and its rationale, many years ago.

Adherence to positive-rights when considering the production and distribution of certain basic private goods like nutrition, shelter, medical care, and so forth, in a world with large income dispersion, provides a clear argument for allocation in kind. It is allocation in coupons which requires justification. If we have for many years thought otherwise, it is because we have ignored positive freedom, and thus positive-rights, in our moral thinking.

6

Hayek on the Market Economy and the Limits of State Action

JOHN GRAY*

1. Introduction

In the work of F. A. Hayek we find the most systematic and comprehensive twentieth-century statement of the classical liberal conception of the role and limits of the State. As a classical liberal conception, Hayek's account of the State and its relations with the market economy is to be contrasted, not only with social-democratic and liberal-interventionist perspectives, but also with conservative doctrines of the functions of the State. For Hayek, as for Kant, Adam Smith, and others in the classical liberal intellectual tradition, the functions of the State are strictly limited. They do not include the promotion of any specific moral ideal or the preservation of a particular culture (as they do for conservatives[1]) any more than they comprehend the socialist imposition on society of a preferred pattern of distribution of income or wealth. The chief task of the State is the protection and enhancement of individual freedom. It is because he believes that the market economy is an indispensable condition of individual freedom that Hayek, along with other contemporary classical liberals, sees the principal economic functions of the State as having to do with the maintenance and improvement of the institutions which sustain market processes. Hayek's life-work has been the project of renewing the foundations and repairing the ramifications of this classical liberal conception of the State.

Hayek's conception of the liberal State and his defence of the role within it of an unhampered market economy have several distinctive features, often neglected by his critics, which distinguish them from other similar contributions to classical liberal traditions. In the first place, Hayek's case for the market is one which rests upon the inevitable imperfections of market processes and not upon the barely coherent fiction of perfect competition. It is an argument which focuses on the epistemic functions of the market as an institution for the generation and transmission of information

---

* Fellow of Jesus College, Oxford.
[1] For Hayek's rejection of conservatism, see his 'Why I am not a conservative' in Hayek (1960).

that would not otherwise be available to economic actors. Hayek's model of the market is not that of a mechanism for the allocation of scarce resources to known and competing ends, but instead that of a discovery procedure for the disclosure and co-ordination of preferences. The defence of the market is not, for Hayek, ultimately in terms of its efficiency in generating wealth, but rather in terms of its superiority over available alternatives as a means of co-ordinating preferences non-coercively. It is an argument from liberty, and not primarily from welfare. Second, the conception of government which emerges from this argument is not that of the minimum State. Hayek explicitly rejects the view, defended by such *laissez-faire* liberals as Wilhelm von Humboldt, Herbert Spencer, and Robert Nozick, that the tasks of the State are restricted to the prevention of force and fraud, the protection of property rights and the enforcement of contracts, and the provision of criminal justice and national defence. Along with Adam Smith and the great majority of the classical liberal economists, Hayek argues that the State has positive or service functions which include the supply of some public goods, the provision of a minimum level of security against severe deprivation, and the adoption of measures for the improvement of market competition. If it is not a minimum State, however, Hayek's conception is that of strictly limited government—a conception of *Rechstaat* or government by rules which excludes the kind of interventionist policies which dominated the western world in the three decades after the Second World War.

One of my goals in this paper is to elucidate the distinctive features of Hayek's defence of limited government and the market economy and to respond to criticisms of Hayek's conception which depend upon mis-interpretations of his views. At the same time, I aim to assess critically Hayek's argument and to illuminate some of its weaknesses and limitations. In particular, I shall contend that Hayek's case against State interven-tion in the economy is incomplete in so far as it fails to exploit the insights of the Virginia School of Public Choice into the structure and mechanisms of government failure. Further, I shall submit that Hayek's rejection of social justice (despite its power as a critique of many fashionable distribu-tivist conceptions) neglects the importance of the initial distribution of capital endowments, in the context of a full normative defence of the market. Most particularly, I shall contend, Hayek's case for the market, though it occasionally develops intimations to this effect, fails to identify market institutions as the primary means to the promotion of positive freedom in advanced industrial societies. My claim will be that, once these weaknesses or limitations of Hayek's account are acknowledged and corrected, a defence of limited government and the market economy can be developed which preserves the central insights of the Hayekian perspective and is resistant to the standard criticisms of socialists and interventionist liberals.

2. Imperfect Competition and the Epistemic Functions of Markets

By contrast with neo-classical economic theory in its normative aspects, Hayek does not base the case for the market on any conception of general equilibrium. Indeed, in all his major essays in defence of the market of the 1930s and 1940s, Hayek is explicit, not only that the case for the market does not depend on its approximation to a condition of perfect competition, but that such a state of affairs is hardly conceivable, let alone achievable in the real world. In his earliest writings in economic theory, Hayek had adopted a version of the Walrasian general equilibrium conception, but by the time he addressed himself to questions of socialist calculation and the role of knowledge in economic processes, he had definitely become a theorist of imperfect competition. (The gradual and partial character of Hayek's adoption of a disequilibrium model of market processes creates problems for his explanation of macro-economic discoordination which I shall discuss briefly below.) Crucial to Hayek's later theorizing is the insight that, whereas it may be approximated in a few specialized markets, perfect competition cannot be realized across the economy as a whole because it presupposes uniformity of product, zero transaction costs, and, above all, that firms are in possession of perfect information. None of these conditions exists, or can ever exist, in any real-world economy. In the real world, most products are highly differentiated, search and transaction costs are unavoidable, and knowledge is fragmented among a myriad of actors. This is especially but not exclusively clear in the instance of the provision of services. As Hayek (1948, pp. 96–7) has observed:

Especially remarkable . . . is the explicit and complete exclusion from the theory of perfect competition of all personal relationships existing between the parties. In actual life the fact that our inadequate knowledge of the available commodities or services is made up for by our experience with the persons or firms supplying them—that competition is in a large measure competition for reputation or goodwill—is one of the most important facts which enables us to solve our daily problems. The function of competition is here precisely to teach us *who* will serve us well; which grocer or travel agency, which department store or hotel, which doctor or solicitor . . . The reasons competition in this field is described as imperfect have indeed nothing to do with the competitive character of the activities of these people; it lies in the nature of the commodities or services themselves.

Even outside of the provision of services, perfect competition theory neglects the heterogeneity of goods and the fact that the knowledge which each producer has of the market for his goods is local, partial, and fallible. Many of the activities engaged upon in competitive markets are explicable only by reference to these very factors of imperfect knowledge and information—so that, as Hayek (1948, p. 96) tersely puts it, '"perfect" competition means indeed the absence of all competitive activities'.

In his most pragmatic statement on these questions, Hayek (1948, p. 104) remarks that 'The argument in favour of competition does not rest on the conditions that would exist if it were perfect'. On what, then, does it rest?

The argument for market competition depends primarily on the thesis that market institutions can, better than any other, utilize the knowledge that is dispersed throughout society. Such knowledge cannot successfully be gathered, collected, or put to use by any central authority for several reasons. It is, in the first place, knowledge of circumstances that are often transitory and ephemeral, and so it becomes quickly dated. Knowledge of price relativities and of entrepreneurial opportunities often comes in to this category. Such information, even if it could be centralized by a public authority, would have lost much of its practical value by the time it had been collected. But second, the knowledge that the market makes available is often local and tacit knowledge—knowledge, that is to say, of local conditions which is stored or embodied in practices, skills, dispositions, and traditions rather than expressed in theories or propositions. Practical knowledge of this kind[2] typically can be only partially articulated or theorized about, and there are, for this reason, insuperable limitations on its being made publicly accessible in any propositional form. Market institutions, by contrast with central planning institutions, allow such practical knowledge to be expressed in action and use—in the preferences and decisions of economic agents. There is a third and final point to be made about the uses made of decentralized knowledge by market institutions. Inasmuch as they yield products and opportunities that would not otherwise exist, market institutions serve to generate knowledge about preferences that would not otherwise exist either. By opening up in an unplanned way an array of goods and services which consumers had not hitherto envisaged, market institutions act as a discovery procedure for preferences which they themselves help to evoke. It is not only that market institutions put to use dispersed knowledge or information that could not be as well exploited by any other institution, but also that they generate information about preferences which would not otherwise exist.

Hayek's conception of the market, then, may be characterized as that of an epistemic machine—an institutional device for the transmission of fragmented social knowledge in a form which makes it generally accessible

[2] For the idea of tacit or practical knowledge, see Polanyi (1951).

and usable. The role of market pricing, in this conception, is as much a signalling device for the expression of dispersed social knowledge as it is a mechanism for reporting resource scarcities. The economic problem to which market institutions are the most adequate institutional solution, in Hayek's conception, is indeed the problem of economizing on ineradicably scarce knowledge, rather than that of allocating known resources to known but competing ends. Hayek's case for the market is not understood until it is acknowledged that in the real world—as distinct from the circumstance modelled in neo-classical economic theory—neither available resources nor human preferences can be known to any single agent. In so far as we have any knowledge of resources and preferences, it is that mediated to us via the institutions of the market itself.

In its original formulation, Hayek's defence of the market was developed as a critique of various socialist schemes of central economic planning (and, in particular, of the Lange–Lerner scheme of market-simulating socialism[3]). It was in this formulation that Hayek's argument (building on the related, but in important ways distinct, arguments of Mises) achieved a decisive intellectual victory over his socialist opponents. In his later works, however, Hayek seeks to generalize his argument against the possibilities of socialist calculation—the argument, that is to say, against the feasibility of central economic planning—into an argument against government intervention in the economy of the sort practised by post-war governments throughout the western world. It is here that the ground of Hayek's argument shifts and becomes less clear. It is not, indeed, contrary to a conventional view, expressed by Sen[4] among many others, that Hayek rests his case against such governmental intervention primarily on the claim that it has unintended consequences, since it is obvious enough that any policy, be it one of intervention or of non-interference, will have unintended, unpredicted, and unpredictable consequences— some of them desirable and some of them not. It is an error in the interpretation of Hayek to suppose that his argument against government intervention rests primarily on such a truism. Rather, his argument is that *government intervention in the economy generates failures in market co-ordination which would not otherwise occur*. In part, of course, this is a central element in Hayek's argument with Keynes—that Keynes had in general misdiagnosed the sources of market discoordination in failures of macro-economic policy, whereas its real causes lay typically in discoordinations in relative prices (including, crucially, discoordinations in

[3] For Hayek's critique of the Lange–Lerner model of 'competitive socialism', see Hayek (1948, chs. VII–IX).

[4] For Sen's view, see Sen (1983a). For a powerful critique of Sen's view, see Barry (1985).

the price of labour). This insistence on a micro-economic explanation of macro-economic discoordination has been a consistent theme in Hayek's thought over sixty years, and serves to distinguish his theoretical perspective as sharply from that of Friedman as from that of Keynes. It is not, to be sure, that Hayek denies all relevance to macro-economic causes in explaining the mass unemployment of the 1930s, since, with Friedman, he attributes decisive importance to errors in monetary policy in the United States.[5] This is, in fact, entirely compatible with his general view, most clearly and sharply stated in recent writings, that government policy enters the economy chiefly as an exogenous disturbance and does not typically assist a return to co-ordination. As he has recently put it (Hayek, 1978, p. 98),

... monetary policy is much more likely to be a cause than a cure of depressions, because it is much easier, by giving in to the clamour for cheap money, to cause those misdirections in production that make a later reaction inevitable, than to assist the economy in extricating itself from the consequences of over-developing in particular directions. The past instability of the market economy is the consequence of the exclusion of the most important regulator of the market mechanism, money, from itself being regulated by the market process.

This last statement of Hayek's condenses a complex argument about the effects of macro-economic policy on market co-ordination. In one of its aspects, Hayek's argument is the argument he advanced against Keynes, when he maintained that, since market discoordination consists typically in a micro-economic discoordination of relative prices, it will not usually be corrigible by changes in macro-economic policy. Elsewhere in his works, Hayek has maintained that government interventionism of the Keynesian type is likely in the long run to be self-limiting and indeed self-defeating, since its success depends upon beliefs and attitudes, such as money illusion, which its operation over a generation or so is likely to erode. In its most general form, however, Hayek's claim is that government intervention in the economy generates signals or noise, which make the task of economic agents in selecting lines of production for which there is a real demand harder rather than easier. This is to say, simply put, that government intervention characteristically introduces further uncertainty and disturbance in an already discoordinated economy.

There is, in addition, a further vital element in Hayek's analysis of government failure in the context of macro-economic policy, which he rarely makes fully explicit, but which is essential to his case against

[5] As Hayek (1978, p. 97, footnote 2) puts it, 'The long depression of the 1930s . . . was wholly due to the mismanagement of money by government before as well as after the crisis of 1929'.

intervention. It is that the incentive structure of modern political institutions makes errors in policy prohibitively difficult to correct and, for that
matter, embodies a mechanism in which erroneous policies are likely to be
preserved. In unhampered markets, there is a quasi-automatic error-
elimination process whereby maladaptive firms and practices are likely to
be filtered out. This is the basis of the analogy, much explored in recent
theorizing,[6] between market competition and evolutionary selection. That
this analogy is manifestly imperfect does not deprive it of value, since
Hayek's chief point is that in government institutions the selection
mechanisms that exist are ones which are likely to stabilize and entrench
harmful and failed practices. When we ask what these mechanisms are, on
the other hand, we find no systematic answer in Hayek's writings, but
must turn instead to the theorizers of the Virginia School of Public Choice.
Here, and pre-eminently in the work of James Buchanan,[7] we find a
theoretical perspective which goes far to explain the otherwise remarkable
fact that many interventionist policies remain in force even when the
theoretical case for them has been abandoned by everyone. The explanation for the persistence of rent control, when its theoretical basis has been
undermined by economists of virtually every persuasion, is in the fact that
the groups that would be hurt by its abolition are small, concentrated, and
so politically effective, whereas the much larger group which would benefit
is diffused, unorganized, and so politically impotent. There is an inherent
likelihood, for this reason, that any form of government intervention
which benefits particularly those groups that are concentrated, easily
organizable, and whose common interests are readily identifiable will
prove politically prohibitively costly to abandon, even when its adverse
effects on the economy as a whole (and thereby on the public interest) are
manifest to all. This is, however, only one instance of the perverse effects of
the political incentive structure on policy. As the mechanisms of this
selection process have been analysed by Buchanan, Olson (1965), and
others, they reveal a structure in which collusive groups will typically be
able to rig policies in their favour and inhibit changes in policy which injure
their perceived interests. Government failures, unlike all but the worst
market failures, are likely to become unalterable features of the landscape
once they occur. Only catastrophic changes in the entire system, such as
those that occur as a result of defeat in war, appear able to dislocate the
political leverage of such collusive groups on public policy.

In its most explicit sections, Hayek's argument against government
intervention in the market is one that relies very heavily on epistemic
considerations. As such, it may be a powerful argument in so far as it

---

[6] See, for example, Nelson and Winter (1982).
[7] See, most particularly, Buchanan (1975).

establishes that large-scale government intervention in the market demands knowledge of price relativities that are known and knowable by no one agency. It is powerful, also, in illuminating the neglected fact that interventionist policies often serve to confuse and disorient economic agents by producing signals which direct activity further into areas in which it is not sustainable in terms of the real economy. Powerful as they are, these arguments of an epistemic sort are not sufficient to yield a conclusive case against interventionism. For they neglect the possibility of a macro-economic discoordination that is endogenously caused and which (at least in some historical circumstances) can arguably best be overcome by government action. As far as Hayek's argument goes, it suggests only considerations against intervention, which would need to be weighed case by case. In particular, it would seem to have little force against the sort of endogenous discoordination theorized by Hayek's great and neglected pupil, Shackle,[8] in his brilliant generalizations of some of Keynes's deepest insights. The possibility of such a crisis in the market process cannot, after all, be excluded altogether by Hayek, if he follows Shackle in abandoning Walrasian general equilibrium for a conception of markets as being constantly in dynamic disequilibrium. At the same time, Hayek never confronts directly the possibility of a crisis of this sort, principally because he fails to follow to the end the implications of the disequilibrium model. He thereby generates a fundamental question for his theory: if large-scale discoordination can be produced by factors internal to the market process itself, how can there be any demonstrative argument against government intervention?

We move close to such an argument, I believe, when Hayek's epistemic arguments are supplemented by arguments to do with the incentive structure of modern political and governmental institutions of the sort theorized systematically in the Virginia School. The upshot of these latter arguments is that, except in rare circumstances where policy is made (as perhaps it was by Keynes) by a disinterested and politically invulnerable élite, a case-by-case approach to government intervention in the market will produce an ever larger number of policies which, once instituted, cannot be abandoned for political reasons, and which over the longer term are manifestly damaging to market co-ordination. It is this perspective on the reality of political life in the modern State which is typically neglected by those who favour a piecemeal evaluation of interventionist proposals. They neglect the conservative tendency of political élites and government bureaucracies when confronted by well-organized, collusive interest groups and the inherent tendency of interventionist policy to conceal its mistakes. Most specifically, they neglect the fact that the control of the

[8] See Shackle (1972), his master-work.

information available to government is itself characteristically in the hands of such groups, who lack any incentive to transmit information injurious to their interests. It is these considerations which support Hayek's argument for a general (if not a universal) prohibition on intervention by government in the market economy, where his epistemic arguments, taken by themselves, do not. What kind of political order, however, would be necessary in Hayek's view for the implementation of such a ban? How is Hayek's conception of a non-interventionist order related to others in the classical liberal tradition, and how satisfactory is it?

3. The Principles of a Liberal Social Order: Hayek's Constitution of Liberty

At one extreme of the liberal intellectual tradition stand the defenders of *laissez-faire*. These doctrinaire liberals—Bastiat, Spencer, and Nozick, for example—hold that the just functions of the State are exhausted by the provision of national defence and of those services necessary for the maintenance of civil and criminal justice. This minimum-Statist or, as it is sometimes called, *minarchist* position is one that Hayek has always rejected. As he puts his position in his master-work (1960, p. 231):

The range of variety of government action that is, at least in principle, reconcilable with a free system is thus considerable. The old formulae of laisser-faire or non-intervention do not provide us with an adequate criterion for distinguishing between what is and what is not admissible in a free system. There is ample scope for experimentation and improvement within that permanent legal framework which makes it possible for a free society to operate most efficiently.

Elsewhere (Hayek, 1948, p. 110), he has gone so far as to remark that

it would not be altogether untrue to say that the interpretation of the fundamental principle of liberalism as absence of state activity rather than as a policy which deliberately adopts competition, the market and prices as its ordering principle and uses the legal framework enforced by the state in order to make competition as effective and beneficial as possible—and to supplement it where, and only where, it cannot be made effective—is as much responsible for the decline of competition as the active support which governments have given directly and indirectly to the growth of monopoly. It is the first general thesis which we shall have to consider that competition can be made more effective and more beneficent by certain activities of government than it would be without them . . . Where the traditional discussion becomes so unsatisfactory is where it is suggested that, with the recognition of the principles of private property and freedom of contract, which indeed every liberal must recognise, all the issues were settled, as if the law of property and contract were given once and for all in its final and most appropriate form . . .

Hayek's conception of the proper role of government, then, is far removed from the libertarian ideal, found in Nozick and even in Friedman, of the minimum State. It has much in common with, and indeed stands in the tradition of, the liberal-conservatism of such thinkers as Tocqueville, Constant, and de Jouvenel—all of whom acknowledged the necessity and desirability of governmental action for the promotion of individual liberty and market competition. But what, then, in Hayek's view, are the proper economic functions of the State?

We can begin to answer this question by noting, as a fundamental feature of Hayek's political philosophy, the absence of any theory of natural property rights. Following Hume rather than Locke, Hayek treats property rights as artefacts, conventions necessary both for economic welfare and personal independence, rather than as eternal verities given us by natural law. Accordingly, the detailed content of our system of property rights is never immune from emendation or revision and is, in fact, permanently open to reform. One of the chief economic tasks of the State is, for this reason, to subject the received inheritance of property rights to a critical revision so as to make sure they conform to the requirements of a competitive system. It is in this connection that Hayek has argued for reform of the law of patents, corporations, and trade unions, for example.[9] His argument is that the existing legal framework has diminished market competition and promoted monopoly—by granting legal immunity to trade unions and by imposing a tax regime which favours established producers. It is in such perverse legal policies, and not in any inherent logic of the market, that the tendency to market concentration is explained, and the task of government is accordingly that of reshaping the legal environment so that it positively favours market competition. The role of the State is not here passive or conservative, but instead active and reformist, in seeing to it that the detailed content of property rights coheres well with the necessities of free competition.

Because Hayek's political thought does not repose (as does Nozick's, for example) on any conception of natural or fundamental rights, his account of the just limits of State activity is not framed in terms of respect for rights, but rather in terms of procedural justice. Hayek's thought is that justice is done when government follows first procedures, chief among which are the provisions of the rule of law. Now Hayek's account of the rule of law is complex, disputable, and in parts certainly indefensible,[10] but it is not my purpose here to assess it. I wish to remark only that Hayek's conception of political justice, and thus of the tasks of the State, whereas it is Humean in

---

[9] See Hayek (1948, pp. 113–14, 116) and Hayek (1960, ch. 18).
[10] I have myself discussed critically Hayek's account of the rule of law in Gray (1984a, ch. 3).

its acknowledgement of the conventional character of property rights, is Kantian in that it sees State coercion as justified chiefly by a consequent diminution of coercion in society and a corresponding enlargement of liberty. Hayek is explicit that it is, in general, only the defeat of private coercion that warrants coercion by the State.[11] At the same time, he is no less clear that government has many functions, above and beyond the Kantian one of defeating coercion, which are of a service variety and which involve the provision of goods which would not be provided in the market. By contrast with all doctrines of minimum government, Hayek's contention is that government may supply any good or service desired by a democratic electorate, *provided that its doing so involves no coercion beyond that entailed in its being funded from taxation*. As he puts it programmatically (1960, p. 223):

Though government must not use its power of coercion to reserve for itself activities which have nothing to do with the enforcement of the general rules of law, there is no violation of principle in its engaging in all sorts of activities on the same terms as its citizens. If in the majority of fields there is no good reason why it should do so, there are fields in which the desirability of government action can hardly be questioned ... Included (among these) ... are the activities which Adam Smith described as 'those public works, which, though they may be in the highest degree advantageous to a great society are, however, of such a nature, that the profit could never repay the expense to any individual or small number of individuals.'

Hayek here affirms that, in addition to initiating legal reform where this is required by the conditions of market competition, the State may provide those public goods which, in virtue of the Smithian free-rider problem, would not be supplied by markets or voluntary agencies. Hayek is not specific about whether these public goods would have to satisfy technical criteria of joint provision and non-excludability, but it is apparent from his discussion of detailed cases—in which he allows that the provision of parks and subsidies to the arts and sciences may be allowable within a liberal State[12]—that he does not intend the publicness of public goods to be construed too strictly. Indeed, always providing that the coercion involved in any such measure does not exceed that required for its public funding, Hayek insists that such policies as the provision outside of the market economy of a safety net to stave off hardship for those without marketable skills, together with the provision of educational opportunities for the

---

[11] See Hayek (1960, p. 144): 'freedom demands no more than that coercion and violence ... be prevented ... The problem of the limit of coercion is not the same as that concerning the proper function of government. The coercive activities of government are by no means its only tasks'.

[12] Hayek (1960, pp. 223, 377 *et seq.*).

poor, may be indispensable rather than merely desirable conditions of a flourishing market economy.[13]

In Hayek's conception, then, much is allowed by way of service functions to the liberal State. Having gone so far, we may ask, how does Hayek avoid himself travelling down that road to serfdom which he had described in his most controversial book? How, in general, is State activity to be contained, if so much of it is allowable in a liberal order? Here it must be pointed out that when, in his *Road to Serfdom*, Hayek argued that economic planning and individual liberty were ultimately irreconcilable, the economic planning to which he referred was that envisaged at the time, encompassing measures such as price controls and direction of labour. History has not corroborated Hayek's argument, since even very extensive State intervention in the economy has nowhere resulted in the extinction of basic personal and political liberties.[14] Nevertheless, the interventions condemned by Hayek as leading down the road to serfdom are clearly distinct from the extensions of State activity beyond the individualist minimum sanctioned in *The Constitution of Liberty* and elsewhere in his writings. The latter form a distinct class of governmental activities inasmuch as none of them involves the kind of coercion necessarily entailed by wartime measures whose transference to peacetime economic management Hayek opposed.

All these points having been taken, there remains a clear need for the kinds of State service activities allowable in Hayek's conception to be subject to some sort of rational discipline. It is a need of which Hayek (1960, p. 224) is acutely conscious:

There is considerable justification for the distrust with which business looks on all state enterprise. There is great difficulty in ensuring that such enterprise will be conducted on the same terms as private enterprise; and it is only if this condition is satisfied that it is not objectionable in principle. So long as government uses any of its coercive powers, and particularly its power of taxation, in order to assist its enterprises, it can always turn their position into one of actual monopoly. To prevent this it would be necessary that any special advantages, including subsidies, which government gives to its own enterprises in any field should also be made available to competing private agencies. There is no need to emphasize that it would be exceedingly difficult for government to satisfy these conditions and that the general presumption against state enterprise is thereby considerably strengthened.

Here Hayek adduces an argument for the privatization of many, perhaps most, services currently supplied by interventionist governments, always provided that such privatization encompassed a genuine return of the

---

[13] Hayek (1960, chs. 17 and 19).
[14] I have criticized Hayek's 'road-to-serfdom' thesis in Gray (1984b, ch. 2).

industries concerned to the market (and not merely the creation of private monopolies, as in the present British case). In the most general terms, Hayek gives in this passage his overall remedy for excessive State activity in the limited State he favours. It is that the activities of the liberal State be regulated, so far as is practically possible, *by strict rule rather than by discretionary authority*. This is the rationale behind Hayek's support for the regime of fixed exchange rates in the aftermath of the gold standard. Hayek's opposition to the Friedmanite proposal for floating exchange rates expresses his conviction that, because of insoluble problems in the measurement of monetary aggregates, no fixed rule for monetary growth can be formulated or adhered to in practice. In the real world, floating exchange rates will always be 'dirty', involving a mixture of market forces with political expediency, bureaucratic mismanagement, and monetary nationalism.[15] (It may be worth noting in passing that Hayek's support for currency competition and free banking expresses his growing conviction that a regime of strict rules cannot of itself contain the growth of the modern State, which must itself be disciplined in its activities by market competition. Similarly, Hayek has seen the possibility of migration as a practical limit on governmental expansion, particularly in respect of local government.[16] His view now appears to be that a regime of rules is a necessary, but not a sufficient, condition of the containment of State power.) It is the avoidance of arbitrariness that forms the rationale for Hayek's proposal that the system of taxation as a whole be proportional, rather than progressive, in incidence and should conform to a fixed rule limiting the maximum rate of direct taxation to the total burden of taxation. 'The most reasonable rule of this kind', he avers, 'would seem to be one that fixed the maximum admissible (marginal) rate of direct taxation at that percentage of the total rational income which the government takes in taxation.'[17] Hayek's argument for proportionality in taxation is that, in the absence of any rational principles for the determination of the rate and incidence of progressive taxation, such taxation cannot be other than arbitrary (and will, in practice, entrench the interests of dominant electoral coalitions). By contrast, the virtue of proportional taxation is that it can be designed in accordance with strict rules, and so avoid arbitrariness.

On both the expenditure and the revenue side, then, Hayek's ideal is that of a *Rechstaat*, or government by rules, in which the State's activities would be regulated by strict principles. There would, in this conception, be

[15] See on this Hayek (1978, ch. XX).

[16] For Hayek on the role of migration in protecting liberty and promoting efficiency in local government, see Hayek (1982, vol. 3, p. 146).

[17] Hayek (1960, p. 323). For an alternative view, see Kay (this volume).

a considerable margin of freedom for liberal governments of a democratic constitution. Even though taxation could not be substantially progressive, the system of benefits might nevertheless be highly redistributive from the majority to the poor—if the majority proved ready to will this outcome. What is precluded under a Hayekian regime of rules is not redistribution from the affluent majority to the disadvantaged minority, but rather that perverse redistribution from the margins to the middle which appears to be the norm in unlimited democracies.[18] Further, there is in the Hayekian constitution of liberty an explicit recognition of the necessity, under a regime of rules, of provision for emergency action by governments. It is compatible with Hayek's project of restraining governmental activity by strict rules that constitutional provisions be enacted which would allow for discretionary State action, not only in wartime, but also in some circumstances of massive economic disturbance.[19] In general, however, the project is that of confining discretionary State activity to the achievable minimum. The justification for such restraint is that only if government is subject to the discipline of strict rules does it become the guarantor, rather than the invader, of individual liberty. This is, indeed, Hayek's version of the liberal doctrine of non-interference. He recognizes (as the defenders of *laissez-faire* did not) that a normative criterion is needed to identify what constitutes 'interference' in the first place, and he proposes that those governmental rules and public policies which aim to protect or benefit identifiable sectional interests be characterized as constitution interference. Conversely, if they are general rules applicable equally to all, the laws of a liberal State will not constitute interference, but instead a constitution of liberty. Without such a regime of rules, according to Hayek, there can be neither individual liberty nor effective market competition.

4. Liberty, Justice, and the Agenda of a Liberal State

Having set out the main outlines of Hayek's conception of the scope and limits of State action, it may be possible to recapitulate his principal contentions so as to bring out the most distinctive features of his position. We began by noting that Hayek's defence of the market process has its inspiration in a theory of imperfect competition and not of general equilibrium. The role of the market is that of co-ordinating human activities by enabling dispersed information to be exploited without recourse to central planning. In fact, whereas the justification of the market

---

[18] On this, see Nozick (1974, pp. 274–5).
[19] See Hayek (1982, vol. 3, pp. 124–6).

economy for Hayek is in its consilience with individual freedom rather than as a mechanism for wealth-maximization, he argues that by economizing on imperfect information, the market can achieve a better allocation of resources to preferred uses than could any central planning mechanism. The positive functions of the State allowable in Hayek's conception concern partly the refinement of the institutions and legal arrangements which shape the market process, and partly the provision of goods and services which the market itself is unlikely to provide. In both of these last areas, however, the justification for a more extensive State activity is not any utilitarian conception of collective welfare. It is that such positive action enhances the prospects for market competition and so increases the opportunities for the citizens of a liberal polity, including its poorest members, to express their preferences by participation in market activity.

Whereas Hayek's defence of the market economy often comprehends claims about the beneficial consequences in terms of prosperity of reliance upon market institutions, these are justified in the end by their promotion of individual liberty. It is this which is their undergirding rationale and which gives to the liberal State its agenda of policy. One element of Hayek's defence of the market economy—not the most important or original, but consistently corroborated by historical experience—is his observation that we have no instance of political or personal liberties flourishing in the absence of economic liberty as embodied in extensive market institutions. Hayek's more fundamental defence of a regime of private property and free markets within the rule of law is in his claim that it is a necessary condition of an assured sphere of personal independence. Here we come upon a feature of his argument that is generally overlooked and which is insufficiently stressed by Hayek himself. For whereas, on the one hand, the private-property, free-market regime entrenches and protects the negative freedom from coercion which is a core value of classical liberalism, it also in Hayek's conception embodies the value of positive freedom as autonomy. Inasmuch as the private property regime equips individuals with resources with which to implement their plans of life and express their values without recourse to any procedure of collective choice, we may even say that (in Hayek's conception of it) private property embodies positive freedom in its most primordial form.[20] In his recognition of private property as a vehicle for the expression of positive freedom, Hayek stands in an authentically Kantian tradition in which private property is recognized as a guarantor of autonomy as much as a shield against coercion.

[20] I have argued this myself in Gray (1986, ch. 8).

It is not true of Hayek, even if it may be true of other thinkers in the classical liberal intellectual tradition, that the regime of private property and free markets under a limited government is defended primarily on grounds of negative liberty. For in Hayek, as in Kant himself,[21] freedom has two faces: it encompasses both protection against coercion and the possibility of self-determination. In Hayek, again as in Kant, the freedom of self-determination or autonomy is secured chiefly through the institution of private property. For it is by using one's own property according to one's own values and goals, without the necessity for consultation with one's neighbour, or any collective authority, that one can most nearly approximate the status of an autonomous agent. In this (often tacit or implicit) defence of the market economy for its contribution to positive freedom, Hayek expresses a deep insight that is neglected or misunderstood by most critics of classical liberalism. These critics take for granted that State action enhances positive freedom, whereas market processes facilitate freedom for coercion, but fail to argue for this view in any compelling way. In Hayek's conception, however, it is in a society such as ours, which comprehends a variety of incommensurable value-perspectives and a diversity of cultural traditions, that the institution of private property is most needed and best justified. By contrast with the unforeseen and unencumbered uses of private property, State action for the promotion of positive liberty or autonomy will often turn out to be paternalist or culturally imperialist in effect, involving an imposition of the values of ruling élites or majorities on the rest. For this reason, the regime of private property and free markets is to be defended as the best embodiment of positive freedom in a context of value-pluralism and cultural variety—and not merely or primarily as the institutionalization of negative freedom.

This defence of private property, implicit rather than manifest in Hayek (1960, pp. 140–2) confronts him with a problem which is not addressed in his thought, namely the problem of legitimating the underlying structure of property holdings in a market order. We have seen that, in Humean conservative fashion, Hayek treats property rights as conventions, grounded in historic acceptance, and as perpetually revisable but not radically criticizable. Further, Hayek has in recent years (1982, vol. 2) been concerned to deflate the ideal of social justice, which he believes to be an only partly coherent conception, functioning primarily as an ideological rationale for interest-group competition in interventionist States. In its rejection of Lockean absolutism about property rights, and in its incisive demolition of many fashionable distributivist conceptions, Hayek's work on property and social justice embodies powerful insights.[22] It nevertheless

---

[21] For the recognition of Kant as a positive libertarian, see Gray (1984c).

[22] For a useful discussion of Hayek's thought in these areas, see Brittan (1983a, ch. 3).

neglects the fundamental question, suggested by a defence of the market order in terms of positive freedom, about the legitimacy of the existing distribution of assets and the position of those in the market order who lack a holding in property. It seems clear that the normative defence of the market order is complete only when it is acknowledged that redistribution of property holdings may be mandated by the concern for autonomy which is the chief ethical rationale for the market. This is a subject on which classical liberals have thus far said little—though it is once again in Buchanan's work[23] that we find the best guidelines for future thought. It is a subject which must be on the agenda of a liberal State, nevertheless, and it is one which Hayek's project—the project of strengthening the foundations and repairing the ramifications of the market order—naturally supports. It is to be hoped that, both among classical liberals and their critics, this question of the legitimation of the underlying structure of assets in a market order will in future come to supplant concern with the merits of the market process itself as the chief focus of normative inquiry.[24]

[23] See, in particular, Buchanan and Brennan (1985).
[24] I have myself considered the normative justification of the market economy by reference to the justice of the underlying set of holdings in Gray (forthcoming).

7

Keynes and the State

ROBERT SKIDELSKY[*]

1. Introduction

Helm (this volume) has rightly pointed out that in the design of economic policy, it is not enough to point to market failure as a justification for government intervention. The costs of market failure have to be balanced against those of government failure. One of the main criticisms of Keynes is that he failed to take the possibility of the latter seriously. For example, Harris (1955, p. 79) accused him of failing to 'reconcile his dislike and distrust of politicians with his determination to thrust upon government serious additional responsibilities'.

What I propose to argue is that Keynes did not in fact want to thrust significant extra responsibilities on politicians as such. First of all, he never wanted government to take on many of the things it has been doing since his death (for example, ownership of industries) and would not have been in the least surprised to learn of 'government failure' in such areas. But second, he meant by the State something very different from what the modern economist or political scientist means by it. Both think of it, roughly, as the government; the economist, in its role as supplier of goods and services; the political scientist, in its role as a monopolist of coercion. For Keynes the distinguishing characteristic of the State was not mechanism or function, but motive. He meant by it a nexus of institutions working for the public good. These institutions could be privately owned; they could supply goods and services through the market. But their tradition, prestige, or situation was such that those who managed them were constrained to take the public good into account in making their decisions. Given the strong Victorian tradition of public service—which was not at all the same as working *in* the public service—Keynes's motivational definition of the State was well grounded in contemporary thought and experience. It also reflected what he wanted the State to do; and thought it could do well.

[*] Professor of International Studies at the University of Warwick.

2. The Agenda and Non-Agenda of the State

In his 1924 Sidney Ball Lecture at Oxford, Keynes followed the embryonic 'public goods' approach of the classical economists in distinguishing those goods and services that are 'technically social' from those that are 'technically individual'. The agenda of State action related 'not to those functions which private individuals are already fulfilling, but to those decisions which are made by no one if the State does not make them' (Keynes (1926)). He then gave three examples of the modern agenda: (a) 'the deliberate control of the currency and of credit by a central institution' to counteract 'risk, uncertainty, and ignorance'; (b) a 'coordinated act of intelligent judgment' as to the amount of national savings and the channels into which they should flow; and (c) a State population policy, paying attention to both quantity and quality.

By 1936 the agenda had been narrowed to the single point of providing enough consumption and investment to maintain full employment. In the last chapter of the *General Theory* Keynes writes that 'there is no objection to be raised against the classical analysis of the manner in which private self-interest will determine what in particular is produced, in what proportions the factors of production will be combined to produce it, and how the value of the final product will be distributed between them'. He concludes that 'apart from the necessity of central controls to bring about an adjustment between the propensity to consume and the inducement to invest, there is no more reason to socialise economic life than there was before' (Keynes (1936)).

The ambiguous phrasing of this last sentence might suggest that Keynes was alive to other kinds of failure which could justify other kinds of 'socialisation'. But in fact this turns out to be not the case. Keynes saw no important market failure arising from monopoly or collusion, a point to which we shall return; nor was he ever a nationalizer on socialist grounds. He was a moderate redistributor of the Asquith–Lloyd George kind; at the end of his life he welcomed the Beveridge Plan. But redistribution of wealth and income was never a passion with him.

All this raises interesting questions about the relationship between Keynes's economic theory and political values. As Durbin (1985, p. 11) has rightly pointed out, 'the focus on particular problems, the choice between different economic means, and even the use of one economic model rather than another, may . . . be affected by the values of the policy adviser'. Keynes's refusal to draw large interventionist conclusions from the existence of 'risk, uncertainty, and ignorance'; his insistence on the allocative efficiency of market capitalism; his relative indifference to questions of equality and social justice, all reflect a certain type of liberal inheritance which he was loathe to jettison.

Keynes was a Liberal, with both a large and a small 'l'. By the former I mean he was a lifelong member of the Liberal party; what is implied by the latter is more difficult to specify. By the 1920s and 1930s—with 'the historic party questions of the nineteenth century . . . as dead as last week's mutton' (Keynes (1925b))—his liberalism defined itself chiefly against threats from, or in distaste for, the right and the left. He castigated the Tory die-hards for their hostility to the reforms necessary to save 'individualistic capitalism' from catastrophe (Keynes (1925b)); and feared the left for exalting the 'boorish' proletariat over the educated bourgeoisie (Keynes (1925c)). In the second half of the 1920s, Keynes is one of a group of liberal-minded intellectuals and politicians searching for a politics of the Middle Way—by which they meant a way of keeping the existing social order going by surrendering some of the outworks to collectivism. The liberalism of this group is extraordinarily embattled. Unlike their early-nineteenth-century ancestors who aggressively evolved the doctrines of individualism and *laissez-faire*, they felt that perhaps history was not on their side and that heroic feats of intellect and management were needed to preserve a free society.

It is worth noticing here that Keynes has a place in another history, not usually told by economists, but which throws light on his economic endeavours: that of the intellectual reconstruction of liberalism in the 1930s to meet the challenge of the dictators. In this story he takes his place alongside such anti-Keynesians as Hayek and Schumpeter, as well as with thinkers like Popper, Mannheim, and Lippmann. Keynes was at one with Schumpeter in his elitist theory of democracy; and he warmly endorsed Hayek's warnings about the dangers of collectivism (Harrod (1951, p. 436)). Keynes's analytic quarrel with the two other economists in this group reflected, not disagreement about political values, but a different judgement concerning the economic means needed to sustain liberal values. In a nutshell, Keynes thought that a mild dose of collectivism was a necessary inoculation against the more virulent forms of the disease, whereas Hayek especially thought of it as the thin end of the wedge.

This intellectual movement of the 1930s may be called the second liberal revival, to distinguish it from the New Liberalism at the turn of the century. Unlike the New Liberalism, it made no serious attempt to reshape the philosophical foundations of liberalism. A central preoccupation of New Liberals was with the question of moral capacity as affected by possible distributions of wealth, income, and initial endowments. This led them to justify interferences with existing property relations. By contrast, the second wave of liberal thinkers tended to take existing property relations as given; what they did (Hayek excepted) was to impose a managerial philosophy on the theory and practice of 'classical' liberalism. This reflects a much greater institutional timidity in face of the violent rearrangement of property relations that had taken place in Russia; and a faith, which may have been born of desperation, in the ability of the social sciences to 'solve' problems.

Keynes is a 'classical' liberal in this sense. Characteristic is his defence of the market system as the best safeguard of 'personal liberty' and 'variety of life', which in turn was a condition of progress (Keynes (1936)). As he told Kingsley Martin, there was a 'profound connection between personal and political liberty and the rights of private property and private enterprise' (Keynes (1939)). The one area in which State intervention needed to go further to improve the conditions of freedom was in guaranteeing access to the labour market. Underlying Keynes's rejection of the main tenets of the New Liberalism was not just an aesthetic objection to Oxford Hegelianism—the New Liberals were Oxford-trained to a man—but his own Victorian belief that capacity is an inherited attribute of individuals and that disabling poverty—the crucial case of involuntary unemployment apart—is the result of character, not market, failure. Although Keynes favoured heavier death duties, there is no suggestion in his writings that the existing distribution of wealth was an important cause of moral, physical, or intellectual disablement. In any case, arguments along these lines never engaged his passions. Keynes thus saw no inconsistency between his liberal values and what he called the system of 'individualistic capitalism' at the micro-level.

It is never possible to assert categorically that an economist's political or moral values caused him to do his economic analysis in a certain way. But we can make suggestions that seem plausible. Schumpeter believes that Keynes's theory was a response to the problems of England's sclerotic capitalism. 'So he turned resolutely to the only "parameter of action" that seemed left to him, both as an Englishman and as the kind of Englishman he was—monetary management. Perhaps he thought that it might heal' (Schumpeter (1952, p. 275)). We can be more specific. Talking about money, or later about demand, was a way of avoiding talking about supply, i.e. about institutions.

From the start, Keynes set out to deal with the 'financial factor' in unemployment ahead of the structural factor (Keynes (1924)); and made monetary management the centre-piece of his up-to-date liberalism. 'For the most violent interferences with stability and with justice', he wrote, 'were precisely those which were brought about by changes in the price level. But the consequences of these changes . . . are intolerable to modern ideas and modern institutions' (Keynes (1925b)). Specifically, Keynes regarded his own explanation of unemployment in terms of demand failure as superseding explanations based on supply-side imperfections, and thus as undermining the left-wing case for planning and public ownership, and the right-wing attack on trade unionism.

3. Keynes's Concept of the State

As Helm (this volume) points out, Keynes's case for extending the economic boundaries of the State rested entirely on failures of macro-economic co-ordination. The position I now want to argue is that in elaborating his case for State intervention along these lines, Keynes made a crucial distinction between the government (or politicians) and the State. This is how he tried to reconcile the inconsistent positions attributed to him by Harris (1955).

Keynes's contempt for politicians is well known. In the first volume of my biography (Skidelsky (1983, p. 260)), I quoted his remark in 1911 to Duncan Grant: 'You haven't I suppose ever mixed with politicians at close quarters . . . their stupidity is inhuman'. In 1917 he confessed to working for a 'criminal' government (Skidelsky (1983, p. 345)); the calling of a general election in 1918 he considered 'an act of political immorality' (Keynes (1919)). Keynes was fully aware that politicians acted for political reasons. 'Even if economists and technicians knew the secret remedy', he wrote in 1922, 'they could not apply it until they had persuaded the politicians; and the politicians, who have ears but no eyes, will not attend to the persuasion until it reverberates back to them as an echo from the great public'. There is little warrant in these remarks for calling Keynes naïve about politicians.

Keynes's earliest demand for extension of State responsibility had to do with monetary policy. In the 1920s, as we have seen, he was a monetary reformer. He wanted to liberate monetary policy from the strait-jacket of the gold standard, and use it to stabilize the price level. The attraction of this mode of macro-economic management—and the quantity theory of money on which it was based—was, as he saw it, that it brought the State in, while keeping the government out. Keynes wanted the Bank of England to do what the Federal Reserve Board in Washington was doing—managing some aggregate in the interests of social stability and without political interference.

Although the Bank of England is not part of the government, Keynes clearly regarded it as part of the State, other parts being the ancient universities, the semi-autonomous public utility corporations, perhaps even *The Times* newspaper (Keynes (1925a)). The common characteristic of these institutions is that they are legally private but public-spirited; as Keynes often put it, they were 'socialised', or were in the course of becoming 'social'. Keynes (1926) wrote of the 'trend of the Joint Stock Institutions, when they have reached a certain size, to approximate to the status of the public corporation rather than that of individualistic private enterprise'. The central thread of his argument has to do with the divorce of management from ownership, and the consequent substitution of the 'public service' for the money-making motive: he estimated that two-thirds of the capital of large-scale undertakings could not be classed as private any more (Keynes (1927)). Keynes welcomed these developments as ridding capitalism of its 'casino' features, while avoiding the dead hand of bureaucratic governmental control. But Keynes did not rely on the evolutionary process alone: 'our task must be to decentralise and devolve wherever we can, and in particular to establish semi-independent corporations and organs of administration . . .' (Keynes (1925b)).

I think we can see why Keynes was not interested in the standard political analysis of private monopoly. While left-wing thinkers saw in the concentration of private capital a powerful argument for public ownership, Keynes believed that it made it unnecessary, since the 'managers' were no longer short-term profit maximizers. The same argument was later to be used by Crosland (1964, pp. 15 f.). If large-scale industry was already 'socialized', a change in its legal status was superfluous.

What distinguishes the State from the non-State sector is motive, not legal status. When Keynes talks about the economy 'socialising' itself, he has mainly in mind the growth of the public service motive at the expense of the private profit motive. By the State he means that group of institutions, private and public, that pursue public aims. He believed that the State in this sense was a growing force in economic life. As he wrote, 'Time and the Joint Stock Company and the Civil Service have silently brought the salaried class into power' (Keynes (1934)). In so far as politicians were motivated by public purposes, they were part of the State; in so far as they served their own interests through politics, they were part of the non-State. Governments were a mixture of both. Although Keynes was highly mistrustful of politicians as a class, he thought that standards of probity and disinterestedness in government had gone up, particularly compared with the eighteenth century.

Keynes's way of talking about the State seems quite strange to us; but it has its roots in the past, when the sovereign or prince was both ruler and private landlord, with public and private interests intertwined. The difficulty Keynes had in expressing his ideas in clear language also testifies to the lack in Britain of any clear theory of the State. In constitutional law, the State in Britain is the Crown-in-Parliament and its servants; but in medieval times sovereignty was fragmented through the system of vassalage, by which grants of land were invested with juridical and political powers. In the capitalist era, property escaped from vassalage to become fully 'privatized', its public functions being taken over by the Crown-in-Parliament. In effect, Keynes suggested that this tendency was now reversing itself. The State was no longer rigidly separated from private property and private enterprise; a corporate relationship was developing and should be promoted further.

It is in the light of these ideas that we need, I think, to interpret Keynes's call for the State to have a determining influence on the level of investment. In Chapter 12 of *The General Theory*—'The State of Long-Term Expectations'—Keynes writes: 'I expect to see the State, which is in a position to calculate the marginal efficiency of capital goods on long views and on the basis of the general social advantage, taking an ever greater responsibility for organising investment'. And on page 378 Keynes looks forward to a 'somewhat comprehensive socialisation of investment'. As I see it, these are not demands for greater political intervention in the economy, whether through public ownership, planning, or fiscal fine-tuning. Rather, Keynes believes that a group of institutions which he calls 'the State' is well placed to implement the full employment investment policy suggested by *The General Theory*. Keynes's aim, in other words, is not to enlarge the government, but to enlarge what Walter Lippmann called 'the public philosophy'.

Two footnotes need to be added to this. The first is that Keynes (as opposed to post-war Keynesians) intended that demand should be 'managed' through monetary, not fiscal, policy. He relied on the 'socialisation of investment' in the way we have been describing to raise the level of activity in the economy; and monetary fine-tuning to even out fluctuations round that level. This is very different from what happened.

Second, although Keynes was not in favour of public ownership, he saw that it might be made into an instrument for the 'socialisation of investment', given the Labour party's commitment to it. Thus in discussion with Labour party leaders he tried to shift the criterion for public ownership from the existence of natural monopoly to the 'importance of the industry as a source of demand for new investment' (Keynes (1931)). This is an example of the way Keynes tried to realign the political project of Labour with his own purposes. But he never deviated from the view that public ownership was, basically, an irrelevance.

4. Conclusion

The following summary seems appropriate. Keynes did not draw the economic borders of the State in the way we do. Keynes's 'State', being defined by the relative absence of the self-serving motives, is both larger and smaller than the contemporary one. It includes bodies that are legally private, but that consciously serve the public interest; it excludes self-serving individuals, whether or not these happen to be politicians.

This view of the State helps explain why Keynes appeared to attach a low probability to the risk of political failure. He was, of course, fully aware that politicians had political motives. In Keynes's political economy, the politician does not suddenly become benevolent. He is not the controller of Keynes's State.

Keynes's concept of the State was adapted to the work he wanted the State to do. There was to be a higher plateau of investment, self-generated by the 'semi-public' corporations. Monetary fine-tuning and exchange-rate policy would normally be left to the Bank of England and the Treasury. The politicians (government) would be called on to intervene decisively with 'pump-priming' measures only in the event of a deep slump, which the new permanent regime was designed to make far less likely.

We know that the post-war 'Keynesian State' was not the same as 'Keynes's State'. The logic of its borders, and therefore of its behaviour, was importantly different from what he envisaged. Do his ideas help us to think more clearly about what the State ought to be doing today?

One area seems particularly fruitful, but to approach it, a common misconception needs to be dispelled. This is that Keynes's State relies on a special (and unrealistic) view of human nature; namely that its controllers are altruistic and therefore we do not need regimes, constitutional or otherwise, to constrain their behaviour. Keynes never believed anything as silly as this. His controllers were constrained to serve the public good by the conventions and traditions of the time and the institutions they manned: in other words, by the systems of incentives in operation. He would hardly have been surprised by Buchanan's discovery that 'people [are] rational utility-maximisers in all their behavioural capacities' (Buchanan (1978)).

The issue lies not here but elsewhere: was Keynes relying on a moral legacy which the further progress of capitalism was itself depleting, as Schumpeter believed? Essentially Keynes was trying to weld a new managerial philosophy onto the Victorian code of public service. It could be argued that he failed to foresee that the public service tradition in which he grew up was dying, not growing; that he and his fellow-mandarins were Victorian survivors—products of Marshall's age of 'earnestness'.

Contemporary capitalism, godless and hedonistic, no longer produces a sufficiently numerous class of people who get their personal satisfactions out of serving the public good to man Keynes's State, much less the post-war Keynesian State.

The logic of this line of argument points in three possible directions. We may hope to compensate for a depleted moral legacy by an increase of knowledge or wisdom. In other words, our controllers may be less incorruptible, but grow to be more competent. This is a new version of the old dream that social science will replace ethics. Alternatively, we may seek some new sources of moral capital—for example, through a system of rewards and punishments such as socialism might provide. Finally, we may try to compensate for the decline in the public service motive by extending the scope of markets and individual contracts, restricting the State even more than the Victorians did: the solution of the New Right. I do not know the answer; but this is the kind of discussion that Keynes would have enjoyed and enriched.

8

Contemporary Conservatism and the Borders of the State

GILLIAN PEELE*

1. Introduction

... in the country where Socialism has been less talked about than any other country in Europe, its principles have been most extensively applied. (Morley (1881) i, 303)

... the middle ground turned out to be like the will-o'the-wisp, the light which flickers over marshlands by night beguiling the weary traveller: as he moves towards it the currents of air he sets up by his movement send it dancing away from him, and he goes on following, stumbling deeper and deeper into the mire. (Sir Keith Joseph (1975))

The question of the borders of the State—of what are the proper limits and purposes of governmental activity—is currently the central one in British political debate. That so fundamental and general a question should be on this country's political agenda at all is a reflection of the changes which have occurred in the political system over the past fifteen years. In particular, it reflects changes which have occurred within the Conservative party which, under Mrs Thatcher's leadership, has enjoyed a remarkable degree of electoral success and has been able to set the terms of the political argument.

Much of this argument concerns the capacity of the State to control and shape economic policy. But much of it is concerned with the extent to which government itself has a duty to provide a wide variety of welfare services and the extent to which public provision of those services is more efficient than private provision or some mix of the two. It is therefore an argument about both means and ends, about values and strategies for promoting them. For much of the period in which this debate has been conducted, the Conservatives, who have challenged previous assumptions about the scope of State intervention, have been in office. As a result, the political framework within which public policy is made—the structures and values which subtly constrain the choices of decision-makers at all

---

* Fellow and Tutor in Politics, Lady Margaret Hall, Oxford.

levels—has been altered profoundly. In this article I shall try to explain how the Conservative party came to be the vehicle of what in the British context seemed to be radical changes of attitude and policy. And I shall explore some of the ways in which this departure from the consensual assumptions of British politics affected the machinery of government and the handling of policy. By exploring some of these questions, it is hoped that some light can be shed, not merely on the character of the current debate about the role of government in the economy and society, but also about whether any agreement is likely to emerge about where the borders of the State should be drawn.

2. The Conservative Party and the Growth of the State

The borders of the British State were extended steadily from the nineteenth century onwards, regardless of which party was in power. The Liberals, for all their adherence to the doctrine of free trade, were convinced by the arguments of social reformers who wished to implement a more positive form of freedom than that which appealed to John Stuart Mill.[1] The Conservatives, despite their attachment to the rights of property, believed in a strong government which could regulate to correct abuses of private economic power, could protect particular interests, and could intervene in a range of arenas if such intervention seemed electorally popular.[2] Labour from its inception wished to see public authority—central and local—used to produce a fairer distribution of wealth and a more just society.[3] Pragmatism, not ideology, was the dominant factor in what functions the State accepted, although once the State had acquired a new area of responsibility, it was rarely abandoned. As a result, although the further growth of government from the late nineteenth century onwards is undeniable, this advance followed no blueprint or plan: a variety of problems, reforms, reorganizations, and experiments constituted the tributaries feeding the tide of collectivism which so worried critics of the process such as Dicey (1962).

War was above all the great engine both of State expansion and of centralization. The condition of would-be recruits at the time of the Boer War revealed a range of social problems and stimulated thought about the

[1] On nineteenth-century attitudes to government in particular see MacDonagh (1977) and Lubenow (1971). For an overview which takes account of these developments see Gash (1979). For an excellent introduction to liberal social thought after J. S. Mill see Freeden (1978). Freeden notes in particular the importance of utilitarianism in overcoming the nineteenth-century hostility to the State.

[2] For a magisterial survey of the components of the British political tradition which illuminates the different forces within Conservatism, see Greenleaf (1983).

[3] On the elements of Labour's attitudes see Cole (1953–60) and Foote (1985).

extent to which the machinery of government was equipped to meet the demands made upon it.[4] The First World War saw the transformation of the system of Cabinet government and governmental intervention in the economy, to a degree which changed the character of the British political system. After 1918 it was not possible to ignore the ubiquitous presence of the State in British economic, commercial, and social life, even though elements in the Conservative party in particular looked upon many of the new developments with suspicion.[5] By comparison the Second World War was less of a turning-point, though it obviously involved a massive addition to the government's powers to control and plan the economy and accelerated the trend towards public responsibility for a range of welfare functions.

The experience of the Second World War, followed by a period of Labour government between 1945 and 1951, created a consensus both about the best methods of handling the economy—where Keynesian insights encouraged politicians to believe that by manipulating demand they could ensure the full employment to which successive governments had explicitly committed themselves since 1944—and about the broad outlines of the Welfare State.[6] This was the so-called 'post-war settlement' which endured until the mid-1970s, embodying consensus about the need for an extensive, indeed expanding, role for government in Britain. This consensus bound the Conservative party to an acceptance of the existing bonds of State ownership and an approach to matters of economic management and social policy which made its rhetoric and programmes little different from those of any European social democratic party. Less surely, perhaps, the consensus also bound the Labour party to the mixed economy. Yet, doubts about the merits of this 'settlement' began to emerge even in the 1960s. When the Conservatives went into opposition in 1964, there was some radical revision of party policy, and Edward Heath came into power in 1970 promising a 'quiet revolution'[7] to make Britain more entrepreneurial and its industry less dependent on government. The experience of government quickly led Heath to abandon the more radical elements of his election programme and to adopt a style of government which continued the 'corporatist' trend of all previous administrations.[8]

---

[4] For a discussion of this point see Greenleaf (1983) and Beloff (1984). Also Beloff (1969).

[5] For further discussion of the post-1918 period see Middlemas (1979).

[6] On the nature of the settlement see Addison (1975). For the commitment to full employment see HMSO (1944a).

[7] For a somewhat hostile account of the Heath Government see Holmes (1982). On the quiet revolution see Gardyne (1974).

[8] On corporatism in British politics see Smith (1979) and the more recent analysis by Middlemas (1986).

Efforts to reduce the amount of government intervention in the economy were explicitly abandoned as unemployment began to rise, underlining the apparently incontrovertible fact that no government could afford the electoral consequences of abandoning the industrial sector to its fate or of allowing prices and incomes to be determined by the market alone.

The loss of the February 1974 general election (which Heath had called in the context of a miners' challenge to his incomes policy) prompted a much greater intellectual reappraisal throughout the Conservative party than had the loss of the 1964 and 1966 elections. This was partly because new intellectual forces were already having some impact around the periphery of the Conservative party and in the quality Press. Thus the Bow Group, which had always been seen as on the left of the party, embraced monetarism, while newer pressure groups such as the Selsdon Group articulated an even more robust free market approach to public policy.[9] Influential journalists such as Samuel Brittan and Peter Jay attacked the already weakened tenets of Keynesianism, and the Institute of Economic Affairs, from being a voice crying in the wilderness, found its ideas acquiring a new audience. The reappraisal also occurred because many Conservatives doubted whether—given the hostility of the trade union leadership to the Conservative party—any corporatist measures could be suitable for a Conservative government since the price of bringing the unions into policymaking was to give them at least a partial veto over public policy.

3. The Challenge to Conservative Orthodoxy

These developments would perhaps have led in any event to a marked shift towards a different style of political philosophy from that which had hitherto marked the Conservative party, especially given the extent to which oil shocks of the early 1970s and the policies of the Wilson/Callaghan Governments underlined the weakness of the British economy.[10] But two other factors were vital in transforming the character and style of Conservative ideology in the 1970s. The first was the role of Sir Keith Joseph and Margaret Thatcher in developing a coherent and appealing alternative to existing Conservative assumptions. The second was the unpopularity on the Tory back-benches of Edward Heath—an unpopu-

[9] These developments are covered to a large extent in Kavanagh (1987). On the Bow Group, reference should be made to Brittan and Lilley (1977). Lilley, who became MP for St Albans and PPS to the Chancellor of the Exchequer in 1984, was Chairman of the Bow Group 1972–5; Samuel Brittan was an early advocate of neo-liberalism.

[10] On the Wilson–Callaghan years see Holmes (1985a).

larity which was to result in his displacement as leader by Margaret Thatcher.

Sir Keith Joseph's role in the recasting of Conservative party ideas and attitudes after 1974 was crucial. When the Conservative party lost the February 1974 general election, Sir Keith, along with Margaret Thatcher, raised money to finance a new organization—the Centre for Policy Studies. This organization became the focal point for developing a radically different approach to Conservative philosophy and policy. As Edward Heath became more defensive about the consensus he had tried to build around the corporate policies of the second half of his administration, Sir Keith Joseph was spelling out the fundamental premisses of his version of Conservatism—one in which the role of the State was greatly reduced.

The burden of Sir Keith's re-evaluation of political principle was that the so-called 'consensus' or 'settlement' of post-1945 Britain should be abandoned. The search for the middle ground of politics, which so many Conservatives believed had delivered electoral success, was a mistaken one. For Sir Keith, the middle ground entailed compromises which displayed no logic and could therefore offer no solution to Britain's seemingly intractable economic problems, especially inflation. Worse still, the middle ground was not a position of the Conservatives' own making. It was constantly moving in a collectivist direction both because Labour was itself moving towards more left-wing policies and because the initiatives of a Labour government were rarely reversed when the Tories returned to power. There was thus a ratchet effect in British politics, so that every Labour government saw Britain move a further notch to the left while the Conservatives merely consolidated the status quo ante.[11]

The middle ground, according to Sir Keith, was very different from the common ground which represented the shared values of the British people. This 'common ground' governments *should* seek. But above all, governments needed to recognize their own limits and to acknowledge that they could not manage every aspect of social and economic life. Conservatives had to fight a battle of ideas and there needed to be a new emphasis on the importance of the individual pursuing his own self-interest and of the market as the best way of integrating those choices efficiently. As Sir Keith put it in December 1975:

Until recently, government was expected to confine its role to setting the framework within which people would be free to pursue their own mixture of

[11] It is difficult to convey the breadth of Sir Keith Joseph's arguments in a few short paragraphs. For an introduction to his thought at this time, reference should be made to his collections of speeches *Reversing the Trend* (Joseph (1976a)) and *Stranded on the Middle Ground* (Joseph (1976b)).

self-interest and altruism, with a safety net for the failures from whatever cause. Within this framework people would make their decisions, great and small, and take the consequences, confident that the rug would not be pulled from under their feet, and that if government had any role at all it would be a stabilizing one . . .

But recently government had assumed it could do far more than this— that it could reduce inequalities, redistribute income, set prices and incomes, and generate full employment. Yet, as Sir Keith suggested, it had to be recognized that 'there were limits to what governments can do for people, to the decreasing returns and counter-productive nature of government provision and intervention beyond a certain point'.

Sir Keith's economic ideas as he elucidated them in speeches and pamphlets over the period 1974–5 had clearly been influenced by Milton Friedman and by the rather different ideas of the Austrian school represented especially by Ludwig von Mises and Friedrich Hayek. But the significance of his intellectual challenge was that it went much beyond matters of economic policy alone. For what Sir Keith was anxious to do was to transform the climate of opinion in Britain and to reverse the trend away from collectivism and towards individualism and entrepreneurialism. His argument for a social market economy was but a part of a wider vision of Britain in which the State would play a very much reduced role.[12]

The intellectual challenge by Sir Keith might have done little more than open an interesting but rather academic debate within the Conservative party. The ability to translate ideas into policy in the Conservative party depends crucially on the leadership and its receptivity to new thought. Edward Heath was fully aware of the initiatives of Sir Keith Joseph and Margaret Thatcher, although he clearly did not at the time foresee the impact they would have. What did become increasingly clear, however, was that Heath had inspired little affection among the general run of Tory back-benchers so that once the February 1974 general election was lost, there was immediate speculation about the future of his leadership. Only the imminence of another general election postponed a leadership challenge; but once the Conservatives failed to win the October 1974 election, it was certain that some move would be made to oust him. The way in which it was done and the personality of his successor were,

[12] The notion of the social market economy has caused some confusion. It was originally used in West Germany by the Christian Democrats to signify a vigorous market-orientated economic policy tempered by welfare provision. It became consensual between the parties. It was presumably both the emphasis on the market and the consensual aspects of this ideology which Sir Keith wanted to transfer to Britain. Later usage neglected the original point of the term and almost suggested that the emphasis was on the word social.

however, to have major consequences for the future style of the Conservative party and for the British political system as a whole.

When Edward Heath had succeeded to the Tory leadership in 1965, he was the first beneficiary of the party's change from a non-elective to an elective system for choosing the leader. The rules had, however, been designed to apply when the leadership was vacant. That was not, of course, the situation in 1974 since Heath had no intention of resigning the leadership voluntarily. Those who wished to make it easier to challenge an incumbent leader therefore urged a change in the rules. In 1974 this was done so that, as in the Labour party, a Tory leader now has to be re-elected each year (even when the party is in office), thus allowing, at least in theory, the possibility that he (or she) might be challenged, a fact which Mrs Thatcher emphasized during the 1987 election campaign when she was challenged on how long she intended to stay as leader.[13]

After the loss of the 1974 election there was pressure for someone to run against Heath. Yet there were few likely candidates for the succession who would do this. Those who might in normal circumstances have been thought of as potential successors were too loyal to threaten Heath's position and, while Sir Keith Joseph might have run in order to offer an alternative version of Conservatism, he had by that stage decided that on personal grounds he would not seek the leadership. The only senior politician willing to challenge Heath was Margaret Thatcher, whose candidacy was seen very much as the offering of an alternative brand of Conservatism although in her campaign she tried to appeal to as broad a constituency as possible. Initially her chances of winning were seen as negligible. Certainly, Edward Heath thought he would have no difficulty in beating Mrs Thatcher, who had after all only held major office once—as Secretary of State for Education from 1970 to 1974. What had been underestimated, however, was the personal hostility to Heath on the backbenches and the efficiency of the Thatcher electoral machine which was largely master-minded by Airey Neave.[14] On the first ballot Mrs Thatcher defeated Heath by 130 votes to 119 and, although new candidates came forward at the second ballot, it was too late to stop the Thatcher bandwagon.[15] The Conservative party thus acquired in 1975 a new leader who was in a very different mould from previous leaders. Apart from the fact that she was the first woman to lead a major British political party, Mrs

[13] On the selection of Tory leaders generally see Fisher (1977) and Beloff and Peele (1985).

[14] The growth of dissidents within the Conservative party in the early 1970s can be traced in Norton (1978).

[15] The Thatcher campaign for the leadership is documented in various biographical studies of which the best is probably Brock and Wapshott (1983).

Thatcher was in almost every way an outsider. Like Heath, she had come from a modest background and was a meritocrat. Unlike Heath, she had not acquired the tastes and values of the Conservative establishment or indeed any other establishment. Her voice was the authentic voice of the commercial middle classes: she valued self-help and independence, not paternalism and 'one-nation' interdependence. So far from moderating the Conservative message, she wanted to clarify it; and in the work which she and Sir Keith Joseph had initiated through the Centre for Policy Studies (of which she was vice-chairman), she had signalled that she was open to a variety of new influences and ideas. With her election to the leadership, the way was open for the Conservative party to become the vehicle of a very different view about where the borders of the British State should be drawn.

4. The Conservative Party in Opposition

Despite the direction in which Mrs Thatcher and Sir Keith Joseph had been moving in 1974, the advent of Mrs Thatcher to the leadership created a new climate of opportunity for a variety of different groups on the right, and not just for those who were wedded to Sir Keith Joseph's views of the free market values and neo-liberalism of Friedman and Hayek.

At the risk of over-simplification, three broad strands vied for influence while the party under Mrs Thatcher was in opposition. First there was the traditional party élite. By this I mean those who had acquired positions of influence in the Conservative party in Parliament and the country *before* the Thatcher leadership and who assumed that they would be able to retain their influence afterwards. While this group had no particular ideological axe to grind, it is probably fair to say that they were pragmatists who saw their role as a moderating one in order to prevent the dominance of any single ideology or doctrine. The second strand was that of the economic liberals and free marketeers who wished radically to change a number of features of the British economy and society—most crucially in the directions of eliminating government controls and responsibilities. Finally there was a strand which is difficult to label but which may best be described as the 'cultural right'. The thinkers in this mould, who included Roger Scruton, Maurice Cowling, and Edward Norman, as well as journalists such as Ronald Butt, were interested in asserting the importance of moral and religious values in Conservatism as well as in rejecting some, if not all, aspects of the claims to equality made by such minorities as blacks, gays, and women.[16] Many of these thinkers were

[16] The flavour of this strand of Conservatism is probably best acquired by reading *The Salisbury Review*.

associated with the Conservative Philosophy Group and they published a journal—*The Salisbury Review*—which gave them additional publicity and coherence. Their emphasis on authority and historical continuity as opposed to reason and individual choice as the source of political enlightenment made them ultimately at odds with the neo-liberal free marketeers. Yet in the atmosphere that prevailed within the party in the years of opposition, such inconsistencies did not matter all that much. The different strands overlapped and interacted, and the vocabulary and rhetoric of authors such as Milton Friedman, Friedrich von Hayek, Ludwig von Mises, Michael Oakeshott, and Irving Kristol percolated down into reaches of the party where such abstract works were not normally read.[17]

Although Mrs Thatcher created her own synthesis of all these tendencies and impulses and added her own instinctive appeal to popular opinion to them, the influence of the free market and neo-liberal strand of opinion deserves further examination. It was by far the most coherent intellectually and the most self-confident; and it offered what many Conservatives wanted by 1975—an ideology which could at once inspire them and offer solutions to the problems which the Heath Government had found so intractable. This the free market creed did, with its emphasis on the freedom of the individual, on the perfection of the market mechanism, on the need to sweep away the dead hand of bureaucracy and special interest groups, especially the unions. Above all, it offered an alternative economic paradigm to Keynesianism and one which was not the preserve of a minority but which was being taken increasingly seriously beyond the circles of the right.

There is detailed discussion of the ideas of monetarism elsewhere in this book (see articles by Helm and by Allsopp). The point which needs to be made here is that monetarist ideas, in addition to their promise to solve the problem of inflation, appealed to Conservatives for a variety of other reasons. (It may, of course, be doubted whether many politicians were able to understand the subtlety of the theories rather than simply taking the broad outlines of the doctrine and translating them into political nostrums.) What was important for many on the right was the role of the State and the relationship between the public and the private sector which monetarism entailed. This broader ideology—political monetarism as it is sometimes called—took the economic critique of Keynesianism as its starting-point. But its real significance was the extent to which it allowed a robust celebration of capitalism, a rebuttal of egalitarianism, a rejection of State intervention, and a justification of individualism. Thus between 1975 and 1979 the Conservatives acquired not merely a different set of

[17] For an overview see Green (1987). American developments are covered in Peele (1984).

economic policies from those that had marked the Heath years; they acquired also a disposition which made them more suspicious of governmental activity in the social and economic arena than they had been at any time since 1939.

At the level of economic and industrial policy, monetarist theory did of course entail a major withdrawal of the State. According to the monetarist theory, inflation occurred as a result of there being too much money in circulation. Money, like any other commodity, was subject to the laws of supply and demand, and an increase in supply (faced with a given demand) would diminish the value of the good, and hence the price level would rise. As the money supply grew, in excess of the growth of the economy, inflation would occur. Governments which wished to prevent inflation should devote themselves to the task of ensuring that the increase in the amount of money in circulation did not exceed the growth of the real economy. This goal, the monetarists argued, government could achieve, whereas the other purported remedies for inflation—for example prices and incomes policies—prevented the natural, and hence the proper, adjustment of relative prices, thus distorting the micro-economics of the (goods) market. It is easy to see why such a message should have been especially attractive to Conservatives between 1975 and 1979, given that the difficulties of defining the money supply and the problems with controlling it had not yet surfaced in the popular debates.[18] Monetarism offered them a way out of incomes policies and hence of the need to bargain in a corporatist manner with the unions. Of course, no government could afford to ignore public sector pay—i.e. pay where the government was to some extent itself the paymaster. However, monetarism offered an escape route from the endless round of negotiations with trade union leaders over norms and guidelines and with companies over pay limits— activities which seemed to many observers on the right to be both futile and demeaning.

There were, however, two other aspects of monetarism which had wide political appeal in the climate of the opposition period between 1975 and 1979. The first was the emphasis which the monetarist theorists placed on ensuring that the operation of the economy was not impeded by monopolies of either capital or labour. Not merely did the withdrawal of government from macro-economic employment policy promise a new relationship with the unions; there was also the strong suggestion that the influence of the unions should be reduced in order to generate economic efficiency. Just what role the government should have in breaking down the power of the unions was unclear between 1975 and 1979, but the new approach promised a battle which a Conservative government had a better

---

[18] For the difficulties associated with monetarism see Smith (1987).

chance of winning than the approach epitomized in Edward Heath's Industrial Relations Act of 1971.

The second aspect of monetarism which was appealing was the extent to which it urged control of the public sector borrowing requirement. The suggested theoretical relationship between monetarism and the public sector borrowing requirement (PSBR) is both complex and ambiguous and is dealt with in detail elsewhere in the book (see Allsopp). Suffice it to say here that the proposal to reduce public spending was popular for a number of reasons in the Conservative party. There were those who believed that the private sector ought to be given additional stimulus to make the whole economy more efficient, and they could join hands with those who regretted the growing demands of welfare services in particular on the public purse. Such services, it was argued in some circles in Britain and more widely in the United States, were not merely costly but they also made the problem of poverty worse by contributing to a syndrome of welfare dependence.[19]

High levels of public expenditure had of course to be funded, and the Conservative party in this period was especially aware of the arguments of the supply-side economists in the United States who advocated sweeping reductions in taxation in order to generate additional economic activity. The Conservatives were also conscious of the growing dislike of high levels of taxation which had led to new parties and right-wing resurgence in Scandinavia, to referendum and initiative challenges including Proposition 13 in California, and to drives to change the balance between direct and indirect taxation.[20] In Britain the protest against rate rises in the early 1970s had led to the establishment of the Layfield Committee and eventually to a commitment from Margaret Thatcher to abolish the existing system of rates.[21] The demand for lower taxation had also been recognized in the Labour party when the Callaghan Government under direction from the International Monetary Fund (IMF) had brought the PSBR under control and announced tax cuts of £2 billion in 1978.[22] Lower taxation was good populist stuff, and for the Tories it had the appeal of promising long-term economic benefits as individuals were stimulated to work harder.

On three levels, then, the period of Conservative opposition from 1975

[19] See for example Murray (1984). The point about welfare dependency was also made at length in a book based on a Channel 4 television series presented by Professor K. Minogue. See Graham and Clarke (1987).

[20] On tax rebellions in America see Citrin and Sears (1985).

[21] See Layfield Committee (1976). Mrs Thatcher's commitment to rate reform ultimately led to the proposal to replace rates with a poll tax.

[22] For a discussion of Labour's economic strategy see Smith (1987), especially pp. 56–71; Holmes (1985a); Barnett (1982); and Donoghue (1987).

to 1979 promised to produce a different role for the State. First, by distancing government from the detailed control of prices and incomes and by concentrating government attention on the control of the money supply, it promised a very much reduced role for government in the daily management of the economy. Second, by focusing on the overall levels of the PSBR and by attempting to stem the growth, if not to cut public expenditure, there was signalled a new attitude to public provision—one that was bound to be restrictive rather than expansive. (The initial goal of the government in 1980 had been to cut the PSBR in real terms; this by 1983 had been changed to a goal of holding it steady in real terms, and by 1986 the aim had become to reduce public spending as a percentage of gross domestic product (GDP).[23]) Finally, the emphasis which both major parties would put on the reduction of taxation in the period 1974–9 encouraged the Conservatives to promise radical reform in the structure of taxation and reductions in income tax.

Together these three elements of the new Conservative creed would have spelt out a swing away from collectivism for the party. Yet such a swing was not altogether unfamiliar in opposition. On the whole, Tory leaders in opposition do retreat to a recipe of greater freedom and more private initiative, less bureaucracy and more entrepreneurial activity. What made this period of opposition different from both the 1945–51 period and the 1964–70 period was the personality of the leader and her own deep commitment to achieving radical change in Britain.[24]

Mrs Thatcher's personal convictions led her to combine the insights and theories of the monetarists and of those who like Sir Keith Joseph argued for a change in the balance between the public and private sector with a rhetoric which emphasized home truths about the recipe for Britain's economic recovery. This approach was thus intellectually inspired and populist at the same time, and it certainly alarmed her critics on the left of the Conservative party who thought that a more pragmatic approach to economic policy was in order. As Jim Prior (1986, p. 119) put it:

Margaret's economic policy was dictated by the belief that 'sound money' was the essential requirement for a successful and stable nation. As far as she was concerned, inflation was a much greater social evil than unemployment, and in any case, in her eyes, you could only cure unemployment by controlling inflation. She thus felt free to castigate all post-war governments, Labour and Conservative, because she reckoned their policies had made our problems progressively worse . . . The idea of pumping money into the economy to reduce unemployment was anathema. If only a better balance could be achieved between the public sector and

[23] For an accessible approach to public expenditure problems see Likierman (1988).
[24] Apart from biographical studies, reference should be made to Young and Sloman (1986).

the private, with less public spending, the economy would expand in response to market forces. It was a very simplistic approach, a combination of her own instincts founded in the corner shop at Grantham, laid over by a veneer from Hayek and Friedman.

Even in opposition, Mrs Thatcher's style of leadership and her commitment to defined policies were more reminiscent of a crusade than of the normal pragmatic decision-making of the Conservative party.[25] To some extent, this clarity and conviction in the leader was an asset which inspired confidence in the troops; at the same time, it made it difficult, to say the least, to debate policy matters in a dispassionate and rational manner. This was perhaps unfortunate because it obscured the extent to which many of the questions which it was legitimate to place on the political agenda—for example, about the best way of running the economy and the best way of managing medical and welfare services—were indeed open ones to be resolved by empirical evidence. The creation of a mood of evangelism impeded the objective analysis which many Conservatives wanted to apply to public policy.

In the period of opposition, there were forces working to constrain the new style of Conservatism. The Conservative Research Department, although it was later to be brought more directly under Central Office control and had already lost some of the intellectual initiative to groups such as the Centre for Policy Studies and the Institute of Economic Affairs, was still responsible for much of the work that went into the manifesto and for the preparation of ministers for office. Chris Patten, who was head of the Research Department until becoming MP for Bath in 1979, was an extremely able man whose sympathies were with the Tory moderates, not the 'neo-liberals' and free marketeers. Without the authority which being Prime Minister was to bring to her, Mrs Thatcher still had to pay attention to senior party figures such as William Whitelaw, James Prior, and Sir Geoffrey Howe. The documents written for the 1979 general election were therefore something of a compromise between those who wanted to make the tone and style of Conservatism substantially different from past interpretations of the Tory creed, and those who favoured continuity with the 'one-nation' Conservatism of R. A. Butler and Harold Macmillan. Yet it was difficult to ignore the extent to which the change of leadership had created a new mood in the Conservative party and the encouragement which had been given to those who wanted to break with the earlier tradition of Conservatism and to place more emphasis on the values of the individual, freedom, and the market.

The Conservatives won the general election of 1979 with a majority of

[25] For two excellent accounts of the impact of Thatcherism on the style of policymaking see Riddell (1983) and Keegan (1984).

43 over all other parties. They thus became responsible for the activities of
the State, and the question then became to what extent the new influences
within the Conservative party would affect policies in government.

5. Conservatives in Government: Rolling Back the Borders of the State?

Although there was no doubt that the Conservatives had been subject in
opposition to important new personal and philosophical influences, their
ability to translate these influences into policy in government was less
certain. All governments find their radical ideas conceived in opposition
are tempered in government both by reality and by the advice of Civil
Servants who have the sobering facts at their command. And, as time
passes, all governments become absorbed with the daily routine of
administration and find it more difficult to generate new initiatives. Yet
there was in 1979 a sense that *this* government would be different from its
predecessors in its determination to follow through on its radical vision, a
somewhat odd inversion of the normal assumptions about the source of
radicalism within the British political system. Leo Pliatzky, a senior Civil
Servant who has documented many of the problems associated with
economic decision-making in British government, predicted the magnitude of the change which was about to come over Whitehall; he saw Mrs
Thatcher's entry to 10 Downing Street as bringing about 'a revolution'
(Pliatzky (1982)).

Why was the Thatcher Government not subject to the normal forces
that tend to erode an incoming government's commitment to its programme? Several factors must be taken into account. First, there was the
obvious determination of the Prime Minister herself and her vision of
changing the character of British political life. Her personality was a strong
one and she was unwilling to be deflected by conflicting advice. There
would be, she had stated, no room for disagreement in her Cabinet.[26] The
Press, which had become convinced by much of the rhetoric of the new
Conservatism and had itself espoused much of the monetarist thinking,
was supportive for the most part, and where it was not, it could be dis-
missed as irrelevant. The Labour opposition was in a state of disarray and,
being absorbed with the constitutional struggles that were ultimately to
produce the breakaway Social Democratic Party, there was little likelihood
of it offering the government much pause for thought.[27] This is not to say
that the total implementation of the party manifesto, much less the
broader vision of the Prime Minister and her closest ideological colleagues,
was achieved—far from it. But the determination of the Thatcher Govern-

[26] For a study of Mrs Thatcher's style of premiership see Hennessy (1986).
[27] See discussion in Keegan (1984).

ment to engineer profound changes in the political and economic system was marked, and those who were responsible for carrying out Conservative policy were aware that the mood was a very different one from that which prevailed at the beginning of most new administrations.

Nowhere was the 'revolution' predicted by Pliatzky more felt than in the Civil Service.[28] When political scientists look back at the long-term effects of the Thatcher years, the change in the position of the Civil Service and its mores may well come to be seen as the most significant alterations of all in the political system. The role of the Civil Service was, of course, crucial for a variety of reasons. Its growth had symbolized the extension of collectivist values. The high calibre of its recruits represented the prestige of public service by comparison with the private sector. Its permanent officials were the symbol of the post-war consensus which Mrs Thatcher, like Sir Keith Joseph, so criticized. And the clever men of Whitehall were suspect because of their presumed ability to modify and dilute the plans of an elected government.

Mrs Thatcher herself was unusually hostile to the Civil Service as an institution. Like many leading Conservatives who had fallen under the influence of new right theory, she was aware of the argument that bureaucracies develop goals other than the pursuit of the policies of their government—goals which often have more to do with consolidating the bureaucrats' own position and protecting existing programmes than with any objective pursuit of the public good.[29] (Whether she had actually read these works is not clear and of course it could well be argued that private organizations display the same tendencies.) Mrs Thatcher had also been unimpressed with her Civil Servants at the Department of Education and Science when she had been Secretary of State from 1970 to 1974. Although supportive of Civil Servants who gained her confidence, she disliked what she saw as the Civil Service style—detached and consensual. In short, she wanted a more managerial Civil Service, trimmed in size and capable of implementing her radical policies.

A reduction in the number of Civil Servants had already been set in motion by the Callaghan Government. Mrs Thatcher's aim was to cut the number of Civil Servants still further, and by 1987 a cut of 19 per cent had been achieved—a figure which represented a fall in numbers of 137,300. The cuts were implemented in a variety of ways; some of them were achieved by improving efficiency, others by transferring functions away from central government or shifting them to the private sector. It was not, however, merely the size of the bureaucracy that the Conservatives attacked. They also wished to reduce the privileges attached to Civil

---

[28] For discussion of the Civil Service in modern Britain see Beloff and Peele (1985).

[29] For the new right's theories of bureaucracy see for example Tullock (1976).

Servants' pay and conditions, to secure greater efficiency by introducing some of the ethos of the best parts of the private sector of the economy (a wish which was shared by President Reagan in his handling of the bureaucracy), and to limit the extent to which the Civil Service could hijack government policy initiatives.[30]

Mrs Thatcher's determination to ensure that the official machine implemented her policies produced some major changes in the conventional relationship between the Civil Service and ministers. Although Mrs Thatcher had initially been opposed to the introduction of personal advisers into Whitehall, she came to sanction this development and indeed imported some key advisers from outside—for example Terry Burns and Alan Walters—into major economic policymaking roles.[31] She was more interventionist than many other Prime Ministers had been in the process of promotions; and the early promotion of Sir Peter Middleton to be Permanent Secretary of the Treasury to succeed Sir Douglas Wass was generally seen as a manifestation of her personal influence. And in 1981 Mrs Thatcher abolished the Civil Service Department which had been concerned with personnel and machinery-of-government questions but which many Conservatives saw as defending the special privileges and position of the Civil Service.

Pay was another area highly sensitive for the relationship between the government and the Civil Service. This was perhaps inevitable given the government's emphasis on the control of public expenditure and the abandonment of comparability procedures in favour of cash limits. But the situation was not improved by the explicit hostility to the public sector voiced in some Conservative circles. A militant leadership emerged in the Civil Service unions and there was already a major strike in prospect by 1981—which may in turn have influenced the decision to abolish the Civil Service Department. Problems associated with the criteria for deciding Civil Service pay led the government to establish a committee under Mr Justice Megaw to devise a new system of Civil Service pay. Its report in July 1982 suggested that comparison with scales outside the Civil Service should have a less important role in the future and that greater attention should be paid to market forces.[32]

The period 1979–87 thus saw a major politicization of the Civil Service,

[30] On recent developments in American bureaucracy see Levine (1985).

[31] Sir Terence Burns was the first director of the London Business School's Centre for Economic Forecasting and an early advocate of the use of a medium-term financial strategy which would set targets for the money supply. He became the Chief Economic Adviser to the Treasury and Head of the Government Economic Service in 1980. Sir Alan Walters became a full-time personal economic adviser to Mrs Thatcher in 1981, although after 1983 he remained in the post on a part-time basis.

[32] Megaw Committee (1982).

not simply in the sense of the government attempting to make the machinery of government more responsive to political leadership, but also in the sense of the Civil Service itself responding to government initiatives in a way that was more like that of an ordinary union than of the special public service it had once been.

If the reduced size of the Civil Service was one important signal of the government's change of direction with regard to the role which the Conservatives wanted the State to play, so too was their first budget, of June 1979, which reflected the thinking which had gone into the manifesto itself and into the earlier document *The Right Approach to the Economy* which reflected Terry Burns's and James Ball's ideas about how to implement monetarism. The basic rate of income tax was reduced from 33 per cent to 30 per cent despite the unhealthy 'state of the books' which the Conservatives found on entering office, although this was balanced by the introduction of a 15 per cent rate of value added tax (VAT). The first round of public expenditure cuts were announced, totalling £1.5 billion for 1979/80 compared with Labour's plans.[33] Monetary policy was also tightened, with a target set for M3 of 7–11 per cent for 1979/80 compared with the Labour range of 8–12 per cent. However, it was not until the budget of March 1980 that the Chancellor of the Exchequer made the outline of Conservative economic policy clear and announced the vehicle through which he intended to control the money supply—the so-called Medium-Term Financial Strategy (MTFS).[34]

The MTFS (which encapsulated David Laidler's concept of gradualism) became the centre-piece of the government's economic policy for a short period. Within the MTFS itself, at first the monetary target dominated, but came to be increasingly displaced by the PSBR. The strategy as a whole came under increasing challenge as the exchange rate rose sharply (under-mining the manufacturing sector) and then subsequently collapsed. By the end of 1983/4 some commentators suggested that the UK had effectively moved to an exchange rate target. In both cases it was difficult to establish the precise role which these concepts played in the government's overall economic policy, and for many who thought that policy ought to be adjusted to take account of the rapidly rising unemployment, there was a feeling that they had become totems rather than a guide to sound economic management.[35]

The decision to pursue a deflationary course was bound to be contro-versial within the Conservative party as well as on the opposition benches.

---

[33] Smith (1987).

[34] See *The Times*, 27 March 1980.

[35] For further discussion of monetarism see Smith (1987). For David Laidler's ideas see Laidler (1985a); also Laidler (1985b). Also pertinent are Burns (1977) and Walters (1986).

Many pragmatic Conservatives were sceptical of the nostrums of monetarism and fearful that unemployment would lead to electoral disaster. They were joined in their opposition by a number of Conservatives whose philosophy was such that they did not necessarily prefer low levels of inflation to full employment, and among senior party figures there were many who remembered the legacy of mistrust which the Conservatives had inherited from the 1930s. Inside the government, however, Mrs Thatcher was determined that the monetarist experiment should be pursued consistently and without faltering. Although her initial Cabinets contained a number of persons who were not committed to her philosophy, she ensured that the key economic posts went to like-minded Conservatives. Sir Geoffrey Howe as Chancellor was backed by John Biffen as Chief Secretary and Nigel Lawson as Financial Secretary. Sir Keith Joseph, Mrs Thatcher's early intellectual mentor, went to the Department of Industry. Only James Prior represented the 'wetter' strand of Toryism at the Department of Employment and he had major fights within the party to ensure that his strategy of reforming industrial relations law in a step-by-step manner was accepted.

The Treasury's repeated attempts to cut the level of public expenditure inevitably generated resistance from those at the heads of the spending ministries. This is hardly surprising because however much a minister may agree in theory with an overall strategy of cutting public expenditure, he earns a reputation within his department and outside it by defending the departmental programmes against cuts. This phenomenon (which could be seen in both Mrs Thatcher and Sir Keith Joseph when they were in charge of high-spending departments between 1970 and 1974) did not cease to operate under Mrs Thatcher. The 1981 budget, which saw a new series of demands from the Treasury for cuts, caused real divisions within the Cabinet and a demand for a revision of the procedure whereby the crucial budget decisions were taken. This in turn led to the establishment of the so-called 'Star Chamber', a committee of the Cabinet presided over by Whitelaw before which ministers hammered out their budgetary arguments.[36]

It has been noted that 1981 in many ways marked a change in the character of Mrs Thatcher's premiership.[37] Initially she had been dependent on a number of senior Cabinet ministers who were not of her political persuasion. But, with the reshuffles of that year, she was able to dominate the Cabinet more effectively. The Falklands War and the subsequent election victory of 1983 greatly reinforced her position. While there was some discussion of her position as party leader—especially after

[36] Holmes (1985b).
[37] Holmes (1985b).

Michael Heseltine challenged her style of premiership in the wake of the Westland affair at the end of 1985—there was never any serious threat to oust Mrs Thatcher. Although her style of leadership was made an issue in the election, there was no challenge to her before the poll.[38] And the election victory of 1987—which gave Mrs Thatcher an unprecedented third term of office—again reinforced her dominance of the Cabinet and the party.

The original economic philosophy offered by the government reflected the critique worked out in opposition. Although Sir Geoffrey Howe as Chancellor from 1979 to 1983 was a strong adherent of that philosophy, his successor, Nigel Lawson, expounded an even more robust vision of the economy in Mrs Thatcher's second term. Indeed, the shakier some of the doctrinal foundations of monetarism became, the more flamboyant and self-confident was the Chancellor's defence of the government's economic strategy. Lawson used the 1986 budget to spell out that vision when he combined the idea of reduced direct taxation with a theory of popular capitalism. Thus apart from reducing the basic rate of direct tax from 30 per cent to 29 per cent, Lawson promised to spread the ownership of stocks and shares more widely than ever before and suggested a future in which far more ordinary members of the public would have a direct stake in the capitalist system.[39]

The concept of a people's capitalism was in a very real sense the complement to the Conservative rolling-back of the borders of the State by public expenditure cuts and privatization, and represented an attempt to change popular attitudes so as to make them more supportive of the private sector, less reliant on the public sector, and more entrepreneurial. Although there were many facets to the Conservative campaign, the two key ones were profit-sharing and privatization. The profit-sharing idea entailed encouraging companies to develop schemes whereby workers could be paid in the form of shares in the company. Such shares would attract tax relief and would, it was hoped, enhance the workers' commitment to the firm's profit-making capacity. At the same time, in order to encourage the small investor, the rate of stamp duty payable on share transfers was reduced, reinforcing the fall in transaction costs which the new technology had brought.

The central policy, however, was privatization, which neatly brought together a number of ideological and pragmatic facets of the Conservatives' new philosophy. It represented a strong desire to alter the balance between the public and the private sector and find permanent ways of changing the borders of the State. The Labour party in the early 1970s had

[38] For a discussion see Tyler (1987).
[39] Nigel Lawson's own ideas can conveniently be gleaned from Lawson (1980, 1982).

spoken of making a permanent transfer of power to working people and their families. Now the Conservatives, conscious of Sir Keith's warning of the ratchet effect of Labour governments, hoped to bypass the normal process of adversary politics by giving individuals a stake in the system of private enterprise.[40] As has been pointed out, privatization is not a simple concept but rather an umbrella term for a range of policies designed to strengthen market forces as opposed to the forces of the State.[41] Whether by developing policies to reduce the role of the public sector in the economy, by using public policy to encourage the private sector to grow, by increasing market pressure on public sector organizations, or by seeking new mixes of public and private sector resources to solve problems, the intention of the government was clear. It believed that on grounds of efficiency and morality, the private sector's role should be enhanced. And, as one recent commentator has put it, 'privatization . . . transformed a government in office into a radical government with a political ideology' (Veljanovski (1987)). Initially the Conservatives were committed only to reversing the most recent of Labour's public ownership initiatives—not to trying to reform the State's role in industry by selling off a wide range of nationalized industries. However, the early success of share sales convinced ministers that a more radical policy of privatization might be electorally popular, would bring financial relief to the government, and would deal with the persistent problem of running the nationalized industries. By 1983 the government had divested itself of interests in 25 companies and had set in motion sales for many more, including two major public utilities of gas and telecommunications.

The goal of extending share ownership was important to the policy-makers. The British Gas and British Telecom shares were put on the open market, with some shares specifically reserved for the small purchaser, especially those who used or worked for the relevant utilities. (Survey evidence suggests that about one million people—half of the total of those who sought shares in British Telecom—had never owned shares before.) Taken together, the sale of shares is calculated to have raised assets worth £6,957 million between 1981/2 and 1985/6, although clearly many would criticize the way these sales of assets were integrated into the national accounts. Following the sale of British Gas, the State sector of industry, according to the government, accounted for 8 per cent of GDP, whereas in 1979 it had accounted for 11.5 per cent.[42]

In addition to the spectacular and radical attempt to create a wider share ownership and to reduce the role of the State, the Conservatives were

[40] Kavanagh (1987).
[41] For discussion see Heald and Steel (1982).
[42] These figures on privatization are taken from HM Treasury (1987, vol. II, p. 30).

aware of the importance of another way of building support for the values they represented—through the housing market. Housing policy was, in fact, seen as crucial to the political battle after 1979. Apart from such steps as raising the proportion of a mortgage which could earn tax relief to £30,000 to encourage home-ownership, the Conservatives pursued a vigorous policy of council house sales. Selling council houses to sitting tenants in fact constituted one of the earliest experiments with privatization and, of course, brought in money to the State sector. Home-ownership has been growing steadily in Britain since 1964, but between 1979 and 1987 the proportion of home-owners rose from 57 per cent to 64 per cent.[43] Until 1979, however, the number of council tenants had also been rising because what had been declining was the private rental sector, largely as a result of the laws designed to protect private tenants. After 1979, however, home-ownership grew at the expense of the council sector.[44] In 1986 a further development occurred with the announcement that New Town Corporations would be privatized.

There was of course a strong political motive behind the housing policies adopted by the Conservatives after 1979. It may be that, as some commentators have noted, a correlation between political attitudes and housing tenure tells us nothing about the direction of causation in the relationship.[45] Certainly it would be naïve to assume that a new house-owner changes his political views simply on the purchase of a house or that a former council tenant would alter political preferences on being given the option to purchase his home. This is not to say, however, that long-term attitudes may not be affected by changes in the pattern of housing tenure in Britain.[46]

From the point of view of Conservative strategy, four broad benefits may be hypothesized. First, the expansion of the number and range of owner-occupiers extends the numbers of those with a stake in society and in the free market system. Second, the sale of council houses, apart from adding to the number of home-owners, would break up homogenous working-class communities and presumably reduces the likelihood of there continuing pockets of hostility to Conservative values. Third, the sale of council houses ought to make occupational mobility easier than before when complicated council house transfers had to be arranged, although it should be recognized that differences in price between the housing markets of different areas clearly remain an important factor. Finally, of course, the

[43] This is the figure given in HM Treasury (1987, p. 154).
[44] For a discussion of the impact of housing tenure on voting see Heath, Jowell, and Curtice (1985), especially pp. 44–57.
[45] Heath, Jowell, and Curtice (1985).
[46] For an examination of housing policy see Holmans (1987).

spread of council house purchase would give many voters a stake in resist-
ing the return of a Labour government which might attempt some rever-
sion to the status quo ante.

Housing policy reflected a number of strands in the contemporary
Conservative party. Support for home-ownership had of course been an
important element in the party's credo since the time of Churchill's post-
war administration. The decision to move forcefully on council house sales
showed the radical populism of the Conservative party, the willingness to
use the levers of central government to force local authorities to adopt
national policies in areas which had hitherto been seen as primarily local.
And it also indicated the ambitious vision of the party by 1979; for its eyes
were not merely on the short term but on transforming the character of
British society.

With housing policy, the Conservatives were clearly extending the
private sector in a way which attracted a vast section of the population,
although there emerged substantial criticism of the extent to which the
housing stock was being neglected and the continuing plight of the
homeless. However, in those areas where the Conservatives had hoped to
reduce the extent of the public sector either by cutting back expenditure
unilaterally or by attempting to encourage a different mix of public and
private resources, the problem turned out to be more difficult. Public
opinion, it seemed, was perversely in favour of a high level of expenditure on welfare services—or at least on those welfare services which most
people believed they might be likely to use at some time in their lives.
The debate about the National Health Service was a particular case in
point.

The National Health Service (NHS) enjoys a special place in the affec-
tions of those who support an extensive Welfare State. Founded by
Aneurin Bevin in the immediate post-war period, it commands a great deal
of popular support.[47] Yet there has also been increasing concern about the
principles on which the service is operated—concern which is not confined
to those who want to see a vigorous free market in health care. The
problem of the NHS is the extent to which growing demand for health care
can be met from public resources.

The debate when the Conservatives initially came to office was not
prosecuted with vigour. The question of whether the NHS would be better
funded from insurance rather than taxation had been raised from time to
time but not pursued for fear of political reactions. Any general concern
about Conservative commitment to the NHS was allayed by the statement
that it was not the party's intention to reduce spending on the NHS—a

---

[47] For attitudes towards the National Health Service see Bosanquet (1984).

statement which was echoed by Mrs Thatcher's famous comment that 'the NHS is safe with us'.[48]

Many Conservatives on the right of the party were interested in revamping an insurance-based approach to welfare services, including medicine, rather than continuing the existing comprehensive version of the Welfare State which had strong redistributive connotations and also involved the use of a State bureaucracy. The appeal of the idea—which was also applicable to pension reforms—was that it appeared more flexible and could allow variations in provision. Yet any suggestion of wholesale reform of the National Health Service on this basis was politically dangerous and ministers were careful to handle proposals for change very circumspectly.[49]

By the time of the 1987 election, however, it was clear that the issue of major reform could not be avoided if the Conservatives were not to be permanently vulnerable on the issue. There is a major conflict between the generalized health care envisaged under the original system and the increasingly expensive treatments which can now be made available by modern technology, for example dialysis and transplants. Very few major changes had been made to the structure of the NHS, and indeed by what was the last session of the 1983 Parliament the Conservatives had committed themselves to spending more resources on the Service. Yet this hardly stemmed public criticism of flaws in the system. Whether a way can ever be found to restructure the NHS without alienating public opinion remains to be seen; but the review which had promised an opportunity for radical solutions to be canvassed by 1988 had rejected major change.[50]

It might have been assumed that the experience of two terms of government would have diminished the Conservative party's appetite for radical reform. Yet the party entered the general election of 1987 with a manifesto which promised further initiatives designed to alter the role of government in Britain. Some of these initiatives were extensions of the government's privatization plans—so that, for example, electricity, the British Airports Authority, and water were targeted for sale to the public. Other initiatives were more controversial. A radical overhaul of education was promised and included a proposal to allow schools to opt out of local authority control in certain circumstances. The first government grants to education had been in 1833 and the State's growing involvement in the provision of education mirrored the intellectual and ideological battles of the

[48] For a general study see Klein (1983). For an interesting study of the impact of competitive tendering in the NHS see Milne (1987). Also Witney (1988).

[49] On the Central Policy Review Staff see Hennessy, Morrison, and Townsend (1985).

[50] For a recent argument for introducing more competition into the NHS see Green (1985).

nineteenth and twentieth centuries. There were also plans to improve the efficiency of the private rented sector of the housing market by relaxing controls and regulations. Although the Labour party attacked the Conservatives for these proposals and suggested that they were but part of a more general strategy to undermine the Welfare State, the Conservatives were re-elected in 1987 with an overall majority of 101 seats over all other parties—a majority which makes it likely that many of the Conservative manifesto proposals will be translated into legislation.

6. Conservatism and the Constitution

It has already been suggested that one of the first institutions to feel the impact of the Conservatives' desire after 1975 to create a new balance between the public and the private sectors was the Civil Service. Other political institutions in the United Kingdom were also affected by the reassessment of the activities of government, however. Indeed there was something of a paradox in the impact which Mrs Thatcher's initiatives had on the British system of government. For, while it is true that her intention was to reduce the power of government generally, especially by transferring more responsibility and choice to the individual, she found that this could only be done by strengthening central government. Thus any balance between central and local government which existed before 1979 was eroded as a result of Conservative policies.

This centralization of power in the British political system after 1979 came about more by accident than by design. By and large the Conservatives had, until the mid-1960s, been suspicious both of suggestions for constitutional reform and of organizational theory. Pragmatic and *ad hoc* adjustments had been accepted but the party had been slow to embrace even initiatives such as the Parliamentary Commissioner for Administration which were designed to eradicate maladministration. Edward Heath's period as leader saw a quickening of interest in reform of the machinery of government and in the application of management techniques to Whitehall's administrative processes. His 1970–4 administration saw a series of organizational experiments with such innovations as 'super-departments' and the 'hiving off' of discrete governmental functions to other agencies. The establishment of the Central Policy Review Staff under Lord Rothschild epitomized Mr Heath's belief in the need for long-term policy research and planning of a different nature from that undertaken within the departments.

In opposition between 1974 and 1979, some Conservatives emphasized the need for constitutional reform including a written constitution and a bill of rights. This interest reflected concern that Britain was becoming more difficult to govern and that the electoral and party systems were producing governments whose policies were manifestly out of line with the majority of public opinion. However, the rise of neo-liberalism within the Conservative party and change of leadership meant a diminution of interest in constitutional reform as a method of precluding the abuse of State power. The more radical solution of transferring functions to the private sector and relying on the market to protect freedom replaced arguments that essentially involved relying on complicated systems of checks and balances. Mrs Thatcher herself was far less interested than her predecessor had been in machinery-of-government questions; she believed that such issues were peripheral to the question of policy. Admittedly, some on the right were impressed by Hayek's arguments about the need to provide rules to govern the conduct of economic and political activity, but such concerns tended to be ignored in the press of practical policy concerns.

In government, however, the Conservatives found that their policies could not be implemented fully without fundamental alterations in the political system, specifically in the network of relationships which existed between central and local government. On one level, this meant taking powers to impose a duty on local authorities to implement such policies as council house sales. More generally, it entailed increasing erosion of the financial independence of local government. And, ultimately, it involved the abolition of the metropolitan counties when it became clear that they were going to be used by Labour as bases to oppose the expenditure controls which were so crucial to the government's economic strategy.

Those who opposed Conservative policy saw Mrs Thatcher's initiatives as a dangerous attack on the system of local government. Those who supported her argued that the government had a mandate to implement certain policies and that it was unacceptable to permit ideologically motivated local authorities to frustrate that mandate. As with so many issues in British government, the debate focused not on attempting to achieve a proper balance between central and local government, but rather on the partisan preferences of the debate's protagonists—preferences which might in the past (or indeed in the future) lead them to advocate quite different positions with respect to the balance of local and central power.

One final point should be made about the approach to the constitution under Mrs Thatcher. Although the Conservatives wanted to reduce the powers of the State in relation to the control of the economy and the provision of welfare, they wished to see the authority of the State maintained in the sphere of defence and law and order. Both of these basic functions of the State became highly salient to the political debates of the 1980s. Defence became an important electoral issue as the Labour party moved towards unilateral disarmament. Law and order was important both because of the Conservatives' perception that this theme was important to the general public and because the other parties were seen as vulnerable on the issue. (Labour's radical elements had developed an anti-police stance which Neil Kinnock had to counter in the 1987 campaign.) There was thus, in addition to a reassessment of the role of the State in the economy and in relation to welfare, a strengthening and indeed a centralization in relation to State functions which Conservatives saw as fundamental. Some might see this as a somewhat odd blend between the neo-liberal and the populist strands of contemporary Conservatism; yet, if not entirely consistent, it proved electorally popular.

7. Conclusions

The State's role had increased in Britain over the twentieth century as a result of those who thought the power of central government the best instrument to create a more just and a more efficient society. That expansion of governmental activity created a political culture in which it was assumed that government could and should solve a wide range of problems. Although the Labour party believed in using governmental power more extensively than did the Conservatives, both parties were, until the mid-1970s, committed to a positive role for the State and relatively unenthusiastic about the role of the market. In the 1970s, however, the Conservative party became the vehicle for a general questioning of the existing balance between the public and the private sectors in Britain. Although the Conservative party's adherence to the tenets of monetarism was modified in government, the accompanying emphases on public expenditure restraint and on lower direct taxation were sustained. Over a period of three administrations, the government was able to promote the values of individualism, ownership, and entrepreneurialism in a way which had a distinct impact on the political climate. And while the attempt to introduce market values into areas such as the National Health Service were not very successful, some policy initiatives were extremely popular—most notably those in the field of housing.

Could it be said that a new consensus has been created either within the Conservative party or between the parties? Within the Conservative party there have been opponents of specific policies and, more generally, of the tolerance of high rates of unemployment and the refusal to use governmental powers extensively to try to redress disparities between different parts of the United Kingdom. Some of the criticism has come from senior figures such as Francis Pym, Sir Ian Gilmour, and James Prior who had long been in disagreement with Mrs Thatcher; other criticism has been focused on the back-benches through groups such as Conservative Action to Revive Employment (CARE), the One Nation Group and the Tory Reform Group. But dissident activity has been sporadic and the balance of opinion within the Party has moved right. Thus there is probably now a general bias towards market solutions and a general suspicion of collectivist ones. This does not mean that such ideas would never be readopted for, as has been pointed out, the majority of Conservatives are agnostic on economic policy;[51] it simply means that at the moment the climate within Conservative ranks is anti-Statist.

The success of the Conservative party and its new policies has forced the Labour party to reassess its position on a range of issues. It now seems likely that Labour will abandon its traditional commitment to the form of nationalization which it introduced in the period 1945–51; and it is unlikely to try to reverse Conservative initiatives on council house sales. It may not be precisely a new consensus, but in these areas the nature and form of State involvement will never be the same again. The extent to which Labour rethinks its central strategies on taxation, industrial policy, and the Welfare State remains to be seen, but it would be surprising if it did not move towards new formulae in these areas, reflecting perhaps the demand for greater individual choice and a new partnership between the public and private sectors.

In conclusion, the last decade has seen an intellectual shift which has caused a redrawing of the borders of the British State. Whether the new borders are permanent or temporary only time will tell. It would be surprising, however, if they were ever again drawn in the same place as in 1979.

[51] Norton (1987).

9

The Macro-economic Role of the State

CHRISTOPHER ALLSOPP[*]

1. Introduction

Most discussions of markets versus planning, or of compromises such as the 'mixed economy', focus on the role of government intervention in the allocation of resources and in the promotion and distribution of economic welfare. There is, however, another aspect of government which came to particular prominence in the post-war period—the role of the State in setting the macro-economic framework within which markets have to operate. Thus the 1950s and 1960s—and arguably the 1970s and 1980s as well—were periods of active macro-economic management in pursuit of goals such as full employment, price stability, and balance of payments equilibrium. In parallel with changing views about the role of markets, this policy activism came to be widely questioned. Perceptions about what governments can and should do at the macro-economic level have swung about to an extraordinary extent as economic conditions have deteriorated.

This article is about the case for and against active macro-economic management. The questions raised, and the types of economic theory involved, are rather different from those that arise in considering resource allocation and the distribution of income at the micro-economic level. Clearly, however, macro-economic and micro-economic attitudes interact, and not just at the political level. Thus, in much of the 'monetarist' tradition, markets are viewed not only as the best way of coping with micro-economic interactions, but also as ensuring macro-economic performance as well. Macro-economic objectives are subsumed under a general attitude of market optimism. (That indeed is the chief characteristic of this type of economics.) At the other end of the spectrum, heavily interventionist strategies—replacing the market—may also repress macro-economic issues, since macro-economic objectives are part of the planning process. The most interesting issues thus arise in the middle ground.

* New College, Oxford. I am extremely grateful for helpful comments from Andrea Boltho, Dieter Helm, and Tim Jenkinson. The usual disclaimers apply.

Specifically, is there a case for macro-economic intervention by the State which transcends the usual reasons for intervening at the micro-economic level?

Given the large scale of the topic, the approach in this paper has to be selective. Section 2 looks at the development and practice of Keynesian ideas, focusing on the divergences that arose between theory and political practice. It is argued that the Keynesian diagnosis and prescription, properly interpreted, lead to a specific and limited role for State intervention, different in many respects from the post-Keynesian consensus, which itself evolved over time. Section 3 considers the underlying issues involved in the monetarist 'counter-revolution', again trying to distinguish between theoretical preconceptions and political practice. Section 4, building on the earlier analysis, looks in more detail at the emerging 'consensus' of the 1970s and early 1980s, which, it is argued, is more apparent than real. Section 5 re-evaluates the macro-economic role of the State, suggesting that the range of issues, which narrowed in the 1970s and early 1980s, is now widening again as governments, especially in Europe, attempt to get to grips with the problem of persistent unemployment. The situation is reminiscent of the widening policy agenda of the inter-war period. Section 6 is a brief conclusion.

2. Keynesian and Post-Keynesian Economics: Theory and Practice

The most important political aspect of 'Keynesian' economics lies not in a particular model, but in a *diagnosis*. In contrast to the prevailing paradigm of the inter-war period, Keynes (and of course others such as Kalecki or Myrdal) saw unemployment as arising, not for the usual classical reasons, but because of a deficiency of demand or spending.

From a policy point of view, once that diagnosis is made, then the general prescription of raising demand follows, and the mechanics of multipliers, of fiscal policy, or of monetary effects are really a detail. Again, from a policy point of view, the diagnosis is basically optimistic: it suggests that economic management can get rid of unemployment relatively quickly with little pain or cost. This message contrasts with the pessimism of the classical (or neo-classical) position. This suggested that a cure for unemployment would necessarily involve a reduction of structural problems, a better functioning labour market at the micro-economic level (increased flexibility, in the current jargon), and lower *real* wages. All these prescriptions, which arise, of course, from *ad hoc* explanations of unemployment, due, ultimately, to imperfections and market failures, would require fundamental long-term change, and almost no one, in the inter-war period or at present, could expect rapid improvements.

Furthermore, against the broad policy options apparently offered by the classical diagnosis—the improvement of markets with a return to competition *or* detailed intervention to replace the market system—the Keynesian prescription offered the perfect political compromise: limited intervention by the State to improve the macro-economic environment, whilst leaving resource allocation largely to the market system. This kind of intervention could be seen, not as supplanting the capitalist system, but as saving it from itself. The Keynesian message had considerable political power.

This political aspect is stressed since it is probably true to say that it was the *idea* of a macro-economic role for government that shaped the post-war consensus rather than the specific advocacy of demand management. Thus, though the General Theory is concerned with macro-economic problems in a closed economy, it is natural to extend the framework to include the avoidance of inconsistencies and other problems arising at the international level—with the prescription of co-operation and co-ordination of policies. Moreover, a glance at the experience of countries other than the UK suggests that it was the commitment to macro-economic management in general rather than demand management *per se* that was important in the 1950s and 1960s.

It also needs to be stressed that, though the post-war consensus is often described as 'Keynesian', at least in the Anglo-Saxon literature, there were many aspects of it that were not. The development of Welfare States, industrial intervention, and public expenditure programmes (analysed elsewhere in this volume) has little to do with macro-economics, or, for that matter, with the economics of Keynes. That said, these developments do affect the macro-economy, in terms of the constraints or problems faced and in terms of the instruments available. (Thus, as noted, in a fully interventionist economy, macro-economic problems *per se* may become degenerate.) Moreover, many problems—such as international payments problems, or regional and sectoral difficulties—are, so to speak, only 'semi-macro'. It is necessary, however, not to lose sight of the fundamental point that the original message was minimalist in spirit: limited intervention by governments at the aggregate level was seen as necessary to set the macro-economic framework in which markets could operate.

The fundamental questions are thus about why markets may fail at the macro-economic level whilst remaining viable at the micro-economic level. Macro-economics is about co-ordination failures, and the macro-economic role of the State is to avoid them.

(a) Co-ordination

When economic units, such as individuals, firms, sectors, or countries, interact, co-ordination problems can arise. Thus, for example, with oligopolistic interdependence between firms, where the actions of one firm affect the others, the result will depend, often sensitively, on whether they compete or collude, on the information available to the different units, and on the precise nature of the strategic interdependence. Often such interdependence leads to a case for intervention, for example to discourage monopoly practices, or to co-ordinate research and development, or to meet strategic threats from foreign competitors. Market failure, due to strategic interactions and information deficiencies, may, as argued elsewhere in this volume, be pervasive.

This approach contrasts with the typical paradigm case of perfect competition, or general equilibrium, where co-ordination is achieved, at the micro- and at the macro-economic level, by an appropriate set of prices. As is well known, the conditions under which such an equilibrium could be established are stringent—and indeed the paradigm is frequently used 'backwards' to illustrate and illuminate the situations likely to lead to market failure. Even within the paradigm, there is a problem as to how the equilibrium set of prices comes to be established: what is it that co-ordinates the system as a whole? (Various devices such as the 'Walrasian auctioneer' or the 'Edgeworth recontract process' have been put forward as idealized 'thought-experiments' to dodge the implications—see Helm in this volume.) With oligopolistic interdependence and information failures at the micro-economic level, co-ordination failures at the macro-economic level are more likely to arise.

The classic failure at the macro-economic level for a closed economy stressed by Keynes was a potential failure of co-ordination between the savings decisions of households, on the one hand, and the investment decisions of firms, on the other. This, it is argued below, can be seen as a market failure of a particular kind, justifying macro-economic intervention to avoid deleterious outcomes such as unemployment or a fluctuating price level. It amounts to the denial that this particular co-ordination requirement can safely be left to the market, via fluctuations in a particular relative price—the interest rate.

There are, however, other potential failures at the macro-economic level. A particularly transparent and important case—which has the advantage of bringing out in a direct way some of the gaming or strategic problems—is the problem of international co-ordination. The economic policies of individual countries interact and they interact in a strategic way.

Co-ordination and co-operation may be necessary to avoid deleterious outcomes for the system as a whole.

(b) An Example: International Co-ordination

The example to be considered is particularly simple, and may be stated as a question for policymakers: 'What happens if countries try to run balance of payments surpluses relative to each other, and what is the appropriate policy to avoid deleterious outcomes?'.[1] (This of course was a practical question faced by the architects of the post-war international order, including, of course, Keynes.)

To keep the thought-experiment simple, assume there is only one international asset which is fixed in supply—call it gold. Assume further that all gold is held by the governments as reserves. We know immediately that balance of payments surpluses and deficits must add up, over the several countries, to exactly zero (the counterpart to this is that the stock of gold is fixed). For an individual country, a balance of payments deficit would imply an outflow of gold; a surplus would imply an inflow.

Without loss of generality, it may be assumed that the system starts in equilibrium in the sense that each country is in international payments balance *and* that governments are content with the stocks of gold that they hold (i.e. suppressing any consideration of the private sector, the system is in stock and flow equilibrium). What then happens if governments decide that they want to hold more gold reserves and that they want to build them up by running payments surpluses?

Obviously the system is then in disequilibrium. Without more assumptions about what governments do, little more can be said. However, if we have the feeling that whatever they do in such circumstances is likely to be bad (intuitively plausible, since they cannot succeed), we already have a policy recommendation, Trivially, but importantly, the recommendation is that they should not try to do this: they should co-ordinate their policies, and not try to do the impossible. There is a role for macro-economic co-ordination.

In fact, we can make a good guess at what governments *might* do to try to improve their payments position or build up reserves. It is not one thing, but several. One thing they might do is to introduce trade restrictions, leading to a trade war with costs all round. Another is competitive de-

---

[1] Recent work on international policy co-ordination has focused on more complex issues such as international compatibility of the mix between monetary and fiscal policy, the difficulty of providing credible commitments over time, and at a more practical level, the benefits of alternative schemes such as 'target zones' or 'multilateral surveillance'. (See, for example, Buiter and Marston (1985) for papers on many of the issues.)

valuations, if each currency can be devalued in terms of gold. A third is competitive deflations which, if prices and wages are sticky, would lead to world recession and unemployment. Policymakers in the post-war reconstruction phase were acutely aware that *all* these policy actions had occurred in the inter-war period, and were concerned to prevent a repetition. They clearly saw a need for international co-operation, both on objectives and on the rules of the game.

Whilst the main point is that the mere diagnosis of a problem (countries trying to run balance of payments surpluses relative to each other) may be sufficient to suggest a policy response (don't), it is useful to pursue the example a little further. Economists like to model the results of changes in parameters—like the change in the desire to hold reserves assumed above. In particular, there is a question as to whether economic actions would lead to the establishment of a new equilibrium.

It is clear that the trade-war case would be hard to model in detail. It may, however, lead to a new equilibrium—of a sort. Countries could get into a situation where, given the other countries' trade restrictions, their own position was the best they could achieve. This would be a non-cooperative equilibrium. This would be worse than the co-operative equilibrium they started with, since the game is non-zero-sum. Co-operation and co-ordination thus have clear benefits in getting to, or in maintaining, the better outcome. Such strategic interactions are one of the most fundamental reasons for believing in a macro-economic role for the State.

Competitive devaluations in relation to 'gold' would not be popular in practice, but may lead to a new equilibrium. If they lead to the price level falling in each country relative to gold, the gold stock is effectively revalued. When this has gone far enough, the value of the gold stock is high enough to satisfy the higher demand for reserves, leading to the possibility of a new equilibrium. This result is 'monetarist' in spirit: effectively the price level is flexible downwards. (There is an analogy with the more normal case where an increase in the domestic demand for money leads to a fall in prices and a new equilibrium.) In practice, measures to increase the stock of 'gold', for example by paper gold such as 'bancor' or SDRs, or to co-operate on raising its price would generally be preferred to uncoordinated devaluations, even if these were realistically possible. (Thus, on a 'dollar' standard, the example breaks down.)

The most 'Keynesian' case is competitive deflations. There is a gaming element here too. If the reason for these reactions is to build up reserves, the outcome if all do it is self-defeating. On the other hand, one country may gain, if it acts in isolation. Even more importantly, if one country does not deflate, whereas others do, that country may lose reserves and suffer heavy losses. The situation has the form of a 'prisoner's dilemma'. It may be optimal for the individual country to deflate whether others deflate or whether they do not. The equilibrium is a bad outcome for all. Co-operation breaks the dilemma. Even without formal co-operation, the co-operative solution may be achieved in repeated plays, but there is a presumption that it would be fragile, especially in the face of major shocks.

More conventionally, the process of competitive deflationary moves is closely analogous to the disequilibrium process of 'multiplier' adjustment familiar from elementary textbooks. It leads to successive rounds of deflation. A new (quasi-)equilibrium may be achieved, if, in terms of the governments' overall objectives, increasing unemployment or decreasing output lowers the desire to build up reserves. The end-point of the multiplier adjustment would come about when output or employment had fallen enough to reduce to zero the desire to build up reserves. Often, the (disequilibrium) process of adjustment is suppressed and attention focused simply on the new underemployment equilibrium (the comparative static or comparative equilibrium method).

There is a far-reaching parallel between the multiplier story and the outcome of a non-cooperative game. After the shift in the desire to build up reserves, the co-operative solution is for no action to be taken, since it would be self-defeating. The non-cooperative outcome is reached when there is no further benefit to the individual country from further deflation. A sufficient condition for this is that the reserves held are in line with desired holdings, which is also the end-point of the multiplier adjustment.

The end-point of the multiplier reaction was referred to as a 'quasi'-equilibrium since it effectively depended upon prices and wages being fixed in terms of 'gold'. If this is not the case, then it may not be the end of the story. Specifically, if low output and high unemployment lead to wages and prices falling (balanced deflation), then the effective gold supply rises, ultimately to the point where the desire to hold reserves is satisfied. Thus there is something special about the 'monetarist-type' adjustment, and it could be said to be *the* new equilibrium of the system. The Keynesian problem could be said to arise from inflexibility of wages and prices. Whether this theoretical point is relevant to policy depends partly upon the speed of reaction. Even if it were very rapid, however, (and many 'monetarists' of the new classical school assume continuous market clearing) policymakers might very well prefer to alter 'the supply of gold' or international liquidity to satisfy the demand for reserves—especially if the demand for reserves were to fluctuate. That is, they might prefer to *offset* the problem rather than rely on markets, since a fluctuating price level or gold price might be regarded as costly and undesirable.

The desirability of offsetting action depends upon there being something to offset. In the example, a policy problem arose precisely because the demand for reserves changed. But why did it change? It was plausible, perhaps, because governments are often thought to be arbitrary in their decision-taking. In the Keynesian economic framework, the private sector is also typically assumed to indulge in such arbitrary shifts—the analogy is with an increase in the desire to save. If this does not happen or happens only very slowly, then the policy problem may simply not arise. The literature is full of solemn demonstrations that stabilization policy is not needed if there is nothing to stabilize. We return to this below.

Two further points may be made. The first is that the problems posed by the example do not seem to depend upon the small number of economic agents assumed. If desires to hold reserves change in a correlated way, then non-cooperative outcomes seem more, not less, likely if the number of agents is large. Competition does not ensure that a group of individual agents will never try to do the impossible. It may or may not make it more likely that the price response (as opposed to trade wars or deflation) would be rapid.

The second is to emphasize how the analysis depended upon one simple consistency condition, which relates to the nature of the equilibrium and disequilibrium concepts being used. The weakest concept of equilibrium is, in the example, that the aggregate desire to hold reserves equals the total supply. Nothing is said about whether individual countries are in equilibrium. Even if plans are consistent in aggregate, much adjustment could be going on 'underneath'. A stronger condition would be that each individual country should be in equilibrium. Beyond that, that each individual agent should be in equilibrium in each and every country. Much macro-economics is based on aggregate consistency relationships and the consequences of their violation. Consideration of individuals, and individual markets, is often suppressed. (Thus, in the above, almost no structure except of the broadest and intuitive kind was given to the private sectors.) This is highly unsatisfactory to theorists who like to cast their analysis in terms of general equilibrium. However, one thing that is known about general equilibrium is that it never happens. Ultimately, many disputes in economics are about the relevance or otherwise of equilibrium results to practical policy.

(c) Demand Management and Unemployment

The pervasive legacy of the General Theory is the diagnosis of unemployment as due to aggregate demand failures, solvable in principle if the government can manipulate expenditure. It should be noted that such a

diagnosis/treatment combination is somewhat circumscribed and conditional: there may be other reasons for unemployment not susceptible to
this treatment and there may be other reasons why demand cannot or
should not be manipulated. In practice, the remedy of demand management was always seen as conditional on the avoidance of other problems,
such as inflation or external difficulties.

One way of characterizing the policy message is to note that in simple
Keynesian models (often more influential than complicated ones), the level
of output and unemployment is *indeterminate* and thus dependent on the
stance of policy. For example, in the simple Keynesian multiplier model
(extended to include government expenditure), output and unemployment
can be manipulated by varying government spending, or by varying investment if investment depends on interest rates and interest rates can be
controlled. Likewise, taxes affect consumption spending. Indeterminacy of
this kind, an unattractive feature to the theorists, is a policy advantage. It
gives scope for action and a macro-economic role to the State. The policy
problem is essentially simple. Given the objective of full employment, the
policy instruments are set accordingly.

Extensions are possible. Thus, analysis of the 1950s and 1960s recast
the policy problem in the framework of multiple objectives and multiple
instruments. Trade-offs, such as the Phillips curve (relating inflation and
unemployment), were introduced. Basically, however, the analysis continued to offer policymakers a set of choices, choices that were quite
different from those implicit in the equilibriumist or neo-classical framework. It was when the reality of those choices came to be seriously doubted
from the late 1960s onwards that the consensus on economic management
broke down.

Such a characterization of the policy framework of the consensus years
may seem unduly mechanistic (though mechanistic models are surprisingly
durable—witness the continuing popularity of the Hicksian 'IS–LM'
framework). In many ways, a 'market failure' approach is more illuminating, and probably more true to the way in which Keynes thought. Thus,
just as 'classical' unemployment can be seen as arising from the wrong
constellation of real wages—especially a general level of real wages that is
too high—Keynesian unemployment is frequently seen as arising from a
level of *nominal* wages and prices too high relative to the money supply
(here standing for those factors that affect the flow of nominal spending or
demand). Correction would involve *either* lower nominal wages (and a
lower price level) *or* an increase in the money supply (more generally an
increase in demand).

As is well known, Keynes did not favour cuts in nominal wages as a way
out of recession, arguing instead for a rise in demand. But the form of

Keynes's argument against cutting nominal wages was not so much that it would not work (though he doubted the efficacy, given, he assumed, seriously deleterious expectational effects) but that it was far easier to raise the money supply or lower interest rates than to lower nominal wages. Thus, at this crucial point, Keynes's argument was pragmatic: it was easier to manage demand than to affect the wage bargain.[2] Unfortunately, that is not an argument that carries weight if there is an objective of curbing inflation.

It might seem from the above that Keynesians should be prepared to accept the so-called neo-classical synthesis—that the Keynesian model applies to the special case of rigid nominal wages and that nominal wage flexibility would eliminate any tendency to Keynesian unemployment. It suggests, moreover, that the interesting question is, as so many theorists have suggested, what it is that accounts for nominal wage inflexibility. This, however, would be to over-simplify, especially if we are concerned with the policy message and the justification for macro-economic intervention.

Keynes had remarkably little to say about labour market failures, at either the micro- or the macro-economic level. On the contrary, his view seems to have been that that part of the economic system functioned pretty well, well enough at least that failures could be ignored for the purposes of analysis. (Keynes would probably have regarded himself as trying to get away from the *ad hoc* nature of the classical diagnosis of unemployment, resting as it did on imperfections and market failures in the labour market.) The market failures that he was principally concerned with were those involving savings, investment, and finance.

Thus the classic 'Keynesian' problem is the wrong interest rate, determined by liquidity preference. The policy message is immediate: if bankers and speculators set up the wrong interest rate, then it is up to the authorities to intervene to set the right one. (It is easy these days to make the same point about the determination of international exchange rates, and, of course, Keynes himself spent the later years of his life almost entirely concerned with trying to set up a rational exchange rate system.)

Though Keynes was clearly not optimistic that 'finance' would 'get it right' from the point of view of the real economy, it is useful to probe a little more deeply into the 'failures' that might be envisaged. The first is simply the possibility of speculation leading to the wrong prices for assets—the wrong interest rate in simple versions of the Keynesian model. Keynes's distaste for the stock market is well known—he referred to it as a casino—and he thought that its time-horizon was short-term and that

---

[2] Indeed, it is worth recalling that for Keynes, stability of nominal wages was often taken as a policy objective. (Cf. Keynes, *General Theory*, ch. 19.)

expectations were not based on a view of the economic 'fundamentals'. This is where he applied his famous 'beauty contest' analogy to suggest aggregate irrationality from the interaction of rational individuals.

We are not concerned here with whether this diagnosis is, in some fundamental sense, right—the kind of behaviour described has proved difficult to model—but with drawing out the implications if it is right. Broadly, if it is, then unrestrained financial markets may generate the wrong set of interest rates and asset prices, and, what is more, may generate fluctuations. (Thus, for Keynes, the liquidity preference schedule determined the interest rate but not necessarily at the 'full employment' level, and was subject to shifts reflecting waves of optimism or pessimism.) On this diagnosis, there is a role for government in controlling the interest rate and in preventing fluctuations. The latter would require offsetting shifts in liquidity preference by central bank action. The parallel between this set of views and worries in the 1980s over the level and volatility of unrestrained floating exchange rates is obvious. (Note that, in both cases, the desirability of State action depends upon the efficacy of the instruments the State has available and on it being able to take a wise and far-seeing view of the fundamentals.)

Whilst the above argument is based on the motivations, expectations, and interactions of operators in financial markets, the second argument, though related, is perhaps more fundamental. Recall that in the 'classical' scheme of things, the role of the interest rate was to balance savings and investment at full employment. Thus, if an increase in the desire to save is considered—the impact that Keynes often seems to have had in mind—the classical view had it that interest rates would fall, stimulating investment. This Keynes denied. If interest rates do not adjust as they should, then (short of a change in the price level, see below) deflation and unemployment would result. Thus the question of whether a rise in the desire to save *signals* through to a fall in interest rates and thus to investment is fundamental to the dispute.

This is often treated as an empirical question: do interest rates or incomes and output react more quickly? There is more to it than that, however. Is the *information* available to financial markets to make the required adjustment?

An increase in the desire to save is an increase in the desire to accumulate assets. 'The problem arises . . . because of an increased desire for wealth as such' (Keynes, *General Theory*, ch. 16). Asset stocks are, however, given in the short term. Thus the initial impact we are concerned with is the attempt by the private sector to do something that it cannot do (i.e. this situation is like the international example discussed above). The private sector could accumulate assets, however, if investment were to rise (i.e. if interest rates were to fall), for then asset stocks would rise as a counterpart to the increased investment. Thus, it may be asserted, *if* interest rates do fall, all may be well and the economy remains at full employment, whereas if they do not, the Keynesian failure results.

The problem Keynes was concerned with was that the increased desire to save (excess supply of savings) would not signal through to the financial markets. Unless investment does rise, there is no increase in *actual* savings, no flow of money into financial institutions, no increase in liquidity. How then are the 'bankers' to know that they should lower interest rates? The increased desire to save expresses itself simply as a reduction in consumption *spending*. (Hicks introduced the refinement that the reduction in spending would lead to a reduction in the demand for money and a fall in the interest rate; this qualification does not, however, alter the fundamental point, since such a decline in interest rates is conditional on the reduction in spending. It mitigates the downward movement of the economy, rather than eliminating it.) The problem is that the excess supply of savings, which should lead to lower interest rates, is 'notional' rather than actual. It does not lead to an information flow (for example, a flow of money) that could actually cause the market to adjust.

There is, of course, a potential way out of this problem. If financial markets *anticipate* the decreased consumption and increase in potential (i.e. full-employment) savings, then they could act to lower interest rates and increase investment spending (i.e. the goods market would clear). The Keynesian view can be seen as denying that this process would work, since financial markets would not have the relevant information about potential savings, and would in any case be unlikely to adjust on the basis of potential as opposed to actual outcomes. (A banker who adjusted the interest rate on the basis of where it ought to be to ensure full employment would lose money unless everyone else did it as well.) The impasse could be broken, however, by the authorities intervening on the basis of a longer-term and essentially normative view of the economy. Thus, fundamentally, the Keynesian prescription for monetary policy can be seen as the need to intervene and guide financial markets to offset a particular kind of information failure.

The two problems—financial speculation and the inability of financial markets to adjust savings and investment at full potential output—whilst distinct, can be taken together. It seems that Keynes felt they would interact unfavourably in unregulated systems. Thus a recession could be caused (say) by some piece of bad 'news' which would (1) cause financial markets to favour liquidity, tending to raise the interest rate, (2) if anything, tend to raise the propensity to save, and (3) lower business confidence, leading to a fall in investment. Thus financial operators try to increase their holdings of money in a situation where they cannot, and savers increase their desire to hold assets in a situation where the supply of assets to hold is likely to fall due to a cut in investment (compared with previous trends). The tendency to recession could be *offset* by monetary and fiscal policy: increases in liquidity preference by open market operations, and savings/investment imbalance either by monetary policy or by fiscal policy. (In the latter case, a budget deficit—equals dissaving by the government—can be seen as offsetting a divergence between potential savings and investment, or equivalently, in stock terms, as supplying the assets to satisfy the public's increased desire for 'wealth as such'.)

The Keynesian diagnosis can thus be seen as displacing the origins of unemployment from failures in the labour market, to failures in the goods and financial markets requiring government action of a macro-economic kind to overcome them. The case for stabilization does not really depend upon rigidity of money wages, though if money wages are rigid, the problems of the economy will appear as fluctuations in unemployment.

To see this, consider the (no doubt unrealistic) case where the wage and price levels can move up and down sufficiently quickly to lead to continuous market clearing in the labour market. The way this would work, at least in theory—Keynes for one doubted the efficacy in practice—is that a sufficient fall in wages and prices would raise the effective real value of nominal asset stocks (such as, but not exclusively, money), satisfying the increased demand for assets that would otherwise cause problems. Thus, in the presence of the type of failures Keynes was concerned with, the price and wage level would fluctuate undesirably, constituting a case for stabilization policy to stabilize *prices*. (Indeed, the *Treatise on Money* was concerned with price fluctuations.) Persistent unemployment would, however, not be a problem.

To summarize, the Keynesian diagnosis shifted attention to potential failures in financial and goods (savings/investment) markets, and away from labour markets. The case for stabilization policy was to offset fluctuations that, it was assumed, would otherwise occur. Beyond this, if important prices or quantities have a tendency to get stuck in the wrong place—as in some rationing models—then policy action is more generally needed to set the appropriate constellation of macro-economic influences. The government needs to play an active role in co-ordinating the economy.

(d) *Macro-economic Intervention in Practice*

This general message, that the government needs to set the macro-economic climate, was, it seems, more important in the post-war period than the Keynesian diagnosis of unemployment *per se*. It led to the deployment of a range of policy instruments, with differing emphasis between countries, directed towards the maintenance of high employment growth. Although the general thrust of policy is frequently described as Keynesian, it could equally be described as a commitment to management in general and went far beyond a simple faith in demand management as a cure for all ills. (Seen in this way, nearly all countries were Keynesian in the broad sense, though not in the narrow.) The breakdown, when it came, was not the end of demand management but a more serious and comprehensive change away from the idea that purposeful macro-economic management was needed or that it could achieve the goals of full employment and growth.

This view of the influence of Keynesian ideas on post-war policy is, it can be argued, supported by the way in which the techniques were introduced in the context of the time. First, one of the main lessons from the inter-war period was negative: the need to avoid policy errors of a de-stabilizing kind. Avoidance of error, whilst it implies the importance of macro-economic policy, has a different connotation from the more positive belief in demand management that developed later. (This was nowhere more clear than in the setting up of the Bretton Woods system and associated international organizations.) Moreover, the perceptions of the errors to be avoided differed between countries, depending in part on earlier experience.

Second, the techniques were not, on the whole, initially applied to the problem of Keynesian unemployment: demand management was explicitly applied in wartime to mitigate *excess* demand. (Thus, Keynes's pamphlet 'How to pay for the war' was, in some ways, more influential than the *General Theory* itself.) When so-called Keynesian techniques were applied to the problem of generating growth and full employment, they were combined with a battery of other controls and policies associated with the reconstruction phase. (No one could ignore supply-side problems in the immediate post-war years.) Thus, what came to be seen as the paradigm case of Keynesian policy—the use of demand management and deficit finance to remove persistent Keynesian un-employment—was not really tried in practice. When unemployment of a persistent kind did arise in the 1970s, worries over inflation and over debt effectively precluded policy responses of the simple Keynesian kind.

Over time, the perceived macro-economic role of the State tended to expand. In part, this no doubt reflected the increasing ambition of the authorities. In part, it represented responses to new problems as they arose. The policy framework also became more mechanical, with positive attempts to manage the economy replacing attempts to offset its failures. And, in the 1960s, governments, especially in Europe, became more generally interventionist with the development of industrial, labour market, and regional policies, going far beyond a co-ordinating or off-setting role for the State. Thus, when problems, such as inflation, arose for which the consensus economics seemed to have no ready answer, this led, not to a search for new policies, but to a much more radical questioning of the role of macro-economic policy.

(e) *Inflation*

The real significance of the assumption in the Keynesian model of fixed or rigid money wages is not that it gives rise to unemployment equilibria, but that the model effectively has nothing to say about the price level or about inflation.

This does not mean, however, that no policy prescription was implied. Obviously the framework leads to the presumption that excess demand—what Keynes called an 'inflationary gap'—should be avoided. Thus the policymakers' job was to manage demand to avoid either excess—which by common consent would be inflationary—or deficiency—which would lead to unemployment. In line with the general neglect of labour market problems characteristic of this framework, the assumption seems to have been that if excess demand were avoided, then the wage and price level would look after itself. There was still no detailed theory, however, about what would happen to inflation if policymakers were to get it wrong.

In practice, policymakers were, from the first, far less sanguine about inflation, the control of which was often seen as a *necessary* condition for successful policy action elsewhere. One problem is how the 'full employment' level of demand should be defined and determined empirically. Views can, and did, differ markedly over the effective minimum that should be aimed at. The target rate of unemployment, if thought to be under the government's control, is also a number that is more or less bound to become politicized and subject to interest group pressures.

When it came to policies to deal with inflation, there were always, in effect, two broad approaches—and there still are. One, plausibly enough, is to accept higher unemployment and a lower pressure of demand. Few would doubt that, *ceteris paribus*, inflation is harder to control with low unemployment than with high. The other is some form of direct intervention in the wage formation process—incomes policy of one type or another. Many of the early demand managers felt that control over wages and prices would be a necessary condition for the maintenance of high employment growth.

Against this background, the Phillips curve, relating inflation to the level of unemployment, is bound to seem something of an aberration. It suggested a trade-off for policymakers between inflation and unemployment, contrasting with earlier and later views that inflation control was necessary for the success of other aspects of policy. In the 1960s, the apparent trade-off worsened dramatically as inflation rose, leading to a substantial change in policy perceptions.

Specifically, the policy problem was reformulated in terms of various versions of what might be called the 'accelerationist thesis'. Instead of a trade-off between inflation and unemployment, it was suggested that an inflationary disequilibrium would lead, not to steady inflation, but to rising inflation. Eventually, it was argued, the authorities would have to act with non-accommodating policies: there would, to use the cliché, be no alternative.

This switch from the idea of a trade-off between inflation and unemployment to the idea of no trade-off in the long run is, arguably, the most important change in policy perceptions of recent years. Though it represented a change in theoretical preconceptions, it also reflected practical policy problems as conditions deteriorated. The time was, so to speak, ripe for theories that accounted for these difficulties. The intuition behind most versions of the thesis is straightforward, though it sometimes appears paradoxical.

The key aspects of the theory are, first, the importance of expectations and, second, the *un*importance of inflation. The first suggests that if inflation has been going on for some time, then anticipated price rises will become built in to economic behaviour (especially wage- and price-setting behaviour). The second suggests that inflation, by itself, does nothing to remove the underlying cause of the disequilibrium. Together, they suggest that inflation, if it persists, will tend to get worse.

This latter can be illustrated in terms of the conventional demand-pull and cost-push explanations of the cause of inflation. If inflation is due, say, to excess demand in labour and product markets (i.e. an inflationary gap), and if inflation, as it occurs, is *accommodated* by the authorities with passive monetary (and fiscal) policies (including, in an open economy, toleration of exchange rate falls to offset international inflation differentials), the excess demand simply persists over time. Acceleration is very likely. If the problem stems from wage-push or 'competing claims' in imperfect markets, similar considerations suggest that inflation *per se* would do nothing to mitigate the underlying problems. Here, the mechanism leading to acceleration with accommodating policies is transparent: real wage aspirations are frustrated as unanticipated inflation erodes the real value of nominal settlements, leading to higher claims next time. There are many other versions of varying degrees of sophistication, but all stress expectations and the absence of money illusion in the longer term.

Out of equilibrium, i.e. when inflation is accelerating, the process is inevitably hard to model: the disequilibrium will be sensitive to lags in the system, and the order of 'acceleration' could 'shift gear'—for example, if accelerating inflation itself were to become anticipated. This does not really matter, however, for the usual reason that the diagnosis of a problem is often sufficient to indicate the policy response. Here, the obvious policy response, sooner or later, is non-accommodating policies which stop the process of acceleration and stabilize the rate of inflation. This in turn leads to the Natural Rate of Unemployment thesis (NRU) of Friedman (1968) and Phelps (1967).

The natural rate of unemployment, sometimes called the NAIRU, standing for the 'non-accelerating inflation rate of unemployment', is that level of unemployment that arises if the government stabilizes the rate of inflation, for example, in simple models, by setting a stable rate of growth of the money supply. (It is usually taken to be independent of the steady rate of inflation fixed upon, though it need not be.) With steady, anticipated inflation, rising prices have, it is usually assumed, no effects on the real economy—or at least have only small effects.[3] Thus inflation does not matter (much). On the other hand, a higher rate of inflation, if steady, would not help the real economy: the authorities might as well go for a low rate of inflation as for a high one. Paradoxical as it may seem, inflation matters because it does not matter, and because it does not matter it should be set at a low level.

The actual characteristics of the natural rate of unemployment depend, however, on the underlying diagnosis of what it is that would lead to accelerating inflation in the absence of non-accommodating policies. Thus, if inflation were previously thought of in terms of (say) a Keynesian inflationary gap, non-accommodating policies lead to the elimination of that gap, and the resulting unemployment would be the level of unemployment corresponding to zero 'gap', i.e. 'full employment'. In monetarist models (see below), inflation depends upon the rate of growth of the money supply, and changes in unemployment usually depend upon mistaken expectations (for example, affecting real wages). A steady rate of growth of the money supply, anticipated by the private sector, eliminates these expectational errors. In the 'cost-push' or 'competing claims' tradition, unemployment rises to the point where cost-push pressure is *contained* by high unemployment. (Sometimes the acronym NAIRU is reserved for this latter, to get away from the 'full' employment connota-

---

[3] Friedman (1977) in particular suggests deleterious effects from high rates of inflation. See also Cross (1987).

tions of the NRU.) Thus, there can be considerable disagreement over the causes and characteristics of a given level of unemployment resulting from non-accommodating policies.

The important issue of the diagnosis of the reasons for unemployment is further discussed below. Here, the notable result of the accelerationist thesis is the effect it has, if taken as true, on the (broadly Keynesian) policy framework of the consensus years.

The Keynesian framework initially suggested considerable freedom for policymakers to select the appropriate level of employment. (To be sure, this was circumscribed by other constraints, often regarded as separable problems.) The set of policy choices was substantially narrowed when trade-offs were recognized, as with the Phillips curve. With the accelerationist thesis, implying no trade-off in the long run (a vertical Phillips curve), perceived policy choices were further narrowed. Indeed, except in the short run, macro-economic policy of the conventional kind had no bearing on the level of unemployment. To the extent that macro-economic policy had a role, it was to set a stable financial framework to ensure steady inflation at an acceptable level.

Another way of describing the change is to note that the post-Keynesian framework becomes, with the addition of the accelerationist thesis and its cousin the 'natural rate of unemployment', an equilibrium model. It is thus close, or at least much closer, to the 'classical' or neo-classical model. It is not surprising that the policy implications appear similar. Unemployment, if it exists at a high level, becomes the result of malfunction in the labour market. And the macro-economic role of the State is the traditional one of looking after the exchanges, and, via financial policies, controlling inflation.

It is argued below that this is too simple a characterization. Before doing that, however, it is necessary to sketch some of the important features of what came to be known as monetarism.

3. Monetarism

There are almost as many versions of monetarism as there are monetarists. As with the Keynesian framework, this section seeks to highlight some aspects which appear most important in considering the macro-economic role of the State.

It is useful to start with a theoretical problem. The conventional paradigm of value theory (which comes in versions of various degrees of sophistication, starting with 'supply and demand', taking in 'classical' or (more strictly) neo-classical economics, and culminating in the Arrow–Debreu model of general equilibrium) determines the allocation of resources and *relative* prices. It has nothing to say about the price level or the rate of inflation.

One of the simplest ways of filling that gap is to add some version of the 'quantity theory of money'. From the theoretical point of view, if it is assumed that there is a fixed or controlled stock of money, and if there is a well-determined demand for that stock of money dependent on the price level, then the equilibrium price level will be determined and, by extension, so will the rate of inflation. This is perhaps the simplest version of monetarism.

There is, of course, much more to be said. There are, for example, questions about why there should be a stable demand for money, and about how a change in the quantity of money actually affects prices in 'disequilibrium'. Here we are mainly concerned, not with the theoretical difficulties, but with the policy implications of this type of approach.

Broadly, in practical terms, there are two essential elements. First, that the real side of the economy (the allocation of resources and relative prices) will, so to speak, look after itself. This can be seen as a belief in the relevance of equilibrium economics, both at the micro-economic and at the macro-economic level. Less formally, it implies a high degree of optimism about the functioning of markets at the micro and the macro level.

Second, that the price level is determined by the quantity of money. In Friedman-type versions, this may be expressed as the hypothesis that nominal expenditure (i.e. the flow of expenditure in money terms) is determined by the stock of money in circulation, which means that since real expenditure is determined from the supply side, the price level is determined. Equally important is the implied negative. It is only money that determines the price level; other things, such as fiscal or exchange rate policy, do not, or at least do not in equilibrium.

Practical qualifications need to be made. Markets may take time to adjust, and may be subject to imperfections and failures. (Thus, the paradigm applies to a competitive system.) Similarly, the equilibrium price level or rate of inflation may not be established immediately. These qualifications were characteristic of monetarist ideas in the 1960s. Later versions of monetarism require correct or rational expectations for equilibrium: unanticipated changes will have real effects. The common thread, however, is the belief in the importance of markets in determining real performance, and belief in the importance of money in determining inflation. Of the two elements, though it is the latter that gives monetarism its name, it is the former that is the more fundamental.

It is useful to contrast monetarism with the Keynesian paradigm. Taking unemployment first, the monetarist explanation has similarities with the 'classical' diagnosis. Thus unemployment arises from the behaviour of labour markets. It is necessary to be careful here. Extreme monetarists, especially those who believe in the empirical relevance of market clearing, must diagnose unemployment, if it exists, as 'voluntary' or as in some sense optimal. Thus, if unemployment benefit is high, unemployment will arise from 'voluntary leisure', i.e. rational individuals will choose not to work at going wage rates. 'Search' unemployment will result from a rational approach to seeking information on job opportunities. Less extreme monetarists admit frictional and structural effects of a more informal kind, as well as imperfections, such as trade union structures, which may lead to real wages being too high in detail or in aggregate. Not too much violence is done to an admittedly complex set of ideas if the monetarist diagnosis of unemployment is seen as essentially similar to the classical diagnosis, attacked by Keynes.

The policy prescriptions are similar and derive from the diagnosis. Thus, they include measures, such as provision of information, to make labour markets work better; and beyond this, the reduction of institutional and legal rigidities. The prescription is usually that wages need to be more flexible and lower in real terms. Sometimes, but not always, trade unions are blamed for rigidities or for keeping wages above their market-clearing levels. At the time when monetarist ideas started to be influential in the 1960s, however, unemployment levels were not high enough to seem a serious policy problem.

Of more significance initially was the denial by monetarists and their allies of Keynesian problems in goods and financial markets. This can be seen as fundamental to the macro-economic role of the State. If, for example, the monetarist framework is accepted, but the demand for money is thought to swing about endogenously (as suggested by Keynes), then a case for stabilization policy—offsetting action by the central bank—follows. Moreover, if savings/investment balance is not thought to be subject to intertemporal co-ordination failures, fiscal and monetary policy to offset these failures is not required. One could add that if exchange markets function well, or if, under fixed exchange rates, the wage and price levels are flexible, international control and co-ordination are not needed either.

Thus, more than anything else, the set of ideas broadly called monetarism is optimistic about the macro-economic functioning of the market system. (There is, it should be noted, a darker version of monetarism, principally associated with Hayek, which is not optimistic about the performance of markets, especially in the presence of such institutions as trade unions, but which nevertheless argues against a macro-economic role for the State on the grounds that the State would make even more of a mess of things, i.e. government failure is worse than market failure.)

Monetarism denies the co-ordination failures, central to Keynesian economics, partly by denying the shifts in behaviour that would give rise to the need for co-ordination in the first place.

There is, however, a limited role for the State in the monetarist framework. The price level and the rate of inflation are indeterminate until the level and rate of growth of the money supply are fixed upon. Thus the characteristic monetarist prescription is that monetary growth should be controlled to give a stable and predictable rate of inflation.

In policy terms, the denial of the need for Keynesian policies was not particularly important or influential until the consensus was threatened by rising inflation. (Why abandon policies that seem to be working, and which, even if not needed, do not seem to be doing any harm?) With rising inflation, however, the policy message was quite different, and bore a remarkable similarity to the Keynesian message of an earlier time. Monetarism offered the optimistic hope that inflation could be controlled, relatively easily and with little cost, simply by a change in the perceived role of the State. All that was needed was that the money supply should be brought under control. This optimism, now over inflation, contrasted strongly with the pessimism implicit in the Keynesian framework. For Keynesians, inflation posed a problem for which there appeared to be no easy answer.

(a) *Some Problems*

More than with most other bodies of economic theory, there is a problem about the relevance of monetarism to practical policy issues. One reason for this is a direct result of the method commonly adopted. It is assumed that a restricted version of equilibrium economics, based on rational choice and competitive markets, is relevant, and little attention is given to strategic interactions or to real world adjustment processes—which relate to the stability, uniqueness, and hence relevance of equilibrium. The conditions under which rational individuals, interacting, lead to optimal results for the system as a whole are, as noted, extraordinarily stringent. Thus monetarism asserts the absence of co-ordination problems, rather than demonstrating their unimportance.

Further problems arise over the concept of money itself. In part, these are also theoretical. In the Arrow–Debreu system, there is no role for money or any other assets: contracts, made 'now', obviate the need. With sequences of budget constraints, however, money and other stores of value have a role (Hahn (1984)). These are interesting issues, but are not pursued here. They do, however, relate in a general way to more practical difficulties. Thus the question of what money is and why it is demanded is of considerable practical as well as theoretical significance.

In the theoretical monetarist paradigm, it is probably best to think of money as something concrete, like a stock of notes and coins, controlled by the government. Money pays no interest and is quite different from other assets such as Treasury bills or bonds. This is blindingly unrealistic as a description of 'money' in a modern economy. (It should be noted that the Keynesian approach is similarly unrealistic, but the unrealism may be less crucial to the system properties.) Specifically, there is a serious practical problem about the concept of money in the real world to which the label 'money' should be applied. (Should it be M_1, M_2, M_3, or what?) Recall that it is 'money' that matters, and other things do not, so this labelling problem is far from being a quibble. A related difficulty is that, though the quantity theory of money may make sense as an equilibrium relationship, monetarism requires more: money must be under the control of the authorities, and the causal mechanisms must run from money to spending. In practice, money may not be easily controllable—especially if it pays interest and is supplied, not by the authorities, but by the commercial banking system—and the transmission mechanisms remain empirically obscure. (Concentration on equilibrium results obscures the importance of mechanism and causality.)

Friedman suggested that the test of the quantity theory should be empirical: give or take a few lags, the system worked, he argued, *as if* equilibrium results applied. Unfortunately, the empirical base of monetarism is not strong either. Hendry and Ericson (1983) have shown that the quantity theory works no better than a random walk—it does not work.

These are serious difficulties and they are practical ones which surfaced as monetarist ideas and presumptions came to be applied in the 1970s and 1980s.[4] Arguably, however, their main bearing is on the less important aspects of monetarism. The more important aspect is the implicit view of markets, which sees a role for government in controlling prices and inflation, but no macro-economic co-ordinating role for government in relation to real activity or unemployment. This message proved much more durable and influential in policy debates than 'technical' monetarism.

---

[4] For a discussion of the difficulties that emerged in the United Kingdom see Allsopp (1985) and Laidler (1985b).

4. Consensus and Dissent

This section considers two broad issues. The first is alternative explanations of the rapid growth period in the 1950s and 1960s. The second is the degree of consensus that emerged in the late 1970s and early 1980s, which is more apparent than real.

(a) *The Role of Policy in the Long Boom*

For monetarists and their allies, there is no problem in explaining the long boom. On the contrary, full employment growth is regarded as the natural tendency of the system, so long as policy actions are not destabilizing. The contrast with the inter-war difficulties is usually explained in terms of the avoidance of error. Similarly, the rise in inflation in the 1960s is explained by over-ambitious policies, especially lax monetary policy, which, though it may have lowered unemployment initially, led to inflation as expectations adapted. Government interference of a more general kind, such as support for declining sectors, labour market legislation, and rising welfare benefits, tends to be seen as raising the 'natural rate of unemployment'. Lax policies and government interference thus account for the difficulties that ensued. It has already been noted that this reading of history provided a basically optimistic message for policymakers, given that unemployment, at the time, was not high.

Such a stylization of the facts contrasts sharply with the Keynesian consensus. In that framework, the inter-war difficulties served as a model of what would happen with uncoordinated policies and without macro-economic control. Post-war success was ascribed, at least initially, to purposeful policy action. Breakdown when it came was due to new problems and uncoordinated policy responses.

Nevertheless, there are problems with the Keynesian story. Whilst policy action was extremely pervasive and powerful in the early post-war years, going well beyond demand management, it is harder to explain the maintenance of the long boom as due to policies of a Keynesian kind. In many countries, it is not obvious that active demand management policies were applied (especially in some of the most successful, such as Germany), and where they were applied, as in the UK, there is evidence that they were destabilizing at least in the sense of accentuating rather than attenuating the cycle. Policy actions do not seem large enough to account for the degree of success achieved. It is well known that, compared with the inter-war period, it is the buoyancy of private investment that is the major feature of the post-war years. Deficit finance was not resorted to on a large scale. In most countries, national debt was low or, as in the UK, falling. Attempts to explain high employment growth in terms of public expenditure trends are also subject to well-known difficulties.

This is, of course, the merest sketch of the problem. It is, however, perhaps sufficient to indicate the difficulties that Keynesians had in arguing against the more supply-side orientated explanations of their opponents. The argument that Keynesian actions were not large enough or widespread enough to account for success is, however, far from decisive. It arises from an extremely mechanical view of Keynesian economics. If, as suggested above, the Keynesian message is seen as the need to have policies in place to avoid potential macro-economic difficulties arising from co-ordination failures, success may not seem so hard to account for. The argument would then be that it was precisely *because* governments were acting as co-ordinators of the system that the Keynesian difficulties were largely avoided, and hence were not observed. The Keynesian message, it was argued, was minimalist in spirit: it prescribed macro-economic action of a limited kind, internationally and domestically, in order to allow markets to work. If the purpose of a policy is to avoid problems, the policy can hardly be attacked on the grounds that it was successful.

It is necessary to go a little further. One aspect of Keynesian economics that was stressed was the need to offset endogenous swings in private sector behaviour. This is so, if they occur. But if the system is being successfully co-ordinated, the likelihood of such swings in behaviour—reflecting perhaps gaming difficulties and correlated responses—is much reduced. If economic agents believe in a stable world, they are likely to behave in a stable way. Paradoxically, a successful strategy would need to be only lightly applied, and if anticipated, success would tend to breed success. The expectation of high employment and growth is likely to be conducive to the maintenance of favourable responses by the private sector: confidence is particularly important in generating high investment.

Such reasoning suggests that the commitment to economic management and international co-operation may have been the most important aspect of the economic framework of the 1950s and 1960s. That commitment, by and large, existed. Moreover, with the apparent success of the 'new economics', the commitment became credible. If governments are believed to be aiming for full employment growth, and if they are believed to have the policies available to achieve that goal, private sector responses are altered. There is, moreover, a good deal of evidence that private sector expectations did reflect this kind of optimism. Thus, medium-term forecasts for the world economy were remarkably accurate in the late 1950s and 1960s. Phenomena such as labour hoarding, characteristic of the 1960s, suggest the expectation that recessions would be short-lived.

Of course, appeal to expectations and the perceived 'policy regime' in operation requires a number of qualifications. It only makes sense if expectations are broadly validated by experience, and if the authorities are seen, from time to time, to be successful in avoiding difficulties and in meeting their objectives. This presupposes the absence of really serious problems, which appear insoluble, arising at the international level or domestically. It also presupposes that the supply response is forthcoming; that is, that the supply side is sufficiently flexible and profitable. There is a certain fragility about a growth path thus established. But the characteristic of the consensus years was that problems were thought to be soluble, and by and large, though there were difficulties, this seemed to be borne out by experience.

What this means is that we are left with two broad hypotheses about the role of policy during the consensus years, between which it is very hard to discriminate on empirical grounds. One view, the neo-classical or monetarist view, is that favourable real performance reflected the natural buoyancy of the economic system combined with favourable supply-side developments. Financial policy had little to do with the success achieved, except later on when over-ambition led to inflation. The other view is that the policy framework was crucial in getting the process started and in maintaining a climate of favourable expectations. Given that framework, however, the responses to be expected would be hard to distinguish from those implied by more supply-side orientated hypotheses. In particular, the financial and goods market failures, characteristic of the Keynesian theory, would be attenuated by successful co-ordination. But though the results, in broad terms, might be similar, the implications for the macro-economic role of the State are, of course, poles apart.

One way forward is detailed study of the experience of different countries during the consensus years, focusing especially on episodes of successful and unsuccessful policy intervention. At the detailed level, discrimination between hypotheses should be possible, though the difficulties are quite great. (Consider, as an analogy, the difficulty of testing whether lender-of-last-resort facilities, put in place by central banks, are important: if they work, they are not needed.) The problem is that what would have happened in the absence of policy, or with different policy (i.e. the counterfactual) is not directly observable. Generally, it may be asserted, the period of rapid post-war growth is not a very good test bed for sorting out alternative hypotheses about the macro-economic role of the State.

The opposing views do, however, (at least in their extreme form) have markedly different implications for the type of problems that would be expected if consensus broke down and if, for one reason or another, co-ordination were to fail. Thus, an extreme monetarist view would, as already noted, see inflation as easily controllable with appropriate monetary policies, at little cost to the real economy. By contrast, 'Keynesians' would expect serious problems and possibly heavy unemployment. Here we may note that the experience of the 1970s and 1980s is in many ways easier to explain on the 'Keynesian' hypothesis. Once economies are knocked off track and expectations turn sour and become unstable, one would expect a series of problems to arise, not singly but in combination. It would be hard to re-create a climate of confidence and co-operation. And the implication would be, not that policy was not required, nor that it was ineffective, but that policy actions would need to be more closely co-ordinated and generally more powerful whilst the economy was in disequilibrium. But if this is the case, there is a serious danger of the wrong policy message being derived from the experience of the long boom.

(b) *Inflation and a New Consensus?*

The consensus framework of the 1950s and 1960s ran into trouble with the worsening of inflation, especially from the late 1960s onwards. It was vulnerable to the new policy problems, for which there seemed no easy policy answer, and to the increasing influence of 'monetarist' ideas, which offered an easy solution to inflation and denied the need for a co-ordinating role for the State except in the limited area of monetary control. Shocks, such as the oil crises of the 1970s, which only a few years earlier would have been seen as requiring strongly offsetting action, hastened the move towards generally non-accommodating policies with priority given to bringing down inflation.

Whilst it is often maintained that the consensus economics had no solution to inflation, we have seen that this is not strictly true. It is more accurate to say that it had two solutions, neither of which was palatable. The first, unsurprisingly, was to fight inflation with deflation, accepting the resulting unemployment. Many felt that the costs would be very heavy, perhaps so heavy as to be politically infeasible. The second was some form of incomes policy, designed to attack labour market problems directly. Such intervention, whilst welcomed by some, and of course practised in many countries on a temporary or longer-term basis, involved a different kind of intervention from the original 'Keynesian' conception. That, as argued above, could be seen as shifting the focus of attention away from the labour market to difficulties in goods and financial markets. The diagnosis of inflationary problems as arising in the labour market shifted the focus of intervention back again.

These two alternatives, non-accommodating policies and labour market intervention, are fundamental in understanding the policy responses of the 1970s. Different countries—reflecting in part their different institutional structures and historical experiences—tried different methods; and within countries, policy swung from one route to the other with many a U-turn. Over time, however, policy became more and more focused towards non-accommodation of inflation, as incomes policies ran into difficulties or broke down, and as international difficulties arose. Though the responses to the first oil crisis were extremely diverse, by the second, at the end of the 1970s, practically all developed countries were attempting inflation control by non-accommodation and deflation. In most countries, the levels of unemployment reached would have been 'unthinkable' a decade or so earlier, apparently fully justifying the pessimism of the so-called Keynesian policymakers of the 1950s and 1960s.

The prevailing policy vision in the late 1970s and early 1980s can, without doing too much violence to the complexities of the real world, be summed up in terms of the 'Natural Rate Hypothesis' or the NAIRU, discussed above in Section 2. If an inflationary disequilibrium leads to accelerating inflation (so that inflation control becomes a necessary condition for other aspects of economic policy), then non-accommodating policies lead to unemployment becoming endogenous—reflecting some kind of equilibrium of the system. Problems, previously seen in terms of inflation, come to be seen in terms of unemployment. To the extent that unemployment is at its equilibrium level, the power of the authorities to alter it is circumscribed and the menu of policy choices, characteristic of the 1950s and 1960s, shrinks. A reduction of unemployment would, in this framework, require fundamental long-term change. Attempts to use demand management to lower unemployment would simply lead to rising inflation, with, at best, temporary benefits.

In this modified framework, the distinction between 'Keynesian' and 'classical' unemployment tends to break down. Upward pressure on money wages against non-accommodating financial or demand manage-ment policies could lead either to nominal wages being too high in relation to (say) the money supply, or, if firms cannot react by putting up prices, to low profitability and a type of classical unemployment. Indeed a mixed response is likely, with the business sector suffering both reduced profita-bility and lower demand, and with different sectors, subject to different competitive pressures, reacting differently. (Thus, those subject to intense international competition might, in an open economy, be particularly vulnerable.) Thus unemployment of different types can arise from the same basic causes (Morris and Sinclair (1985)).

The acceptance in most countries of at least part of this story seems to account for the consensus over economic management that had emerged

by the 1980s. Governments had not given up the objective of full employment, but felt powerless to do anything about it without inflationary (and
also exchange rate) consequences. Macro-economic policy could do little
to improve the situation. The main hope was that when inflation was
brought under control, unemployment would then decline—as suggested
by Friedman (1977). (Thus, paradoxically, the heavy costs led, if anything,
to a hardening of policy attitudes against inflation, seen as part-cause of
the problem.)

The above account has stressed the *diversion* of the demand management instruments of policy away from their traditional role of maintaining
high employment, to counter inflation. From a policy point of view, a
rather similar story can be told which is more monetarist in spirit. On that
view, over-ambition and developing supply-side rigidities led to the
inflation problems of the late 1960s. Monetary control had to be re-
established. When it was re-established, the economy would settle at the
'natural' or full employment level. Quite explicitly in this case, the
government had no role in promoting full employment via active macro-
economic management. Unemployment in equilibrium would reflect
supply-side problems and inflexibilities.

The two explanations are, from a political point of view, remarkably
similar. Both stress inflation, and especially rising inflation, as the origin of
sharply worsening performance. Both stress non-accommodating policies
as a necessary response. Both see the resulting unemployment as some kind
of equilibrium phenomenon. One can go further. The supply-side
rigidities, especially in labour markets, put forward by many monetarists
to explain unemployment are also appealed to by Keynesians to explain
worsening cost-push pressure. Similarly, Keynesians and monetarists alike
tended to see increased levels of government intervention and interference,
especially in the late 1960s, as worsening private sector responses, leading
to inflationary pressure and/or unemployment. Moreover, the question of
whether the policy response should focus entirely on controlling the money
supply or should be more broadly based, with monetary and fiscal policies
both playing a deflationary role, was liable to seem somewhat esoteric and
unimportant. In short, policymakers did not need to agree on the underlying economics to agree at least roughly on the desirable thrust of policy.

(c) *Dissent*

Though monetarist and Keynesian approaches to explaining the deteriora-
tion in performance in the 1970s and 1980s have much in common and, so
to speak, march together over much of the terrain, they imply quite
different views about the role of the State. Most obviously, they fly apart

over the question of incomes policy. They are different in other respects as well.

For monetarists and others in that tradition, the origins of unemployment lie on the supply side. Inflation results from an excessive growth of the money supply, a failure of policy. Unemployment tends to be seen as either voluntary, or micro-economic in origin. Either of these may also reflect excessive government intervention (for example, too high a rate of unemployment benefit, or structural problems due to government interference). Incomes policies would, if anything, worsen unemployment by introducing further rigidities. A reduction in unemployment requires a fall in the natural rate of unemployment, which would come about by better-functioning markets.

A difficulty—which illustrates the many versions of monetarism—arises over trade unions. A common version of 'classical unemployment' sees it as arising due to real wages that are too high, in turn due, perhaps, to trade union power. In principle, an incomes policy, if it served to lower real wages, could be helpful. In practice, most monetarists, even when they admit the influence of trade unions (and many do not), usually argue against incomes policies (often seen as making labour markets more imperfect, and as strengthening union power) and in favour of liberalizing labour markets.

By contrast, neo-Keynesians frequently see the origins of inflation as arising from real wage pressure. For them, the NAIRU is a rather different concept from the supply-side orientated 'natural rate'. It arises as that level of unemployment that is necessary to choke off excessive wage demands. If these wage demands can be curbed some other way, then the NAIRU declines. Incomes policies, if successful, are just what is needed to lower unemployment. (Note that demand management may be needed as well, to take full and immediate advantage of any reduction in wage-push pressure—see Layard and Nickell (1986).)

Thus the apparent consensus over economic policy in the early 1980s conceals quite different attitudes to incomes policy. It is not surprising that much of the political debate was precisely over that set of questions. In the NAIRU/natural rate framework, the role of incomes policies is the most obvious area of remaining disagreement.

Despite this, it is not hard to account for the pessimism that developed in the 1980s over unemployment prospects. Effectively, there was consensus that the difficulties originated in the labour market—and in that respect the diagnosis was similar to the prevailing diagnosis in the inter-war period. The policy choice centred on ways of improving or offsetting labour market malfunction. On the one side, the monetarists and 'new' classicals pointed to the need to improve the functioning of labour markets, curb trade unions, etc. As in the 1930s, few could believe that such improvements would be rapidly forthcoming. On the other side, the cost-push/NAIRU framework required either an improvement in function or a *permanent* incomes policy. Despite many suggestions—such as tax-based incomes policies—the difficulties of achieving a long-term incomes policy seemed, in most countries, extremely great, given only limited, and usually short-term, success in the past.

The important point to stress at this stage is that such pessimistic attitudes arise almost inevitably from a diagnosis of unemployment that originates from labour market failures. Labour market failures, by their nature, seem hard to put right. The 'Keynesian' revolution displaced the diagnosis of unemployment from the labour market to other aspects of the economy, more susceptible to policy action. It offered no solution to labour market failures if they were present. With the onset of inflation, the prevailing paradigm swung back to where it had been before. I question later whether this consensus view of unemployment in the 1980s is any more justified than the consensus view of the inter-war years.

Before that, however, it is necessary to indicate briefly other elements of disagreement over economic policy in the 1970s and 1980s. The first point is that the monetarists, initially at least, denied *all* macro-economic failures. Thus, obviously, they did not see the need for co-ordination in financial and goods markets—contrasting with the Keynesian consensus—and frequently did not see the need for international co-ordination either. Most importantly, however, they laid little stress on labour market failures: this accounted for their optimism that, give or take a few adjustment costs, inflation control would not lead to high unemployment.

This optimism has hardly survived the test of experience. There is a problem for those working in this tradition to explain how it is that the 'equilibrium' rate of unemployment—the natural rate—could have risen as much as it apparently has, especially in Europe. Present levels of unemployment are vastly higher than those of the 1950s or early 1960s, and with inflation roughly stable, should correspond to the natural rate. What is it that accounts for the enormous rise in the 'full employment' level of unemployment? The usual answer, though it is not convincing, is that imperfections must have been much worse than had previously been thought, requiring even more urgent action. This, now pessimistic, version of monetarism has strong similarities to the classical diagnosis of the inter-war years.

As far as monetary policy itself is concerned, it is questionable whether the simple paradigms of monetarism were ever particularly influential. Certainly, the problems of monetary control turned out to be much greater than the enthusiasts initially anticipated, and even monetary targetry (which can be justified on grounds other than monetarism) has come to be used in a highly pragmatic way. More importantly, the neglect of other aspects of policy—such as fiscal and exchange rate policy—has not survived the developing problems of the 1980s: though some of the policies that this aspect of monetarism led to were bizarre. (Thus, the neglect of fiscal deficits by the Reagan administration can be seen as arising in part from this set of ideas, as can the neglect before 1985 of the exchange rate and current account position. In Europe, in sharp contrast to North America, fiscal policy soon reappeared as a centre-piece of policy, but with fiscal deficits being controlled in order to control money.) Generally, macro-economic policy in the 1980s was, in sharp contrast to popular perceptions, highly active, in pursuit of financial objectives. Most recently, financial market failure—especially in the international markets—is very much back on the political agenda.

On the face of it, Keynesians, especially those working in the cost-push tradition, have less to be ashamed of and have had to modify their theories less comprehensively to keep up with emerging events. Thus, the cost-push/incomes policy wing of the profession was always pessimistic about the likely consequences for unemployment if the demand management instruments were turned against inflation without incomes policies. They believed that uncoordinated responses, internationally and domestically, could lead to major difficulties, which would be hard to put right. Compared with some of the more pessimistic monetarists, they even look optimistic, offering as they do at least the possibility of a marked improvement in performance if incomes policies can be designed and put in place and international co-ordination re-established.

However, the neo-Keynesian consensus enshrined in the cost-push version of the NAIRU is subject to the same difficulties faced by the monetarists. What is it that accounts for the apparent rise in the NAIRU? Is the concept of an equilibrium rate of unemployment—so important in generating a certain set of policy attitudes and prescriptions—meaningful at all? And if it is not, or if the NAIRU concept needs substantial modification, what are the policy implications?

5. The Macro-economic Role of the State: A Widening Agenda

If unemployment is regarded as an equilibrium or quasi-equilibrium phenomenon, the macro-economic role of the State in dealing with unemployment is sharply constrained. Either the macro-economic policy has effectively no role—the view of monetarists and many others—or macro-economic intervention requires some kind of incomes policy. This latter, further discussed below, can be seen as macro-economic co-ordination of responses in the labour market, to deal with labour market failure.

But is the idea of equilibrium, implicit in the NAIRU-type framework, tenable? More importantly, is it the only way in which high and persistent unemployment can be explained? If it is not, what are the policy implications of alternative diagnoses?

As far as the first of these questions is concerned, there is no doubt that unemployment could arise for supply-side reasons and/or for cost-push reasons, as the theory assumes. There is a direct analogy here with the classical diagnosis of the inter-war period and the Keynesian response. The classical diagnosis was one possible explanation of unemployment: it was not the only one, and Keynes suggested another where the problems arose elsewhere. Similarly with the NAIRU/NRU framework. It constitutes a possible explanation, but there are others which, from a theoretical point of view, may be equally plausible.

From an empirical perspective, the NAIRU/NRU framework has, as noted, not stood up well. A concept of equilibrium unemployment is only convincing if equilibrium unemployment is reasonably constant. In practice, for the theory to fit, the NAIRU must have risen dramatically in a way which is hard to explain.

Suppose, as an extreme response, that it is assumed that the NAIRU simply does not exist and that from an empirical point of view the concept is empty. The problem then would be to find other explanations of persistent unemployment. One obvious one is straightforwardly Keynesian. The origin of unemployment could lie in goods, financial, and international markets, and in the failure of policy to correct for such co-ordination problems. As in the original Keynesian framework, however, there would be a further problem in explaining how such problems led to unemployment.

To sharpen the analogy with Keynesian economics, assume in an *ad hoc* way that the rate of nominal wage inflation is just given. If it were, and the authorities did not pursue the correct macro-economic policies, internationally and domestically, then unemployment would result. We would be back to the Keynesian policy framework in all essentials. The NAIRU, being definitionally the rate of unemployment consistent with a steady rate of inflation, would be 'indeterminate'. It could be reduced by appropriate macro-economic policies. The chief danger would be that unemployment would be misread by policymakers as reflecting structural and other real phenomena in the labour market, so that appropriate policies were not adopted.

The analogy is over-simplified but nevertheless demonstrates that in the

1980s, as in the inter-war period, the origins of unemployment do not *have* to be seen as arising in the labour market. There are other possibilities which may, or may not, be empirically relevant. Now, as then, other possibilities have markedly different policy implications.

The fixed nominal wages/exogenous inflation story can, moreover, be qualified and made potentially more realistic. First, as in the Keynesian model of the textbooks, excess demand can be regarded as inflationary, and as leading to acceleration of price rises for too low a level of unemployment. (Since the point at which this would happen is hard to establish, this leaves open the question of whether accelerating inflation in the late 1960s and 1970s was due, in part at least, to excess demand.) Moreover, it may well be true that nominal wages and inflation are rigid or sticky in a downward direction. (Such an asymmetry is not usually built into the conventional NAIRU/NRU story—as stressed by Solow (1986).) If so, attempts to lower inflation by downward management of demand may lead to heavy unemployment, as was certainly assumed by many Keynesians. Shocks, such as the oil crises, and policy mistakes could intensify adjustment problems, and lead to unemployment. The NAIRU/NRU could take a long time to establish itself.

In fact, the question of whether the NAIRU is determinate or not is directly analogous to the question of whether the Keynesian economic model leads to underemployment equilibrium. If it does, the performance of the real economy is, in a sense, indeterminate and depends on policy. Similarly, if the NAIRU does not exist, or if there are multiple equilibria, there is, in principle, a role for policy in determining unemployment. And, as in the case of the Keynesian model, there is a question, especially from the policy point of view, as to whether the possibility of underemployment equilibrium is essential to the policy message. In particular, even if the NAIRU concept is retained for the long term, slow adjustment would have rather similar policy implications for the short term.

Recent experience of persistently high unemployment has greatly weakened the power of the NAIRU concept. As a direct result, the policy agenda is expanding.

(a) *Qualifications to the NAIRU Framework*

It is useful to indicate, necessarily in an informal way, some of the qualifications to the NAIRU framework that seem most relevant to the policy debate and to an assessment of the macro-economic role of the State.

Starting with the 'supply side' of the picture, it is clear that there may, in practice, be an important question of causality. Given that supply-side rigidities can be observed as accompanying high unemployment in many advanced countries, should these be regarded as the explanation of unemployment, or should they be regarded as the result of policies? It is clear, for example, that if a recession is prolonged, businesses would adjust the capital stock to the prevailing level of output, and the situation would appear 'capital'-constrained. In practice, this observation has led to the suggestion that policies to expand output need to be 'supply-side friendly', i.e. that simple demand management would be dangerous if it were to lead to bottle-necks.

More generally, there are a number of factors, often pointed to as a reason for unemployment and rigidity in labour markets, that could, with equal plausibility, be regarded as the result of problems originating else-where. Thus, job protection schemes, which may be stabilizing when the economy is in the region of near full employment, become expensive and dangerous when unemployment rises. Public deficits and excessive public sector claims can likewise be the result of poor performance rather than the cause of it. Inevitably there is a danger of the wrong implications for policy being derived. (This is not to assert that the factors described are not linked to unemployment, but that they might not be.)

Similar points can be made about the labour market itself. Prolonged unemployment leads, almost inevitably, to ills, to discouragement, and to segmentation. In principle, these deleterious effects may be reversible. There may, however, be permanent losses. Where the economy gets to depends upon its past history. Certainly, a distinction may need to be made between short-run and longer-term supply potential, and with it a distinction between short-run and longer-run 'equilibrium' unemployment.[5]

It is notable that the theory that connects accelerating or decelerating inflation with unemployment is often *ad hoc*. We have already noted that there may be asymmetries in the wage response. Perhaps even more seriously, from a policy point of view, the question has to be raised of whether measured unemployment is a good proxy for the forces that contain wage pressure. There are many reasons why it might not be. One obvious point is that changes in unemployment—say rises—may be a more widespread influence on wage aspirations and settlements. This would imply that the time-path was important. (And, in the limit, if changes were all that mattered, the NAIRU is indeterminate.) Generally, segmentation, differences between insiders and outsiders, different behaviour in the core sectors from the periphery (Mayhew (1985)), and so on may suggest a complex and historically determined relationship between unemployment and wage pressure. The power of the concept of the NAIRU is greatly

---

[5] The issues are discussed in Morris and Sinclair (1985). Path dependence leading to multiple equilibria or indeterminacy of the NAIRU is frequently termed 'hysteresis'; see, for example, Blanchard and Summers (1986).

weakened. The strength of 'wage-push' may itself be subject to shifts as political conditions change.

The political implications of accepting even some of the above qualifications are startling. At a general level, they suggest that unemployment at high and persistent levels is not 'inevitable' and that policy of various kinds could influence it. The State re-emerges as having a decisive role in determining unemployment.

The change in the potential policy agenda can be simply illustrated by two important examples. First, if a group of the unemployed labour force—such as youth or the long-term unemployed—are ineffective in influencing the wage bargain, a range of policies, special schemes, and the like can be directed towards aiding them without worsening inflationary pressure. (Such schemes are on the agenda of all political parties in the UK.) One can go further. Training schemes and other proposals that help the disadvantaged groups to compete effectively in the labour market may actually reduce inflationary pressure, and with it equilibrium unemployment. There is, in effect, a double benefit. Targeted reflation, special schemes, and the like are not an option under a strict interpretation of the NAIRU: they become an option as the concept itself is weakened.

The second example concerns incomes policy. In the NAIRU framework, a permanent improvement of unemployment requires a permanent incomes policy. This is not true if the NAIRU itself is indeterminate or if there is a difference between the short-run NAIRU and the long-term equilibrium. Instead, the focus may be on the problems of *transition* from high to low unemployment. It is during the transition that supply-side difficulties would be most likely to arise, and labour market pressure may be most intense when employment is expanding. This suggests that *temporary* incomes policies—which are far easier to believe in—may have an important role in a programme to reduce unemployment. The pessimism, implicit in the NAIRU/NRU framework, may not be warranted.

(b) *The Role of Incomes Policy*

As we have seen, the question of the role of incomes policies became crucial as western countries faced problems of inflation and labour market difficulties. There remains, however, a difficult set of issues over what kind of problems incomes policies should be designed to mitigate. In turn, this depends upon what labour market processes are assumed to lie behind inflationary or unemployment difficulties. A distinction needs to be made between what might be termed 'real' problems and those that stem entirely from co-ordination failures—though, in practice, the situation will frequently contain both elements. That a distinction is necessary is supported by the observation that over the years many policymakers have tended to stress *nominal* wage restraint, whereas many models posit real wage pressure (or more generally 'competing (real) claims').

In the usual NAIRU framework, the specification is in terms of real wage pressure, which is contained, *ex post*, if the economy is in equilibrium, by unemployment. *Ex post*, real wages may or may not be 'too high' or 'too low' in relation to the notional full employment position. An incomes policy, if it allows a move to higher (equilibrium) employment, may or may not involve a fall in real wages. (Thus the distinction often made between 'Keynesian' and 'classical' unemployment is not very useful. The *ex post* real wage is, as it was for Keynes, endogenous.) Nevertheless, *ex ante*, real wage pressure is the origin of the problem in imperfect markets (as, for example, in Layard and Nickell (1986)).

An increase in the NAIRU could come about for several reasons. Obviously, an increase in wage aspirations—the target real wage—would be one possibility. An increase in the degree of imperfection—though hard to make precise—is another. Finally, a reduction in the capacity of the economy to fulfil aspirations, for example because of a supply shock, could be another. Similarly, an incomes policy could work by reducing aspirations (the consensus-forming element in many practical schemes is obvious), by containing those aspirations by competition or by restraint other than through unemployment, or, in principle, by allowing favourable developments in supply. Very broadly, incomes policy works either by making people want less or by containing those aspirations. In short, an incomes policy is intended to do something real.

The point can perhaps be made more transparent if a change, such as exchange rate depreciation, is considered. Since, if effective, this will lower potential real wages, it would be ineffective in lowering unemployment if inflation is to remain under control. Real wage resistance, in this case *ex ante* real wage resistance, precludes devaluation as a remedy.

In contrast, upward wage pressure could arise purely from *co-ordination* difficulties in the labour market, even in the absence of real wage resistance, either *ex ante* or *ex post*. For example, if wage bargainers are mainly concerned with relativities, there may still be a problem with the going (nominal) rate, as each takes into account the expected developments elsewhere. It is this case which leads to the most obvious case for devaluation as a policy instrument: it is far easier to co-ordinate a general reduction in wages by altering the exchange rate than by agreeing thousands of individual wage bargains. (This is analogous to one of Keynes's main arguments for believing that it was far easier to raise demand via macro-economic policy than to raise it by wage restraint.)

The basic point, however, is that nominal wage rises, expectationally generated, may be just as much a problem for policymakers concerned with controlling inflation as those generated by some sort of real wage pressure. Moreover, the co-ordination game may be insensitive to unemployment. This leads to the idea of an incomes policy which stresses the co-ordinating, as opposed to the containing or controlling, role of the State. It is important to separate out the idea of incomes policy as a 'freeze' from the idea of incomes policy as a 'squeeze'.

The idea of the State as a co-ordinator in the labour market to prevent upward movements in nominal wages is directly analogous to the case for macro-economic intervention in other markets. The State can be seen as trying to ensure a co-operative solution to the dilemmas implicit in decentralized systems. As suggested, this may involve a pure co-ordination role—like agreeing to speak a common language. Or it may involve more: the imposition of restraint on real wage aspirations, or agreement to limit them on the grounds that all can see that, in aggregate, the system cannot deliver more than can be supplied. The NAIRU too can be seen as the outcome of a non-cooperative game, when co-operation has broken down.

6. Conclusion

The original Keynesian message, it has been argued, was minimalist in spirit. It could be seen as displacing the diagnosis of unemployment away from problems in the labour market, to co-ordination and other failures elsewhere—in goods, financial, and international markets. The role of the State was to set the framework within which markets could effectively function.

Policy in the consensus years went far beyond this limited role for State intervention. Nevertheless, the way to avoid unemployment continued to be seen in terms of avoiding macro-economic difficulties, by purposeful management of the economy and by international co-operation. The consensus started to fall apart as genuine labour market difficulties started to be experienced. Initially, these appeared as inflation, for which the consensus framework had no easy solution.

The experience of inflation, in a situation where unemployment was low, set the stage for what became known as monetarism, which in its purest versions admitted no market failures, requiring co-ordination to overcome them. Inflation was seen as arising from government failure, especially over-ambition on unemployment. The message was optimistic in that it suggested an easy cure for inflation with small cost in terms of unemployment.

The monetarist message contrasted with the previous consensus view on inflation control. Labour market problems were seen as inherently difficult to deal with, requiring an extension of intervention into the labour market (incomes policies) or heavy unemployment. The experience of the 1970s led to developing consensus that non-accommodating policies against inflation were the only option—though there was continuing debate over the possible role of incomes policies. Unemployment again came to be seen as reflecting labour market problems, either due to wage-push or due to supply-side rigidities and inflexibilities.

In the 1980s, the policy agenda has been widening rapidly. Faith in uncoordinated markets has been rapidly eroded. International co-ordination is now widely seen as necessary. Monetary and fiscal policies are, in most countries, being used in a pragmatic way. Finally, the diagnosis of unemployment as arising in labour market failures is beginning to be questioned. At the very least, macro-economic intervention and international co-operation are now seen as adjuncts to successful labour market strategies.

One possibility is that a further shift will take place, similar to the shift to macro-economic management after the war. This would involve displacing the focus of policy attention, away from the labour market, to domestic and international financial policy. It is perfectly possible that the prevailing diagnosis of unemployment as arising from problems in the labour market is wrong. That indeed would be an optimistic conclusion.

It appears more likely, however, that labour market problems will continue to restrain policy. What is required is an extension of the macro-economic role of the State to labour market co-ordination. Here too the role of the State can be seen ideally as minimalist, setting the framework within which markets can function.

Inevitably, however, co-ordination of price- and wage-setting behaviour is difficult, far more difficult even than co-ordinating international responses or ensuring that domestic financial conditions are conducive to expansion. The alternative, however, is unemployment or coercion. Ultimately, the case for incomes policies is, as it always was, the fear of something worse.

10

The Economic Functions of the Tax System

JOHN KAY[*]

1. Introduction

Why do governments raise taxes? When should they impose taxation, in preference to other instruments of economic intervention? At first sight, the answers to these questions appear obvious. The purpose of taxation is to raise revenue. But this answer, although correct in a limited sense, is evidently inadequate. The traditional role of government was to provide public goods, such as defence and police, and to obtain funds for the purpose with minimum fuss or cost. But this is now a minor part of total fiscal activity in all western economies. Much of government expenditure is now devoted to the provision to users, at prices well below cost, of services such as health and education which could be privately provided and which normally were privately provided before public expenditure achieved its present scale. Direct grants to individuals through social security expenditures form another major element of public budgeting. These three services alone—health, education, and social security—now account for over half of UK government spending. Most of the financial transactions of government now involve either taxing some activities to subsidize others, or taxing some people to subsidize others by means of redistribution among individuals or households. The traditional separation between revenue and expenditure, which remains characteristic of British budgetary procedures, dates from an era in which the activities of public authorities were very different in both scope and scale.

Thus most fiscal activity is accounted for by objectives other than government need for revenue. And even if revenue were a primary objective, an approach which adopted this as starting-point would leave us no criteria for discriminating between the alternative means of imposing taxation. The current revenue requirements of the British government are of the order of £4,000 per adult per year. If we contemplate raising that sum as a poll tax, some immediate conclusions can be drawn from the

* Director, Centre for Business Strategy and Professor of Industrial Policy, London Business School.

obvious impracticality of the proposal. One is that even those who might query the legitimacy of redistribution as an objective of fiscal policy, or seek to minimize its extent, cannot escape analysis and assessment of the distributional aspects of their proposals. A second is that both equity and enforceability are central issues in the design of tax structures, and that these are closely linked together.

It follows that there are inescapably multiple objectives in a tax system and that the search for simple structures must be to a degree illusory. It does not follow from this, however, that because taxation structures are inevitably complex, there is no point in choosing between them and we might as well resign ourselves to what we have. Much of the complexity of actual tax systems is the product of attempts to reconcile a mismatch between objectives and instruments by piecemeal adaptation. The evolution of the tax structure resembles the endless alteration of a badly fitting suit, and those who criticize the design are accused of ignoring the immediately relevant problem of the shortness of the sleeves. The purpose of more thoughtful analysis is to see the relation between symptoms and underlying causes.

The first part of this paper attempts to elaborate a framework for examining tax problems within a conventional welfare economics context—the maximization of some essentially individualist social welfare function. This welfarist approach to tax policy is characterized by its emphasis on outcomes, rather than processes, as the primary criteria in choosing between alternative systems. Section 2 describes the main features of the analysis, and Sections 3 and 4 the main types of fiscal issue which are suggested by the approach: efficiency arguments based on market failure, equity questions relating to income distribution.

But it is apparent that in public debate on tax policy, there is concern about process as well as outcome. Section 5 reviews a number of non-welfarist objectives and Section 6 examines questions of enforcement. In Section 7 I try to bring together the implications of the paper for the design of actual tax structures.

2. Taxation and Welfare Economics

The principal purpose of welfare economics is to define conditions under which the achievement of efficiency in production, allocation, and distribution can be decentralized. There is an extensive literature defining these conditions. Perhaps the clearest description is to be found in Koopmans (1957). Some of these conditions relate to the nature of social objectives. They require, for example, that a social welfare function should in some sense represent an aggregation of individual preferences. Others concern the technology of production. If there are substantial economies of scale, for example, competitive solutions may not exist, or if they do exist, they may not be efficient. Still other conditions relate to the structure of individual preferences and rule out certain kinds of dependence and interdependence between households. Violation of these conditions is described as market failure.

If the assumptions of the model hold, however, then an optimum relative to any particular distribution of resources and endowments across individuals and households can be achieved by the production decisions of competitive profit-maximizing firms. Moreover, any desired optimal outcome can be obtained provided the appropriate initial distribution of endowments between agents is achieved. These results—the fundamental theorems of welfare economics—represent a modern and precise formulation of Adam Smith's mechanism of the 'invisible hand'.

These arguments, in both their old and new guises, are sometimes used, and abused, as justification for conservative policies of *laissez-faire*. But their real significance is not to deny a role for government intervention in economic affairs so much as to define it. The problems of achieving production and distribution in complex modern economies, in ways which reflect the wishes of consumers and the limit of production possibilities, seem considerable. Efficiency in resource allocation would appear to demand the accumulation of very large quantities of information about individual preferences and production possibilities. It would be difficult to develop a structure in which individuals and firms had incentives to reveal such information accurately, rather than to distort their descriptions of what they want or what is feasible in order to obtain outcomes more advantageous to themselves. Even given accurate and complete information, it is necessary to co-ordinate the activities of different producers. It is apparent from the experience of governments operating industrial policies—and even more from centrally planned economies—that these problems are not simply theoretical. The difficulties of obtaining accurate information and of achieving consistence between the plans of different producers are the principal practical obstacles which such governments face.

The significance of the fundamental theorems of welfare economics is that they suggest that the price mechanism may be an efficient method of economizing on information and decentralizing the job of co-ordination. The attainment of efficiency through such a mechanism requires an appropriate initial distribution of endowments across consumers, and, therefore, government will necessarily be involved in the distribution and redistribution of income. Moreover, the conditions required to ensure efficiency will not hold universally. If such market failures are very widespread, then other methods of economic organization must be sought. But if their incidence is limited, the advantages of economy and efficiency in co-ordination of different activities and in the acquisition and use of information may still be attainable. Competitive markets, moderated by selective intervention to deal with particular causes of market failure, may then appear as highly effective means of economic organization.

In a predominantly market-based economy, it would follow that government intervention would fall in two principal areas. It would be involved in the distribution of income between households. And it would be concerned to remedy market failures in areas where the assumptions of the fundamental theorems of welfare economics failed to hold. The government would, in turn, have two principal types of mechanisms of intervention. One category would be the imposition of taxes and subsidies, in which the State seeks to use the signals of the price mechanism to achieve more desirable outcomes. The second type of mechanism suppresses the signalling role of prices in favour of direct control and regulation of aspects of the process of production and allocation. Different means will be called for in different circumstances.

3. Sources of Market Failure

One of the important functions of the fundamental theorems of welfare economics is to draw our attention to specific areas where markets are likely to fail. The assumptions of these arguments rule out, for example, the existence of *public goods*. These are commodities which have two related characteristics. If provided for one member of the community, they are available to all and even those who decline to contribute cannot easily be excluded from their benefits. Defence and broadcasting are two classic examples. Government intervention through tax policies cannot solve these problems, which arise from the absence of effective incentives to suitable private production, although some ingenuity has gone into the design of 'incentive-compatible' mechanisms which might allow decentralization, as in Groves and Ledyard (1977) and Green and Laffont (1977). Nor would subsidy to private producers be sufficient, unless surrounded by other rules and regulatory restraints. Public goods, therefore, represent a deficiency in competitive markets which can be corrected only by direct public intervention in production, and lie substantially outside the scope of tax/subsidy policy.

Externalities arise where the economic activities of one agent affect the enjoyment, or the production possibilities, of another. There are externalities in consumption where one commodity—cigarettes or roses—is of harm or benefit to others. Production externalities exist when the operations of different producers interact physically with each other—as, for example, when smoky factories pollute the activities of their neighbours, or bees pollinate adjacent orchards. In all these cases, competitive outcomes will deviate from efficient levels because the person who chooses output level will not adequately consider these interactions.

Externalities may be dealt with either by regulatory intervention or by tax policies, and in practice both of these are used. Offensive activities are both restricted and taxed. If regulatory authorities had all relevant information about consumer preferences and about production possibilities, they could achieve the same result by either mechanism: they could simply prescribe the optimal quantity or they could level a tax which could induce production or consumption exactly equal to the optimal quantity. Information is generally inadequate, however, and it is the structure of the available information which determines the appropriate remedy. If the externality involves the deposit of noxious waste in the public water supply, the uncertainty surrounding the appropriate quantity of the emission is less than the uncertainty about the size of the tax rate which would produce that quantity; and direct prohibition is the most efficient remedy.

Where the issue is noisy aircraft, however, the question is less clear-cut. The appropriate solution is an intermediate one between freedom and prohibition. Few would argue either that air traffic should be banned altogether, or that airlines should be free to make as much noise as they like. A regulatory authority can seek to adjudicate, but it faces the difficulty that airlines have an incentive to exaggerate the economic costs which noise restrictions will impose on them, while others have an equal incentive to exaggerate the distress which noise causes them. A tax–subsidy based solution—which imposes a charge on aircraft reflecting the level of noise created and redistributes compensation to those affected—has the advantage that it enables airlines to assess the charge against the benefits, residents to balance compensation against detriment, and so relieves these informational problems.

Problems related to *information* are, indeed, a rather general cause of market failure. Difficulties arise where there is asymmetry of information between buyer and seller—used cars, or financial or professional services—or where the product itself is information—estate agency or advertising. In all these cases, tax-based solutions have little to contribute. More direct forms of intervention are required.

Paternalism is a common motive for intervention. Where such paternalism is the product of supposed superior information, regulation is the natural response. We believe that no one would wish to buy heroin or unsafe toys, if they understood what it was they were purchasing, and so we prohibit their sale; we believe that if the benefits of primary education were properly appreciated, everyone would want it and so we make consumption compulsory. This liberal interpretation of paternalism turns it into an issue of asymmetry of information. Often, however, paternalism is just that here we seek to nudge consumers gently in the direction of desired consumption patterns, and here taxes and subsidies are the most effective weapons. We tax alcohol and tobacco and subsidize opera.

Markets can also fail where *ownership rights* are insufficiently well defined. There is no obvious owner of water in rivers, or the airwaves, or the fish in the North Sea, or the oil in the sea-bed beneath them. A mixture of regulation and tax policy is called for here. Regulation is needed to create an ownership structure where otherwise competitive exploitation would lead to inefficient outcomes. Taxation is then called for to extract the rents which this form of public intervention has created. So we have charges for water extraction licences, special tax regimes for broadcasting and North Sea oil, and unresolved problems in fisheries policy.

The existence of monopolies may prevent the achievement of efficient competitive equilibrium. The obvious response is the regulatory one of removing the monopoly. This may not be possible in cases of natural monopoly—where scale economies, or other characteristics of technology, imply that it is impossible or inefficient for more than one firm to exist in the market. Taxation can be used to extract the rents earned by such monopolies for public rather than private benefit, but this redresses the distributional issue without removing the inefficiency which results from price distortion. The monopolist's incentive to restrict output and raise price could only be reduced by tax policy if output were subsidized, rather than taxed: presumably with the subsidy being recovered by a licence fee for the continued exploitation of the monopoly. Aside from the obvious implausibility of the solution, the information required to implement it is the same as that which would be needed to control output directly. So taxation alone can rarely be an adequate answer to monopoly problems.

We have defined six principal groups of cause of market failure. For two—public goods and information asymmetries—tax subsidy policies have few solutions to offer and direct public regulation or production is required. In two cases—paternalism and externalities—taxes and subsidies would commonly be the most appropriate public response. In the remaining two—ownership uncertainty and monopoly—some combination of tax and regulation is normally called for.

4. Taxation and Income Distribution

Models of tax structure derived from welfare economics are based, implicitly or more commonly explicitly, on an individualist social welfare function. The arguments of that function are non-observable utilities, which are in turn determined by consumption. Commonly, however, people discuss the effects of government policies by reference to their effect on the distribution of income. If distribution is a policy concern, what is it the distribution of?

One immediate issue is the definition of the tax unit. Are the welfare functions implied those of households, or of individuals (or indeed some other concept—UK income tax law, in common with some other countries, defines a tax unit which includes husband and wife but not children)? This question is partly a matter of welfarist fact—can one sensibly talk about a common standard of living of a household which is determined by its total resources? It is also a matter of individual rights—it may be felt that the tax system ought to treat taxpayers as individuals even if they are known to share resources with each other. In either case, subsidiary difficulties emerge. The household basis fails to acknowledge needs to define equivalence scales, or some other means of comparing welfare levels of different households with the same resources but different composition. The individual basis needs to recognize the dependence of an individual's standard of living on the circumstances of the household within which he or she lives and so makes pursuit of distributional objectives either expensive or ineffective. It should be no surprise that the appropriate definition of the tax unit is one of the major unresolved issues in the tax systems of all countries, and that the diversity of international practice is almost as complete as is possible.

The use of the word 'resources' in the preceding paragraph is designed to evade a central issue. Utility is a function of consumption. Intertemporal issues can be ignored on the basis that this consumption is the outcome of transactions in a complete set of Arrow–Debreu markets. At this point, both theory and operational practice have to acknowledge that the set of markets which exist is severely incomplete. But consumption of current commodities may be a misleading measure of welfare if it ignores differences in individual capacities to deal with future events and prospective contingencies.

The concept of income is an attempt to deal with some of these problems. The operational difficulties which it has encountered are discussed in some detail in Section 6 below. But some conceptual issues should be noted here. The relevant income measure is a forward-looking

Hicksian concept—an assessment of sustainable prospective consumption. But there is an inherent contradiction here. On the one hand, we use income precisely because incomplete markets preclude direct observation of consumption choices. On the other hand, if markets are indeed incomplete, the actual welfare levels achieved by individuals with the same potential consumption levels will depend, sensitively, on their specific intertemporal preferences and the particular states of nature which in fact arise.

An alternative, extreme, view is to suggest that markets are so incomplete that we should proceed as if intertemporal markets did not exist at all. This would imply that the distribution of income between me aged 30 and me aged 60 raises essentially the same public policy issues as those which arise in comparisons between me aged 30 and someone else aged 30. We take a 'spot' view of personal consumption and regard redistribution across the life cycle as a policy objective as much as redistribution across the community. A tax system based on aggregate current consumption is rather robust to the appropriate specification of the problem. If markets are very incomplete, its short-term perspective is an appropriate one. If they are complete, then current consumption would, from the permanent income hypothesis, be a suitable proxy for lifetime income.

The difficulty of specifying redistributive objectives is paralleled by restrictions on the availability of redistributive instruments. The maximization of whatever specific individualist welfare function is chosen requires that the government can select an appropriate initial distribution of endowments. Such a distribution implies the use of 'lump-sum' taxes which are based on the underlying characteristics of the taxpayer rather than his actual behaviour. It would, for example, mean that tax liability was based on earning capacity rather than on earnings, because a tax on earnings would distort the relationship between consumer and producer prices.

Tax and benefit systems do make some use of information of this kind. The age of a taxpayer will usually affect both his tax payments and his receipt of benefit. Physical disability is generally recognized in fiscal systems. But characteristics such as these account for only a small proportion of the variance of total tax payments by individual households: most of this variance results from differences in actual earnings or in consumption. The extensive use of lump-sum taxes, independent of individual behaviour, is impractical because even if such a system were thought fair and acceptable, it is impossible to derive the information on which it could be based. It is difficult to find measures of earnings capacity better than, or independent of, actual earnings.

What can be said, then, about structures where lump-sum taxes are excluded, and governments have to rely on taxes on directly observable magnitudes such as consumption of particular commodities? An inevitable consequence of this constraint is that society lies inside its welfare frontier; but an important result, due to Diamond and Mirrlees (1971), is that it is still desirable to be on the production frontier. It follows that any distributional objective which could be achieved by changing the structure of production is more appropriately met through the mechanisms of taxes on final commodities or factor supplies. In particular, taxes which fall on intermediate goods will generally be inefficient.

This argument is a good example of a central characteristic of the theory of optimal taxation—the sensitivity of the results to a careful specification of the problem. Another illustration may be found in the Ramsey rules (1927)—which are generally interpreted as justifying high taxation of commodities in inelastic demand. These rules are derived as the solution to the problem of devising an optimal structure of commodity taxes to raise prescribed revenue, in a framework in which lump-sum taxes are unfeasible or where the social welfare function is indifferent to transfers of income between households. But if lump-sum taxes are feasible, there is no evident reason to wish to raise any revenue from commodity taxes at all. And even if lump-sum taxes are not feasible, a uniform lump-sum tax across all households patently is. If the government wishes to raise revenue and is not concerned to identify who it gets it from, a poll tax is the best instrument available.

This argument would seem to reverse a conventional wisdom that assigns distributional objectives to income taxes and the revenue-raising function to commodity taxes. If there were no distributional objectives, it appears that we would not wish to use commodity taxes at all. If there is a distributional objective, then it is still not obvious why one would wish to use commodity taxes, if an income tax is feasible (or, equivalently at the present level of generality, if an expenditure tax is feasible). Certainly the common argument for lower tax rates on specific commodities or distributional groups fails, within this welfarist framework, if an income tax is available. To justify the pursuit of distributional objectives through differentiated commodity taxes, we need to resort to welfarist arguments (as in Section 5 below) or to administrative arguments (as in Section 6 below), and assert 'positive rights' or the impossibility of applying income taxation to a section of the population. Within a general welfarist framework, however, arguments for differential taxation of commodities exist only to the extent that commodity taxation is a proxy for some other, preferred but unfeasible, form of taxation. Commodity taxes may substitute for lump-sum taxes if, for example, high earning capacity is associated with preferences for particular items of consumption. They may be proxies for taxes on non-taxable goods—such as leisure—if they are imposed on complementary commodities.

Although the structure of optimal income tax schedules has been a central concern of the welfarist theory of taxation for the past fifteen years or so, results with practical implications for the design of tax schedules remain relatively scarce. There is an obvious direct conflict between the efficiency components of the welfare objective—which demand low marginal tax rates to minimize the welfare costs of distortion of consumer choice—and the equity objective which demands high marginal tax rates to reduce differentials of income. It is apparent that however high the priority given to equity, rates would not rise to 100 per cent—since lower rates could raise more revenue for redistribution to poorer groups. This hardly original observation, commonly attributed to Arthur Laffer on a Washington napkin, is of limited operational value since the revenue-maximizing rate of tax may very plausibly be only slightly less than 100 per cent. Similar difficulties confront application of the equally striking observation that the marginal tax rate should be zero at both extreme ends of the rate schedule and income distribution. The rationale is that any positive marginal tax rate on the richest man yields no revenue and may discourage effort; a similarly structured argument may be applied to the poorest man. The difficulty is that there is nothing in the argument which excludes high marginal tax rates only a little distance from these extremes.

5. Other Objectives

It is evident that there are a number of characteristics of real tax systems which cannot be accounted for adequately in a welfarist framework. This implies that the choice between tax instruments, or the decision to impose a tax at all, is at least in part the result of features of the instrument itself and not simply of its potential welfare implications.

There are some cases where the way in which the tax is administered is intended to be a central feature of the tax. For example, there is a lengthy tradition in which it is a conscious aim of the benefit system to stigmatize recipients—by confining them to the workhouse, by public humiliation, by requiring them to subject themselves to protracted administrative procedures or to undertake futile exertion. Often the arguments adopted to support this appear to have a welfarist tone—they are intended to offset the disincentive effects to effort which are the inevitable result of benefit provision. It is clear that attaching welfare-reducing conditions to benefits is always a second-best outcome, and in most cases it is one which would seem to be dominated by the alternative of providing a lower level of benefits in the first place. The recipient would generally be indifferent between a higher level of benefit with stigma and some reduced level of benefit, and the reduced benefit would impose lower costs on the rest of the population.

What is the rationale of stigma? If we are unable to distinguish between 'scroungers' (people for whom the marginal disutility of effort is high) and the 'deserving poor' (people with low capabilities), then it might be supposed that requiring benefit recipients to break stones will induce the scroungers to work and leave benefits for the deserving poor. This does not seem to be a welfarist argument, since the scroungers, by definition, find the jobs they are forced to take particularly unpleasant and the deserving poor spend their time breaking stones. (They must be made to break stones, or else the scroungers will be found among them.) This outcome might be defended in welfarist terms—the distress caused to the rest of the population by the possibility of scroungers receiving benefits is so great that reducing it more than offsets the disabilities which the offsetting measures impose on scroungers and deserving poor alike, but this does not really seem to be the heart of the matter.

I think the argument in fact rests on one or both of two premisses. One is that we are not in fact concerned about the welfare of the poor, but about their consumption of food, clothing, housing, etc. Benefit with stigma ensures that these consumption levels are achieved or achievable, and the fact that the resulting programme does very little for the welfare of the poor is of little consequence. Alternatively, or additionally, there are some kinds of preference—such as extreme dislike of work—which are to be discounted by the social welfare function. Both of these are clearly non-welfarist arguments.

Actually, at least until recently, the view that benefits should be stigmatizing had become decidedly unfashionable. Indeed, the opposite problem was apparent; if you have historically associated benefit receipt with public humiliation, some of the disincentive to receive benefit is likely to survive removal of the humiliation. Remedies for this are not easily available and lie mainly in constantly changing the name of benefits and the administrative procedures by which they are operated in order to cover the historical tracks.

An opposite approach goes by the label of universalism. The underlying principle is that a procedure will be more acceptable if everyone is subject to it. At one end of the political spectrum, this is expressed in the view that even the poorest 'ought' to pay some tax (as, for example, in the proposal that all adults should be required to pay at least 20 per cent of a community charge). A different political perspective presents a similar view in its support for universal benefit systems, in which benefits are awarded on the basis of contingency rather than need. The argument is sometimes developed to the point of claiming that the greater acceptability of universalist benefit systems is such that poor households will actually receive more under them—that additional expenditure will more than offset reduced share—although empirical evidence for the proposition seems lacking. Both of these are non-welfarist arguments, in the sense that it would seem that their outcomes could be Pareto-dominated by alternative mechanisms.

It is not easy to explain why it is that almost all countries impose much heavier taxes on alcoholic drinks and tobacco than on most other commodities. The commonly canvassed arguments are patently rationalizations. There is little evidence to suggest that demand elasticities are particularly low, and this is not a good theoretical argument for high tax rates anyway. The health risks associated—particularly—with tobacco were established after heavy tobacco taxation had been introduced, and rates have not risen much since, in real terms. There seem to be many other commodities for which externality arguments for taxes or subsidies are stronger.

One characteristic which alcohol and tobacco do have in common, and which differentiates them from other commodities, is that their consumption is substantially under-reported in surveys of personal expenditure. Consumers seem to be in some way ashamed of their use of alcohol and tobacco; perhaps this guilt is assuaged by the payment of heavy taxation. Surveys of popular attitudes to taxation would support this. While VAT and general commodity taxes are among the most disliked of all taxes, alcohol and tobacco taxation rarely attract adverse ratings, despite the high incidence of tax. There is consequently little political resistance to such taxes. Whether this is a good, or acceptable, reason for having them is difficult to assess.

Taxes may secure, or be associated with, rights and freedoms. At one level, this is enshrined in such slogans as 'no taxation without representation'. This rallying cry is as popular as the view that more taxation should imply more representation, or that nil or negative taxation should imply no representation, is unpopular. This suggests that the question of whether the participants in the Boston Tea Party had proper ground for complaint is one which requires rather more careful analysis. There is, in fact, not much to the argument of 'no taxation without representation'. We would think it odd if spending a night in a French hotel, and thereby paying more French tax than some Frenchmen, entitled us to vote in French elections, and the fact that the residence or citizenship conditions required for eligibility for the electoral register are far more demanding than those needed to establish residence or domicile for income tax purposes generates very little concern.

The American settlers resented the fact that they were exploited in the sense that they believed they contributed more to the UK exchequer than the benefits they derived from it. In this they differ little, however, from rich Englishmen. Our sense of the legitimacy of their grievance seems to derive primarily from a feeling that they paid more, relative to what they got, than Englishmen in a similar economic position. Thus it was a complaint about horizontal equity—the violation of the principle that similar individuals should be treated similarly. Now the weakness of the horizontal equity principle is that there is no objective measure of what constitutes similar circumstances, and hence any attempt to apply the principle can immediately be converted into a different argument. If George III responded that American settlers were clearly not in the same circumstance as native Englishmen, it is difficult to see how to counter his argument. Perhaps the American War of Independence was not about rights, but a welfarist argument about income distribution—the implied social welfare function gave insufficient weight to Americans.

None the less, the horizontal equity issue suggests that there may be limits to the information which it is thought legitimate to use in assessing tax liability. A welfarist tax system would normally use as many pieces of objective information about individuals or households as possible, in order to make as close an approach to lump-sum taxation as is feasible. We feel relatively comfortable with a tax/benefit system that discriminates by age or marital status, more uneasy when it discriminates by sex, more uneasy still if it discriminates by colour or racial origin. In practice, this seems to suggest that we are not unhappy about discrimination as such within tax/benefit structures, but worry when it appears to replicate other, undesirable forms of discrimination in different areas of social behaviour. None the less, if we discovered that having red hair, or being born in Scotland, was positively correlated with earning capacity, would we—as a welfarist argument suggests we should—support higher taxes on those with these physical characteristics or places of birth?

The horizontal equity issue may also be used to rule out randomness in taxation. In general, welfarist arguments do not support random taxation, but Stiglitz (1982) has demonstrated conditions under which they might. Literal randomness in taxation is, of course, unknown, but vagaries in enforcement may have effectively the same result. Where there is a conflict between welfarist and horizontal equity arguments, it is not apparent which should prevail. Two men are in a lifeboat with enough water for one. The horizontal equitable outcome—that both die—is Pareto-dominated by tossing a coin to see who gets the water.

If tax structures may conflict with rights and freedoms, they may also promote them. Negative freedoms are normally more appropriately achieved through regulation than through the tax system. But this may depend on whether they are absolute rights, or property rights to be traded. We may agree, for example, that I should be free to determine whether I sleep on my back or my stomach. But if other people are sufficiently concerned about the matter, am I to be permitted to let them pay to come and turn me over? The issue is at the heart of Sen's (1970a) conflict between liberalism and Paretianism, and the resolution by no means straightforward. I may have a right not to be polluted, but a sensible interpretation of such a right is not that there should be no pollution, but rather that there should be no pollution without consent or adequate compensation. With high transaction costs, however, a tax may secure the outcome more effectively than a structure of rights.

Positive freedoms are more naturally sustained through the tax system. I have already suggested that one motive for stigmatizing benefits is that people are concerned about the consumption, rather than the welfare, of the poor. At its simplest, this can be characterized within a welfarist framework as a straightforward kind of interdependence in which utility is a function of the consumption levels of others. This would imply subsidies, and a typical form might be the provision of a limited quantity at no or negligible cost. Such a take-it-or-leave-it offer is common in housing, health, or education. A choice is offered between a fixed quantity at a lower price or freedom to determine the amount consumed at the cost of paying the full price for the whole quantity. The extension of this kind of interdependence into a concept of rights would imply similar conclusions.

6. Enforcement

Enforcement of a tax system is undermined by both avoidance and evasion. Evasion is simple tax fraud. The taxpayer reports inaccurate information to the authorities, or fails to report at all. Avoidance occurs when the data supplied are correct, but give a misleading impression, since the transaction has been recast in a way which gives a substantively identical result but a different tax treatment.

These problems reduce the effectiveness of the tax system, and also imply resource costs. Such costs may be categorized into direct administrative costs—those incurred by tax authorities themselves—and compliance costs imposed on taxpayers. An alternative subdivision of costs specifies two categories, which might be described as costs of interpretation and costs of reporting. Interpretation involves understanding statutes, applying them in particular cases, and managing tax affairs so as to maximize potential advantages and minimize possible disadvantages.

Reporting is the maintenance of appropriate records and their transmission to the tax authorities. Avoidance is clever interpretation, evasion dishonest reporting. One important aspect of this distinction is that interpretation is a highly skilled activity, requiring the exercise of skill, judgement, and experience. Reporting is essentially a routine clerical function.

Technology has brought about spectacular reductions in the costs of reporting, or more accurately in the potential costs, since many tax authorities—particularly those of the United Kingdom—have been painfully slow to make changes in procedures in the light of these developments. Interpretation, on the other hand, becomes increasingly expensive. These technical changes have begun to influence the design of tax structures—particularly through the adoption of value added tax, which is light on interpretation but demanding of reporting, in most western countries.

At one end of a spectrum of avoidance activities lie wholly artificial arrangements, where the steps involved are convoluted and possibly unknown to the taxpayer himself and there is no commercial intention. At the other are the distortions which arise when I avoid paying tax on whisky by not drinking it, or escape tax on effort by not engaging in it; these represent the familiar welfarist dead-weight losses of taxation from welfare economics. Most real avoidance activity lies, in fact, somewhere in between. It is rarely possible to achieve both the desired outcome and a lower tax liability without some cost.

The existence of such a spectrum largely rules out appeals to the conscience as a means of reducing tax avoidance, although these are often explicitly or implicitly made. It is, presumably, not immoral to stop drinking whisky or smoking cigarettes because taxation has made the price so high. Equally, it would be absurd to contend that avoidance is legitimized by the fact of cost to the taxpayer, however small. There is ample evidence that even evasion of tax is not perceived with the same moral opprobrium attached, for example, to the theft of State property; and that attitudes towards it vary considerably in different countries. Curiously, the further south one travels, the more relaxed attitudes to fiscal fraud appear to be. Any stigma might seem to be related to the degree of departure from current norms, which reflect the degree of effective enforcement by the tax authorities both currently and in the past. Phrases such as 'paying their share' or 'everyone is doing it' represent these attitudes. And this relativist position seems appropriate. What is the honest taxpayer to do in a country where general enforcement activity by the revenue authorities is very lax?

If the degrees of avoidance and evasion are indeed determined in this relativist way, some important implications follow. One is that the possibilities of enforcement are strongly influenced by the perceived equity of the tax system as a whole. This is a long-run, rather than a short-run, observation; it is unlikely that the moonlighting plumber will be induced to abandon his activities by improvements quite elsewhere in the tax system—but it is probable that the acceptability of his activities within the community will be influenced by the design of the system as a whole and the methods of its enforcement. War between the authorities and taxpayer may have very substantial positive or negative effects, depending on whether the war is perceived as just or as arbitrary and selective. A corollary is that politicians and officials should be very hesitant in talking about the so-called 'black economy' without substantial evidence. A prevalent view that 'everyone is doing it' is dangerous if everyone is doing it, and considerably more dangerous if they are not.

It will be apparent that a sharp distinction between avoidance and evasion is difficult to sustain and at some basic level each are aspects of the same problem. Indeed some countries have sought to turn avoidance into evasion by means of a general anti-avoidance statute, which asserts that transactions undertaken only to avoid tax may not be undertaken or do not count. Since the House of Lords decision in *Ramsay* in 1980, something similar applies in the UK. It is hardly necessary to spell out the reasons why such provisions do not work very well—how do the authorities decide in any, far less all, cases which hypothetical alternative state of the world is presumed to have occurred? In practice, their value is confined to some of the extremes of artificial anti-avoidance devices.

The underlying issue here is how to translate the economic concepts determining tax liability into specific and verifiable information. For some potential taxes, this is simply impossible, and that is what, for example, excludes lump-sum taxes. Much of the history of the evolution of tax systems can be seen in terms of attempts to resolve the tension between concepts which were objective but which lacked much welfare significance—number of windows in a house, number of cigarettes smoked— and others—income or wealth—which appeared closer to the arguments of a welfarist objective function but which have proved difficult to define or to measure.

The use of direct welfare indicators is patently outside the capabilities of any tax administration, and 'wealth' is not much better, although many countries do tax some elements of tangible wealth as proxy for the whole. The problem, of course, is that even if some measurable item appears to be a good instrumental variable in the no-tax world, it is unlikely to remain such a good proxy after tax has been imposed on it. Most practical difficulties have centred around the use of income as a variable to be reported and taxed. Consumption is a good deal more straightforward, specific items of consumption more straightforward still, and purchases of particular commodities easy to measure. Other transactions are natural targets, and those—such as real property transfers—which require registration by the State in any event have been particularly attractive targets. Broadly, the closer the intended tax base to a transactions base, the fewer are the practical problems of enforcement.

Income is the borderline case. Less obviously impractical as choice of tax base than one such as 'welfare' which patently depends on the specific preferences of individuals, or one such as 'wealth' which rests heavily on the subjective evaluation of future events, income is nevertheless patently not a readily measurable item like number of cigarettes smoked or the price paid for a property. As a result, it is the measurement of income in both the personal and corporate sectors which accounts for by far the largest part of the 'interpretative' component of tax compliance costs.

Tax law in Britain, as in most countries, eschews definition of income and merely exemplifies it, relying on judicial interpretation to determine what it is should be taxed. Such interpretation has encountered predictable difficulties. The Hicksian definition—which looks at what one can spend without impoverishing oneself—is not an operational basis for a tax system. The Haig–Simons definition—which treats income as accretion to wealth—avoids directly the problem of defining expectations, but still demands an assessment of wealth and conflicts with many common-sense definitions of income. But in the absence of any agreed underlying concept, whether derived from economic theory or everyday experience, both judicial interpretation and revenue practice are intrinsically arbitrary.

It is my view that income is now across the borderline of impracticality. The contrast between the interpretative costs of systems of personal and corporate income taxation and the relatively trivial ones associated with a consumption-based tax such as VAT is striking, and the difference is growing. It has led most countries in the western world to adopt a VAT or equivalent broad-based tax, in the course of the last twenty years. The job of persuading tax authorities that what they have been attempting to do for 200 years is impossible is not, however, an easy one; the chains which bind the slaves of defunct economists to their masters are strong indeed.

7. Precepts for Tax Systems

Implications for the design of actual tax systems fall into two main categories—those which determine the choice of instruments and those which affect the actual rates of tax. A first question to be determined is which kinds of tax are actually feasible. This not only limits the variety of structures available but influences the roles which are to be played by those taxes which can be employed. Lump-sum taxes, which reflect the unobservable endowments of individuals, are impractical because they require information from the taxpayer which he lacks incentive to reveal and the tax authority lacks capacity to verify. This is not to say that lump-sum elements cannot play a role in the assessment of tax liability, and typically they do. All tax systems utilize both contingent information—factual statements about the taxpayer's age, or occupational or marital status— and data about transactions undertaken by the taxpayer.

Many of the enforcement problems posed for tax structures arise because of the difficulty of finding verifiable measures which can be related to underlying, unobservable, economic concepts. There is a spectrum ranging from the ideal, but unobservable (endowment) to the verifiable, but irrelevant (number of cigarettes purchased). The robustness of a tax structure reflects its ability to resolve this tension. Consumption represents a more effective resolution than income—sacrificing little, if anything at all, in relevance, for a decided gain in verifiability.

The choice between income and consumption as the primary tax base is a clearly distinct issue from the choice between direct and indirect taxation. Direct taxation is differentiated by the identity of the taxpayer; indirect by the nature of the transaction. As a general proposition, it is easy to see why one might want to discriminate by reference to the second. But the discussion above has illustrated a number of possible reasons, and a general tax on all commodities may be a convenient mechanism for collecting a general consumption tax.

As far as rates of tax are concerned, uniformity of commodity tax rates is suggested as a starting-point, but a starting-point for deviations. There is a case for differential taxation of goods complementary to leisure or high earning capacity; probably not a case of much practical significance. But the argument for uniformity relates to the taxation of final goods only; in general, intermediate goods should not be taxed. The principal exception to this—that commodities which involve production or consumption externalities should be taxed whether they are intermediate goods or not— translates into an argument for the differential taxation of final commodities as well. There are non-welfarist arguments for the subsidization of limited quantities of some basic commodities and, possibly, for differential taxation of alcohol and tobacco. Marginal rates of income tax should tend to decline at both the top and the bottom of the income range.

The tax mechanism itself may have consequences, but it is appropriate to do no more than suggest what they are and leave the decision to political choice. Universality—the involvement of all taxpayers in the same system—may seem to some an advantage, to others not. Transparency— ready identification by the taxpayer of the amount he has to pay—may be a merit or a weakness of a particular system. Randomness in impact is unlikely to be appropriate on welfarist ground and probably excluded by non-welfarist arguments.

If these seem a limited range of propositions to emerge from a century's study of public finance, consider the specific policy implications. The substitution of expenditure for income taxation; the abandonment of zero-rating of food and fuel; the abolition of business property taxes and, at least in their present form, of corporation taxes; and the inversion of a combined tax and benefit structure which currently imposes very high rates of tax at its extremes. The economic analysis manifesto for tax reform is radical if not necessarily popular.

11

Social Security Policy, Defining the Borders of the State

ANDREW DILNOT[*]

1. Introduction

In 1987/8 more than 25 million of the 56 million individuals in the UK received one or more social security benefits; for 9.6 million the benefit will be State retirement pension, for 12 million child benefit, for 3 million unemployment benefit or supplementary benefit. Some 7 million of the 20 million households in the UK received tested housing benefit. The cost of the whole social security programme was £47 billion, around one-third of total public expenditure, and considerably more than the total revenue from income taxation. The social security programme will cost more than twice as much as the next most expensive area, defence. It would not be unreasonable to think that in this area the State impinges most obviously on the behaviour and well-being of the population; that it is here that the economic borders of the State are most easily seen, and the activity of the State most important to the individuals affected.

For all of these reasons, we might expect there to be a clear rationale behind the structure and apparent aims of the social security system in the UK. It is difficult to see what that rationale might be. As we discuss in Section 2, the system as envisaged by Beveridge in 1942 would have had such a rationale, but the system we face now bears little relation to the Beveridge ideal. The plethora of different structures and benefits which have grown up not only make understanding the system difficult, but through their complex interrelationships impair the straightforward achievement of specified goals.

In the remainder of this article we start from Beveridge and his conception of the State's role, in Section 2. In Section 3 we follow the development of the system through the post-war period, focusing on the problems caused by the mismatch between the original conception and final

* Director of Personal Sector Programme, Institute for Fiscal Studies. Thanks are due to the Department of Economics, Research School of Social Sciences, at the Australian National University. This chapter was written during a visit there in summer 1986. Also to Dieter Helm, for comments on an earlier draft.

implementation. In Section 4 we consider the current system and the roots of the problems we face. Section 5 attempts to draw together the analysis of UK practice in the post-war period, to clarify the distinctions between different social security objectives, and to discuss the types of systems they might imply.

2. Beveridge: The Foundation of the System?

'No document within living memory has made such a powerful impression, or stirred such hopes, as the Beveridge Report' (*Hansard*, 16 February 1943, column 16/8). Thus the minister responsible for commissioning the report took part in the enthusiastic reception it received. The Beveridge Report was followed in 1944 by White Papers (HMSO (1944b, 1944c)) which accepted its main principles, and formed the basis of the post-war legislation on social security. Despite the retreat from the principles advanced by Beveridge which has characterized post-war social security policy, it is worth examining his proposals as an example of an attempt at a coherent structure. It is also hard to understand our current predicament without the background of Beveridge.

The core of the scheme was the concept of social insurance. By social insurance, Beveridge meant a system in which all individuals would make contributions to a National Insurance fund which would provide cash benefits in the event of the contingencies most likely to lead to poverty—sickness, old age, unemployment, etc. These benefits would be sufficient to protect against want.

Consider the first two of the six 'fundamental principles' of the Beveridge plan.

Flat Rate of Subsistence Benefit. The first fundamental principle of the social insurance scheme is provision of a flat rate of insurance benefit, irrespective of the amount of earnings which have been interrupted by unemployment or disability, or ended by retirement. This principle follows from the recognition of the place and importance of voluntary insurance in social security, and distinguishes the scheme proposed for Britain from the security schemes of Germany, the Soviet Union, the United States and most other countries with the exception of New Zealand. The flat rate is the same for all the principal forms of cessation of earning—unemployment, disability, retirement; for maternity and widowhood there is a temporary benefit at a higher rate.

Flat Rate of Contribution. The second fundamental principle of the scheme is that the compulsory contribution required of each person or his employer is at a flat rate, irrespective of his means. All insured persons, rich or poor, will pay the same contributions for the same security; those with larger means will pay more only to the extent that as taxpayers they pay more to the national exchequer and so to the State share of the Social Insurance fund. This feature distinguishes the scheme proposed for Britain from the scheme recently established in New Zealand under which the contributions are graduated by income, and are in effect an income tax assigned to a particular service. Subject moreover to one exception, the contribution will be the same irrespective of the assumed degrees of risk affecting particular individuals or forms of employment. The exception is the raising of a proportion of the special cost of benefits and pensions for industrial disability in occupations of high risk by a levy on employers proportionate to risk and pay-roll. (Beveridge (1942, paras. 304 and 305))

The most important point from the first principle is that no account will be taken of past or present income when paying benefits. The payment is to be related to the contingency, not the circumstances of the recipient. This characteristic mirrors the likely arrangement under a system of private insurance, and is indeed intended to encourage additional private provision for those whose circumstances would allow it. The second principle makes very clear the difference between private and social insurance; under the system of social insurance, 'the contribution will be the same irrespective of the assumed degrees of risk affecting particular individuals'. This statement is akin to a private insurance company charging the same car insurance premiums to two individuals though one drives a Mini and has a twenty-year record of no claims, and the other a Lamborghini which he has crashed on average three times a year over the same period. Under a system of 'social insurance', the State pays benefits in the event of given contingencies. At the individual level, even with uniform flat-rate contributions, it is *not* the case that such an arrangement mirrors a system of private insurance, since it is clear that the risks of unemployment, sickness, and disability are related to individual-specific characteristics which would be taken into account by any private insurer. Private unemployment insurance for a coal-miner in many areas of the UK would have been very expensive in the early 1980s, especially when compared with the cost for a tenured university academic. A scheme of social insurance would have them pay the same contribution, for the same benefit; the redistribution from tenured university academic to unemployed miners implicit in such a scheme is clear. While the Beveridge scheme proposed to take this diversity of risk into account when funding disability benefits for high-risk occupations, it was explicitly ignored in all other cases.

The distinction between private and 'social' insurance is evident in the case of unemployment and sickness. For retirement benefits, the position is less obvious; while there may be some relationship between occupation and the risk of reaching retirement, or the length of life after retirement, the Beveridge scheme for retirement pensions could be seen as a purely commercial arrangement, with payments made by individuals leading to actuarially calculated benefits on retirement.

Beveridge aimed to introduce compulsory contributory retirement pensions, perhaps having in mind the sort of preference failure Helm discusses in this volume, and a system of insurance against 'accident' contingencies such as unemployment where the benefits were made available by dint of prior contribution to the scheme, but at the individual level were not related to the risk of accident and therefore likely call on the benefit system. The latter implied some redistribution in favour of 'high-risk' individuals, which might be justified, especially in the case of unemployment, by seeing the accident as caused by, or at least allowed by, the State. Such a view is particularly easy to imagine in a period dominated by Keynesian ideas of the macro-economy, with one of the roles of the State seen to be maintaining full employment.

The first two principles tell us under what circumstances the benefit will be paid, and how the contribution will be charged; what of the level of benefit?

Adequacy of Benefit: The fourth fundamental principle is adequacy of benefit in amount and time. The flat rate of benefit proposed is intended in itself to be sufficient without further resources to provide the minimum income needed for subsistence in all normal cases. It gives room and a basis for additional voluntary provision, but does not assume that in any case. The benefits . . . will continue indefinitely without means test, so long as the need continues. . . . (Beveridge (1942), para. 307)

So for Beveridge the benefit was to be set at a subsistence level, which he estimated to be, in 1938 prices, 32 shillings per week for a non-pensioner couple, broken up as in Table 11.1.[1]

The poverty line was to be an absolute one, related to subsistence levels of consumption expenditure. This was in many senses as important a feature of the scheme as the concept of social insurance, since it was the absolute nature of the poverty line which would make paying for social security possible. Beveridge assumed, rightly as it transpired, that post-war Britain would experience substantial economic growth. This economic growth would lead to an automatic rise in the real level of tax receipts, which would make possible the increased number of social security payments which would result from the implementation of the Beveridge scheme. This economic growth would only facilitate the payment of benefits under a Beveridge-type scheme if the benefit level did *not* rise in line with economic growth, but only in line with prices; that is, if the poverty line was an absolute one.

[1] See Chapter 1, Appendix C of Dilnot, Kay, and Morris (1984).

Table 11.1. Beveridge's subsistence level

Food	13s.
Clothing	3s.
Fuel, light, and sundries	4s.
Margin	2s.
Rent	10s.
Total	32s.

In Beveridge's view, poverty was caused by the temporary or permanent interruption of earnings, which might come about for a number of reasons. If those reasons could be identified, so could poverty. One response, which is still occasionally put forward, would be to have individuals insure themselves against these contingencies. But Beveridge did not advocate that route, because he saw the responsibility for the existence of the contingencies as lying principally with society rather than the individual. In *Insurance for All and Everything*, written for the 1924 Liberal Summer School, he writes (my emphasis):

In all these five ways, by industrial accident, sickness, unemployment, old age, or by the death of the breadwinner, the income of the family may be destroyed permanently or for a time. They are all threats to security, risks of economic life, disorders endemic in modern society. *They are disorders of society rather than of the individual*, that is to say, they may and do affect perfectly normal persons; they are also to a large extent modern disorders.

This view that the causes of poverty are the result of disorders of society rather than of individual behaviour is enormously important, explaining Beveridge's insistence that contributions not be related to risk. If the individual is not responsible for the interruption of earnings which leads to poverty, he should not be expected to bear a higher proportion of the cost than any other individual.

However, given this view of the causes of poverty, one is bound to ask why Beveridge wanted to indulge in complex 'insurance'-type arrangements. If poverty comes almost at random, and is the responsibility of society rather than the individual, why not merely redistribute to the poor out of general State revenue? Sir William Beveridge was a Liberal, whose ideas on social security were well developed by the early 1920s. The idea of the State merely handing out cash would have been intolerable for someone who saw individual action as essential to human dignity. In the Beveridge Report itself he writes: '. . . benefit in return for contribution, rather than free allowances from the State, is what the people of Britain desire ... Management of one's income is an essential element of a citizen's freedom. Payment of a substantial part of the cost of a benefit as a contribution, irrespective of the means of the contributor is the firm basis of a claim to benefit irrespective of means' (Beveridge (1942, para. 21)). Beveridge may or may not have been right about what the people of Britain desired, but is here faced by inconsistency. The risk of unemployment is not random: many individuals never experience it, while others suffer repeated spells. Within the Beveridge scheme, substantial redistribution from low- to high-risk individuals occurs. High-risk individuals will not have paid 'a substantial part of the cost' of their benefit. Like it or not, the Beveridge scheme fails to ensure 'Payment of a substantial part of the cost of a benefit as a contribution'. And yet this lack of link between contribution and risk arises of necessity out of Beveridge's view of the causes of poverty as 'disorders of society rather than the individual', which requires that the burden be spread evenly across society. The desire to protect individual freedom and responsibility which gave rise to the insurance basis of the scheme, and the view of poverty as not being the responsibility of the individual, simply do not cohere very effectively.

Beveridge wanted the State to ensure a minimum subsistence standard of living for all. It was to do so by requiring uniform contributions from all, and paying uniform benefits to all in the event of given contingencies regardless of any other income. The State would effectively redistribute from low-risk to high-risk individuals. There was no explicit income redistributive element; poverty was identified by events such as unemployment which might cause it, rather than by a shortfall of income relative to need. The individual was not seen as responsible for the onset of poverty, but should feel that a substantial part of his benefit had been paid for by his own contributions.

3. Post-War Social Security—Whither Beveridge?

Three developments since 1948 have swamped and reshaped Beveridge's ideal, so that all that is now left is the common but erroneous belief that our current system is a 'Beveridge' system. One development is the widespread topping-up of National Insurance benefits by various means-tested benefits, contravening Beveridge's view that the safety net of National Assistance should be precisely that, and rarely used. The second is the complete abandonment of flat-rate contributions in favour of contributions related entirely to income, which, as Beveridge (1942, para. 305) wrote in his second fundamental principle, are 'in effect an income tax assigned to a particular service.' The third development is the growth of new categories of poor, especially those in low-paid work with children, and single-parent families. For both of these groups, a complex system of means-tested benefits has been instituted which fits unhappily, if at all, with the National Insurance system.

These developments are not unrelated. Some were inevitable consequences of flaws in the original Beveridge design, some the result of attempting to change the objectives without changing the underlying structures. Perhaps the greatest problem was that of cost, which was bound up in Beveridge's conception of poverty. As noted in Section 2, Beveridge advocated an absolute poverty line. If real earnings were to double in the post-war period, as they did, the poverty line should remain stable. Paying for the more comprehensive coverage of the new system would be made possible by increased tax payments from the higher real incomes of those in work. Beveridge was content to see the relative living standards of those dependent on benefits halve, because he was not concerned to reduce inequality or redistribute income. Rather, Beveridge's aim was to provide those goods which were necessary to subsist, and no more. This view of the poverty line was unacceptable to both governments and voters in the post-war period. The suggestion that the retired should not share in increased levels of prosperity seemed absurd. Since 1948, the real level of retirement pensions has increased by a factor of almost two and a half, while unemployment and sickness benefits have increased in real terms by a factor of almost two. Beveridge had envisaged *no* increase in real terms.

The poverty line is now almost always defined in relative terms, yet such a definition appears to give a somewhat flexible concept of poverty. Sen (1983d) has offered a link between absolute and relative poverty lines. Certainly, he argues, we must see poverty in terms of an absolute level below which no one must fall. But this absolute level should not be defined in terms of commodities as Beveridge and the traditional 'absolute' measures would suggest, but in terms of capabilities. Thus we can see poverty, as did Townsend (1979), as being the inability to 'participate in the activities of the community', but rather than conceptualizing this as a relative poverty line in terms of goods, we can see it as an absolute poverty line in terms of capabilities. The type and amount of goods required to take part in the activity of the community have obviously changed since 1948 when the National Insurance scheme was introduced. The State pension for a couple in the UK is now set at £60 per week. If it were set at £25 per week (around Beveridge's real level), those who depended on it would not be capable of taking a full part in society. This view of poverty ties in with the notion of positive freedom discussed by Dasgupta in this volume—the ability '. . . to be a somebody, not nobody; a doer—deciding, not being decided for, self-directed . . . conceiving goals and policies of [one's] own and realizing them.' This 'absolute capability' approach may have little effect on the practice of measuring poverty in relative terms, but does provide a more watertight rationale for so doing.

The acceptance of a relative poverty line implied inevitable disaster for the Beveridge ideal. Benefit levels were increased in real terms, increasing the costs in line with economic growth rather than allowing the growth to pay for the scheme. As unemployment rose slowly towards the levels assumed by Beveridge, and the number of retirement pensioners increased rapidly, costs spiralled ahead of forecasts. This increase in costs led to increased contribution levels. However, as the contribution level rose, the burden on the lower-paid became unacceptably high as a proportion of their income, because the contribution was at a flat rate. So in 1961, to enable further increases, the contribution became part graduated. By 1975, the contribution was entirely related to income. Beveridge's fundamental principle of a flat rate of contribution collapsed as a result of increased contributions required by increased costs, implied by a relative view of poverty.

The increased levels of contribution were, understandably, unpopular. To soften the blow, higher levels of future benefits were promised, implying still higher costs. Much of the increased future benefits took the form of earnings-related supplements to retirement pensions and unemployment and sickness benefits. Hence, the collapse of flat-rate contributions led also to the demise of the fundamental principle of flat-rate benefits.

The increased benefit levels which stemmed from the relative view of poverty also attacked the principle of adequacy. Beveridge had intended the National Insurance benefits to be set at such a level that those in receipt of them would not need to have recourse to any topping-up from means-tested benefits, especially the safety net of National Assistance. Clearly, the safety net had to be set at a level equal to the poverty line, be it a relative or absolute one. To set the National Insurance benefits at this level would have been excessively expensive. At no time since the introduction of the system has the flat rate of benefit been sufficient to provide resources equal to the supplementary benefit/National Assistance level in the normal case (including housing assistance). Around 25 per cent of all National Insurance beneficiaries, and 50 per cent or more of the unemployed since 1970, have typically received means-tested supplementary benefit in addition to their National Insurance benefit. In addition to supplementary benefit, many households in the UK receive means-tested housing benefit and a large proportion of these are National Insurance benefit recipients. The relative concept of poverty implied benefit levels which were too costly to be paid to all regardless of income, leading to an enormous unplanned increase in the coverage, expense, and complexity of the means-tested benefit system—another nail in the coffin of social insurance in the UK.

Rapidly rising costs were not the sole problem. Social insurance aims to relieve poverty not by tackling poverty itself, but by identifying those contingencies likely to cause poverty. Contributions are extracted from the population which will be sufficient to pay benefits to those who experience the specified contingencies. It is obviously very important to identify accurately the causes of poverty, not just at the inception of the scheme, but many years into the future. Such a task is an almost impossible one, as shown by two groups who were the subject of no particular provision in the Beveridge scheme and yet have become the focus of much anti-poverty legislation in the post-war period. First, the working poor, who are barely mentioned in the Beveridge Report. Beveridge's view was that anyone in employment would be able to support a wife and one child; family allowances for second and subsequent children were all that was necessary. Second, single-parent families, of whom there are around 1 million in the UK today. Beveridge identified the problem, which was then of much smaller quantitative significance, but failed to suggest any response. Around these two groups the worst interactions of the tax and social security systems have grown up, the lowest levels of benefit take-up, and the greatest degrees of complexity as family income supplement, housing benefits, one parent benefit, and 'passported' benefits, among others, have been introduced on an *ad hoc* basis to try to plug unexpected gaps in the system. It would be unfair to blame Beveridge for failing to foresee the changes in the structure of society and the economy which gave rise to poverty among these groups, but it is important to note that such problems will afflict any scheme which relies on identifying *in advance* the causes of poverty.

4. Social Security in the UK—1986/7

In this section we look briefly at the composition of social security expenditure which has developed in the UK, relating the various benefits to their apparent aims, and discuss some of the problems inherent in the current system.

Table 11.2 presents an analysis of expenditure on social security and the number of recipients of each benefit.[2] The National Insurance benefits, which were to be by far the most important in Beveridge's scheme, account

[2] See the annual Government Public Expenditure Plans, HM Treasury (1987) for more detailed information on social security expenditures.

Table 11.2. Social security expenditure and numbers of recipients, 1986/7

	Expenditure (£ million)	Number of recipients[a] (thousands of households)
NATIONAL INSURANCE BENEFITS		
Retirement pension	18,374	9,620
Unemployment benefit	1,570	820
Other	4,737	1,700
Total	24,681	
OTHER NON-MEANS-TESTED BENEFITS		
Child benefit	4,624	12,115
War pension	594	270
Other	1,912	2,080
Total	7,130	
MEANS-TESTED BENEFITS		
Supplementary pensions	1,222	1,745
Supplementary benefits	7,033	3,185
Family income supplement	138	205
Housing benefit (rent)	3,518	4,885
(rate)	1,675[b]	7,135
ADMINISTRATION	2,170	
TOTAL	47,567	

[a] Totals of recipients are not shown, as many receive more than one of the benefits.
[b] Estimate.

for only a little over half of total expenditure. Child benefit is a flat-rate benefit like the National Insurance benefits, but entitlement is not related to prior contribution. Around 25 per cent of benefit expenditure is on means-tested benefits, received by well over 7 million households. Many of the recipients of National Insurance benefits also receive one or other of these benefits, entirely contrary to the spirit of a social insurance system.

We might attempt to split these expenditures by broad function. The first group, National Insurance benefits, especially those paid to the retired, are indeed in the nature of insurance benefits, and might be organized commercially. However, it is important to note that the contributions which give entitlement to these benefits are at present related to income, while the bulk of the benefit is not. Such redistribution would not be a part of any commercial scheme. While the Beveridge scheme of flat-rate contributions and flat-rate benefits might have been transferred to a scheme of compulsory private insurance, the current flat-rate retirement scheme funded by graduated contributions could not be, without a substantial change in its distributional impact.

The second group of non-means-tested benefits is dominated by child benefit, a flat-rate payment for all children. One way of seeing this payment is as a scheme for redistributing income over the life cycle. The period of child-rearing is typically one of low income in relation to needs, thus the payment of child benefit redistributes from those without children to those with them. The argument for State involvement in this redistribution is that the capital markets which would allow individuals to make their own provisions are imperfect, and that they may not perceive the benefits of so doing. Another way of viewing child benefit is as a support to those who take on the valuable role of providing society with people to look after the current generation when it reaches old age. The war pension is a payment from the State to those who suffered in protecting it. Most of the 'other' benefits are payments to those looking after the disabled, such as attendance allowance, or payments to the disabled themselves, such as mobility allowance. These benefits might fit more easily in a social insurance framework, but were not clearly envisaged in the 1940s.

The final group, means-tested benefits, exist with the prevention of poverty especially in mind. Rather than attempt to identify its causes, as do the National Insurance benefits, they aim to identify the condition, and pay sufficient benefit to alleviate it, and no more. They are deliberately redistributive. It is important *not* to think of the means-tested and non-means-tested benefits as excluding one another; as we noted in Section 3, many of the recipients of National Insurance benefits have their income topped up, and therefore determined, by means-tested benefits.

This is not the place for a detailed discussion of the problems of the UK social security system, or analysis of possible routes to reform,[3] but it is worth noting some and relating them to the haphazard development of our system.

The best-known problem is probably the poverty trap. Families with children where one or both parents work can in principle lose more in increased taxes and reduced benefit payments than they gain from an increase in their wages. This problem afflicts only the low-paid in full-time work and single-parent families, the two groups we identified as 'missed'

[3] See Creedy and Disney (1985), Dilnot, Kay, and Morris (1984), and HMSO (1985a) for details of the recent debate and proposals for reform.

by the Beveridge Report, and about whom complex means-tested benefit payments have grown up. The interaction of these benefits with the tax system causes the poverty trap. Related to the poverty trap is the unemployment trap. It is possible for low-paid workers to find that they would be better off, or only slightly worse off, out of work than in work, although the magnitude of this problem is often exaggerated.[4] This trap is also the result of unplanned interactions between the means-tested benefit system, especially supplementary benefit and family income supplement, and the direct tax system.

A third problem is that although the means-tested benefits are received by very large numbers of individuals and families, the take-up rate is often low; many of those entitled to social security benefits are not receiving them. For some benefits, family income supplement in particular, the take-up rate is around 50 per cent, for housing benefit between 60 and 70 per cent, for supplementary benefit around 70 per cent.[5] While there are a number of possible explanations for this, the complexity of the system and the many different benefits to which an individual may be entitled will clearly have some impact. If we think of the supplementary benefit as a safety net, non-take-up of entitlement to it is clearly a cause for some concern.

The government published in 1985 a Green Paper followed by a White Paper which presented a number of suggestions for reform, the structure of which, while not very radical, aimed to alleviate especially the poverty and unemployment traps, and to simplify the payment and calculation of the means-tested benefits. Many of the more dramatic simplifications were abandoned between the Green and White Papers.[6] Perhaps the strongest theme was to give more help to the low-paid with children—precisely the group Beveridge had thought would not need it.

5. How Should We Do It?

Much of the debate on social security policy, in the UK and elsewhere, has been in terms of whether universal or means-tested benefits are the most appropriate method of payment. This question is of great importance, and is vital to the discussion of the size of the public sector and the structure of taxation. However, to a very large extent it is a secondary question and one which avoids the most important issue—what do we want the social security system to do? The reason for the mess which we find the British

[4] See Micklewright (1986) for a survey of evidence in the 1980s.
[5] See Dilnot, Kay, and Morris (1984, p. 49).
[6] See Davis, Dilnot, and Kay (1985), Dilnot and Stark (1986), and HMSO (1985b).

social security system in today is the failure to match desired aims with an appropriate system. Beveridge wanted to pay subsistence benefits to all suffering given contingencies. He was not interested in the poor in work, or in redistribution across the life cycle, or in 'relative' poverty. Post-war governments picked up Beveridge's structure and tried to achieve their own aims with it; many of these aims were not only not Beveridge's, but were incompatible with his. Little wonder that the system has not worked well, and that little of the Beveridge ideal is left.

There are perhaps three obvious groups of objectives for a social security system.

(1) *Social insurance*: The classic Beveridge aim, which, as we noted above, can take two broad interpretations. First, the compulsory intrusion of the State in insuring risks which might be insured in the same way in the private sector—flat-rate contribution for flat-rate retirement benefits. Second, insurance of non-uniform risks such as unemployment, financed by flat-rate contributions. The State intervenes to redistribute from low-risk to high-risk individuals. If these are the objectives and a subsistence level of benefits is acceptable, Beveridge's original scheme, which included a transitional period of twenty years before the full level of benefit was paid, would have served reasonably well, aside from the caveat that not all categories of poverty were insured.

(2) *Poverty prevention*: Here, the aim is to prevent any individual or family falling below a given minimum level. There are many ways of achieving this, from a rigorously means-tested system which pays benefits to all and rapidly withdraws them as individual income rises, to a system which pays benefits to all and effectively withdraws them more slowly through the tax system. The differences between these two approaches to guaranteeing minimum incomes have often been exaggerated recently;[7] the second implies higher government expenditure and taxation than the first—it effectively spreads the band of income over which benefit is withdrawn to the whole of the income distribution—but they are both extremes, and most feasible systems lie somewhere between the two.

(3) *Life cycle distribution/support of socially desirable activity*: Here the aim is to overcome some flaw in the capital market, or encourage individuals to engage in 'good' activities, which may well include having children (or *not* having children—we could even imagine a negative child benefit in an overcrowded country!). Another possible aim in this general area is intra-family redistribution, perhaps to ensure that mothers receive enough to clothe and feed themselves and their children. For such aims as these, benefits payable to all in a given category seem the obvious instruments.

[7] See Parker (1983) for a description of a basic income guarantee.

It will not be a surprise that these three possible aims correspond to the three categories into which expenditure on social security in the UK was split in Table 11.2. We have obviously wanted a little bit of everything at various times in the post-war period. It is also clear that when decisions have been made about social security policy, such ideas as these have not been very close to the forefront of politicians' minds. And yet I would argue that the failure to be clear about the desired role of the State, the position of its economic border, has been the cause of many of our problems. To attempt to use a system of social insurance as a means of preventing relative poverty, within a social security system which was heavily constrained as to the acceptable level of expenditure, was doomed to lead to failure and complexity. Any imminent reform of social security, either in the UK or elsewhere, must be preceded by a clear exposition of the objectives of the new system. Without such an exposition, many of the old errors will be repeated, and blamed on those who set up, with one aim in mind, a system which fails to achieve costlessly a totally different aim which is later imposed on it.

Given the diversity of policies which have been followed in the past forty years, perhaps the best advice we can offer to those designing social security systems is to ensure that they are flexible. The aims of social security will inevitably change with changing political circumstances, as different groups take different views on the appropriate degree of State intrusion. We might expect that in the next forty years there will be both governments wedded to an insurance-based, contingency-related, flat-rate, non-redistributive system, and governments fervent in their desire for redistributive, income-related benefits. The design of a social security structure should aim to make such changes in policy possible without causing untold problems of administration, complexity, and deprivation. We fool ourselves if we think that by enshrining one set of values in a system, we will prevent it being changed; it will merely work very badly when it is changed.

12

Public Ownership: Concepts and Applications

COLIN MAYER[*]

1. Privatization: The Popular Case

The trend towards privatizing State-owned enterprises has become worldwide. Privatization is being actively discussed or promoted in Austria, France, Italy, Japan, and Spain amongst many other countries. In Britain, we have come to expect periods of nationalization to be followed by denationalization as political fashions alter. But even by British standards, the size and scope of recent transfers from public to private ownership have been unusual.

Why is public ownership everywhere in retreat? It is not difficult to list reasons that are commonly advanced for privatization. First among these is the belief that the performance of private enterprises is superior to that of public corporations. This conventional wisdom does not, however, stem from substantive empirical evidence of a difference in performance between State and private enterprises. Indeed most empirical studies suggest little direct relationship between performance and ownership.

Second, even in the absence of enhanced productive efficiency, it is argued that privatization opens up markets to the forces of competition that make firms more responsive to the preferences of consumers. Competitively set prices ensure that the allocation of production and services between different markets reflects consumer demands. But one of the points that the British government's privatization programme has served to emphasize is that there is no direct relationship between ownership and market structure. To date, the British government has resolutely refused, with a few minor exceptions, to instil competition in industries that are being privatized. State monopolies are for the most part being replaced by

[*] Professor of Corporate Finance at City University Business School. This paper is part of the Centre for Economic Policy Research programme, 'An International Study of Corporate Financing'. The project is being supported by the Bank of England, the Esmée Fairbairn Charitable Trust, the European Economic Community, the Japan Foundation, and the Nuffield Foundation. The author is grateful to Dieter Helm and Stephen Yeo for comments.

private, albeit regulated, monopolies. Allocative efficiency is unlikely to be enhanced in the process.

The most immediate benefit that the government derives from privatizations is the revenue from sales. The sale of public assets is particularly attractive during periods in which public expenditure is constrained by limitations on public sector borrowing. However, as with most asset sales, current receipts are only achieved at the expense of future income. The fact that there is a relationship between privatizations and constraints on public sector expenditure merely draws attention to the inadequacies of existing accounting conventions. A set of accounts that correctly measured the economic value of the public sector's assets and liabilities should not inflate current receipts in relation to future forgone revenue.

Recently, wider share ownership has become a major justification for the privatization programme in France and the UK. The success of a few substantial privatizations in attracting applications from a large number of individuals has been hailed as the dawn of 'a share-owning democracy'. The political attractions of this for Conservative governments are clear; but, in addition, it is suggested that private equity markets will benefit from increased individual investor involvement. There can be little dispute with the assertion that the number of private savers holding equity has increased substantially over the last few years in both France and the UK. Leaving aside questions of whether this process is desirable, it is, however, unclear why it should be achieved in this way. The inducement to wider share ownership has been the payment of substantial subsidies in the form of discounts on new issues. There is no reason why subsidies should take this form; indeed, several advantages can be ascribed to the retention of traditional channels of influencing saving patterns through the tax system. A tax subsidy to equity investment avoids the distortion to savings decisions that results from the payment of large discounts on a small number of shares. The Individual Retirement Account in the US suggests that appropriately tailored tax incentives can have substantial effects on private saving decisions.

What emerges then is a set of widely cited reasons for privatization that bear directly on questions of market structure, public sector accounting, and the taxation of savings, but have little direct relevance to ownership. The same criticism applies to the arguments originally presented for State ownership. Monopoly, distribution, quality regulation, public goods, security, and macro-economic policy have all been mentioned in the context of nationalization. But again the relation between these issues and ownership is at best obscure. What we currently lack is a theory of ownership which informs the policymaker of the appropriate degree of public involvement in a particular industry. Without such a framework, fashions that embrace State and private ownership in turn will continue to dictate practice. If for no other reason than the significant transition costs of switching ownership patterns (see Mayer and Meadowcroft (1985)), practices should be determined by more fundamental considerations than fashion. This article will attempt to provide a framework for analysing ownership.

2. An Outline and Summary of the Paper

The approach that this paper follows is straightforward. The central argument is that public ownership is a statement about restrictions on the portfolio allocations of investors: public ownership imposes an equal distribution of equity holdings across the population. Leaving aside problems created by the incorrect pricing of asset sales, a privatization relaxes this restriction, and reallocates equity holdings from an equal to a market-determined distribution.

In justifying State control, we are therefore looking for reasons why individual equity investments should be restricted. As usual when trying to determine whether market processes should be corrected or constrained, we are searching for possible externalities. This paper suggests one important class of externalities arising from differences between the interests of investors and consumers. The paper argues that this conflict and its implications for public ownership can best be considered within an intertemporal framework, through the application of a general class of models concerned with the resolution of the conflict between choice and commitment.

The approach adopted in this paper suggests that three conditions are required to justify public ownership. First, there must be concentration on either the supply or the demand side of the market. Section 3 discusses the externalities that may arise in savings decisions of individuals and argues that there are circumstances in which the imposition of *intermediaries* between investor and firm may be desirable. The intermediary corrects the externality associated with investors' incentives to free-ride on the evaluation of firms' performance: through monitoring and holding a diversified portfolio the intermediary eliminates investors' need to evaluate individual firm performance.

Similar externalities arise in consumption decisions and may lead to the introduction of an *agency* between consumers and producers. Externalities arise, for example, in consumer networks such as communication and computer systems, where the value of services provided to a particular individual depends on consumption decisions of others. In certain circumstances, co-ordination of consumption by a central agency may therefore be desirable. An agency may also be required to undertake analyses of heterogeneous products whose quality cannot be readily identified by consumers, such as health care or financial services. The same free-rider problem that afflicts investor monitoring undermines consumer quality assessments.

Such intermediaries and agencies provide the basis for concentration in supply or demand, which creates the potential for abuses of power. Although concentration is a product of monitoring and co-ordination, these alone do not justify public ownership. It is only when the analysis is extended beyond a single period in Section 4 that ownership becomes an issue. In a multi-period context, intermediaries can abuse their monopoly positions to the detriment of investors. These potential abuses may make allocations of ownership and control relevant considerations, but not if such abuses can be stemmed by the creation of appropriate contracts. The second condition necessary to justify public ownership is that complete contracts should be infeasible or costly.

The nature of the potential abuse is readily illustrated. Suppose, for example, that an agency exists on the consumption side of the market. Consider first the case in which savers are committed to the portfolio allocations that they make in the first period. In the second period, consumption decisions are co-ordinated by the agency, which can choose its supply from a range of producers, each of which has capital in place that is dedicated to production in this sector. This imbalance in flexibility between producer and consumer permits the consumer agency, by threatening to take its purchases elsewhere, to prevent producers earning normal returns on the value of first-period savings. Since in the second period capital invested has no value in alternative employment, the agency can drive producers' returns to zero. If this is anticipated in the first period then there will be under-investment. While the interests of consumers are furthered by the maintenance of flexibility in production and distribution, restrictions on flexibility are required to promote investment. The relative merits of private and public ownership can therefore be seen as a resolution of this conflict between consumer and investor.

The appropriate allocation of property rights should reflect the relative importance of flexibility and commitment. The greater the benefit to be derived from flexibility in co-ordination of second-period consumption, the greater the value placed on consumer control. In cases in which there are externalities in consumption and there is uncertainty surrounding second-period preferences, the avoidance of commitment to particular distributions may be of substantial value. On the other hand, the greater the effects of choice of first-period investments on second-period performance, the stronger is the case for retaining investor control and limiting second-period flexibility. In this case, commitment is required to elicit appropriate investment decisions.

Private ownership provides the property rights required to encourage participation in first-period investments. Public ownership, on the other hand, maintains greater flexibility in responding to second-period demand requirements of consumers. Social ownership is thus of proper concern in circumstances in which the property rights of private ownership do not adequately reflect subsequent demand requirements of consumers. Conversely, public ownership does not create the incentives for first-period investment. The third condition for public ownership is therefore that considerations of flexibility should outweigh those of commitment.

In Section 5 the paper applies these ideas to patterns of ownership that are observed in several industries in different countries. The theory should be able to explain a number of stylized observations about ownerships: (1) public ownership is consistently higher in some industries than others; (2) in certain industries there are considerable variations in ownership patterns across countries; (3) with some notable exceptions, proportions of domestic production that are State-owned are broadly similar in several countries; and (4) privatization is particularly actively pursued in certain industries.

The theory suggests that public ownership is most prevalent in industries in which technical innovation is slow, investment expenditures are modest, and demand requirements are unpredictable. This is consistent with observed patterns; for example, postal services and railways display the highest degree of State control across countries of any of the industries examined. Moreover, ownership patterns are unlikely to be stable over time: periods of technical innovation will be most closely associated with private ownership. The relevance of public ownership will also be, at least in part, related to the size of economies and the development of their capital markets. The paper suggests that observed patterns of ownership across countries and across industries can in large part be explained in terms of the trade-off between the benefits of flexibility and of commitment.

Section 5 ends on a note of caution. The association of private property with commitment and public ownership with flexibility may be undermined by imperfections in capital markets and by the organization of government. In particular, once a separation between ownership and control is introduced, then the same problems of commitment that are a feature of public ownership may occur in private companies. Competition in financial markets may discourage investors from making long-term credible commitments. Conversely, the stability of bureaucracies and their procedures for evaluating and rewarding performance may permit governments to make credible commitments to invest in industry. State-controlled organizations might then be able to implement investment projects that private capital markets could not.

The arguments in this paper have been alluded to in two previous papers (Mayer (1985a, 1985b)); this is an elaboration of the issues raised there. The paper is an application of a general class of models concerned with the resolution of the conflict between choice and commitment. This topic has been discussed in several other contexts and is being actively pursued as part of an international study of corporate finance and investment (see Mayer (1987)). The presentation here is informal, but more formal models are becoming available (see Bray (1986)).

The main results of the paper are:

(1) Public ownership should only be contemplated in industries in which monitoring or co-ordination create concentrated markets, and the abuses to which such concentration may give rise cannot or should not be avoided by contractual arrangements.

(2) Where a *prima-facie* case for public ownership exists, consideration should be given to the relative importance that should be attached to flexibility in production or distribution and commitment to investment plans.

(3) Neither private nor public ownership can be expected to be universally appropriate.

(4) Public ownership is associated with industries in which flexibility is of dominant concern, and private ownership will be preferred where commitment is required to encourage investment.

(5) Changes in ownership will frequently be justified by technical innovation. A life cycle of ownership patterns may emerge.

(6) Patterns of ownership across industries in different countries can be broadly explained by considerations of commitment and flexibility.

(7) Sizes of product and capital markets will both influence preferred ownership patterns.

(8) It is rarely appropriate for ownership to be the same at all stages of production in an industry. The preferred form of ownership is frequently opaque in circumstances in which disintegration is not an option.

(9) The fundamental principles of ownership summarized in (1), (2), and (4) will not apply in circumstances in which financial markets fail to encourage corporate investment. Conversely, the structure of government administration may permit public corporations to make investment commitments.

3. The Organization of Production and Consumption

The question that we want to answer is: 'under what circumstances is it desirable for the portfolio allocations of investors to be constrained?'. We begin by considering a single-period model in which there are no transaction costs, taxes, information asymmetries, or costs of switching between firms or customers. Portfolio theory informs us that there exist optimal portfolio holdings of investors which reflect individual preferences between risk and return. For example, in two-factor models, all investors hold the same portfolio of equity holdings but allocate different proportions of their portfolios between risky and riskless assets. More generally, holdings will reflect individual consumption and asset return patterns. Constraining portfolio holdings in this context unequivocally imposes welfare costs.

Firm-specific earnings are irrelevant because diversification of portfolios eliminates all but systematic risk components (risk that is common to firms). But specific components no longer remain irrelevant if they can be identified *ex ante* or their *ex post* identification influences performance. If they can be, then *ex ante* selection and/or *ex post* outcomes can be improved. In the presence of quality variations and costly monitoring, insufficient monitoring will occur in the absence of a mechanism for internalizing the externality. That mechanism may take the form of an intermediary. In the former case, performance can be improved through screening. In the latter case, the improvement comes from relating incentives to performance, thereby diminishing the costs associated with moral hazard. Screening or incentives therefore make identification of individual qualities desirable. If identification is a costly process then the private collection of information on firm-specific performance may be insufficient. There is an incentive to free-ride which creates an externality in information collection.

This can be illustrated in terms of a diagram of investors and firms. In the absence of selection or incentive considerations, portfolio diversifications encourage individual holdings that are related to consumption requirements and expectations of investors (Figure 12.1). Restrictions on allocations will be welfare-diminishing. But if evaluations of individual firms can only be achieved at cost, then the imposition of an intermediary between investors and firms is desirable (Figure 12.2). The intermediary internalizes the externality associated with the incentive to free-ride on screening or performance evaluation. The intermediary undertakes monitoring and, through holding a diversified portfolio, eliminates the requirement on investors to identify individual firm performance (see Diamond

Investors

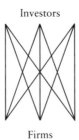

Firms

Figure 12. 1

Investors

Intermediary

Firms

Figure 12.2

(1984)). Alternatively, firms conglomerate and introduce a hierarchical structure. Whether the intermediary is debt- (a bank) or equity- (a conglomerate) financed depends on the ability of investors to identify certain components of risk at low cost.

There is a second class of reasons for imposing an intermediary or layer of hierarchy between investors and firms. There may be an externality on the investors' side. The size of markets as measured by the number of shareholders may not be uniquely determined (Pagano (1987)). The extent to which portfolios can be diversified, and thus the attraction of equities for risk-averse investors, are dependent on the number of participants in the market. Large markets are efficient in absorbing trades with small price adjustments, and individuals only participate if they do not face inelastic supply schedules. This circularity creates the 'network' effect of consumer markets in savings decisions.

Turning to the consumer side, freedom of choice is usually perceived as enhancing consumer welfare. But externalities in consumption undermine this result. Most obviously, externalities arise in consumer networks (for example, communication and computer systems) where the value of services provided to a particular individual is dependent on consumption

Firms

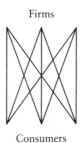

Consumers

Figure 12.3

Firms

Agency

Consumers

Figure 12.4

decisions of others (see Farrell and Saloner (1985)). More generally, interrelationships in consumption occur in the presence of economies of scale and scope in production. In that case individual purchase decisions affect the costs of production of goods and services sold to others. In certain circumstances, co-ordination of consumption by a central agency is therefore required, and the pure market relationship of Figure 12.3 should then be modified to the agency structure of Figure 12.4.

There may be other reasons for agencies. Analogous to the role of an intermediary in undertaking comparative firm evaluations, an agency is required to undertake analyses of heterogeneous (differentiated) products whose quality cannot be readily identified by consumers (for example, health care or financial services). The *raison d'être* of the agency rests on the superior skills of agents in undertaking quality analyses and avoidance of duplication of effort in assessments. The same free-rider problem that afflicts investor monitoring undermines consumer quality assessments. As Figures 12.1 to 12.4 suggest, there is a close symmetry between the factors encouraging the formation of agencies and intermediaries.

We have thus identified four classes of economy: the pure market economy of Figures 12.1 and 12.3; the intermediated or hierarchy economy of Figures 12.2 and 12.3; the agency economy of Figures 12.1 and 12.4; and the non-market economy of Figures 12.3 and 12.4. The appropriate structure for a particular product or economy involves a comparison of the relative benefits of freedom of choice in consumption and savings, monitoring of corporate performance and quality of consumer services, networks in consumption and savings, allocation of capital resources, and economies of scale and scope. Intermediation and agency may therefore be justified; but as yet we have not provided a justification for the public ownership of these institutions.

4. A Question of Ownership

The failure to identify ownership arises from the absence of a distinguishing feature of savings or investment. This deficiency is a consequence of the single-period nature of the discussion. The simplest way of rectifying this omission is to imagine savers as making portfolio allocations in a first period which augment capital assets of firms in the second period. Consumers make their purchases on the basis of observed characteristics and prices of goods in both periods.

The pure market economy then corresponds to the standard textbook competitive market. Production and consumption can be separated and consumption allocated between the two periods with the normal welfare properties associated with a competitive economy. This is not true of the agency economy. Consider first the case in which savers are committed to the portfolio allocations that they make in the first period. In the second period, consumption decisions are co-ordinated or influenced by the agency. The agency has choice of supply from a range of producers each of which has capital in place that is dedicated to production in this sector. This imbalance in flexibility between producer and consumer permits the consumer agency to bid down prices offered in the market to the point at which only variable costs are covered. By threatening to take purchases elsewhere, the agency can not only prevent producers earning normal returns on the value of first-period savings but, since in the second period capital invested has no value in alternative employment, it can drive returns down to zero. If this is anticipated in the first period then there will be no savings (assuming positive time preference). More generally, the imbalance between producers and consumers will result in under-investment.

There are two ways in which this problem may be alleviated. First, if savers are not committed to portfolio allocations then the imbalance is eliminated. Sunk costs are now widely appreciated to be the complicating feature of capital and their absence allows desirable welfare properties to be re-established. However, the discussion in the first section has indicated why mobility between markets may be limited, i.e. why the market is monopsonistic. The presence of the agency restricts the number of alternative outlets for the producer's goods. Second, contracts may be written that limit the second-period discretion of the consumer agency. Indeed, given the first-period under-investment, consumers may well wish to be able to commit themselves to, for example, a second-period allocation of purchases. Therefore contracts will be sought that precommit consumers as well as producers. But these will only be available if outcomes in the second period are observable and verifiable. As Grossman and Hart (1986) have noted, the interesting issues of ownership surround unobservable or unverifiable, not observable, outcomes.

Reversing the argument suggests a similar problem facing consumers in the intermediated economy. Here the choice of the consumer is limited by the horizontal integration created by the intermediary. Competition in supply can only be achieved at cost and the advantages of integration present the consumer with monopoly supply. The distortion comes from the commitment of consumers to a particular producer without the reciprocal commitment being made by the producer. The producer can expropriate monopoly rents by threatening to transfer supply elsewhere.

In the absence of complete contracts, ownership can be used to resolve questions of jurisdiction over states for which contracts have not been written. In the first period, ownership is established, which allows the party in control to determine actions in the second period. The other party is induced to participate through compensating payments in the first period. The question that arises is: 'where does ownership reside?'. In the context of our analysis of consumers and producers, if the relevant description is anything other than the pure market economy, either consumer or investor ownership may be appropriate.

As is well known from standard welfare analysis, the problem of investor control is the inadequate account taken of consumer interests. This is captured in the dead-weight loss of excessive pricing and insufficient output. But consumer control introduces its own distortion of inadequate regard for the returns to investment. The essential conflict that this analysis highlights is between achieving desirable allocations across individuals in a particular time period and appropriate intertemporal allocations. Pre-contracting can only resolve this to the extent that adequate information exists on which to base settlements. If this is infeasible then control has to be established a priori.

The allocation of property rights is determined by the relative importance of flexibility and commitment. The greater the benefit to be derived from flexibility in co-ordination of second-period consumption, the greater the value placed on consumer control. In cases in which there are externalities in consumption and there is uncertainty surrounding second-period preferences, the avoidance of commitment to particular distributions may be of substantial value. On the other hand, the greater the effects of choice of first-period investments on second-period performance, the stronger is the case for retaining investor control and limiting second-period flexibility. In this case, commitment is required to elicit appropriate investment decisions.

The case for social ownership rests on the failure of private ownership to achieve appropriate levels of both first-period investment and second-period distribution. Ownership patterns that are the product of private investment decisions in the first period will elicit inadequate investment in circumstances in which externalities in second-period consumption warrant co-ordination of consumer behaviour. The potential expropriation of returns by the consumer agency undermines attempts to separate the investment and consumption decision. Conversely, the intermediated economy permits the investor to capture returns to savings but only at the expense of second-period consumption. In both cases, ownership patterns that are established by private savings decisions are inappropriate. Consumers in the agency economy should take greater account of first-period investment requirements; the interests of investors in the intermediated economy should be more closely aligned to those of second-period consumers. There are therefore externalities in ownership that provide a prima-facie case for adjustments to private ownership patterns.

Social ownership will be defined as appropriate in circumstances in which first-period private ownership patterns should reflect second-period social consumption preferences. The above discussion has suggested the conditions under which it will be warranted. First, externalities in consumption and savings decisions create monopoly or monopsony market structures. Second, costs or infeasibility of contracting prevent the signing of complete contracts. Third, the assignment of property rights to either consumers or investors will not elicit appropriate investment or consumption decisions. Flexibility in second-period decision-taking necessitates limitations on investor control; conversely, consumers have to display a degree of first-period commitment to investment decisions. Were the latter not true then State involvement to correct an externality would be warranted but not public ownership. The greater the benefits of flexibility, the larger the divergences from private ownership; the greater the benefits to be derived from commitment, the closer should a market or economy approximate to private ownership.

It should be noted at the outset that regulation does not avoid the ownership questions that are raised here. Where regulation takes the form of pre-specified rules pertaining, for example, to rates of return, then this is no different from pre-contracting over specific aspects of an industry's activities. As usual, to the extent that contracting is feasible and not restrictive, it probably dominates public ownership. The valid concern that is usually expressed about regulation is that the restrictions associated with this form of contracting are usually far from innocuous. Outcomes may well justify different prices, more or less favourable to investors. This observation that rules are frequently inappropriate is hardly surprising in the light of the function of flexibility that we are associating with public ownership.

Alternatively, regulation may take a more discretionary form. This has recently become a common feature of the privatization process in the UK. The powers conferred on OFTEL (the Office of Telecommunications) and OFGAS (the Office of Gas Supply) extend beyond the implementation of pricing rules, to broader issues concerned with the maintenance of the public interest. There are two possible scenarios. The first is that the regulatory body is effective, in which case the same problems of expropriation of returns to private investors that are normally associated with agency markets are encountered. The second is that the regulatory agency is ineffective, in which case flexibility is not achieved.

Likewise, other procedures that have been proposed for avoiding abuses of private ownership really only disguise the central issues. For example, franchising may prevent investors from earning predictable monopoly rents but does not correct the abuses that can stem from unpredictable events. The motorway restaurant that benefits from unanticipated declines in oil prices is not prospering in an *ex ante* sense but is still mispricing *ex post*. If continuous franchising is feasible then the distortion is eliminated but a problem of inadequate investment is created.

To summarize, it has been argued that issues of ownership arise in circumstances in which concentration of the allocation of savings or consumer resources is justified by the desirability of co-ordinating investor and consumer behaviour or undertaking comparisons of firm behaviour, either from the perspective of quality of investment or quality of production. Where contracts can be written that adequately account for future outcomes, ownership is again not at issue. However, where this is infeasible then the resolution of outcomes in the event of unforeseen or unverifiable states is achieved through prior allocation of property rights. In general, the allocation is not a matter of indifference since the benefits of control will not be the same for the two parties. In particular, the conflict between consumer and investor is one of appropriate cross-sectional as against intertemporal allocations. In certain cases, the benefits of flexibility outweigh those of commitment; in others, the ordering is reversed. The appropriate allocation of ownership is dependent on this ranking: private property rights provide commitment; public ownership retains flexibility.

The above analysis defines circumstances in which ownership questions arise and the appropriate allocation of ownership. The implication is that neither public nor private ownership should be expected to be universally appropriate. The conditions giving rise to monopolistic and monopsonistic market structures, the ease with which contracts can be written, and the benefits to be derived from commitment as against flexibility can be expected to vary across markets, time, and localities. The next section of the paper therefore turns to an application of the principles described above to specific cases in which public ownership is frequently discussed.

5. Ownership Patterns in Practice

A first look at ownership is, to say the least, confusing. To take the electricity industry as an example, ownership varies between the Austrian, French, and British cases of virtual complete State control, through the Dutch, German, and Swedish cases of predominantly State and local ownership, to the private domination of the Belgian and Spanish industries. On the other hand, telecommunications have been State-controlled, with the notable exceptions of Canada, the US, and now the UK.

Within industries, there are substantial variations in ownership. The transmission of electricity is predominantly a public activity in most countries, while its production and distribution have a significant private component in Belgium, Germany, Spain, and Sweden. Gas transmission is entirely privately controlled in Germany and partially privately owned in Belgium and The Netherlands. Gas is at least in part privately produced in Italy, Spain, and Sweden, as well as Belgium, Germany, and The Netherlands.

A more careful assessment reveals some common features of ownership. Table 12.1 records ownership patterns of a number of industries. At one extreme, postal services are almost universally in public ownership. Railways are the next most widely publicly controlled industry, with complete public ownership in all the countries shown with the exceptions of Canada, Japan, and the US. Telecommunications, as noted above, have been predominantly in the public sector of most countries. Airlines, electricity, and gas display a substantial degree of public ownership in a number of countries, but little or none in others. At the other extreme, cars, coal, oil, shipbuilding, and steel are State-controlled in only a few countries.

Table 12.1. Public ownership in OECD countries, 1985

	Airlines	Cars	Coal	Electricity	Gas	Oil	Posts	Railways	Shipbuilding	Steel	Telecommunications	Country average
Australia	3	1	1	5	5	1	5	5	n.a.	1	5	3.2
Austria	5	5	5	5	5	5	5	5	n.a.	5	5	5.0
Belgium	5	1	1	2	2	n.a.	5	5	1	3	5	3.0
Britain	4	3	5	5	5	1	5	5	5	4	1	3.9
Canada	4	1	1	5	1	1	5	4	1	1	2	2.4
France	4	5	5	5	5	n.a.	5	5	1	4	5	4.4
West Germany	5	2	3	4	3	2	5	5	2	1	5	3.4
Holland	4	3	n.a.	4	4	n.a.	5	5	1	2	5	3.7
Italy	5	2	n.a.	4	5	n.a.	5	5	4	4	5	4.3
Japan	2	1	1	1	1	n.a.	5	4	1	1	3	2.0
Spain	5	1	3	1	4	n.a.	5	5	4	3	3	3.4
Sweden	3	1	n.a.	3	5	n.a.	5	5	4	4	5	3.9
Switzerland	2	1	n.a.	5	5	n.a.	5	5	n.a.	1	5	3.6
United States	1	1	1	1	1	1	5	2	1	1	1	1.5
Industry average	3.7	2.0	2.6	3.6	3.6	1.8	5.0	4.6	2.3	2.5	3.9	3.4

Note: Degree of public ownership—1 = less than 25%; 2 = 25%; 3 = 50%; 4 = 75%; 5 = greater than 75%.
Source: *The American Express (AMEX) Bank Review* (1986).

Furthermore, while there are important variations in ownership patterns within industries, total shares of public corporations are quite similar across several countries. There are serious problems involved in trying to undertake international comparisons of the sizes of public enterprises. Definitions of public ownership differ across countries and the allocation of particular enterprises between the public and private sector is frequently arbitrary. Data are not always available: for example, Belgian statistics do not record output of public enterprises. In some cases output is measured in terms of value added and in others by gross output. Figures on the relative shares of public sectors, therefore, have to be treated with considerable caution. But to the extent that they can be taken seriously, they do not suggest pronounced variations in the contribution of public enterprises to domestic production for the countries shown (Table 12.2). However, referring back to Table 12.1, it is clear that there are some exceptions: Canada, Japan, and the US have an unusually small share of their domestic production in the public sector.

Table 12.2. Percentage of output and investment attributable to public enterprises, 1982

	Output	Investment
Austria	17.8	21.1
Belgium	n.a.	15.0
France	17.6	34.3
Germany	10.7	14.7
United Kingdom	11.2	17.1

Source: Parris, Pestieau, and Saynor (1987).

There are, therefore, a number of stylized facts that the theory discussed in the previous sections should be able to explain. First, some industries display very much more pronounced public ownership than others. Second, there is considerable variation in ownership patterns across countries in certain industries. Third, with some notable exceptions, there are broad similarities in the proportion of domestic production of several countries that is publicly owned. Finally, privatization has been more widely advocated for some industries than others. In particular, privatization of telecommunications is currently under discussion or has recently been implemented in France, Italy, Japan, Spain, and the UK, and liberalization is in prospect in several others. Privatization of electricity is being seriously contemplated in Germany, Spain, and the UK.

Table 12.3 attempts to apply the three criteria of ownership discussed in the previous section to a number of the industries mentioned above. It categorizes industries by market structure, ease of contracting, and relative importance of commitment and flexibility. Inevitably, these classifications are broad-brushed and open to debate. They do, however, illustrate how the principles of ownership described above can be applied in practice.

We begin with the industry that displays the highest level of public ownership: the post office. The primary public good aspect of postal services comes from the consumer network system. In terms of the above discussion, this justifies the existence of an agency that co-ordinates services provided. The major uncertainty in the industry comes from levels of demand for specific services, and this uncertainty requires flexibility in supply and allocation of resources. There has to date been little

Table 12.3. Determinants of ownership in five industries in integrated and disintegrated form

	Structure of market	Ease of contracting	Relative importance of flexibility and commitment	Ownership
Post office	Agency	Limited	Flexibility	Public
(i) Counters	Market	n.a.	n.a.	Private
(ii) Sorting	Agency	Limited	Flexibility	Public
(iii) Delivery	Market/agency	Limited	Flexibility	Unclear
Railways	Agency	Limited	Flexibility	Public
(i) Permanent way	Agency	Limited	Flexibility	Public or contracted
(ii) Rolling stock	Market	n.a.	n.a.	Private
(iii) Stations	Agency	Limited	Flexibility	Public
Telecommunications	Agency or intermediary	Difficult	Flexibility or commitment	Unclear
(i) Local	Market/agency	Difficult	Flexibility	Unclear
(ii) Network	Agency	Difficult	Flexibility	Public
(iii) Equipment	Market	n.a.	n.a.	Private
Electricity/Gas	Agency or intermediary	Difficult	Flexibility or commitment	Unclear
(i) Generators	Intermediary	Difficult	Commitment	Private
(ii) Grid	Agency	Difficult	Flexibility	Public
(iii) Local distribution	Market/agency	Difficult	Flexibility	Unclear
(iv) Appliances	Market	n.a.	n.a.	Private

technological innovation, though with electronic mail it is likely that this will change appreciably over the next few years. In the absence of techno-logical uncertainty, there is limited scope for contracts to specify responses in different circumstances, but this is restricted by demand uncertainty. An industry in which there is an important role for a co-ordinating agency and little technological uncertainty is, according to the above discussion, precisely one in which public ownership is likely to be appropriate.

There are, however, several questions that have to be pursued further. First, to the extent that technological uncertainty is increasing in impor-tance in the postal industry, the balance of ownership will shift in the direc-tion of private control. We illustrate this in relation to several industries below. Second, so far we have taken the definition of the postal industry as given. It is by no means obvious that the form of ownership of all parts of a post office should be the same. The network nature of postal services arises at two levels—collection/delivery and sorting—and is more relevant to letters than parcels. Contractual arrangements cannot be used to avoid the distortions that might arise through demand changes necessitating supply responses. In such circumstances, a monopolist supplier of networking services will be able to exploit its position in relation to final consumers. The maintenance of the public interest argues in favour of the retention of these activities in the public sector. Peripheral services, such as counters and special deliveries, could then be competitively supplied, provided that the public agency's monopoly could not be employed to the detriment of the suppliers of these services.

The above description of an industry in which there is a core component that has a network quality with input and output activities operating around it is relevant to several cases. In railways, the primary network component obviously comes from the permanent way. But in addition it arises at the consumer end in the form of stations. Railways are therefore agency markets in which demand considerations require flexibility in recontracting and there is only limited scope for the introduction of a private element. Where there may be room for privatization is in the provi-sion of passenger and freight services. The operation of private rolling-stock on both private and public tracks is a feature of some overseas rail systems (for example, in Japan). But even here there is an important public good in the form of timetables. Until technical innovation becomes more pronounced, railways will probably for the most part be retained in the public sector.

Telecommunications illustrate the way in which technical progress can alter the appropriate form of ownership. Until recently they have displayed most of the features of an agency industry described above, with networks in the form of national transmission and switching systems. But technical progress has been faster in this industry than in those described so far. As a consequence, the form of uncertainty is no longer restricted to considerations of demand. Technical changes have been particularly prominent at the domestic and value-added network service (VANS) end of the market. But in addition, changes in exchange equipment and the introduction of cable and satellite communication have introduced an element of technological uncertainty into the transmission and switching activities of the industry. While therefore until the 1980s the public ownership of telecommunications could be justified on the same network considerations as the other utilities industries, this is now far from evident. Encouragement of investment in the industry may have swung the balance of ownership in favour of a private one that permits the gains from investments to be captured. It is not, then, surprising to find that the primary motivation behind the government's decision to privatize British Telecom related to the ability of the company to raise capital for investment.

This change in ownership is particularly appropriate if abuses of monopoly can be avoided through structural changes in the industry. Recall that the question of public ownership only arises in circumstances in which intermediaries or agencies are required. There are few grounds for believing that monitoring of investment or production decisions of telephone companies justifies monopoly supply or monopsonistic purchase. The only area in which a public ownership question would appear to arise is in the networking service associated with the transmission system itself. But even here it has been noted that technological innovation has in many cases diminished the costs of introducing competition. Optic-fibre as well as satellite services offer alternatives that could, at least in part, avoid the worst abuses of monopoly in national and local networks. Whether this is indeed the case depends on the way in which competition is fostered between the different systems. The involvement of British Telecom in the newly established cable systems and limitations on competition between cable and telecommunications services have cast doubt on the extent to which competition will emerge in the UK.

The cases of gas and electricity differ on account of the large capital expenditures involved in generation. The grounds for introducing private property rights are therefore stronger in these industries than postal and railway services and telecommunications before the technical innovations of the 1980s. They are, however, complicated by the imposition of the national grid between producer and consumer. Not unexpectedly, then, the choice between private and public ownership has proved less clear-cut in these than in other industries. But technical progress is tending to shift the balance of advantage in these industries too. Here the major innovations are coming from the introduction of international trade in gas and electricity, which is diminishing the distortions that are otherwise associated with public ownership of the national grid and permitting the privatization of other parts of the industry.

Telecommunications, gas, and electricity illustrate the fact that the size of the product market is intimately related to appropriate ownership patterns. Section 3 noted that the size of a capital market is an important determinant of its efficiency in absorbing trades in securities without sustaining price fluctuations. The ability of industries to accommodate more than one producer is therefore dependent on the sizes of both capital and product markets. This goes some way towards explaining the smaller shares of public enterprises in Canada, Japan, and the US. It might also not be entirely unrelated to the observation that the country in which privatization is being most actively pursued is the one in which capital market innovations are most pronounced.

In sum, both patterns of ownership observed in different countries and the forces prompting change are readily explicable within the framework outlined above. Public ownership is common in industries in which externalities in consumption are combined with a requirement that there be flexibility in responding to demand requirements. Private ownership dominates in circumstances in which technological advances and production requirements necessitate capital expenditures. The property rights of private ownership encourage risk-taking and investment, but then introduce a rigidity in subsequent production and distribution activities. What might then be expected to be observed is a life cycle in ownership patterns, with private ownership occurring in the early phases of technological innovation and public control being exerted thereafter as investment considerations diminish in significance in relation to demand responses.

There are, however, two important assumptions implicit in the above: (1) capital markets succeed in bearing risks and (2) the government is not an institution that can credibly make commitments. The justification for the former was the establishment of property rights. That right can, of course, be abused; however, such explicit forms of expropriation take us outside the subject of this article. The reasoning behind the latter was that public control in large part reflects current preferences. Obviously, there are forms of government that avoid the implementation of public preferences, but again that is not in the spirit of this article. Even leaving aside these extremes, there are serious questions that should be raised about the stylized contrast between private commitment and public flexibility. These introduce broader considerations about the function of public ownership.

I have argued at length elsewhere (Mayer (1987)) that there are features of capital markets that may make them inherently poor at risk-taking. The reasoning behind that statement comes from the observation that the providers and users of risk capital are frequently different groups of individuals. In our characterization of the capital market, we viewed ownership and control as residing with investors. If that is not the case then account has to be taken of the relationship between investor and manager in terms of commitments and flexibility. The term that is usually used for flexibility in financial markets is liquidity and liquidity is invariably associated with market efficiency. The primary motivation behind financial innovation and deregulation has been the extension of market liquidity. But stated in these terms liquidity may not be consistent with the advantages that we have associated with the establishment of property rights. What liquidity does is to undermine the ability of investors to commit themselves to particular investment decisions made by firms. This is reflected in the absence of commitment in short-term financial instruments and in equity capital in which there is an active market for companies.[1]

The problem that markets encounter is that competition encourages the provision of financial services that have high current valuations. *Ex ante*, investors would like to be able to commit themselves to investments that offer high returns and are willing to provide the incentives for firms to implement such projects. *Ex post*, there is an incentive on investors to bid down the returns to corporate risk-takers. This gives rise to what are widely perceived to be capital market failures. Limitations on the provision of financial services and corporate control can encourage the development of longer-term relationships. But capital markets will not of their own accord restrict competition in this way. There is an externality arising from the divergence of current private interests from wider longer-term considerations.

This conflict is avoided through the establishment of institutions which are not subject to the competitive forces of market processes. The classic example of such an institution is the Civil Service. Its primary characteristics that permit it to fulfil this function are an absence of a market in corporate control and its lifetime tenure system of employment. Performance of employees is not as a consequence measured in short-term considerations that are the basis of success and failure in private employment. In particular, rewards are not in large part based on out-turn performance but inputs of effort and skills. In terms of the discussion of the previous sections, rewards reflect *ex ante* assessments of inputs, not *ex post* measures of output. The monitoring and incentive systems that are a feature of many governments therefore act to encourage precisely the aspects of commitment that we have associated with private ownership.

[1] The reader is referred to Mayer (1987) for a more detailed discussion of these points.

At the end of the day, there is some irony in concluding that the basic rationale behind private ownership may in fact justify public control. The function of the market in encouraging risk-taking and investment may be undermined by capital market failures that have very fundamental underlying causes. The resolution of these failures may be found in restrictions on competition that are a feature of many government bureaucracies. The conclusion that governments may be called upon to provide the commitments required for long-term investments accords with some popular conceptions. What acts to undermine this conclusion is competition in the electoral process, replacing a market for corporate control with its political counterpart. Elected governments may be able to establish reputations that make commitments credible, but competition in the electoral process would appear to limit this possibility. Where the balance of advantage in long-term decision-taking lies is therefore seen to be intimately tied up with the political process and institutional structure of a particular country.

These considerations clarify why public involvement in financial systems is so often associated with economic development. Such involvement may be explicit, as in the case of France and Italy, or more implicit, in the case of Japan. The justification for public ownership of the financial sector goes beyond simple statements about monopoly control over the payment system or distributional considerations, to more fundamental questions about the inducements to long-term investment. Restrictions on competition can, of course, merely encourage inefficient practices. But the naïve assertion that public provision is inefficient and private provision is efficient misses the point. Efficiency is inappropriately measured by currently observed criteria. What is efficient in the present period may be highly deleterious in the longer term. In any event, the industries that are the subject of study of this article are precisely those in which competition in production is undermined by co-ordination and monitoring considerations. The central question is what institutional structure is best placed to undertake the monitoring of activities that are not supplied in the market-place. While economic theory suggests that this is the proper function of private ownership and the capital market, practice might well dictate otherwise.

6. Conclusion

This article has attempted to establish a case for public ownership from first principles. It has argued that the only factor that is relevant to ownership *per se* is control. Public ownership is a restriction on equity investments in corporations, and a rationale for public ownership has to be sought in a justification for such restrictions. The myriad of other issues that have been discussed in relation to privatization only serve to cloud the debate.

The approach of this paper has been to define circumstances in which a prima-facie case for public ownership can be provided. It noted that a basic requirement is that considerations of co-ordination and monitoring warrant the involvement of an intermediary between investors and firm or an agent of consumers. The issue of public ownership does not arise where the pure market description of an industry or economy applies. In the intermediated, agency, or non-market economy, attention has to be given to contracting and ownership.

Again, ownership is not the relevant consideration in circumstances in which contracts can be written that establish appropriate outcomes. The interesting cases are those in which contracts are infeasible or impose an unwarranted inflexibility in future relationships. Where competition is circumscribed and contracting limited, the relative merits of public and private ownership have to be carefully balanced. What private ownership provides is protection of property rights that encourages inputs of investment and effort. What public ownership supplies is a greater degree of flexibility in determining production and distribution in subsequent periods. The conflict between public and private ownership is therefore the familiar one between commitment and flexibility.

This leads to a powerful set of predictions as to the circumstances in which one form of ownership will be preferred. Public ownership is expected to be most widely associated with industries in which (1) technical innovation is slow, (2) investment expenditures are modest, and (3) demand requirements are unpredictable. These considerations lead to a ranking of public ownership which is quite consistent with observed patterns; for example, postal services and railways displayed the highest degree of State control of any of the industries examined.

The analysis points to a number of predictions. First, ownership patterns are unlikely to be stable over time. Periods of technical innovation will be most closely associated with private ownership. Life cycles of ownership will probably be encountered as technical progress intensifies and wanes. Second, the relevance of public ownership will be at least in part related to the sizes of economies and the development of their capital markets.

When then should be our verdict on the current wave of privatization? The first implication is that changes in ownership will periodically be warranted. The Conservative Government in the UK has not discovered a new principle of ownership. It is merely responding to strong pressures of technical change in product and financial markets. Its drive to extend the process to industries in which such innovation is less in evidence is more questionable. A clear case for one particular ownership pattern has not emerged in circumstances in which these industries remain integrated. This would not have been true had a more radical approach been pursued in which the constituent parts of the relevant industries had been separated.

But the above analysis of patterns of ownership is complicated by inefficiencies in financial markets and the process of government. The association of commitment and flexibility with private and public ownership respectively may not apply. The very forces that promote efficiency in financial markets may undermine their ability to take long-term decisions. Conversely, the stability of bureaucracies and their procedures for evaluating and rewarding performance may permit governments to make credible commitments. The significance of this reversal of roles requires considerably more research, but this article should at least serve as a bench-mark against which ownership changes can be assessed.

13

The Decentralized State: The Economic Borders of Local Government

DIETER HELM AND STEPHEN SMITH [*]

1. Introduction

The borderline between the State and the private sector has come under intense political scrutiny during the 1980s. Other papers in this volume have analysed the philosophical basis of the recent reappraisal of the role of the public sector by the 'new right', and have discussed the economic basis for State involvement in various aspects of the economy. In the introductory paper, Helm argues that the appropriate division of activity between the State and the private sector is, at a deep level, a question of values. Nevertheless, once the objectives have been set, there remains the instrumental question of the most efficient method of achieving these objectives. This is essentially a matter for empirical and pragmatic resolution. Where the borderline between the State and the market should lie depends on weighing up the costs of leaving things to the market, against the likely improvements from government intervention.

Both sides of this equation are more complex than conventional approaches may have implied. On the one hand, market failures pervade much of the economic system. On the other, government failure may also be a problem, and the ability of governments to intervene effectively in market allocations may depend critically on the development of appropriate institutional and organizational structures. Much of State activity is conducted by local rather than central government, and a sizeable literature has grown up around the concept of 'fiscal federalism', analysing the contribution that decentralization in government can make to the effectiveness of government activities and interventions.[1] This literature has examined the reasons for decentralizing government decision-making, the

[*] Dieter Helm is Fellow in Economics at Lady Margaret Hall, Oxford and a Research Associate at the Institute for Fiscal Studies. Stephen Smith is Director of the Public Sector Programme at the Institute for Fiscal Studies. The authors would like to thank Christopher Allsopp and Patrick Lane for detailed comments on an earlier draft. The usual disclaimers apply.
[1] King (1984) provides a good introduction to this literature.

organization of decentralized governments, and the relationships (especially in the area of finance) between central and local government. The literature thus provides many of the ingredients for a reappraisal, from an economic standpoint, of the role of decentralized government.

At the same time, it is clear that, from a political standpoint, the role of decentralized government in the UK is, at present, unusually open to redefinition.[2] During its period of office, the Conservative government has made radical changes to the environment within which local government operates. First, it has tightened central control on the level of local authority spending through changes to the block grant and, more recently, rate-capping. Second, it has abolished the Greater London Council (GLC) and other upper-tier authorities in metropolitan areas. Third, it has forced through a much wider use of tendering and subcontracting for local government services. And finally, it has launched into a wholesale reform of local government finance, based on the programme outlined in the 1986 Green Paper, *Paying for Local Government*. This includes centralizing control over non-domestic rates, and replacing domestic rates with a new household tax, the 'Community Charge', to be paid at a flat rate by all adults.[3]

These changes have resulted in a major shift of effective discretion over policy, if not of power, away from local government towards the centre. Much of what the government has done has been motivated simply by its objective of reducing the level of public expenditure. Nevertheless, it has also maintained that the actions it has taken are consistent with its view of the proper division of responsibilities between central and local government, and more fundamentally its preference for individual choice rather than governmental allocation. In the 1986 Green Paper, the government argues that 'a clear distinction between the roles of central and local government' can be drawn, as follows:

The main task of central government is to establish national policies and priorities for defence, foreign affairs and the economy as well as for public services—such as education—which are provided locally, but where there is a national interest in standards. Within this overall national framework the main role of local government is to provide services in a way which properly reflects differences in local circumstances and local choice.

---

[2] The post-war period has seen a succession of inquiries into aspects of local government and its finance, including the major report by the Layfield Committee (1976). Apart from the introduction of rate rebates which followed the report of the Allen Committee (1965), and the major structural reorganization of local government following the Redcliffe-Maud Report (1969), most of this steady stream of analysis has met with little response.

[3] See Smith and Squire (1986) for a summary of the main proposals.

In this paper we consider the economic issues underlying the division of economic functions between central and local tiers of government, and the implications both for financing local government and for the degree of influence which central government should seek to exert over local government's activities. We begin with the fundamental question, why are some decisions best made at the local level and others at the national level?

2. The Rationale of Decentralized Government

The theory of the perfectly competitive market economy, which forms the core of the conventional neo-classical economic theory, analyses the implications of extreme decentralization in decision-making. It considers the conditions under which individual, rather than collective, decision-making would yield an optimally efficient allocation of resources. Individuals would have to be *fully informed* about the choices open to them; there would be *no monopoly power*, *no externalities*, and *no public goods*. Property rights would need to be *perfectly defined* and *costlessly enforced*, and both capital and labour would have to be *perfectly mobile*.

The need for government arises when the market fails to meet these stringent conditions. In addition, government action may also be necessary to secure the desired distribution of income. The Pareto-optimal/perfect competition paradigm is agnostic with respect to the distribution of income, being concerned only with economic efficiency. Since markets are unlikely to produce the desired distributional outcome, governments have a key role in redistribution.

The failure of market mechanisms in these various respects creates a rationale for government intervention. But the mere fact that the market fails does not guarantee that the government can do any better. Much depends on the capacity of government to respond sensitively to the needs and preferences of individuals and communities, and on its ability to obtain and process the necessary information. 'Government failure' could occur—through lack of information, through technical and allocative inefficiency, or because the bureaucracy chooses to pursue its own interests rather than those of the community.[4] These possibilities limit the ability of governments to respond to market failure.

Whether governments can improve on the failures of the market will vary from case to case. An important element in the ability of governments

---

[4] We do not pursue the latter possibility here. Following Niskanen (1971), a considerable literature has explored the implications of a 'budget-maximizing' bureaucracy. See, for example, Mueller (1979, ch. 8).

to process information and to make the appropriate decisions is the organizational structure of government. It is here that we find the main economic justification for decentralization in government.

Decentralized government is likely to be better informed about the needs of particular individuals or communities. Decentralized democracy may also be better able to reflect the preferences of individuals. However, both of these advantages of decentralization must be weighed against the advantages of centralization in terms of administrative economies of scale, the benefits of equal and consistent treatment of individuals in welfare provision, and the need for central or national solutions to some of the problems of market failure. In different areas of policy, these considerations are likely to have different weight; how the balance is struck in each case should determine the allocation of particular functions to central or local level. There is thus no a priori right answer to the question of the proper degree of decentralization, independent of the characteristics of the goods and services provided.

The following sections consider the major factors bearing on the decision to allocate functions between different levels of government. In the first, we consider the role of central and local government in promoting allocative efficiency and in providing 'public goods'—goods where market failures inhibit individual, market, provision. In the second, we consider the role that redistributive considerations play in the functions of central and local government and how they affect the organization and allocation of functions. Finally, we consider efficiency in administration—the ability of centralized and decentralized systems to operate economically and effectively.

(a) *Efficiency, Market Failure, and Local Public Goods*

The classic motivation for the collective provision of goods, common to economists and political scientists of the left and the right, is the existence of 'public goods'. A pure public good is one which is characterized by non-excludability, and non-rivalry in production and consumption. Public goods arise at a number of different levels, from national cases like defence and, at the international level, customs unions, through to very local public goods such as village notice-boards. Once they are provided for one individual, it costs no more to extend the benefits to other individuals (non-rivalry), and, moreover, it would be costly or even impracticable to try to deny the benefits to other individuals (non-excludability). For goods displaying these characteristics, collective provision is appropriate.

The analysis of local public goods differs in two important respects from the analysis of pure public goods at the national level. First, it is sometimes suggested that many local public goods are in fact 'impure' public goods, which can be provided by the market through the creation of 'clubs'. The *laissez-faire* approach to the problem may thus result in a more adequate level of provision than with pure public goods, and the possibility that State intervention could improve on the market level of provision may be correspondingly less. Second, although provision of local public goods by government is subject to many informational and decision-making problems which arise in the case of provision of public goods of any sort, an additional mechanism has been suggested, whereby population mobility may ensure that individual preferences about local public goods are more accurately reflected in the levels of provision.

Markets and Local Clubs

The market solution to the provision of public goods, whether local or national, addresses the non-excludability characteristic. Non-excludability stems from the absence of property rights,[5] which are themselves a prerequisite of markets. Thus the market solution involves the creation of property rights. Where exclusion, by some means or other (a turnstile for a park, scrambling devices for TV), is *technically* feasible at low cost, it becomes possible for the goods in question to be supplied either through voluntary collective provision by 'clubs', or by profit-making firms. In each case a 'membership fee' would be charged to cover the fixed costs of providing the facilities, and, because exclusion is feasible, use of the facilities would be restricted to those who pay the membership fee.[6]

Clubs are, of course, a common method of collective provision in a number of areas—notably in the provision of sports facilities, golf courses, and angling clubs. Not all public goods will be suitable for club provision—the benefits of planning and environmental policies are largely non-excludable, and club provision would fail, owing to the free-rider problem. (Some of these areas of policy are, in addition, coercive, and therefore only feasible for organizations with the coercive power of governments.) Other services provided by local government are excludable, and could in principle be provided by clubs. Their provision instead by local government may reflect either distributional objectives (education, social services) or the savings in administrative costs (billing, revenue collection)

[5] A property right entitles the owner to exclusive enjoyment over the returns from the asset, good, or service over which it is defined. It follows that others must be excludable. This feature of excludability gives the asset value, and hence a price. See Furubotn and Pejovich (1972).

[6] For an accessible survey of club theory, see Sandler and Tschirhart (1980). For a more theoretical treatment, see Cornes and Sandler (1986). Berglas (1976) and Lane (1987, pp. 42–6) discuss the possibility that firms can replicate the club solution.

from provision by an existing local government structure, that could not be reaped from separate club provision.

Public Goods Decision-making

The optimal level of provision of a public good occurs where the sum of the marginal rates of substitution (MRS) in consumption is equal to the marginal rate of technical substitution (MRT) in production (Samuelson (1954)). The informational requirements for the State to be able to identify the optimum are substantial because the State needs to know each individual's marginal rate of substitution. Thus the central practical problem with the Samuelson result is obtaining accurate and detailed information about individual preferences.

Attempts to discover individual preferences for public goods are liable to be affected by the free-rider problem. Depending on their beliefs about how the demands they express for public goods will affect the amounts they are called upon to pay towards their provision, individuals may be tempted either to overstate or to understate their demand. In general, if they believe that their share of the financing of the public good is unaffected by their declared demand, they may overstate their demand, expecting that the cost of additional provision will fall largely on others. On the other hand, if they believe that their contribution to the cost of the public good will be an increasing function of their stated demand, they may understate their demand, hoping to free-ride on the public goods that others are prepared to pay for. A number of ingenious methods of overcoming this demand revelation problem have been proposed, each trying to doctor the underlying incentive structure.[7]

However, it is notable that very few direct voting methods are, in practice, applied at the individual public good level. One reason for this is their complexity, rendering many of them impractical. A further reason concerns the aggregation of individual preferences. Public goods are rarely provided in isolation, and individuals are typically offered a range of alternatives. At the local or national level, this choice is organized by elections and voting. The purpose of voting is to identify a social ordering of alternatives out of individual preferences. The construction of such a social ordering is not, however, straightforward. It is well known that, where there are at least three individuals, and three social states to choose from, voting paradoxes may result (Arrow (1951a)).[8] People rank the importance of such services as health education, broadcasting, and defence

---

[7] See Thompson (1966), Clarke (1971, 1972), Groves (1973), and the survey in Mueller (1979, ch. 4).

[8] See Sen (1970b) for the standard exposition, and Sugden (1981) and Mueller (1979) for less formal treatments.

in different ways, and the use of simple majority voting may fail to produce a consistent social ordering.

Neither demand-revealing procedures nor voting will therefore provide a perfect basis for the provision of local public goods. Whilst both procedures may in principle provide some of the information necessary for local decision-making, the process of decision-making is inevitably far from ideal. It will be observed, however, that these deficiencies of demand-revealing and voting mechanisms apply to democratic decision-making in general, and are not specific to local government decision-making. However, the third possible solution to the problem of ascertaining individuals' preferences about public goods is a mechanism which is only applicable to decentralized government—the role of population mobility, or 'voting with one's feet', in matching individuals to localities supplying the pattern of public goods they desire.

In a seminal article, Tiebout (1956) suggested that, rather than attempt to provide a voting mechanism to allow individuals within an area to express their preferences, individuals' preferences might be reflected in where they choose to live. If individuals were free to migrate, they would choose to live in a location where the local public goods provided coincided with their preferences. Thus an individual would survey the various combinations available, and decide where to live on the basis of these options. If Liverpool's public libraries were better than those in Scunthorpe, library users might migrate from Scunthorpe to Liverpool if this preference dominated all others for them. A sorting process would then reveal people's preferences by allocating them to locations, rather than adapting the pattern of public goods provided in the various locations to their particular, temporary, population's preferences.

Tiebout laid down the conditions under which the resulting allocation would be perfect, in the sense of Pareto-optimal. The principal assumptions are:

- costless mobility;
- perfect information about the combinations of local public goods available;
- complete given preference orderings, unchanged through time;
- no other market failures, such as monopoly or externalities.

The Tiebout model has often been taken to imply that actual migration will approximate optimality. However, like the more general perfect competition model in neo-classical theory, it actually demonstrates the opposite. Since we know from the model what would have to be true for mobility to yield optimal results, and since we know that these conditions are not met in practice, it follows that we cannot rely on mobility to solve

these preference failures. Mobility will not overcome the revealed preference problem.

The literature has indeed focused on identifying ways in which migration may fail to secure optimality, as a subset of more general market failure. Individuals lack information about alternatives, there are
transactional costs of moving (market failure in housing being perhaps the
most serious), consumers' preferences may change over time, and local
public goods are typically jointly provided. These aspects are surveyed in
Hughes (1987).[9]

The implications for policy of the Tiebout model and the subsequent
literature point in a number of directions. One option would be to
encourage mobility by providing information on available alternatives and
reducing direct and indirect barriers to migration, such as in housing. This,
however, depends on the assumption that the Tiebout result is strictly
increasing—that any increase in mobility necessarily increases welfare by
increasing allocative efficiency. Unfortunately this claim is flawed—
imperfect existing misallocations lead to second-best effects, and a small
increase in mobility in one direction may actually worsen the outcome by
substitution effects with other individuals unable to migrate because
another barrier to mobility constrains them. In addition, migration may
yield externality effects (again, see Hughes (1987)).

Thus we can see not only why 'voting with your feet' will not produce
optimality because of migration market failures, but also that partial
increases in mobility could even reduce welfare. There is, however, a much
more worrying problem with migration solutions—they place an upper
bound on tax-raising potential. If the rates or Community Charges in
Liverpool rise too much, individuals and firms will move elsewhere. This
impact of migration brings the efficiency aspects of the rationale for local
government into conflict with distributional considerations, to which we
now turn.

(b) Distribution and Local Government

An efficient economy, in the neo-classical sense, is not necessarily one
which is distributionally fair or just. Considerations of distribution and
liberty can conflict directly with those of efficiency.[10] It has long been a
central rationale for State intervention to reallocate the outcome of the

---

[9] The Tiebout model has subsequently given rise to a voluminous literature. Amongst
the most important developments are Buchanan and Goetz (1972), Pestieau (1977), Oates
(1972), McGuire (1974), Berglas and Pines (1981), and Berglas (1984).

[10] See the papers by Helm and by Dasgupta in this volume. See also Sen (1970a, 1979b,
1982d) for more detailed analysis.

market in terms of income and wealth to provide for the relief of poverty. Such redistributional policies may take one of two forms. First, there are policies designed to provide basic social primary goods (or merit goods) to individuals. These might include, for example, the provision of minimum standards of health care and education. Second, policy may be directed towards income maintenance, providing transfers of income through the tax and social security systems.

These two approaches to redistribution may need to be implemented in rather different ways. The first approach considers the needs of individuals, and aims to provide a minimum standard of access to basic social primary goods. Since individuals' needs vary, this may involve treating people unequally to produce a more equal outcome. As Dasgupta (1986b) argues, it may require the direct provision of goods rather than income support. The second approach aims to redistribute income, rather than to ensure access to specific commodities. The two approaches to redistribution require different sorts of information about individuals, and also may have different implications for the allocation of policy between different levels of government.

It is widely argued by writers on fiscal federalism (for example, King (1984)) that policies for redistribution are most appropriately set and implemented at national level, by the central government. This argument partly reflects a view that it should be a *single* level of government which is assigned the role of determining the extent of income redistribution. Otherwise, if redistributive decisions were made independently by a number of levels of government, we might find one level attempting to 'undo' the redistributive actions of another. In addition, the case for the assignment of redistributive functions to the national level reflects the costs in terms of efficiency that might arise if local redistributive policies provoked population movements between local government areas. As we noted above, if local government in Liverpool opted for a higher level of redistributive spending than did local government in nearby Chester, there might be a tendency for the richer residents of Liverpool to move to Chester, where they would not have to pay for redistributive policies, whilst the poorer residents of Chester might move to Liverpool. The costs of achieving a given level of redistribution in Liverpool would rise; and higher travelling costs and other welfare losses may be incurred as a result of these fiscally-induced population movements. A similar Tiebout process of migration could restrict the use of redistributive taxes by local government. In both cases, migration imposes an upper limit on the feasible extent of independent redistributive policies at local level, and may lead to costs in terms of efficiency.

The arguments for assigning redistributive policymaking to the national level rest on a rather sharp theoretical separation of efficiency and distribution, which may be considerably less straightforward in practice. Many of the relevant services are mixed goods, containing public good elements but also provided in part on distributional grounds. In the case of education, for example, distributional considerations may be of primary importance, but both national and local public good aspects can be identified. (The latter may include, for example, the teaching of Welsh in Wales, greater attention to multicultural education in certain areas, training for the specific needs of local industries, etc.) Where the local public good aspects of mixed goods are considered of substantial importance, assignment to local government may be appropriate, despite the redistributional aspect. Various devices, including central financial contribution to local spending, may help to ensure that spending is provided to the intended level and that the efficiency costs of induced migration are minimized.

Other writers, including Hochman and Rogers (1969) and Pauly (1973), have taken the opposite view, arguing that income redistribution is itself a local public good. The argument rests on the assumption that redistribution is essentially a preference by some individuals over others which displays 'public' characteristics, i.e. non-excludability and non-rivalry in consumption. Equity and efficiency objectives can thus be combined by defining a Pareto-efficient amount of redistribution.

However, whilst altruism of this form may ultimately play an important part in redistribution, its impact depends on the precise content of preferences and the appropriateness of redistribution through individual rather than collective action. Furthermore, preference information is merely one source of welfare judgement, and a number of alternative non-efficiency criteria have been given more widespread support. Equality is best considered as a rival concept to efficiency, not a subset of it (see Sen (1980) and Dasgupta (1986b)). Redistribution is not therefore best regarded as a local public good, but as a separate objective, which could, in principle at least, be pursued by governments at any level.

Local government in the UK is involved in a considerable amount of spending that is redistributive in effect. However, the justification for this cannot be in terms of the assignment of the 'redistributive function' of government to the local level—there are, as we have noted, efficiency obstacles to this (Tiebout), and may be practical obstacles connected with the erosion of revenue-raising powers through migration. Nor does the allocation of redistributive functions to local government necessarily imply that local government's own redistributive preferences should enter substantially into policy, although inevitably, as a result of assigning these policies to local government, this may happen to some extent. The principal justification for assigning redistributive functions to local government would, in our view, be an administrative and informational one—and it is to the administrative rationale of local government that we now turn.

(c) The Administrative Rationale of Local Government

The growth of national government's functions and services has required a concomitant rise in its administrative functions. Just as large firms often decentralize the administration of plants, so central government has decentralized many of its own functions to local government, to regional health authorities, and to the Scottish and Welsh Offices.

Although organizational and political theorists have analysed the characteristics of decentralization of administration, there has been little attempt in the economic theory literature to apply general decentralization and control theory to this administrative aspect of local government. Yet there exists an extensive literature on decentralization in firms which, we shall argue, has applications to the local government case.[11]

Decentralization of administration arises because of informational economies. It is difficult for any large organization to keep its members adequately informed of each other's activities. As the number of members rises arithmetically, the number of potential links between each of the individuals rises more steeply. To maintain full communication, one link is required between two people, three between three people, six between four people, and so on. Such member-to-member co-ordination rapidly becomes impractical, and various organizational structures can be set up to economize on the number of informational links. These structures can be classified into two broad groups: those where a vertical hierarchy is set up, and those where a horizontal and/or vertical separation of function is created.[12] Central government can delegate tasks to subsidiary authorities (like local government) and/or it can separate out its different functions into different national departments augmented by local or regional sub-branches (health, social security).

From this standpoint, decentralization is a method by which better information can be gathered for decision-making, and processed at lower cost than would be possible with a fully centralized organization. However, at the same time as providing a better informational basis for decision-making, decentralization also can lead to costs in terms of the loss

[11] The theory of the internal organization of the firm has developed as a result of dissatisfaction with traditional black-box profit-maximizing models. The pioneering early paper by Coase (1937) was followed much later by a study conducted by Cyert and March (1963) on the internal organization of firms. Notable subsequent work includes Alchian and Demsetz (1972), Williamson (1975), Arrow (1974), and Radner (1985).

[12] In the organizational literature, these are referred to as M-form and U-form. See Williamson and Bhargava (1972).

of central control over the decisions that are taken. The objectives of the central decision-makers may not be shared by those given the task of implementing policies at local level. Delegating to lower tiers the responsibility for implementing centrally determined policies carries with it the risk that the local agents may choose to pursue their own objectives rather than those of the centre. In considering the administrative advantages of decentralization, there is thus a trade-off between the informational gains from decentralization and the weakening of central control.

Viewed as a form of administrative decentralization, local government may be seen to possess certain informational advantages, but the problems of control are acute. Some of these control problems can be analysed as instances of the general principal–agent problem—how to provide decentralized agents with incentives to pursue the central government principal's objectives.[13] The problem is complicated by conflicting objectives of local agents, and by the lack of information on the part of central government about local costs and population characteristics. Furthermore, central government's attempt to gain information in order to evaluate the performance of a local council is complicated when each has markedly different political objectives.[14]

Again, pursuing the analogy with the literature on the similar principal–agent problems that arise in theory of the firm, central government can ameliorate the monopoly of information possessed by the local agent by seeking independent 'yardstick' information (see, in the economics literature, Shleifer (1985)). This is provided by comparing performance between local authorities, and aids the monitoring of administrative efficiency. If more dustbins are emptied per kilometre for a lower cost in Southend than Gateshead, central government has useful information for appraisal. Such yardstick information suffers from two drawbacks. First, it provides an indication only of relative efficiency rather than absolute efficiency, and second, its usefulness depends on local authorities facing relatively similar cost functions. Nevertheless, despite these drawbacks, yardsticks can provide useful information for monitoring performance, especially in areas where the decentralized agent is restricted by legal or procedural rules to only a limited range of choices.

(d) Evaluating the Case for Decentralization

We have described a number of economic functions that local government can perform. Much of the conventional thinking about the economic

[13] On the principal–agent problem, see Fama (1980) and Rees (1985).
[14] The literature on principal–agent games between nationalized industry Boards and central government has interesting parallels. See Rees (1984).

function of local government has focused on the role of local government as a kind of 'club', providing local public goods. Local, rather than centralized, decision-making about the level of provision of local public goods means that residents' preferences are met more accurately. But the provision of local public goods is not the sole function of local government in the UK—or, indeed, the main one. The 'public good' element in much local spending is quite small. Education spending, for example, may give rise to positive or negative externalities, but it is clear that the benefits from education spending are largely excludable, and consumption of education largely rival. A substantial level of education spending would occur without the involvement of government. Similarly, many of the local services such as public cleansing provided by local authorities may involve externalities, but some level of private provision would occur in the absence of local government provision.

Many local services thus involve the public provision of private goods, either because of the externalities they generate or for distributional reasons. As we have already argued, the distributional priorities of government are most appropriately set at national level, but the information requirements of administration may mean that implementation would be more efficient at a lower level of government. In certain cases, where the informational requirements of operating policies with a substantial distributional content are great, it may be appropriate to make use of the benefits of decentralized administration, and accept the various problems that arise from assigning redistributive services to local governments.

Considerations of this sort would seem to be consistent with the assignment of education and social services to local government in the UK. In both cases, and especially in the operation of social services, there is a need for knowledge of local requirements and conditions in administration. Policies aimed at discriminating between the different needs of individuals, rather than providing a general level of income support, are likely to have particularly substantial informational requirements. National objectives regarding these services might therefore best be attained by decentralized decision-making, subject to nationally-set guidelines and rules.

Of course, local government is not the only form of decentralized decision-making that can reflect local needs and conditions. An alternative form of decentralization is given by the operation of the National Health Service, where a decentralized bureaucracy is given the task of implementing national objectives in the light of local needs. Clearly there are disadvantages in choosing local governments, rather than decentralized bureaucracies, to implement national priorities; local governments may choose to implement their own priorities, especially their own distributional priorities, in place of national government's priorities. What are the offsetting advantages from devolving decision-making over the implementation of policies with a distributional content to local governments?

The actual pattern of decentralized decision-making in the UK may be largely a matter of historical accident. However, the justification for choosing local government rather than decentralized administration must be the greater capacity of local voters, compared with central decision-makers, to evaluate relative performance. It would seem plausible that voters' comparative advantage in this would be greatest when important dimensions of performance involve relatively unquantifiable aspects of service 'quality', and least where effective quantitative indicators of output could be devised.

Nevertheless, whilst these considerations may explain the role accorded to local democratic decision-making, they do not immediately explain the need for local revenue-raising powers. Thus, for example, national priorities in education could be administered by a series of local, elected school boards, managing centrally-set budgets. The allocation of decentralized administration of national redistributive services to local governments with revenue-raising powers may merely reflect economies of scale in local administration—it may be cheaper to give the task to the bodies already in existence to provide local public goods than to establish a separate set of elected boards without revenue-raising powers. Alternatively, and more convincingly, the need for local revenue-raising powers may arise because the informational incapacity of central government is so great that even budget-setting is beyond it. If this is so, local taxation may be needed as a safety-valve, to enable local authorities to correct the imperfect financial allocations made by central government. Either of these interpretations has clear implications for the financial resources appropriate to local government, and it is to this issue that we now turn.

3. Finance

UK local government has available to it only one source of tax revenue—rates—together with a certain amount of scope for charging for some identifiable local services—council housing, school meals, and commercial refuse collection in particular. Roughly half of UK councils' spending is financed from central government grants—in other words, paid for from national rather than local taxation. A similarly substantial reliance on transfers from central government is a feature of State and local governments in many other countries.

(a) *Grants*

The role of central government grants in local financing merits attention both because of their quantitative importance and because of the influence that the grant allocation has had on the financial position and behaviour of local authorities.[15]

The need for central contributions to local spending may arise for a number of reasons. The need for grants may be a straightforward consequence of 'fiscal imbalance': the allocation of taxation and spending functions to different tiers of government on the basis of administrative efficiency can result in a quite predictable discrepancy between the expenditures and revenues of local authorities. Second, grants may be used to reflect externalities—the interests that the residents of other local authorities, or the nation as a whole, have in the spending decisions of a particular authority. Third, grants may be used for 'equalization' between authorities. We consider each of these aspects of grants in turn below.

Fiscal Imbalance

One factor in the allocation of taxes to different tiers of government will be a set of administrative and technological criteria similar to those involved in any decision to centralize or decentralize certain administrative functions within large corporations, and certain spending functions within governments. Economies of scale are likely to be achieved in centralized administration of taxation, at least up to a point.[16] Choosing the most efficient level of government for taxation and spending functions may then leave lower levels of government with insufficient powers of taxation to finance the spending responsibilities they have been allocated, and financial transfers between levels of government may be needed to correct this fiscal imbalance.

Externalities, Public Goods and Spill-overs: The Efficiency Problem

Central contributions to local spending may also be used to reflect the interest that central government or the residents of other localities might have in particular aspects of an authority's spending. In a number of areas of local government activity, expenditure externalities may be important— spending on road maintenance, for example, will tend to benefit road-users living outside the local authority area as well as road-users within the area. Spending on education may need to reflect national priorities as well

[15] See Foster, Jackman, and Perlman (1980), Livesey (1987), and Gibson and Watt (1987).
[16] Netzer (1974) presents some US data suggesting that the economies of scale in tax administration are substantial.

as local preferences. One reaction to externalities from local authority spending would be to centralize spending decisions—to internalize the externality. But, as we have described in Section 2, this may be administratively inefficient, and may fail to allow spending choices to reflect local preferences and priorities.

An alternative approach to spending externalities might be adopted— that of providing a central contribution to local spending to reflect the value that non-residents would place on extra spending by the local authority. Such a grant contribution has clear parallels to Pigovian externality taxes and subsidies; it attempts to adjust the cost of local spending to local residents and voters so that local spending decisions correctly take account of spending benefits accruing to non-residents.

The purpose of central grant contributions reflecting externalities is to ensure economic efficiency in local spending decisions. The aim would be that voters making decisions about local spending should face the true costs of local spending, and should take into account all the benefits of local spending, including those accruing to non-residents. The contrast with Pigovian taxes and subsidies in individual decision-making is, however, instructive. In the individual case, the taxes and subsidies ensure that the individual faces the full costs and benefits of his or her actions. In the case of local authority decisions, a more stringent set of conditions will tend to apply. The nature of these conditions will depend on the way in which decisions are made, and which individual voters influence those decisions. But the form of the local tax, and the distribution across local residents of the benefits of local spending, will clearly be as important as the central grant contribution in determining the spending decisions that voters make at local level.

Foster (1986) places considerable emphasis on the need for marginal local spending to be financed entirely from local revenue sources, and the 1986 Green Paper, too, argues that the marginal tax revenue should come entirely from the proposed local household tax, the 'Community Charge'. Such an approach would be consistent with the view that the spill-over benefits of local spending are negligible. But the requirement that marginal local spending should be financed entirely from local sources will, strictly, only ensure that local spending choices reflect the true costs and benefits of additional spending if a similar balance between costs and benefits of local spending is also reproduced at the individual level. A uniform per caput tax, for example, would only ensure efficiency in spending decisions if the benefits from local spending were similarly spread equally across individuals. Given the redistributive characteristics of a considerable proportion of local spending responsibilities in the UK (such as education and social services), it is highly unlikely that this will be so.

Equalization: The Tax Base and Redistributive Spending

Although recently overlain with a pattern of spending disincentives and penalties designed to influence the overall level of local authorities' spending in line with the objectives of central government, the basic structure of the UK grant allocation aims to achieve uniformity in the range of tax and spending choices facing local authorities. Local authorities differ widely, both in terms of their tax base (in the UK largely due to the uneven distribution of non-domestic rateable value) and in terms of a number of 'need' characteristics, influencing spending levels. In order to ensure that local authorities are able to offer residents the same range of options about combinations of service levels and taxation levels, the distribution of the central grant aims to compensate local authorities both for any deficiency in their revenue base and for differences in the spending needed to provide a standard level of services—the authority's 'Grant-related Expenditure'.

The need for compensation or 'equalization' mechanisms of this sort may be seen in terms of some notion of equity (that similar individuals in different local authorities should be able to choose from the same range of local spending/taxation combinations, or that the level of provision of certain local services should be independent of the wealth of local authority residents[17]). Alternatively they may be seen as necessary to prevent fiscally-induced migration. As we saw in Section 2, where local government aims to provide services with a significant redistributive content, fiscally-induced migration may limit the ability of authorities to provide such services to the level desired.

The need for some form of 'resources' compensation may arise when the local tax base per caput varies between authorities. It will generally be greater in the case of local taxes on businesses rather than on persons, due both to the generally greater concentration of business activity and to the possibility that business taxes may be only partly incident on local residents. Certain patterns of decentralized administration may call for greater resource equalization—for example, if local authority boundaries separate inner-city areas from residential areas.

'Needs' equalization in the UK system has been the source of considerable difficulty. The requirement for needs equalization arises because of the responsibilities placed on UK local government to provide services of a redistributive nature. Where the 'need' for such redistributive services is higher, the difference between authorities is compensated by additional payments of central grant. Problems have arisen in the assessment of differences in spending needs: the use of regression analysis to relate

[17] See Tobin (1970).

indicators of need to spending levels was criticized for implicitly validating local overspending, whilst the present methods rely heavily on the Department of the Environment's judgement. Instability in the measure of needs has been an acute problem leading to uncertainty in local authority budgeting. But, as Bramley (1987) argues, it is by no means clear how best to resolve this instability. Nevertheless, the case for stability in grant allocation far overrides the case for precision in needs assessment (Kay (1982)). Whatever the burden of inaccurate needs assessment, it may be partly capitalized in property prices.[18] Adjustments to the needs formula which seek to fine-tune the distribution of central government grant may thus result in little improvement in the equity of the local finance system, whilst running the risk of a greater and possibly damaging effect on the pattern of capitalization.

(b) Local Taxation

Criteria for Local Taxes

The above discussion of central government grants to local authorities has already indicated the relevance of the theoretical framework of analysis developed in Section 2 to the analysis of local finance, as well as of local spending responsibilities. Administrative questions, and issues of economic efficiency (spill-overs) and equity (equalization) have all been discussed. Similarly, all three considerations bear on the choice of local taxes.

For a tax to be *administered* at the local level, it is necessary for the object of the tax (transactions, property, or individuals) to be unambiguously allocable to local authorities, and for feasible administrative arrangements to be devised which permit local authorities to set, and collect revenue from, different local rates of tax. Property taxes such as rates have clear advantages as local taxes, in that the tax base can unambiguously be allocated to local areas—but international experience shows a wide range of other taxes used as local taxes (McLure (1983)).

As in the choice of taxes at the national level, *economic efficiency* in local taxation may in practice best be promoted by neutrality in taxation—in other words, the use of taxes which modify as little as possible the choices that the private sector would have made in the absence of tax. In assessing neutrality, the relationship between individual taxes within the overall UK tax system should be considered. Thus, domestic rates in the UK might appear, if considered in isolation, to be a distortionary tax on

---

[18] Barnett and Topham (1980) discuss the possibility that capitalization effects on property prices may provide an alternative to needs equalization payments.

housing, but viewed as part of the overall UK tax system may in fact contribute to neutrality by taxing housing consumption, which is otherwise largely untaxed.[19]

The issue of efficiency is extended, in the case of local taxes, by considerations of two sorts. First, there is the possibility that the incidence of some local taxes could, to an appreciable extent, fall outside the local authority area. Some of the burden of paying for a local authority's spending may then be passed on to the residents of other local authorities. The result may be a tendency to excessive levels of public expenditure, since the voters in each local authority can choose higher spending, whilst bearing only a proportion of the cost. Where such externalities in taxation are substantial, local spending choices may fail to reflect the true costs of the chosen level of spending. Thus, for example, one of the criticisms that may be made of non-domestic rates as a source of local government finance in the UK is that part at least of the burden of non-domestic rates may be borne by non-residents of the local authority area receiving the revenue. Non-residents are effectively taxed to pay for local services, and the link between taxation and public spending choices is weakened.

Second, the possibility of population mobility between local authorities opens up a further area in which taxation could affect—and distort—individuals' behaviour. This yields a further set of efficiency criteria beyond those applicable to national taxes. If the scope for mobility between local authorities is great, neither taxes nor spending at the local level can be redistributive—or else the losers from redistribution will simply move to other authorities, where less redistributive policies are pursued. Mobility may thus place limits on local policies, and may involve undesirable erosion of local tax bases in poorer areas. In practice, population mobility is unlikely to be great enough in the UK—given the size of most authorities—to rule out any use of income-related taxes for local government. Nevertheless the possibility of population mobility does indicate that the local taxes should generally be *less* redistributive than those chosen at the national level.

The *equity* characteristics that should be displayed by local taxes—that is, the distributional incidence of the local tax burden—are thus constrained, from one side, by population mobility. Even within a State aiming at a high level of income redistribution, this requirement for comparatively non-redistributive local taxes may cause little difficulty, since the distributional incidence of local taxes can be substantially offset by greater progressivity in national taxation.

However, this does not imply that the redistributional incidence of local

---

[19] This issue is discussed by Hughes (1980, 1982, 1987), King and Atkinson (1980), and Smith and Squire (1987).

taxes should be a matter for indifference. There are limits on the extent to which national redistribution can correct a regressive distributional pattern of local taxation. With a heterogeneous local population, some individuals are always likely to prefer less, and some more, of the local service than is actually chosen. Only where distributional considerations are ignored will it be a matter of indifference that poorer residents are compelled, as a result of the majority decision, to 'purchase' larger amounts of local services than they would wish to pay for.

For this reason, a lump-sum tax, or other highly regressive local taxes, would appear to be unacceptable at the local level. Variations in the rate at which the tax would be levied mean that poorer residents of high-tax areas would be particularly adversely affected, and it would not be possible to compensate for this in the national tax system. If a tax containing a substantial lump-sum element is chosen, some form of rebating for poorer households is essential.

This argument against uniform per caput taxation at the local level turns on the compulsory nature of local taxation, and holds even if the benefits of local government spending are equally distributed per caput. The crucial point is the absence of any real opportunity—aside from the very limited scope for population mobility—to decline to purchase the package of local spending and local taxation which is on offer (Smith and Squire (1987)).

Such objections do not, of course, apply to genuine charging for services by local government, where these charges are voluntary (in the sense that residents can choose not to use the service, and hence not to pay), and where alternative suppliers of services are available. In these circumstances, charging may be an appropriate instrument for ascertaining demand and financing local expenditure when the services in question meet a number of criteria. First, services must be separable, without substantial elements of joint provision. It must be possible to identify clearly the relevant costs upon which to base the charges. Second, individual usage of the services must be variable and measurable. Third, charging may be appropriate where supply is competitive. Competitors place an independent constraint on monopoly pricing and cost inflation. Finally, charging is more appropriate for goods which are relatively distribution-insensitive. Where these conditions are met, finance through charging may have considerable advantages.

4. Conclusions—Functions and Financing

In this paper we have discussed the role of local government in supplying local public goods, in income redistribution through spending and taxation, and as an agent of central government, administering national policies in the light of local needs and conditions. There is a complex tension between these different roles. The more that central government makes use of devolved administration of national policies, the greater the danger that local governments will begin to impose their own priorities, especially their own distributional priorities, on the policies that they are called on to administer. On the other hand, if central government tries to retain control over the execution of these policies (setting uniform minimum standards for education and welfare, or maximum levels of spending on redistributive policies), there is a danger that local government's ability to reflect the legitimate difference in preferences of its residents over local public goods may be compromised. One sort of government failure must therefore be weighed against another.

We have argued that it is not desirable that there should be independent redistributive policies at local level, competing with national redistributive priorities. However, local government in the UK clearly does have a substantial involvement in the provision of redistributive services. The justification for assigning these policies to local level is the greater administrative capability of local government in assessing and responding to local needs and circumstances. However, if redistributive functions are assigned to local level, they should not be dependent on local financing— or else population movements might begin to erode the effectiveness of the policy. The 'losers' from local redistribution would simply move elsewhere.

There is thus a need for equalization payments from central government to even out differences between authorities in the cost of national (redistributive) policies implemented at local level. However, given that the rationale for decentralizing these policies in the first place is the informational disadvantage of central government, it should be recognized—and the system of financing should recognize—that this equalization, whilst better than nothing, may be highly imperfect.

Our argument leads to two important conclusions of immediate policy relevance. First, if the reason for assigning policy functions with a redistributive element to local government is the inadequacy of the information available to central government, then it follows that central government is also unlikely to be in a position to evaluate the effectiveness of individual local authorities in discharging their responsibilities. Central government can, of course, monitor the attainment of particular qualitative and quantitative targets—for example, it could assess whether local authorities are meeting particular minimum targets for pupil/teacher ratios, and could measure the percentage of council houses standing empty. But the logic of decentralizing these functions implies that central government is not in a position to evaluate the overall *effectiveness* of local administration of redistributive policies—and, *a fortiori*, that central government is not in a position to judge whether local authorities are spending 'excessive' amounts in pursuit of these policies. The notion that central government can make judgements about local 'overspending' sits very uneasily with the rationale for decentralizing redistributive functions to local government in the first place.

The second policy conclusion is about local taxation. Because of the likely imperfection of the central grant allocation, central grant is unlikely to cover precisely the amount necessary to finance the redistributive spending responsibilities assigned to local government. Thus, the rather 'tidy' arrangement that might have been hoped for, with central grant covering the costs of redistributive policies assigned to local government, and local taxes paying for the costs of local public goods, is likely to be much more blurred in practice. Given the 'mixed' nature (part public good, part redistributive) of much local spending, it is unlikely to be an easy matter to identify the size of the redistributive and public good elements within local budgets. Local taxes are then going to be required to finance not only the public good function of local authorities, but also an unknown residual element of the costs of their redistributive spending.

In this context, the suggestion that a poll tax might be the appropriate basis for financing local government seems particularly unattractive. The services financed out of local taxation are unlikely to be consumed in equal amounts by all local taxpayers. Even if they are, the fact that a poll tax is compulsory makes it significantly different from a charge for local services. Genuine charging, as we have argued, may have a role to play in financing certain local services. But where payments are compulsory, they bear particularly heavily on poorer households. These distributional effects depend on the level of taxation in each authority, and cannot therefore be fully compensated by offsetting adjustments to national taxes. It is therefore entirely appropriate that at the local level, as at the national level, the distribution of the tax burden should take account of the taxpayer's ability to pay.

Bibliography

Addison, P. (1975), *The Road to 1945*, London: Cape.

Alchian, A. A. and Demsetz, H. (1972), 'Production, costs and information', *American Economic Review*, **62**, 777–95.

Allen Committee (1965), *Committee of Inquiry into the Impact of Rates on Households: Report*, Cmnd 2582, London: HMSO.

Allsopp, C. J. (1985), 'Monetary and fiscal policy in the 1980s', *Oxford Review of Economic Policy*, **1**, 1, 1–20.

—— and Helm, D. R. (1985), 'The political economy of public policy', *Times Literary Supplement*, December.

American Express Bank Review (1986), 'Privatisation: a powerful worldwide trend', 13.

Archibald, G. C. and Donaldson, D. (1976), 'Non-paternalism and the basic theorems of welfare economics', *Canadian Journal of Economics*, **9**.

Arrow, K. J. (1951a), *Social Choice and Individual Values* (2nd edition: 1963), New York: Wiley.

—— (1951b), 'An extension of the basic theorems of classical welfare economics', in J. Neyman (ed.), *Proceedings of the Second Berkeley Symposium on Mathematical Statistics and Probability*, Berkeley, California: University of California Press.

—— (1963), 'Uncertainty and the welfare economics of medical care', *American Economic Review*, **53**, 941–73.

—— (1971), 'Political and economic estimation of social effects of externalities', in M. Intriligator (ed.), *Frontiers of Quantitative Economics*, **1**, Amsterdam: North-Holland.

—— (1974), *Limits of Organisation*, New York: Norton.

—— (1978), 'Nozick's entitlement theory of justice', *Philosophia*, **7**, 265–79.

—— and Hahn, E. H. (1971), *General Competitive Analysis*, San Francisco: Holden-Day. Republished 1979, Amsterdam: North-Holland.

Bacharach, M. (1976), *Economics and the Theory of Games*, London: Macmillan.

Barnett, J. (1982), *Inside the Treasury*, London: André Deutsch.

Barnett, R. R. and Topham, N. (1980), 'A critique of equalising grants to local governments', *Scottish Journal of Political Economy*, **27**, 235–49.

Barry, B. (1965), *Political Argument*, London: Routledge Kegan Paul.

Barry, N. P. (1985), 'In defence of the invisible hand', *The Cato Journal*, Spring/Summer, 133–48.

Bator, F. M. (1958), 'The anatomy of market failure', *Quarterly Journal of Economics*, **72**, 351–71.

Bauer, P. T. (1971), *Dissent on Development*, London: Weidenfeld and Nicholson.

—— (1981), *Equality, the Third World and Economic Delusion*, Cambridge, Massachusetts: Harvard University Press.

—— (1984), *Reality and Rhetoric: Studies in the Economics of Development*, London: Weidenfeld and Nicholson.

Baumol, W. J. (1982), 'Contestable markets: an uprising in the theory of industry structure', *American Economic Review*, **72**, 1–15.

Becker, G. (1976), *The Economic Approach to Human Behaviour*, Chicago: Chicago University Press.

Beckerman, W. (1979a), 'The impact of income maintenance payments on poverty in Britain, 1975', *Economic Journal*, June.

—— (1979b), *Poverty and the Impact of Income Maintenance Programmes in Four Developed Countries*, Geneva: International Labour Organization.

—— (1983), 'Human resources: are they worth preserving?', in P. Streeten and H. Maier (eds.), *Human Resources, Employment and Development*, **2**, London: Macmillan.

—— and Clark, S. (1982), *Poverty and Social Security in Britain since 1961*, Oxford: Oxford University Press for the Institute for Fiscal Studies.

Beesley, M. and Littlechild, S. (1983), 'Privatisation: principles, problems and priorities', *Lloyds Bank Review*, **149**, 1–20.

Bellamy, E. (1888), *Looking Backward*, Boston: Ticknor.

Beloff, M. (1969), *Imperial Sunset*, **1**, 'Britain's Liberal Empire', London: Methuen.

—— (1984), *Wars and Welfare*, London: Arnold.

—— and Peele, G. (1985), *The Government of the United Kingdom: Political Authority in a Changing Society*, 2nd edition, London: Weidenfeld.

Berglas, E. (1976), 'On the theory of clubs', *American Economic Review*, Papers and Proceedings, **66**, 116–21.

—— (1984), 'Quantities, qualities, and multiple public services in the Tiebout model', *Journal of Public Economics*, **25**, 299–321.

—— and Pines, D. (1981), 'Clubs, local public goods and transportation models: a synthesis', *Journal of Public Economics*, **15**, 141–62.

Berlin, I. (1958), 'Two concepts of liberty', *Inaugural Lecture*, Oxford: Clarendon Press.

—— (1969), 'Two concepts of liberty', in *Four Essays on Liberty*, Oxford: Oxford University Press.

Beveridge, W. (1924), 'Insurance for all and everything', *The New Way*, 7, Daily News.

—— (1942), *Social Insurance and Allied Services*, Cmd 5404, London: HMSO.

Blanchard, O. J. and Summers, L. H. (1986), 'Hysteresis and the European unemployment problem', NBER Working Paper.

Bosanquet, N. (1984), 'Social policy and the Welfare State', in R. Jowell and C. Airey (eds.), *British Social Attitudes: The 1964 Report*, Aldershot: Gower.

Bramley, G. (1987), 'Horizontal disparities and equalisation: a critique of "Paying for Local Government"', *Local Government Studies*, **13**, 1.

Bray, M. (1986), 'Uncertainty and the cost of capital: a multi-period model of bank lending', mimeo.

Brittan, S. (1983a), *The Role and Limits of Government: Essays in Political Economy*, London: Temple Smith.

—— (1983b), 'Hayek, freedom and interest groups', in S. Brittan, *The Role and Limits of Government: Essays in Political Economy*, London: Temple Smith.

—— and Lilley, P. (1977), *The Delusion of Incomes Policy*, London: Temple Smith.

Brock, G. and Wapshott, N. (1983), *Thatcher*, London: Fontana.

Buchanan, J. M. (1965), 'An economic theory of clubs', *Economica*, February, 1–14.

—— (1975), *The Limits of Liberty*, Chicago: University of Chicago Press.

—— (1977), *Freedom in Constitutional Contract*, Texas A & M University.

—— (1978), 'From private preferences to public philosophy: the development of public choice', *Institute of Economic Affairs Readings*, **18**, 3–20.

—— (1983), 'Rights, efficiency and exchange: the irrelevance of transactions cost', mimeo, Center for Study of Public Choice, George Mason University.

—— and Brennan, G. (1985), *The Reason of Rules*, Cambridge: Cambridge University Press.

—— and Goetz, C. J. (1972), 'Efficiency limits of fiscal mobility', *Journal of Political Economy*, **1**, 25–43.

—— and Tullock, G. (1962), *The Calculus of Consent*, Ann Arbor, Michigan: University of Michigan Press.

Buiter, W. H. and Marston, R. C. (eds.) (1985), *International Policy Coordination*, Cambridge: Cambridge University Press.

—— and Miller, M. H. (1983), 'Changing the rules: the economic consequences of the Thatcher regime', *Brookings Papers on Economic Activity*.

Burns, T. (1977), 'How much reflation?', *Economic Outlook*, October.

Cairncross, A. (1986), *Years of Recovery: British Economic Policy 1945–51*, London: Methuen.

Calabresi, G. and Bobbitt, P. (1978), *Tragic Choices*, New York: Norton.

Chester, N. (1975), *The Nationalisation of Industry*, London: HMSO.

Citrin, J. and Sears, D. (1985), *Tax Revolt*, Cambridge, Massachusetts: Harvard University Press.

Clarke, E. H. (1971), 'Multipart pricing of public goods', *Public Choice*, **11**, 17–33.

—— (1972), 'Multipart pricing of public goods: an example', in S. Mushkin (ed.), *Public Prices for Public Products*, Washington: Urban Institute.

Clarke, P. (1978), *Liberals and Social Democrats*, Cambridge: Cambridge University Press.

Coase, R. H. (1937), 'The nature of the firm', *Economica*, NS, **4**, 386–405.

—— (1960), 'The problem of social cost', *Journal of Law and Economics*, **3**, 1–44.

Coase, R. H. (1974), 'The lighthouse in economics', *Journal of Law and Economics*, October.

Cohen, G. A. (1978), *Karl Marx's Theory of History*, Oxford: Clarendon Press.

—— (1979), 'Capitalism, freedom and the proletariat', in A. Ryan (ed.), *The Idea of Freedom: Essays in Honour of Isaiah Berlin*, Oxford: Clarendon Press.

—— (1981), 'Illusions about private property and freedom', in J. Mepham and D. Ruben (eds.), *Issues in Marxist Philosophy*, Hassocks: Harvester Press.

Cole, G. D. H. (1953–60), *A History of Socialist Thought*, five volumes, London: Macmillan.

Cooter, R. (1982), 'The cost of Coase', *Journal of Legal Studies*, 11.

Cornes, R. and Sandler, T. (1986), *The Theory of Externalities, Public Goods, and Club Goods*, Cambridge: Cambridge University Press.

Creedy, J. and Disney, R. (1985), *Social Insurance in Transition*, Oxford: Oxford University Press.

Crosland, C. A. R. (1964), *The Future of Socialism*, London: Jonathan Cape.

Cross, R. (1987), 'Hysteresis and instability in the natural rate of unemployment', *Scandinavian Journal of Economics*, 89.

Cyert, R. M. and March, J. (1963), *A Behavioural Theory of the Firm*, New Jersey: Prentice Hall.

Dasgupta, P. (1980), 'Decentralization and rights', *Economica*, 47, 107–24.

—— (1982a), 'Utilitarianism, information and rights', in A. Sen and B. Williams (eds.), *Utilitarianism and Beyond*, Cambridge: Cambridge University Press.

—— (1982b), *The Control of Resources*, Oxford: Blackwell.

—— (1986a), 'The silent food war', *E. S. Woodward Lectures*, University of British Columbia Press, forthcoming.

—— (1986b), 'Positive freedom, markets, and the Welfare State', *Oxford Review of Economic Policy*, 2, 2, 25–36.

—— (1988), 'Trust as a commodity', in D. Gambetta (ed.), *Trust: Making and Breaking Cooperative Arrangements*, Oxford: Basil Blackwell.

——, Hammond, P., and Maskin, E. (1979), 'The implementation of social choice rules: some general results in incentive compatibility', *Review of Economic Studies*, 46.

——, ——, and —— (1980), 'A note on imperfect information and optimal pollution control', *Review of Economic Studies*, 47, 857–60.

—— and Ray, D. (1986a), 'Inequality as a determinant of malnutrition and unemployment: theory', *Economic Journal*, 96, 1011–34.

—— and —— (1986b), 'Nutrition and capability: a study of the clinical evidence', prepared for the World Institute of Development Economics Research Project on Poverty and Hunger. To be published in A. Sen (ed.), *Poverty and Hunger: The Poorest Billion*.

—— and —— (1987), 'Inequality as a determinant of malnutrition and unemployment: policy', *Economic Journal*, 97, 177–88.

d'Aspremont, C. and Gevers, L. (1977), 'Equity and the informational basis of collective choice', *Review of Economic Studies*, 44.

Davidson, D. (1980), *Essays on Actions and Events*, Oxford: Clarendon Press.

Davis, E. H., Dilnot, A. W., and Kay, J. A. (1985), 'The social security Green Paper', *Fiscal Studies*, 6, 3, 1–8.

Debreu, G. (1959), *Theory of Value*, New York: Wiley.

Department of the Environment (1986), *Paying for Local Government*, Cmnd 9714, London: HMSO.

Diamond, D. (1984), 'Financial intermediation and delegated monitoring', *Review of Economic Studies*, 51, 393–414.

Diamond, P. A. and Mirrlees, J. A. (1971), 'Optimal taxation and public production', *American Economic Review*, March and June.

Dicey, A. V. (1962), *Lectures on the Relation between Law and Public Opinion in England durng the Nineteenth Century*, 2nd edition, London: Macmillan.

Dilnot, A. W., Kay, J. A., and Morris, C. N. (1984), *The Reform of Social Security*, Oxford: Oxford University Press.

—— and Stark, G. K. (1986), 'The poverty trap, tax cuts and the reform of social security', *Fiscal Studies*, 7, 1, 1–10.

Dobb, M. (1969), *Welfare Economics and the Economics of Socialism*, Cambridge: Cambridge University Press.

Donoghue, B. (1987), *Prime Minister: The Conduct of Policy under Harold Wilson and James Callaghan*, London: Jonathan Cape.

Dorfman, R., Samuelson, P., and Solow, R. (1958), *Linear Programming and Economic Analysis*, New York: McGraw-Hill.

Durbin, E. (1985), *New Jerusalems*, London: Routledge and Kegan Paul.

Dworkin, G. et al. (1977), *Markets and Morals*, Washington: Hemisphere Publishing.

Dworkin, R. (1977), *Taking Rights Seriously*, London: Duckworth.

—— (1981), 'What is equality?', *Philosophy and Public Affairs*, 10.

Economic Progress Report (1986), 'A flexible labour market', 182.

Elster, J. (1980), 'Exploitation and the theory of justice', mimeo, Historisk Institute, University of Oslo.

—— (1983), *Sour Grapes*, Cambridge: Cambridge University Press.

Fama, E. (1980), 'Agency problems and the theory of the firm', *Journal of Political Economy*, 88, 288–307.

Farrell, J. and Saloner, G. (1985), 'Standardization, compatibility and innovation', *Rand Journal of Economics*, 16, 70–83.

Fisher, N. (1977), *The Tory Leaders*, London: Weidenfeld and Nicolson.

Foote, G. (1985), *The Labour Party's Political Thought: A History*, London: Croom Helm.

Foster, C. D. (1986), 'Reforming local government finance', *Public Money*, 6, 2.

——, Jackman, R. A., and Perlman, M. (1980), *Local Government Finance in a Unitary State*, London: George Allen and Unwin.

Freeden, M. (1978), *The New Liberalism: An Ideology of Social Reform*, Oxford: Clarendon Press.

Frey, B. C. (1983), *Democratic Economic Policy*, Oxford: Martin Robertson.

Friedman, M. (1962), *Capitalism and Freedom*, Chicago: University of Chicago Press.

—— (1968), 'The role of monetary policy', *American Economic Review*, **58**, 1–17.

—— (1977), 'Inflation and unemployment', *Journal of Political Economy*, **85**, 451–72.

—— and Friedman, R. (1980), *Free to Choose*, London: Secker and Warburg.

Furubotn, E. and Pejovich, S. (1972), 'Property rights and economic theory: a survey of recent literature', *Journal of Economic Literature*, **10**, 1137–62.

Gardyne, J. B. (1974), *Whatever Happened to the Quiet Revolution?*, London: Macmillan.

Gash, N. (1979), *Aristocracy and People: Britain 1815–1865*, London: Arnold.

Gibbard, A. (1973), 'Manipulation of voting schemes: a general result', *Econometrica*, **41**, 587–601.

—— (1974), 'A Pareto-consistent libertarian claim', *Journal of Economic Theory*, **7**, 388–410.

—— (1976), 'Natural property rights', *Nous*, **10**.

Gibson, J. G. and Watt, P. A. (1987), 'A model of education expenditure change in English local authorities', in H. Thomas and T. Simpkins (eds.), *Economics and the Management of Education: Emerging Themes*, Lewes: Falmer Press.

Graaff, J. de V. (1957), *Theoretical Welfare Economics*, Cambridge: Cambridge University Press.

Graham, D. and Clarke, P. (1987), *The New Enlightenment: The Rebirth of Liberalism*, London: Macmillan/Channel 4.

Gray, J. (1983), *Mill on Liberty: A Defence*, London: Routledge.

—— (1984a), *Hayek on Liberty*, 2nd edition, Oxford: Basil Blackwell.

—— (1984b), *Hayek's 'Serfdom' Revisited*, London: Institute of Economic Affairs.

—— (1984c), 'On negative and positive liberty', in J. Gray and Z. A. Pelczynski, *Conceptions of Liberty in Political Philosophy*, London and New York: Athlone Press and St Martin's Press.

—— (1986), *Liberalism*, Milton Keynes and Minneapolis: Open University Press and University of Minnesota Press.

—— (forthcoming), 'Contractarian method, private property and the market economy', in J. Chapmen (ed.), *Nomos: Justice and Markets*, New York: New York University Press.

Green, D. (1985), *Challenge to the NHS: A Study of Competition in American Health Care and the Lessons for Britain*, London: Institute of Economic Affairs.

—— (1987), *The New Right*, Brighton: Wheatsheaf.

Green, E. J. (1982), 'Equilibrium and efficiency under pure entitlement systems', in A. H. Meltzer and T. Romer (eds.), *Proceedings of the Conference on Political Economy*, **2**, Supplement to *Public Choice*.

Green, J. and Laffont, J.-J. (1977), 'Characterization of satisfactory mechanisms for the revelation of preferences for public goods', *Econometrica*, **45**, March.

Green, T. H. (1894), 'Freedom of contract', *Works*, London: Longman Green & Co.

Greenleaf, W. H. (1983), *The British Political Tradition*, 1, 'The Rise of Collectivism', London: Methuen.

Grossman, S. J. and Hart, O. D. (1986), 'The costs and benefits of ownership: a theory of vertical and lateral integration', *Journal of Political Economy*, 94, 691–719.

Groves, T. (1973), 'Incentives in teams', *Econometrica*, 41, 617–31.

—— and Ledyard, J. (1977), 'Optimal allocation of public goods: a solution to the "free rider" problem', *Econometrica*, 45, May.

Guha, A. (1972), 'Neutrality, monotonicity and the right to veto', *Econometrica*, 40, 821–6.

Hahn, F. (1984), *Inflation and Unemployment*, Oxford: Blackwell.

—— and Hollis, M. (eds.) (1978), *Philosophy and Economic Theory*, Oxford: Clarendon Press.

Hammond, E. M., Helm, D. R., and Thompson, D. J. (1985), 'British Gas: options for privatisation', *Fiscal Studies*, 6, 4, 1–20.

Hammond, P. J. (1982), 'Utilitarianism, uncertainty and information', in A. Sen and B. Williams (eds.), *Utilitarianism and Beyond*, Cambridge: Cambridge University Press.

Hare, R. M. (1981), *Moral Thinking: Its Levels, Methods and Point*, Oxford: Clarendon Press.

Harris, S. (1955), *John Maynard Keynes*, New York: Scribener.

Harrison, R. (1983), *Bentham*, London: Routledge Kegan Paul.

Harrod, R. F. (1951), *The Life of John Maynard Keynes*, London: Macmillan.

Harsanyi, J. C. (1955), 'Cardinal welfare, individualistic ethics, and interpersonal comparisons of utility', *Journal of Political Economy*, 63, 309–21.

—— (1976), *Essays on Ethics, Social Behaviour and Scientific Explanation*, Dordrecht: Reidel.

Hart, H. L. A. (1975), 'The priority of liberty', in R. Daniels (ed.), *Reading Rawls*, Oxford: Blackwell.

Hayek, F. A. von (1944), *The Road to Serfdom*, Chicago: University of Chicago Press.

—— (1948), *Individualism and Economic Order*, Indiana: Gateway.

—— (1960), *The Constitution of Liberty*, Chicago: University of Chicago Press.

—— (1967), *Studies in Philosophy, Politics, and Economics*, Chicago: University of Chicago Press.

—— (1976), *The Mirage of Social Justice: Law, Legislation, Liberty*, 2, London: Routledge and Kegan Paul.

—— (1978), *Denationalisation of Money*, 2nd edition, London: Institute of Economic Affairs.

—— (1982), *Law, Legislation and Liberty*, London: Routledge and Kegan Paul.

Heal, G. M. (1973), *The Theory of Economic Planning*, Amsterdam: North-Holland.

Heald, D. and Steel, D. (1982), 'Privatizing public enterprise', *Political Quarterly*, 53, 333–49.

Heath, A., Jowell, R., and Curtice, J. (1985), *How Britain Votes*, Oxford: Pergamon.

Helm, D. R. (1984), 'Enforced maximisation: competition evolution and selection', D.Phil., Oxford.

Hendry, D. F. and Ericson, N. R. (1983), 'Assertion without empirical basis: an econometric appraisal of "Monetary Trends . . . in the United Kingdom" by Milton Friedman and Anna Schwartz', in *Monetary Trends in the United Kingdom*, Bank of England, Panel of Academic Consultants, Paper 27.

Hennessy, P. (1986), *Cabinet*, Oxford: Blackwells.

——, Morrison, S., and Townsend, M. (1985), 'Routine punctuated by orgies: the Central Policy Review Staff 1970–1983', Strathclyde Papers on Government and Politics.

HMSO (1944a), *Employment Policy*, Cmd 6527, London: HMSO.

—— (1944b), *Social Insurance, Part I*, White Paper, Cmd 6550, London: HMSO.

—— (1944c), *Social Insurance, Part II*, White Paper, Cmd 6551, London: HMSO.

—— (1985a), *Reform of Social Security*, Green Paper, Cmnd 9517, 9518, and 9519, London: HMSO.

—— (1985b), *Reform of Social Security*, White Paper, Cmnd 9691, London: HMSO.

HM Treasury (1987), *The Government's Expenditure Plans 1987–88 to 1989–90*, Cm 56, London: HMSO.

Hobsbawm, E. (ed.) (1964), *Pre-capitalist Economic Formations*, London: Lawrence and Wishart.

Hochman, H. M. and Rogers, J. D. (1969), 'Pareto optimal redistribution', *American Economic Review*, 59, 542–57.

Hodgson, D. (1966), *Consequences of Utilitarianism*, Oxford: Clarendon Press.

Holmans, A. E. (1987), *Housing Policy in Britain*, London: Croom Helm.

Holmes, M. (1982), *Political Pressure and Economic Policy: British Government 1970–1974*, London: Butterworth.

—— (1985a), *The Labour Government 1974–79: Political Aims and Economic Reality*, London: Macmillan.

—— (1985b), *Mrs Thatcher's First Administration*, Brighton: Wheatsheaf.

Hughes, G. A. (1980), 'Housing and the tax system', in G. A. Hughes and G. M. Heal (eds.), *Public Policy and the Tax System*, London: George Allen and Unwin.

—— (1982), 'The incidence of domestic rates and alternative local taxes', *Fiscal Studies*, 3, 1, 23–38.

—— (1987), 'Rates reform and the housing market', in S. J. Bailey and R. Paddison (eds.), *The Reform of Local Government Finance in Britain*, London: Croom Helm.

Husami, Z. (1978), 'Marx on distributive justice', *Philosophy and Public Affairs*, 7.

Johansen, L. (1965), *Public Economics*, Amsterdam: North-Holland.

Joseph, K. (1975), 'The quest for the common ground', speech delivered at the Oxford Union, December. Reproduced 1976 in *Stranded on the Middle Ground*, London: Centre for Policy Studies.

—— (1976a), *Reversing the Trend*, London: Centre for Policy Studies.

—— (1976b), *Stranded on the Middle Ground*, London: Centre for Policy Studies.

Kahneman, D., Slovic, P., and Tversky, A. (1983), *Judgement under Uncertainty: Heuristics and Biases*, Cambridge: Cambridge University Press.

Katz, M. and Shapiro, C. (1985), 'Network externalities, competition and compatibility', *American Economic Review*, 75, 424–40.

Kavanagh, D. (1987), *Thatcherism and British Politics: The End of Consensus?*, Oxford: Oxford University Press.

Kay, J. A. (1982), 'Symposium on local government finance', *Fiscal Studies*, 3, 1, 1–6.

——, Mayer, C. P., and Thompson, D. J. (eds.) (1986), *Privatisation and Regulation—The UK Experience*, Oxford: Clarendon Press.

—— and Thompson, D. J. (1986), 'Privatisation: a policy in search of a rationale', *Economic Journal*, 96, 18–32.

Keegan, W. (1984), *Mrs Thatcher's Economic Experiment*, London: Penguin.

Keynes, J. M. (1919), *The Economic Consequences of the Peace*, London: Macmillan; *Collected Writings* (CW) ii (1971), 86.

—— (1922), 'Reconstruction in Europe: an introduction', *Manchester Guardian Commercial*, 18 May; CW xvii (1977), 427.

—— (1924), speech by JMK to Conference of the League of Nations Union on Unemployment, 25–7 March, London; CW xix (1981), 184.

—— (1925a), letter by JMK to *The Times*, 25 March; CW xix (1981), 347.

—— (1925b), 'Am I a Liberal?', *Nation and Athenaeum*, 8 and 15 August; CW ix (1972), 295–306.

—— (1925c), 'A short view of Russia', *Nation and Athenaeum*, 10, 17, and 25 October; CW ix (1972), 253–71.

—— (1926), 'The end of laissez-faire', Hogarth Press; CW ix (1972), 272–94.

—— (1927), 'The public and the private concern', paper read by JMK to the Liberal Summer School, *Manchester Guardian*, 1 August; CW xix (1981), 696.

—— (1930), *A Treatise on Money*, London: Macmillan.

—— (1931), JMK to W. Milne Bailey, letter of 18 December in the Keynes Papers, King's College, Cambridge.

—— (1934), 'Mr. Keynes replies to Mr. Shaw', *New Statesman and Nation*, 10 November; CW xxviii (1982), 34.

—— (1936), *The General Theory of Employment, Interest and Money*, London: Macmillan; CW vii (1973), 378–9, 413.

—— (1939), 'Democracy and efficiency', *New Statesman and Nation*, 28 January; CW xxi (1982), 493.

King, D. N. (1984), *Fiscal Tiers: The Economics of Multi-level Government*, London: George Allen and Unwin.

King, M. A. and Atkinson, A. B. (1980), 'Housing policy, taxation and reform', *Midland Bank Review*, Spring.

Klein, R. (1983), *The Politics of the National Health Service*, London: Longman.

Koopmans, T. C. (1957), *Three Essays on the State of Economic Science*, New York: McGraw-Hill.

Laffont, J.-J. (ed.) (1979), *Aggregation and Revelation of Preferences*, Amsterdam: North-Holland.

Laidler, D. (1985a), *The Demand for Money: Themes and Evidence*, New York: Harper and Row.

—— (1985b), 'Monetary policy in Britain: successes and shortcomings', *Oxford Review of Economic Policy*, 1, 1, 35–43.

Lane, P. (1987), 'Principal–agent problems: the relationship between central and local government', M.Phil. thesis, Oxford.

Lange, O. (1938a), 'The foundations of welfare economics', *Econometrica*, 10.

—— (1938b), 'On the economic theory of socialism', Minnesota.

Lawson, N. (1980), *The New Conservatism*, London: Centre for Policy Studies.

—— (1982), 'What's right with Britain', first Patrick Hutber Memorial Lecture, London: Conservative Political Centre.

—— (1984), *The British Experiment: The Mais Lecture*, London: HM Treasury.

Layard, R. and Nickell, S. (1986), 'Unemployment in Britain', *Economica*, 53, 121–69.

Layfield Committee (1976), *Local Government Finance: Report of the Committee of Inquiry*, Cmnd 6453, London: HMSO.

Lerner, A. P. (1944), *The Economics of Control*, London: Macmillan.

Levine, C. (1985), *The Unfinished Agenda of Civil Service Reform*, Washington DC: Brookings Institution.

Levitt, M. (1984), 'The growth of government expenditure', *National Institute Economic Review*, May, 108, 34–41.

Likierman, A. (1988), *Public Expenditure: Who Really Controls it and How*, London: Penguin.

Lindahl, E. (1919), 'Just taxation—a positive solution'. For English translation, see R. A. Musgrave and A. Peacock (eds.) (1958), *Classics in the Theory of Public Finance*, London: Macmillan.

Lindblom, C. (1977), *Politics and Markets*, New York: Basic Books.

Little, I. M. D. (1950), *A Critique of Welfare Economics* (2nd edition: 1957), Oxford: Oxford University Press.

—— (1982), *Economic Development: Theory, Policy and International Relations*, New York: Basic Books.

—— and Mirrlees, J. A. (1968), *Manual of Industrial Project Analysis*, Paris: OECD Development Centre.

—— and —— (1974), *Project Appraisal and Planning for Development Countries*, London: Heinemann.

Livesey, D. A. (1987), 'Central control of local authority expenditure', *Oxford Review of Economic Policy*, 3, 2, 44–59.

Locke, J. (1764), *The Second Treatise of Government*.

Lubenow, W. C. (1971), *The Politics of Government Growth*, Newton Abbot: David and Charles.

MacDonagh, O. (1977), *Early Victorian Government 1830–1877*, London: Weidenfeld.

McGuire, M. C. (1974), 'Group segregation and optimal jurisdictions', *Journal of Political Economy*, **82**, 112–32.

McLeod, A. M. (1983), 'Justice and the market', *Canadian Journal of Philosophy*, **13**.

McLure, C. E., Jr. (ed.) (1983), *Tax Assignment in Federal Countries*, Australian National University, Canberra: Centre for Research on Federal Financial Relations.

Malinvaud, E. (1967), 'Decentralized procedures for planning', in E. Malinvaud and M. O. L. Bacharach (eds.), *Activity Analysis in the Theory of Growth and Planning*, London: Macmillan.

Marwick, A. (1982), *British Society since 1945*, Harmondsworth: Penguin Books.

Marx, K. (1973), *Manifesto of the Communist Party*, Harmondsworth: Penguin Books.

—— (1976), *Capital*, I, Harmondsworth: Penguin Books.

Matthews, K. and Minford, P. (1987), 'Mrs Thatcher's economic policies', *Economic Policy*, **5**, 59–101.

Mayer, C. P. (1985a), 'Pitfalls in public policy: profits or props', *Political Quarterly*, **56**, 142–57.

—— (1985b), 'Recent developments in industrial economics and their implications for policy', *Oxford Review of Economic Policy*, **1**, 3, 1–24.

—— (1987), 'New issues in corporate finance', Centre for Economic Policy Research Discussion Paper 181.

—— and Meadowcroft, S. A. (1985), 'Selling public assets: techniques and financial implications', *Fiscal Studies*, **6**, 4, 42–56.

Mayhew, K. (1985), 'Reforming the labour market', *Oxford Review of Economic Policy*, **1**, 2, 60–79.

Meade, J. E. (1976), *The Just Economy*, London: George Allen and Unwin.

Megaw Committee (1982), *Inquiry into Civil Service Pay*, Cmnd 8590, London: HMSO.

Micklewright, J. (1986), 'Unemployment and incentives to work: policy and evidence in the 1980's', in P. E. Hart (ed.), *Unemployment and Labour Market Policies*, Aldershot: Gower Press.

Middlemas, K. (1979), *Politics in Industrial Society: The Experience of the British System since 1911*, London: André Deutsch.

—— (1986), *Power, Competition and the State*, I, 'Britain in search of balance', London: Macmillan.

Mill, J. S. (1859), 'On liberty', London.

—— (1914), *Representative Government*, London: Dent.

—— (1965), *Principles of Political Economy*, London: Routledge Kegan Paul.

—— (1967), *Chapters on Socialism*, London: Routledge Kegan Paul.

—— (1982), *Liberty*, Harmondsworth: Penguin Books.

Milne, R. (1987), 'Competitive tendering in the NHS: an economic analysis of the early implementation of HC (83) 18', *Public Administration*, 65, 145–61.

Mises, L. v. (1920), 'Die Wirtschaftsrechnung in Sozialistischen Gemeinwesen', *Archiv für Sozialwissenschaften und Sozialpolitik*, 47. Reprinted in F. A. von Hayek (ed.) (1922), *Collectivist Economic Planning*.

Moore, G. E. (1903), *Principia Ethica*, Cambridge: Cambridge University Press.

Moore, J. (1983), speech by John Moore, MP, at the Annual Conference of City of London Stockbrokers, 1 November.

Morgan, K. (1985), *Labour in Power*, Oxford: Oxford University Press.

Morishima, M. (1973), *Marx's Economics*, Cambridge: Cambridge University Press.

Morley, J. (1881), *Life of Richard Cobden*.

Morris, C. N. and Preston, I. (1985), 'Measures of inequality and poverty: an empirical application to household survey data for the UK 1968–1983', Institute for Fiscal Studies Working Paper 75.

Morris, D. and Sinclair, P. (1985), 'The unemployment problem in the 1980s', *Oxford Review of Economic Policy*, 1, 2, 1–19.

Morris, W. (1891), *News from Nowhere*, London: Reeves and Turner.

Moulin, H. (1983), *The Strategy of Social Choice*, Amsterdam: North-Holland.

Mueller, D. C. (1979), *Public Choice*, Cambridge: Cambridge University Press.

Murray, C. (1984), *Losing Ground*, New York: Basic Books.

Musgrave, R. A. and Musgrave, P. B. (1976), *Public Finance in Theory and Practice*, 2nd edition, International Student Edition, Tokyo etc.: McGraw-Hill Kogakusha.

—— and Peacock, A. (eds.) (1958), *Classics in the Theory of Public Finance*, London: Macmillan.

Myrdal, G. (1960), *Beyond the Welfare State*, London: Duckworth.

Nagel, T. (1980), 'The limits of objectivity', in S. McMurrin (ed.), *Tanner Lectures on Human Values*, 1, Cambridge: Cambridge University Press.

Nelson, R. R. and Winter, S. G. (1982), *An Evolutionary Theory of Economic Change*, Cambridge, Massachusetts: Harvard University Press.

Netzer, D. (1974), 'State-local finance and intergovernmental fiscal relations', in *The Economics of Public Finance*, Washington DC: Brookings Institution.

Nicholson, J. L. (1974), 'The distribution and redistribution of income in the United Kingdom', in D. Wedderburn (ed.), *Poverty, Inequality and Class Structure*, Cambridge: Cambridge University Press.

Niskanen, W. A., Jr. (1971), *Bureaucracy and Representative Government*, Chicago: Aldine-Atherton.

Norton, P. (1978), *Conservative Dissidents: Dissent with the Conservative Party 1970–1974*, London: Temple Smith.

—— (1987), 'Thatcherism and the Conservative Party: another institution handbagged?', in K. Minogue and M. Biddiss (eds.), *Thatcherism: Personality and Politics*, Basingstoke: Macmillan.

Nozick, R. (1974), *Anarchy, State and Utopia*, Oxford: Basil Blackwell.

Oates, W. E. (1972), *Fiscal Federalism*, New York: Harcourt, Brace and Jovanovich.

OECD (1976), *Public Expenditures on Income Maintenance Programmes*, Paris: OECD.

—— (1985), *The Role of the Public Sector*, OECD Special Studies special issue, Spring, Paris: OECD.

—— (1986), *United Kingdom*, OECD Economic Surveys, 1985/86, January, Paris: OECD.

Olson, M. (1965), *The Logic of Collective Action*, Cambridge, Massachusetts: Harvard University Press.

O'Neill, O. (1979), 'The most extensive liberty', *Proceedings of the Aristotelian Society*, 79.

Pagano, M. (1987), 'Market size, the informational content of stock prices and risk: a multi-asset model and some evidence', Centre for Economic Policy Research Discussion Paper 144.

Pareto, V. (1896), *Cours d'Economie Politique*, Lausanne.

—— (1917), *Traité de Sociologie Générale*, French edition, Paris.

Parfit, D. (1984), *Reasons and Persons*, Oxford: Clarendon Press.

Parker, H. (1983), 'Basic income guarantee scheme', Treasury and Civil Service Committee Sub-Committee 1982–3, 20–I, 424–43.

Parris, H., Pestieau, P., and Saynor, P. (1987), *Public Enterprise in Western Europe*, London: Croom Helm.

Pattanaik, P. K. (1978), *Strategy and Group Choice*, Amsterdam: North-Holland.

—— and Salles, M. (1983), *Social Choice and Welfare*, Amsterdam: North-Holland.

Paul, J. (ed.) (1980), *Reading Nozick*, Oxford: Blackwell.

Pauly, M. V. (1973), 'Income redistribution as a local public good', *Journal of Political Economy*, 78, 572–85.

Peacock, A. and Rowley, C. K. (1979), 'Pareto optimality and the political economy of liberalism', in A. Peacock (ed.), *The Economic Analysis of Government and Related Themes*, London: Martin Robertson.

Peele, G. (1984), *Revival and Reaction: The Right in Contemporary America*, Oxford: Oxford University Press.

Peleg, B. (1984), *Game Theoretic Analysis of Voting in Committees*, Cambridge: Cambridge University Press.

Pestieau, P. (1977), 'The optimality limits of the Tiebout model', in W. E. Oates (ed.), *The Political Economy of Fiscal Federalism*, Lexington, Massachusetts: Lexington Books.

Phelps, E. S. (1967), 'Phillips curves, expectations of inflation and optimal unemployment over time', *Economica*, 34, 254–81.

Pliatzky, L. (1982), *Getting and Spending*, Oxford: Blackwells.

Polanyi, M. (1951), *The Logic of Liberty*, Chicago: University of Chicago Press.

Popper, K. P. (1945), *The Open Society and its Enemies* (4th revised edition: 1962), London: Routledge and Kegan Paul.

Prior, J. (1986), *A Balance of Power*, London: Hamish Hamilton.

Radner, R. (1985), 'The internal economy of large firms', *Economic Journal*, **96**, Supplement.

Ramsey, F. P. (1927), 'A contribution to the theory of taxation', *Economic Journal*.

Rawls, J. (1971), *A Theory of Justice*, Cambridge, Massachusetts: Harvard University Press.

—— (1980), 'Kantian constructivism in moral theory: the Dewey Lectures 1980', *Journal of Philosophy*, **77**.

Redcliffe-Maud (1969), *Report of the Royal Commission on Local Government in England 1966–9*, Chairman: the Rt. Hon. Lord Redcliffe-Maud, Cmnd 4040, London: HMSO.

Rees, R. (1984), 'The public enterprise game', *Economic Journal*, **94**, Supplement, 109–23.

—— (1985), 'The theory of principal and agent, parts one and two', *Bulletin of Economic Research*, **37**, 3–26 and 77–95.

Regan, D. H. (1983), 'Against evaluator relativity: a response to Sen', *Philosophy and Public Affairs*, **12**.

Reiss, H. S. (ed.) (1970), *Kant's Political Writings*, Cambridge: Cambridge University Press.

Riddell, P. (1983), *The Thatcher Government*, Oxford: Martin Robertson.

Robbins, L. (1933), *The Nature and Significance of Economic Science*, London: Macmillan.

Roemer, J. (1982), *A General Theory of Exploitation and Class*, Cambridge, Massachusetts: Harvard University Press.

—— (1984), 'Equality of talent', University of California, Davis, Department of Economics Working Paper 239.

Royal Commission on the Distribution of Income and Wealth (1980), Report 5, 79–99, London: HMSO.

Ryan, A. (1973), 'Utilitarianism and bureaucracy', in G. Sutherland (ed.), *The Growth of Nineteenth Century Government*, London: Routledge Kegan Paul.

—— (1985), 'Utility and property', in R. Frey (ed.), *Utility and Rights*, Oxford: Blackwell.

Samuelson, P. A. (1954), 'The pure theory of public expenditure', *Review of Economics and Statistics*, **36**, 387–9.

—— (1955), 'Diagrammatic exposition of a theory of public expenditure', *Review of Economics and Statistics*, **37**, 350–6.

Sandler, T. and Tschirhart, J. T. (1980), 'The economic theory of clubs: an evaluative survey', *Journal of Economic Literature*, **18**, 1086–91.

Satterthwaite, M. A. (1975), 'Strategy-proofness and Arrow's conditions: existence and correspondence theorems for voting procedures and social welfare functions', *Journal of Economic Theory*, **10**, 187–217.

Sawyer, M. (1976), *Income Distribution in OECD Countries*, OECD Economic Outlook, Occasional Papers, July, Paris: OECD.'

Scanlon, T. (1987), 'The value of choice', Tanner Lecture at Oxford University, mimeographed. To be published.

Schelling, T. C. (1978), *Micromotives and Macrobehaviour*, London: Norton.

Schmeidler, D. and Vind, K. (1972), 'Fair net trade', *Econometrica*, 40, 637–42.

Schumpeter, J. A. (1952), *Ten Great Economists*, London: Allen and Unwin.

Sen, A. K. (1970a), 'The impossibility of a Paretian liberal', *Journal of Political Economy*, 78, 152–7.

—— (1970b), *Collective Choice and Social Welfare*, San Francisco: Holden-Day. Republished in 1979, Amsterdam: North-Holland.

—— (1973a), *On Economic Inequality*, Oxford/New York: Clarendon Press/ Norton.

—— (1973b), 'Development: which way now?', *Economic Journal*, 93.

—— (1975), 'The concept of efficiency', in Nobay and Parkin (eds.), *Contemporary Issues in Economics*, Manchester: Manchester University Press.

—— (1979a), 'Utilitarianism and welfarism', *Journal of Philosophy*, 76.

—— (1979b), 'Personal utilities and public judgements', *Economic Journal*, 89, 537–58.

—— (1980), 'Equality of what?', in S. McMurrin (ed.), *Tanner Lectures on Human Values*, 1, Cambridge: Cambridge University Press. Reprinted in A. K. Sen (1982), *Choice, Welfare and Measurement*, Oxford/Cambridge, Massachusetts: Blackwell/MIT Press.

—— (1981a), *Poverty and Famines: An Essay on Entitlement and Deprivation*, Oxford/New York: Clarendon Press/Oxford University Press.

—— (1981b), 'Ethical issues in income distribution: national and international', in S. Grassman and E. Lunberg (eds.), *The World Economic Order: Past and Prospects*, London: Macmillan. Reprinted in A. K. Sen (1984), *Resources, Values and Development*, Oxford/Cambridge, Massachusetts: Blackwell/ Harvard University Press.

—— (1981c), 'Public action and the quality of life in developing countries', *Oxford Bulletin of Economics and Statistics*, 43.

—— (1982a), 'Rights and agency', *Philosophy and Public Affairs*, 11.

—— (1982b), 'Just desert', *New York Review of Books*, 19, 4 March.

—— (1982c), *Choice, Welfare and Measurement*, Oxford: Basil Blackwell.

—— (1982d), 'Equality of what?', in A. K. Sen, *Choice, Welfare and Measurement*, Oxford: Basil Blackwell.

—— (1983a), 'The profit motive', *Lloyds Bank Review*, 147, 1–20. Reprinted in A. K. Sen (1984), *Resources, Values and Development*, Oxford/Cambridge, Massachusetts: Blackwell/Harvard University Press.

—— (1983b), 'Liberty and social choice', *Journal of Philosophy*, 80.

—— (1983c), 'Evaluator relativity and consequential evaluation', *Philosophy and Public Affairs*, 12.

—— (1983d), 'Poor, relatively speaking', *Oxford Economic Papers*, 35, 153–69.

—— (1984), 'The living standard', in D. Collard, D. R. Helm, M. Fg Scott, and A. K. Sen (eds.), *Economic Theory and Hicksian Themes*, Oxford: Oxford University Press.

—— (1985a), 'Well-being, agency and freedom: the Dewey Lectures 1984', *Journal of Philosophy*, 82.

—— (1985b), *Commodities and Capabilities*, Amsterdam: North-Holland.

Sen, A. K. (1987), *On Ethics and Economics*, Oxford: Blackwell.

Shackle, G. L. S. (1972), *Epistemics and Economics*, Cambridge: Cambridge University Press.

Sharkey, W. W. (1982), *The Theory of Natural Monopoly*, Cambridge: Cambridge University Press.

Shepherd, W. (1984), 'Contestability vs. competition', *American Economic Review*, 74, 572–87.

Shleifer, M. (1985), 'A theory of yardstick competition', *Rand Journal of Economics*, 16, 319–27.

Skidelsky, R. (1983), *John Maynard Keynes: Hopes Betrayed 1883–1920*, London: Macmillan.

Smith, A. (1776), *The Nature and Causes of the Wealth of Nations*, 1st edition. Republished 1910, London: Dent. Reprinted 1925 as *The Wealth of Nations*, London: G. Bell and Sons Ltd. Republished 1976, Oxford: Oxford University Press.

—— (1976), *The Theory of the Moral Sentiments*, Oxford: Clarendon Press.

Smith, D. (1987), *The Rise and Fall of Monetarism*, London: Pelican.

Smith, S. R. and Squire, D. L. (1986), 'The local government Green Paper', *Fiscal Studies*, 7, 2, 63–71.

—— and —— (1987), *Local Taxes and Local Government*, Report Series 25, London: Institute for Fiscal Studies.

Smith, T. (1979), *The Politics of the Corporate Economy*, Oxford: Martin Robertson.

Solow, R. M. (1986), 'Unemployment: getting the questions right', *Economica*, 53, 23–34.

Starr, R. (1973), 'Optimal production and allocation under uncertainty', *Quarterly Journal of Economics*, 87, 81–95.

Statistical Office of the European Community (1983), *Comparison in Real Values of the Aggregates of the ESA, 1980*, Luxemburg: Statistical Office of the European Community.

Steedman, I. (1977), *Marx after Sraffa*, London: NLB.

Steiner, H. (1974), 'Individual liberty', *Proceedings of the Aristotelian Society*, 74.

Stiglitz, J. E. (1982), 'Utilitarianism and horizontal equity: the case for random taxation', *Journal of Public Economics*, 18, 1–33.

—— (1985), 'Information and economic analysis: a perspective', *Economic Journal*, Supplement, 95, 21–41.

Streeten, P. (with S. J. Burki, M. Ul. Hug, N. Hicks, and F. Stewart) (1981), *First Things First: Meeting Basic Needs in Developing Countries*, New York: Oxford University Press.

Sugden, R. (1981), *The Political Economy of Public Choice*, Oxford: Martin Robertson.

Thompson, E. A. (1966), 'A Pareto optimal group decision process', in G. Tullock (ed.), *Papers on Non-market Decision Making*, Charlottesville: University of Virginia.

Tiebout, C. M. (1956), 'A pure theory of local expenditures', *Journal of Political Economy*, 64, 416–24.

Titmuss, R. (1970), *The Gift Relationship*, London: Allen and Unwin.
—— (1976), *Essays on 'the Welfare State'*, 2nd edition, London: Allen and Unwin.
Tobin, J. (1970), 'On limiting the domain of inequality', *Journal of Law and Economics*, 13, 263–77.
Townsend, P. (1979), *Poverty in the United Kingdom*, Allen Lane.
Tuck, R. (1979), *Natural Rights Theories*, Cambridge: Cambridge University Press.
Tullock, G. (1976), *The Vote Motive*, Hobart Paperback 9, London: Institute of Economic Affairs.
Tyler, R. (1987), *Campaign: The Selling of the Prime Minister*, London: Grafton Books.
Usher, D. (1981), *The Economic Prerequisites to Democracy*, New York: Columbia University Press.
Varian, H. (1974), 'Equity, envy and efficiency', *Journal of Economic Theory*, 9, 63–92.
—— (1975), 'Distributive justice, welfare economics and the theory of fairness', *Philosophy and Public Affairs*, 4.
—— (1984), 'Dworkin on equality of resources', mimeo, University of Michigan.
Veljanovski, C. (1987), *Selling the State*, London: Weidenfeld.
Vickers, J. (1985), 'Strategic competition among the few', *Oxford Review of Economic Policy*, 1, 3, 39–62.
Viner, J. (1960), 'On the intellectual history of laissez faire', *Journal of Law and Economics*, 3, 45–69.
Walters, A. (1986), *Britain's Economic Renaissance: Margaret Thatcher's Reforms 1979–1984*, Oxford: Oxford University Press.
Weitzman, M. L. (1974), 'Prices versus quantities', *Review of Economic Studies*, 41, 477–91.
—— (1977), 'Is the price system or rationing more effective in getting a commodity to those who need it most?', *Bell Journal of Economics*, 8, 517–24.
Williams, B. (1973), 'A critique of utilitarianism', in J. J. C. Smart and B. Williams, *Utilitarianism: For and Against*, Cambridge: Cambridge University Press.
Williamson, O. E. (1975), *Markets and Hierarchies*, New York: Free Press.
—— and Bhargava, N. (1972), 'Assessing and classifying the internal structure and control apparatus of the modern corporation', in K. Cowling (ed.), *Market Structure and Corporate Behaviour*, London: Gray Mills.
Winter, S. (1969), 'A simple remark on the second optimality theorem of welfare economics', *Journal of Economic Theory*, 1, 99–103.
Witney, R. (1988), *National Health Service: A Modern Solution*, London: Shepheard-Walwyn.
Yarrow, G. K. (1986), 'Privatisation in theory and practice', *Economic Policy*, 2, 324–77.
Young, H. and Sloman, A. (1986), *The Thatcher Phenomenon*, London: British Broadcasting Corporation.

Index

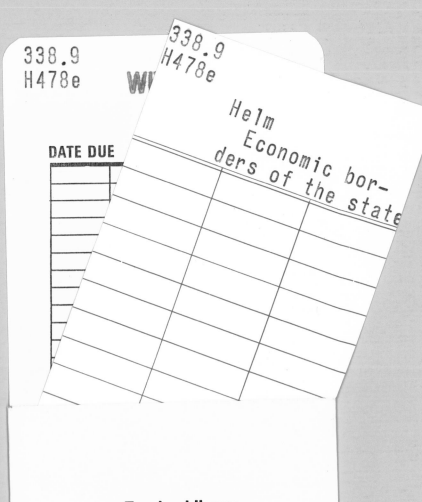